NEW STUDIES IN BIBL

Series editor: 1

Salvation to the ends of the earth

A BIBLICAL THEOLOGY OF MISSION

Andreas J. Köstenberger
and
Peter T. O'Brien

APOLLOS

INTERVARSITY PRESS
DOWNERS GROVE, ILLINOIS 60515

InterVarsity Press, USA
P.O. Box 1400, Downers Grove, IL 60515-1426, USA
World Wide Web: www.ivpress.com
Email: email@ivpress.com

APOLLOS (an imprint of Inter-Varsity Press, England)
Norton Street, Nottingham NG7 3HR, England
Website: www.ivpbooks.com
Email: ivp@ivpbooks.com

InterVarsity Press®, USA, is the book-publishing division of InterVarsity Christian Fellowship/USA®, a student movement active on campus at hundreds of universities, colleges and schools of nursing in the United States of America, and a member movement of the International Fellowship of Evangelical Students. For information about local and regional activities, write Public Relations Dept., InterVarsity Christian Fellowship/USA, 6400 Schroeder Rd., P.O. Box 7895, Madison, WI 53707-7895, or visit the IVCF website at <www.intervarsity.org>.

Inter-Varsity Press, England, is closely linked with the Universities and Colleges Christian Fellowship, a student movement connecting Christian Unions throughout Great Britain, and a member movement of the International Fellowship of Evangelical Students. Website: www.uccf.org.uk

USA ISBN 978-0-8308-2611-7
UK ISBN 978-0-85111-519-1

Set in Times New Roman
Typeset in Great Britain

Printed in the United States of America ∞

 InterVarsity Press is committed to protecting the environment and to the responsible use of natural resources. As a member of the Green Press Initiative we use recycled paper whenever possible. To learn more about the Green Press Initiative, visit <www.greenpressinitiative.org>.

Library of Congress Cataloging-in-Publication Data

Köstenberger, Andreas J., 1957-
   Salvation to the ends of the earth: a biblical theology of mission/Andreas J.
Köstenberger and Peter T. O'Brien.
     p. cm.—(New studies in biblical theology; 11)
   Includes bibliographical references and index.
   ISBN 0-8308-2611-4 (pbk.: alk. paper)
   1. Missions—Biblical teaching. I. O'Brien, Peter Thomas. II. Title. III. New studies in
biblical theology (InterVarsity Press); 11.

BV2073 .K67 2001
266'.001—dc21
                                  2001024039

British Library Cataloguing in Publication Data

A catalogue record for this book is available from the British Library.

P	27	26	25	24	23	22	21	20	19	18	17	16	15	14
Y	25	24	23	22	21	20	19	18	17	16	15	14	13	

With heartfelt gratitude
to Don Carson,
mentor and friend

Contents

Series preface

New Studies in Biblical Theology is a series of monographs that address key issues in the discipline of biblical theology. Contributions to the series focus on one or more of three areas: 1. the nature and status of biblical theology, including its relations with other disciplines (e.g. historical theology, exegesis, systematic theology, historical criticism, narrative theology); 2. the articulation and exposition of the structure of thought of a particular biblical writer or corpus; and 3. the delineation of a biblical theme across all or part of the biblical corpora.

Above all, these monographs are creative attempts to help thinking Christians understand their Bibles better. The series aims simultaneously to instruct and to edify, to interact with the current literature, and to point the way ahead. In God's universe, mind and heart should not be divorced: in this series we will try not to separate what God has joined together. While the notes interact with the best of the scholarly literature, the text is uncluttered with untransliterated Greek and Hebrew, and tries to avoid too much technical jargon. The volumes are written within the framework of confessional evangelicalism, but there is always an attempt at thoughtful engagement with the sweep of the relevant literature.

It is a special delight to see this volume put in its appearance in the series. Dr Köstenberger is one of my former students, and his revised dissertation, published by Eerdmans, attests his longstanding, competent interest in mission as well as in close exegesis. Dr O'Brien, both friend and colleague, is well known not only for his major commentaries, but also for his own publications in the area of mission – the fruit both of scholarly interest and of his own experiences in India and elsewhere.

Together they have written a biblical theology of mission that listens carefully to the biblical texts, and follows the Bible's 'story-line' without flattening the diverse emphases of the various biblical books. Here is scholarship that matters: careful and even-handed, yet of transforming significance for all Christians serious about the mission of the church of Jesus Christ.

D. A. Carson
Trinity Evangelical Divinity School

Authors' preface

The idea for the present volume was conceived while both of us were teaching at Trinity Evangelical Divinity School, Deerfield, Illinois, in 1995. Discovering a common interest in the subject of mission, and having previously published in the area, we decided to pool our resources and attempt to produce a joint treatment on the topic of mission in the New Testament. It soon became clear, however, that this theme could not be examined apart from the Old Testament, and needed to be treated from a biblical-theological perspective as a whole. A chapter on second-temple Judaism was added in order to probe further on a historical level the question of the continuity or discontinuity of the missions of Israel on the one hand and the missions of Jesus and the early church on the other.

Chapters were divided between us, with each producing drafts of our respective chapters which were then submitted to the other for feedback and critique. In this way we aimed to produce a unified treatment that capitalized on our respective areas of interest while issuing in a coherent work on mission in the various corpora of Scripture. Happily, we found ourselves in substantial agreement on all major issues regarding the biblical teaching on mission, particularly the question of whether or not Old Testament Israel was called to mission, whether second-temple Judaism should be characterized as a missionary religion, and whether Jesus limited his earthly mission to Israel or also embarked on a Gentile mission.

Although it has taken us almost five years to complete the project, because of other responsibilities, we are now grateful to present the results of our research. We look forward to the review process in the hope that discussion will further our understanding of this most important of scriptural themes. We view this project not simply as an academic exercise, but as a service to God's people worldwide. It is our sincere hope that our Christian mission, which is first of all God's, will be founded on a biblical theology that takes its cue from the scriptural revelation as a whole. We long for Christ to be exalted among the nations, and that his salvation might indeed reach the ends of the earth. It is our earnest desire that the prophetic vision might be fulfilled so that 'the earth will be filled with the knowledge of the glory of the LORD, as the waters cover the sea' (Hab. 2:14; Is. 11:9).

We would like to express our appreciation to Don Carson for accepting this manuscript into the New Studies in Biblical Theology series, and for his encouragement and firm editorial hand, which have made this a better book. We have pleasant memories of time spent at Tyndale House, Cambridge, during sabbatical leaves in the autumn of 1998. We thank our respective institutions, Southeastern Seminary and Moore Theological College, for their active support of our writing. And we are grateful, last but not least, for our wives' unflinching commitment and partnership in the gospel. May this volume be used in the furtherance of that gospel, as we await the glorious appearing of our great God and Saviour, Jesus Christ (Titus 2:13).

Andreas Köstenberger
Peter O'Brien

Abbreviations

AB	Anchor Bible
AnBib	Analecta Biblica
BAGD	W. Bauer, W. F. Arndt, F. W. Gingrich and F. W. Danker, *Greek-English Lexicon of the New Testament*
BBR	*Bulletin for Biblical Research* (Chicago: University of Chicago Press, 1979)
BECNT	Baker Exegetical Commentary on the New Testament
BETL	Bibliotheca ephemeridum theologicarum lovaniensium
BFCT	Beiträge zur Förderung christlicher Theologie
Bib	*Biblica*
BibRes	*Biblical Research*
BibSac	*Bibliotheca Sacra*
BibToday	*Bible Today*
BJRL	*Bulletin of the John Rylands Library, University of Manchester*
BT	*The Bible Translator*
BTB	*Biblical Theology Bulletin*
BZ	*Biblische Zeitschrift*
CBQ	*Catholic Biblical Quarterly*
ConBNT	Coniectanea biblica, New Testament
CRINT	Compendia Rerum Iudaicarum ad Novum Testamentum, ed. S. Safrai et al. (Philadelphia: Fortress, 1974–)
CTR	*Criswell Theological Review*
CurTM	*Currents in Theology and Mission*
EBS	Encountering Biblical Studies
EHS	Europäische Hochschulschriften
EMZ	*Evangelische Missions-Zeitschrift*
EQ	*Evangelical Quarterly*
ETL	*Ephemerides theologicae lovanienses*
FB	Forschung zur Bibel
FRLANT	Forschungen zur Religion und Literatur des Alten und Neuen Testaments

GNC	Good News commentary
HTKNT	Herders theologischer Kommentar zum Neuen Testament
HTR	*Harvard Theological Review*
IBMR	*International Bulletin of Missionary Research*
IBS	*Irish Biblical Studies*
ICC	International Critical Commentary
Int	*Interpretation*
IRM	*International Review of Mission*
IRT	Issues in Religion and Theology
ITQ	*Irish Theological Quarterly*
IVPNTC	IVP New Testament Commentary
JB	Jerusalem Bible
JBL	*Journal of Biblical Literature*
JETS	*Journal of the Evangelical Theological Society*
JJS	*Journal of Jewish Studies*
JPTSup	Journal of Pentecostal Theology Supplement Series
JR	*Journal of Religion*
JSNT	*Journal for the Study of the New Testament*
JSNTSup	Journal for the Study of the New Testament Supplement Series
JSOT	*Journal for the Study of the Old Testament*
JTS	*Journal of Theological Studies*
KEK	Kritisch-exegetischer Kommentar über das Neue Testament
NAC	New American commentary
NASB	New American Standard Bible
NEB	New English Bible
Neot	*Neotestamentica*
NICNT	New International Commentary on the New Testament
NIGTC	New International Greek Testament Commentary
NIV	New International Version of the Bible
NovT	*Novum Testamentum*
NovTSup	Supplements to *Novum Testamentum*
NRSV	New Revised Standard Version
NRT	*La nouvelle revue théologique*
NS	New Series
NSBT	New Studies in Biblical Theology
NTAbh	Neutestamentliche Abhandlungen
NTS	*New Testament Studies*
PNTC	Pillar New Testament Commentary

ABBREVIATIONS

QD	Quaestiones Disputatae
RB	*Revue Biblique*
ResQ	*Restoration Quarterly*
RevScRel	*Revue des sciences religieuses*
RSV	Revised Standard Version of the Bible
RTR	*Reformed Theological Review*
SANT	Studien zum Alten und Neuen Testament
SBLDS	Society of Biblical Literature Dissertation Series
SBLMS	Society of Biblical Literature Monograph Series
SBS	Stuttgarter Bibelstudien
SE	*Studia Evangelica*
SBT	Studies in Biblical Theology
SJT	*Scottish Journal of Theology*
SNTSMS	Society for New Testament Studies Monograph Series
SNTU	Studien zum Neuen Testament und seiner Umwelt
SR	*Studies in Religion/Sciences religieuses*
ST	*Studia theologica*
Str-B	H. Strack and P. Billerbeck, *Kommentar zum Neuen Testament aus Talmud und Midrash*, 6 vols., München: C. H. Beck, 1926–61
TAPA	*Transactions of the American Philological Association*
TBei	*Theologische Beiträge*
ThStud	Theologische Studiën
TNTC	Tyndale New Testament Commentaries
TrinJ	*Trinity Journal*
TS	*Theological Studies*
TToday	*Theology Today*
TU	Texte und Untersuchungen
TynB	*Tyndale Bulletin*
TZ	*Theologische Zeitschrift*
WBC	Word Biblical Commentary
WMANT	Wissenschaftliche Monographien zum Alten und Neuen Testament
WTJ	*Westminster Theological Journal*
WUNT	Wissenschaftliche Untersuchungen zum neuen Testament
WW	*Word and World*
ZNW	*Zeitschrift für die neutestamentliche Wissenschaft*
ZTK	*Zeitschrift für Theologie und Kirche*

Chapter One

Introduction

Between Eden and the eternal state, between Abraham and Armageddon, between Babel and the beast's confinement to the lake of fire, few biblical topics are as important as mission. This is because mission, while purposed by God prior even to sin, is inextricably linked to man's sinfulness and need for redemption and God's provision of salvation in the person and work of our Saviour, the Lord Jesus Christ. This 'good news' of salvation in Jesus, however, must be made known. Thus mission is the ingredient that both precedes Christian existence and constitutes a major motivation for Christian living: the saving mission of Jesus constitutes the foundation for Christian mission, and the Christian gospel is the message of mission, a mission that is not optional but mandatory.

A biblical-theological approach

Mission has thus far been one of the step-children of New Testament theology. Rarely has this significant biblical theme been given its due in the overall discipline.[1] The present study, while also concerned to deal with larger missiological issues, represents a modest effort to help fill this gap.[2] An attempt is made to explore mission comprehensively throughout the entire sweep of biblical history, including the Old Testament, the second-temple period and the New Testament. The approach followed is *biblical-theological*.[3] Previous treatments of the theme of mission have tended either (a) to be descriptive and to stress the diversity of the different portions of Scripture, or (b) to assume the pre-eminence of mission in a given book of Scripture at the outset, and

---

[1] Note the representative survey by Köstenberger (1999a: 347–362).

[2] *Cf.* O'Brien 1999a.

[3] On biblical theology, see esp. Carson 1995: 17–41. The same author also provides helpful reflections on theological method (Carson 1991a: 39–76). On the need for a biblical theology of mission, see Bosch 1993: 175–192; Goldsworthy 1996: 2–13, esp. 3–4. See now also the suggestive volume edited by Gibson (1998).

then to find these assumptions confirmed in the study of the respective biblical writings. The present work seeks to follow a third path, combining a commitment to a biblical-theological method and a salvation-historical approach with an openness to examine the various portions of Scripture regarding their respective contributions to the biblical theme of 'mission'. This allows for the possibility that certain books may contribute little, or nothing, to the theme. It also makes room for discontinuity between mission in the two Testaments. The difficult question of whether or not second-temple Jews pursued mission likewise must be treated primarily as a historical rather than a dogmatic exercise. For biblical theology is first of all inductive, and thus must be open to diversity.

At the same time, the present study proceeds with the expectation that the message of the biblical writings regarding mission will turn out to be more than a conglomerate of disparate data. A biblical-theological approach may indeed reveal a certain amount of diversity in the scriptural teaching on mission. Since Scripture, however, is ultimately *God's* Word, we may legitimately expect to see an underlying logic and unity in the biblical message on this subject.[4] For Scripture is united by one primary pervading purpose: the tracing of God's unfolding plan of redemption. It everywhere assumes that *this God acts coherently and purposefully in history.*

In claiming that our approach is biblical-theological we recognize that it is neither a systematic-theological nor a missiological examination. This is not to suggest that we have no interest in systematic-theological issues or missiological questions. Quite the reverse. It is hoped that any biblical-theological insights or conclusions may help both systematicians and missiologists in their own study of the issues related to this subject. But in the first instance, at least, we are not addressing the legitimate questions of these related disciplines.

We have conducted our research self-consciously as believers who are committed to the lordship of Christ, rather than as dispassionate, 'neutral' observers.[5] Our interest in the subject at hand is not merely an academic one. Our driving motivation springs from a passion to see God's mission carried out in today's world.

[4] For a helpful treatment of unity and diversity in the New Testament, see D. Wenham in Ladd 1993: 684–719. See also Köstenberger 2000b.

[5] *Cf.* esp. ch. 5 entitled 'The Interpreter' in Maier 1994, and here particularly the discussions under the headings 'Faith as Aid to Understanding', 'The Difference between the Regenerate and the Unregenerate Interpreter', and 'The Work of the Spirit on the Interpreter'.

History, literature and theology

The study rests on three pillars: history, literature and theology. *History* is important, because biblical scholarship should practise the craft of every historian: painstaking historical research.[6] Christianity is an historical religion, and if its historical moorings are uncertain, theological findings will necessarily be undermined. *Literature* has its place, because Scripture has come down to us as a collection of sixty-six books, in the form of literature rather than unmediated historical events. These writings convey history, but they do so by way of *interpreted* history, written by believers who put on their writings the stamp of their convictions as to the significance of the events they record. The best approach to uncover biblical teaching on a given theme, and the one followed in the present study, is therefore a *narrative* one, which traces the way in which teaching on a particular topic unfolds in a given corpus of Scripture.

Finally, *theology* must be given its due. Unlike history-of-religions treatments, which are largely descriptive and comparative in nature, the present study proceeds in the conviction that Scripture is first and foremost a divinely inspired book, setting forth authoritative teaching that provides a framework for Christians' beliefs as well as actions. Thus the primary purpose for the present work is a careful exploration of the biblical-theological interconnections between the different portions of Scripture. No abstract definition is postulated at the outset of this work, if for no other reason than that Scripture itself does not define 'mission' (Stott 1991: 1). We consider that an inductive exegesis leading to biblical theology should come first, after which an effort is made to relate the contributions of the different corpora, and even Testaments, to each other (Köstenberger 1995c).

This does not mean that any of us approaches Scripture on a given topic as a blank slate. We all have a synthetic approximation in mind when we set out to explore biblical teaching on a particular subject. At present our concern is simply to maintain *maximum openness* to the actual scriptural message on mission and *flexibility* throughout the entire process of exploration. On a general level, the criterion for inclusion of a given portion of Scripture for discussion in the present volume may simply be that it relates in a significant way to the proclamation of God's name and of his saving purposes in Christ to the

---

[6] For some reflections still worth pondering (first raised in 1909), see Schlatter 1997: 17–20.

unbelieving world (hence the title *Salvation to the Ends of the Earth*). These passages may ordinarily be accessed through a particular writer's terminology (e.g. 'sending'), and it is in any case important not to lose sight of the connection between biblical *words* and biblical *themes*.[7] Nevertheless, any given scriptural theme is greater than strict verbal boundaries, so that attention to larger overarching concepts must balance terminological considerations.

Moreover, in our commitment to an inductive biblical-theological approach, we come to our task aware that considerable previous work has been done in this area. An acquaintance with the history of biblical scholarship is necessary, for it provides us with many questions that have, not without good reason, set the agenda for scholarly discussion. Was Old Testament Israel called to active missionary outreach similar to the New Testament church? Can second-temple Judaism be characterized as a missionary religion? Did Jesus limit his mission to Israel or did he extend it also to the Gentiles? Did Paul encourage believers to emulate his practice of evangelism and mission, or not? These are just some of the questions that any treatment of mission in Scripture needs to take up and seek to answer as precisely as possible. We recognize the need to be conversant with a wide range of literature, in the fields of biblical studies (Old Testament as well as New Testament) and missiology. Given the magnitude of the task (and space constraints no less), our goal has been to interact with major representative works rather than provide an exhaustive treatment of the whole.

The procedure followed in this work

The plan for this book, then, is as follows. The opening chapter is devoted to an exploration of mission in the Old Testament, focusing on the major theological strands (notably the Abrahamic promises) that lay a foundation for mission in later Scripture. This is followed by a chapter on mission in the second-temple period. Here the question dealt with is whether second-temple Judaism can be characterized as a missionary religion or not. Starting with chapter four, the various corpora of the New Testament will be treated. The three Synoptic Gospels provide the starting point, in the order Mark – Matthew – Luke, based on the tentative assumption of Markan priority. Jesus will not be dealt with in a separate chapter, since we have no unmediated

---

[7] *Cf.* ch. 2 in Köstenberger 1998a which deals more fully with this subject.

knowledge of him and his mission apart from the Gospels (just as the early church will not be treated separately but in the chapter on the book of Acts). Issues of an integrative kind will be taken up in the concluding synthesis.

Luke's Gospel is treated jointly with the book of Acts, in keeping with the two-volume character of this work. This is immediately followed by the chapter on mission in Paul. Treating Luke and Paul's writings in close proximity to each other is particularly helpful in that both share many points of contact. The chapter on Paul is followed by a discussion of mission in John. In keeping with the profoundly theological orientation of John's Gospel, the investigation will constitute a thematic study along narrative lines. The final chapter discusses mission in the General Epistles and the book of Revelation. While grouped together under one heading, the treatment is not monolithic. Still, the circumstances of the church in the second half of the first century AD, in particular the mounting persecution, provided some significant common ground for mission in these writings. A concluding synthesis seeks to assess the way in which the contributions of the various biblical writers relate to each other in terms of diversity as well as underlying unity.

Conclusion

This study of mission in the Bible has been richly rewarding for us. As we have sought to trace the major contours of the scriptural message on this topic, we have come to a deeper understanding of God's gracious salvation in the Lord Jesus Christ for a needy and lost world. It is our earnest desire that this book may lead to 1. a greater appreciation of God's saving plan that moves from creation to new creation; 2. a deeper grasp of the significance of Jesus Christ's sending by the Father and his mission accomplished through the witness of his apostles; and 3. a commitment, as contemporary disciples who follow in the footsteps of the apostles and first witnesses, to the glorious gospel of our great God and Saviour.

Chapter Two

The Old Testament

J. H. Bavinck once remarked: 'At first sight the Old Testament appears to offer little basis for the idea of missions', adding that the 'entire pagan world is portrayed more as a constant threat and temptation to Israel than as an area in which God will reveal his salvation'.[1] But Bavinck rightly recognized that when the Old Testament is studied more closely it quickly becomes obvious that there is considerable concern for the future of these nations. Salvation will one day be their lot, for the divine plan has the whole world in view.[2]

God's creation and his purpose for humankind

Any comprehensive treatment of mission in the Old Testament must begin with God's creation and his purposes for humanity.[3] The notion of mission is intimately bound up with his saving plan which moves from creation to new creation, and has to do with his salvation reaching the ends of the earth.[4] Towards the beginning of the Bible, the call of

---

[1] Bavinck 1960: 11, cited by De Ridder 1975: 14.

[2] Many biblical scholars (as distinct from missiologists), who have written on mission in the New Testament, have failed to examine adequately issues relating to salvation for the nations in the Old Testament. Although this omission has been occasioned, in part, by a narrow definition of 'mission', it is serious nevertheless. So, for example, Hahn (1965: 18–20) devotes only three pages to the subject; Bosch (1991), although touching on several important theological matters arising from the Old Testament, gives four pages to the subject in a book of six hundred, while Kasting (1969: 11) begins his study on mission within Judaism, thus omitting the Old Testament entirely! Senior and Stuhlmueller (1983: 7–138), with their section, 'The Foundations for Mission in the Old Testament', are a notable exception.

[3] This assertion is at variance with the view of many earlier writers who claimed that the beginnings of the biblical teaching on mission are to be found in Israel's election and the exodus, rather than the creation. A representative example is Manson (1953: 257–265, esp. 257), who stated: 'in the Bible the conception of the Church's universal mission is bound up, first and last, with the thought of the Church being "the Israel of God"'. *Cf.* Rowley 1945: 15.

[4] Note how Martens treats this important point at the conclusion of his Old Testament theology (1994: 257–278).

Abram (Gen. 12) is intimately linked with God's dealings with the nations; not surprisingly, the canon of Scripture ends, in Revelation, with a book which speaks about God's purposes for the created order and his concerns for a people of 'every nation, tribe, language and people' (Rev. 14:6). This theme of God's saving purposes reaching the ends of the earth forms a grand envelope that contains the entire story of Scripture.

The first indications of God's plan for the world appear in the creation account of Genesis 1. From the opening verse of this chapter God's control over all creation is asserted. In the first six days eight acts of creation are presented (vv. 3–31). On the sixth day, as his crowning act, God created humankind in his own image and likeness (vv. 26–28). Man as the image of God is installed as his vicegerent over all creation with a mandate to control and rule it on behalf of its maker. Six times God says that specific acts of creation are 'good' (vv. 4, 10, 12, 18, 21, 25), and the divine evaluation of the whole creation is that it is 'very good' (v. 31). While this has been understood in terms of a perfected creation with complete harmony, or good in an ethical or aesthetic sense, the expression probably signifies that it conformed to the divine intention and purpose. 'The world created by God and acknowledged as "good" is the one in which history begins and the one that will reach its goal by fulfilling the divine purpose for which it was created' (Dumbrell 1994: 20). Humankind and the world, as depicted in Genesis 1, corresponded perfectly to the divine intention, the details of which will become clearer in the unfolding revelation.

Genesis 2:1 ends the account of creation: 'Thus the heavens and the earth were completed in all their vast array.' On the seventh day God rested from all his work, not on account of weariness, but because he had completed his creation. The seventh day brings the creation week to an end; the work of creation has been finished. Dumbrell helpfully notes that the verb šābat, rendered 'stop, cease', implies 'the nuance of completion or perfection in the sense of bringing a project to its designed goal', which in the immediate context is explicit.[5] In other words, the notion of rest explains the goal of creation. God enters his rest on the seventh day, a day in which there is no mention of an evening or a morning. It is open-ended or unending. He has entered his rest and humankind is invited to share that rest with him.

To conclude: God created the world and humanity distinct from himself and yet totally dependent on him. Creation is not some emanation of the deity or a part of him. Humankind, while made in the

[5] Dumbrell 1994: 23. Note his discussion on 22–23.

image of God, is not to be understood as descended from him, as many of the ancients thought. Genesis 1 indicates that God's lordship is over the whole creation including all humankind.

The fall of humankind and the spread of sin

Genesis 3 describes the transition from innocence to guilt – the fall of Adam. Man becomes a sinner in this chapter, and the whole story of humankind is disastrously affected by the consequences of his disobedience to God. Man was to live under the divine command (2:16–17), but instead rebels against his Creator. In chapter 3 sin begins with doubt regarding the trustworthiness of God's character, which then leads to the desire for independence from him, and this results in direct disobedience (vv. 1–6). Sin, which is described as a serious moral lapse, is also the reversal of the original order of relationships – God, the man, the woman and the animals (cf. 3:1–6 with 2:18–25) – and thus a deliberate attack on the divine order established at creation.

The sinner finds himself under the wrath of God, and this involves a change in relationships: the intimacy between the man and the woman is broken, the woman will feel the pangs of childbirth (v. 16), and the man is cursed in relation to the ground. His relationship to the environment is marked by frustration and pain (vv. 17–19; cf. Rom. 8:20–23), and he is unable to exercise his dominion over nature in a proper way. Both the man and the woman are banished from the Garden, and their relationship with their Maker now assumes a negative rather than a positive form (vv. 22–24). A bright note, however, appears in verse 15, where the Lord promises that the seed of the woman will defeat the serpent. Christian scholars have understood this as the *protoevangelium*, the first glimmer of the gospel.[6]

The disastrous consequences of the fall and the spread of sin on an ascending scale are traced in the succeeding narratives: Cain and Abel (4:1–16), the sons of God and the daughters of men (6:1–4), the generation of the flood (6:5 – 9:28), and the tower of Babel (11:1–9). The spread of sin and its effects move from Adam to involve his family (Gen. 4), and then the whole of humankind in the flood. Sin has now become universal. The saving of Noah and his family occurs as the result of God's direct intervention. According to Genesis 6:18–21 God

---

[6] Collins (1997: 139–148) and Alexander (1997: 363–367) have recently shown on syntactical grounds that the 'seed of the woman' in Gen. 3:15 'must be understood as referring to a single individual and not numerous descendants' (Alexander 1997: 363).

saves this family and a representative group of animals, birds and reptiles, in order to 'keep' his covenant with them, a statement that apparently refers to the plan which God brought into being at creation (cf. 9:1–7). After the flood Noah and his family are commissioned (9:1–7) in terms recalling 1:28. Despite the ongoing presence of sin, God intends to maintain the covenant with the created order, that is, with man and his world (9:9–13).

The call of Abram and the nations[7]

The divine call to Abram and the promise of blessing to him and his family, as well as to all peoples on earth,[8] are presented against the backdrop of a humankind under divine judgment. Genesis 3 – 11 shows us the disastrous consequences of the fall and the spread of sin on an ascending scale. By the time we arrive at Genesis 11 we have reached the nadir of human existence with a fractured and disastrously broken society that has lost any sense of God-centredness. The account of the tower of Babel concludes on a note of profound despair with humankind utterly unable to fulfil its God-given destiny (11:1–9). Men and women in their proud independence of God have sought a centre for their society which is to be realized completely in themselves (Westermann 1984: 554–555). In a divinely ordered world the Lord's appropriate response to this arrogant human assertion is judgment – the scattering of people over the earth and the confusion of languages (11:5–9).

Yet as in the narratives of the fall (Gen. 3), the murder of Cain (Gen. 4) and the flood (Gen. 6 – 8), judgment is not the final word. Genesis 12:1–3 is God's gracious response which reverses the sin and downward spiral of chapters 3 – 11. So dramatic and magnificent is this response that it is expressed in language similar to that of a new creation.[9] In his summons to Abram God is about to effect a new creative work. In Genesis 1:3 he spoke and called creation into being;

---

[7] Note Muilenburg 1965: 387–398; Dumbrell 1984: 47–79; and Alexander 1998: 191–212.

[8] The theme of mission in the Old Testament, as described above, is a vast subject. Limitations of space prevent us from addressing the subject in a comprehensive way. Our endeavours, therefore, will be much more modest. From a salvation-historical perspective and hopefully as a contribution to biblical theology, we shall attempt to trace through what we believe to be fundamental, namely, the fulfilment of the Abrahamic promises in key Old Testament passages, particularly as they bear on the divine purposes of saving the world.

[9] The divine speech and command at Gen. 12:1 are structurally similar to the speech and implied command at the beginning of creation.

now after a series of human failures God begins again and introduces a new phase of history by summoning Abram into a relationship with himself and blessing him (Gen. 12:1–3).[10]

'Leave your country, your people and your father's household and go to the land I will show you.

> 'I will make you into a great nation
> and I will bless you;
> I will make your name great,
> and you will be a blessing.
> I will bless those who bless you,
> and whoever curses you I will curse;
> and all peoples on earth
> will be blessed through you.'

The Lord summons Abram to leave his native land, his past and his family, in other words, everything that would have been regarded in the ancient world as providing ultimate personal security. The divine speech consists of a command and a series of promises that far outweigh the command, 'showing where the chief interest of the passage lies' (Wenham 1987: 274). The focus of attention is upon what God will do in and through Abram, thereby fulfilling his intentions for his creation (cf. Legrand 1990: 3).

God appoints for Abram a promised land (v. 1) and assures him that his descendants will be a great and significant nation (v. 2). The name for which the builders of Babel had yearned (11:4) is to be *given* to Abram (Kaiser 2000: 18). Furthermore, the name he is to receive will be 'great' (v. 2). Over against the people's attempt to establish a world centre in Babel, Abram is promised that around him and his descendants a great nation will be gathered, a nucleus that will be the company of the redeemed, the new people of God (Dumbrell 1994: 34).

Five times in Genesis 12:1–3 the words 'bless' and 'blessing' occur. Pointedly, they stand in sharp contrast to the five instances of the word *curse* in the narrative describing the spread of sin (Gen. 3:14, 17; 4:11; 5:29; 9:25), and thus underscore the point that in the summons of Abram we have the divine response to the human disaster of Genesis 3

---

[10] Wenham (1987: 270) comments: Gen. 12:1–3 'binds together the primeval and the patriarchal history by presenting the call and blessing of Abram as the answer to the calamities that have befallen mankind in Gen 1 – 11'. *Cf.* Blauw 1962: 19–20 and Sailhamer 1992: 139.

– 11. God blesses Abram (v. 2a) which, we have seen, is bound up with the nation and fame. Abram is to be the embodiment of blessing, the example of what blessing should be (v. 2b).[11] Further, the Lord promises to bless those who recognize the source of Abram's blessing.

The climactic expression, with its final use of the term *bless* (v. 3), promises that Abram will become the means of blessing for all humankind.[12] But how are the peoples of the earth to be brought into contact with Abram? Is Abram's responsibility to reach out to them? This raises the wider theological question that recurs throughout the Old Testament and will impinge on Israel's mission. The answer in relation to Abram turns, in part, on how we translate the final verb *bless* in verse 3. The passive, 'all peoples ... will be blessed' (NIV), suggests that Abram is the mediator of the blessing to all peoples, and this accords with the stress that falls on the last clause. The reflexive 'and by you all the families of the earth shall bless themselves' (RSV), makes Abram the model for rather than the source of blessing, and this interpretation is anticlimactic.[13] However, in order to bring out fully the thought intended, we should probably combine the two and render the verb 'win for themselves a blessing'. 'This climactic rendering would mean that the peoples of the world would find blessing by coming to the Abrahamic descendants, rather than by later Israel's outreach. And this interpretation is consistent with the way mission is presented in the Old Testament – nations come in pilgrimage to Israel's God' (Dumbrell 1994: 35).

The divine summons of Abram and the promises to him are of momentous significance. God's intention to bless him, his seed and all

---

[11] Note the treatment of Dumbrell 1984: 67–68, to whom we are indebted. There is considerable discussion as to the precise meaning of 'blessing, bless' in this context. Although Martens (1994: 37–38, 45) acknowledges that the nuance varies in different contexts, here in Gen. 12:1–3 it signifies 'salvation'.

[12] Muilenburg (1965: 391) rightly observes that the 'stress of the pericope falls upon the last line'. Alexander (1994: 13) states: 'The primary motive behind the call of Abraham is God's desire to bring blessing, rather than cursing, upon the families of the earth. The promise that Abraham will become a great nation, implying both numerous seed and land, must be understood as being subservient to God's principal desire to bless all the families of the earth.' *Cf.* Martens 1994: 237, 242. Further, God's blessing was to be experienced by nations, clans, tribes, people groups and individuals: Kaiser 2000: 19.

[13] In later contexts in Genesis where the Abrahamic promises are repeated, the verb is sometimes rendered as a passive (18:18; 28:14), sometimes as a reflexive (22:18, NRSV; 26:4, NRSV). Muilenburg (1965: 392) prefers the reflexive in Gen. 12:3. Alexander (1994: 13, n. 12) opts for the passive, partly on the grounds that the earliest versions reflect it (*cf.* Kaiser 2000: 19–20). See his discussion and bibliography. For a different interpretation, see Wells 2000: 203–204.

peoples of the world is a reassertion of his original purpose for humankind.[14] Furthermore, the promises made to Abram in Genesis 12:1–3 are paradigmatic. The promise of land and descendants forms the content of what is later known as the Abrahamic covenant (Gen. 15:1–18), and this serves to assure him that God's intentions will be fulfilled. The terms of the Abrahamic covenant are restated in Genesis 17, and ultimately the promise refers to a company of believers of whom Abraham is father (cf. Rom. 4:16–17). The many nations of whom Abraham will be father are not his natural descendants, but because of the divine promises he will become for them the channel of blessing. And, in order to reinforce his promise, God changes the name of Abram ('the father is exalted') to Abraham ('father of a multitude'). Genesis 18, where Abraham intercedes for Sodom, provides us with hints as to how the promise is to be mediated to the outside world.

The patriarchal narratives, which follow the Abrahamic covenant, indicate how Abraham, Isaac and Jacob convey the blessings to their age, and potentially to the world. Each is the bearer of the Abrahamic promises (Gen. 26:2–5; 28:13–15), and these are reaffirmed at the end of the patriarchs' lives (Gen. 22:15–18;[15] 26:24; 35:9–12). Jacob's position is significant for the development of the theme of Israel. On leaving and returning to the Promised Land (Gen. 28:10–17; ch. 32) he is assured that God is with him. He is given the name 'Israel' (32:28), and returns to the Promised Land with this new name, which prefigures his role as the patriarch of the twelve tribes. The terms of the Abrahamic covenant are restated in the Joseph narrative:

> 'The sceptre will not depart from Judah,
>   nor the ruler's staff from between his feet,
> until he comes to whom it belongs
>   and the obedience of the nations is his' (Gen. 49:10).

Although the translation and interpretation of this text are disputed,

---

[14] *Cf.* Wenham 1987: 275 and his discussion in 1994: 202–203. Scobie (1992: 285) comments: 'If, with the call of Abram, the focus in the Old Testament shifts to God's election of and dealings with a chosen people, nevertheless the concern for the entire created order is never lost sight of.'

[15] The divine speech in Gen. 22:16–18 forms an *inclusio* with Abraham's call in 12:1–3 and concludes the main section of the Abraham narrative. What was promised in 12:1–3 is now guaranteed by divine oath. Gen. 22:16–18 includes the additional aspect that the nations will be blessed through Abraham's 'seed', which might point to many descendants, but probably denotes a single descendant (cf. the discussion of Alexander 1994: 18–22).

Genesis 49:10 is thought to be the first messianic declaration in the Old Testament. Ezekiel announces that the promise to Judah, because of the evil behaviour of members of the royal line, is about to be reversed by Nebuchadnezzar's capture of Jerusalem: 'It will not be restored until he comes to whom it rightfully belongs' (21:27). The Septuagint regards verse 27 and its echo of Genesis 49:10 as clearly messianic.

The book of Genesis concludes with the promise of descendants to Abraham in the process of being fulfilled, and that regarding the land as assured. These promises take us back to the position of Adam in Genesis 1 – 2, and will be intimately related to the role of Israel within God's purposes. How they are to be fulfilled in the nation, and in what sense the blessings through Abraham will extend to humankind, will be made clear in the unfolding revelation. The Abrahamic covenant continues throughout the Old Testament as the framework within which relationships between God and his people are presented. We shall see fundamental connections between this and later covenants which will finally lead to all the peoples of the world coming in pilgrimage to the God of Israel.

Israel and the exodus

If God's promise of descendants to Abraham was being fulfilled by the end of Genesis (cf. Exod. 1:12), then the book of Exodus recounts how the Lord began to fulfil his promise of the land to the assembled multitude of Israel. The exodus of his people from slavery to the Egyptians is presented in the song of Moses (Exod. 15:1–18) as a new creation. The appearance of creation motifs in the song suggests that Yahweh's redemption of Israel with a high hand and an outstretched arm is a renewal of the creation mandate. The divine saving purposes for the world are in some way bound up with Yahweh's victory over Egypt at the sea.

Israel's role in the divine purposes

Israel is redeemed for a particular purpose in God's plan, and that role becomes clearer upon the completion of her movement to Sinai, which is the immediate goal of the exodus (cf. Exod. 3:12). Here at Sinai, where the covenant is made, Israel emerges fully as the people of God. Yahweh's future plans for her, and the role she is to play within his purposes, not least with reference to the promises made to Abraham, are described in a passage of great significance: Exodus 19:3–6.

'This is what you are to say to the house of Jacob and what you are to tell the people of Israel: "You yourselves have seen what I did to Egypt, and how I carried you on eagles' wings, and brought you to myself. Now if you obey me fully and keep my covenant, then out of all nations you will be my treasured possession. Although [For] the whole earth is mine, you will be for me a kingdom of priests and a holy nation." These are the words you are to speak to the Israelites.'

Verse 4 summarizes what the Lord has done for Israel in terms of redeeming them from Egyptian bondage ('you yourselves have seen what I did to Egypt'), of guiding and caring for them on the march to Sinai ('how I carried you on eagles' wings') and assembling them at Sinai in order to make a covenant with them ('and brought you to myself').

The following verses (5–6) reveal what the Lord has in mind for Israel. First, the nation is called 'my treasured possession' (sᵉgullâ), an expression that was used in the Old Testament of private property held by royalty (Eccles. 2:8) or David's own personal treasure over which he alone had control (1 Chr. 29:3). The point here is that Israel is Yahweh's special people whom he has chosen 'out of all nations'; they are those over whom he has particular sovereignty.

Secondly, the final words of verse 5, translated by the NIV as a concessional clause, 'Although the whole earth is mine', should be rendered in a causal sense, '*For* the whole earth is mine'. It 'carries the main weight of the proclamation' and sets forth the divine motivation for Yahweh's exodus redemption from Egypt: 'Israel is called because the whole world ("earth") is the object of Yahweh's care.'[16]

Thirdly, the summons to Israel to obey the Lord fully and to keep his covenant (v. 5) does not refer, as many commentators suppose, to the Sinai agreement which is about to be concluded, but is a call to commitment to a previously established covenant. Already in the book of Exodus (2:24; 6:4–5) reference has been made to the patriarchal covenant, and a continuity has been established with this through the revelation given to Moses (ch. 3). Accordingly, the covenant spoken of here in verse 5 is the covenant made with Abraham. The Lord summons Israel to accept wholeheartedly the promises he had made

[16] Dumbrell 1994: 45. *Cf.* Hedlund 1991: 32–33. For Martens (1994: 268), 'The significance of the particular (Israel) is seen in the perspective of the universal.' He adds: 'God's purpose with one people is not restrictive but is inclusive eventually of peoples beyond the Hebrews' (270).

with Abraham and the fathers. So Israel is not entering a covenant of works, that is conditional or provisional, but is responding to a covenant of grace based on divine promises made earlier with Abraham.

Finally, verse 6 sets forth Israel's vocation, that is, her role in the divine purposes which is the result of her election, mentioned in verse 5. As Yahweh's 'treasured possession', Israel is to be 'a kingdom of priests and a holy nation'. The first phrase, 'a kingdom of priests', though disputed in meaning, probably signifies a kingdom that is priestly in character (cf. Schüssler Fiorenza 1972: 114–116), while 'holy nation', which is parallel to the preceding, points to a separated people over whom God rules.[17] Together the two expressions indicate that Israel must serve the world by being separate, as a priest served his society by being distinct from it.

The question of Israel's 'mission' to the nations

Israel's calling in Exodus 19:5 had the whole world in view. The nation was to be holy and to serve the world by being separate. Her life was to give clear evidence of Yahweh's rule over her, and thus to be a model of his lordship over the whole world. Israel had been chosen by the Lord from among the nations of the world which were in rebellion against him. But, in fact, Israel failed to live up to her calling. The nation did not demonstrate Yahweh's rule over her life, or model his lordship for the whole world.

However, a further question needs to be asked: in addition to serving the world by being holy and separate, did not Israel have an obligation to bear witness to her neighbours? Granted that the nation should have provided a model of Yahweh's lordship but failed to do so, did Israel have any further responsibility to the world which belonged to Yahweh? Was the nation to reach out to others, to 'go' as well as to 'be'? Or, to put the question another way: what was the nature of Israel's mission to the nations?

This cluster of questions is one of the most hotly debated among recent interpreters at both a popular and a scholarly level, for it raises a profound theological problem regarding Israel's relationship to the world. If the call of Abraham and the related choice of Israel are to be understood as part of Yahweh's plan for the salvation of all, then how does one explain the almost total absence from the Old Testament of any concern that the people of Israel should go out and share their

---

[17] See further the discussion of mission in ch. 9 on 1 Peter, especially under the heading 'Transference of old-covenant categories'.

knowledge of the one true God with the other nations? Why does Israel not proclaim its knowledge of God to the nations? If Yahweh's choice of this people as his own treasured possession was *because* the whole world belonged to him, why does she not reach out to the other nations of the world? Perhaps even more significantly, why does the Old Testament itself not call on God's people to repent for this apparent lack of concern about the nations? Did Israel truly have a missionary calling within the purposes of God?

A strong tradition of Christian interpretation claims that God gave Israel the task of missionary outreach, and that the failure of the nation to engage in this role is part of the reason why he had to come up with a better plan in the gospel.[18] This common assertion, however, is unsatisfactory both exegetically and theologically. To contend that Israel had a missionary task and should have engaged in mission as we understand it today goes beyond the evidence. There is no suggestion in the Old Testament that Israel should have engaged in 'cross-cultural' or foreign mission. 'The nation of Israel witnesses to the saving purposes of God by experiencing them and living according to them.'[19]

Briefly, Israel related to the nations in two ways: first, *historically* through incorporation, and then *eschatologically* through ingathering (Scobie 1992: 286–292). Concerning the first, Charles Scobie has rightly claimed that 'at most stages of Israel's history provision was made for the incorporation of people of non-Israelite descent' (Scobie 1992: 286). Examples of incorporation include the 'mixed crowd' (NRSV) which accompanied Israel out of Egypt (Exod. 12:38), the adoption of Rahab and her family (Josh. 6:25) and the acceptance of foreigners within the kingdom of David (2 Sam. 11:3; 15:19–23). The Mosaic legislation showed special concern for the *gšr*, the stranger or foreigner who was resident in Israel (cf. Exod. 12:48; 22:21). Ruth the Moabitess was a prime example of this historical incorporation. Indeed, as the great-grandmother of King David, she has an important role to play within God's saving purposes (Ruth 4:13–22).[20]

But although incorporation into Israel was always possible, it had its limits, especially in relation to intermarriage. Nehemiah forbade intermarriage with foreigners such as Moabites in the post-exilic period

---

[18] This position is espoused by Kaiser 1981: 29–30 and 2000: 9–10, 22–24. Note the criticism by Goldsworthy 1996: 3, n. 3.

[19] Goldsworthy 1996: 7. He adds: 'It does not appear that being a nation of priests was ever understood as meaning a nation of evangelists and foreign missionaries' (6–7). On the prophetic conception of Israel's mission to the nations, see below.

[20] On the possibility of 'salvation for people outside Israel's covenant', see the article with this title by Widbin (1991: 73–83).

(Neh. 13:23–27), and Ezra broke up mixed marriages (Ezra 9 – 10). So while certain individuals did come and attach themselves to Israel, the people of God, these were exceptions. By the time of the New Testament, there appears to have been little thought of an active reaching out in order to seek 'proselytes'. And even when this did occur, it meant that the outsider became a Jew. 'Proselytization is resocialization or nationalization.'[21]

The second feature of Israel's relationship to the nations is found in Old Testament eschatological expectation: in particular, the ingathering of the Gentiles. We shall touch on this point only briefly, and reserve a fuller discussion for later. Israel's history, which was marked by disobedience and division within, and by subjection to a series of foreign nations, led to the increasing recognition that Israel's hope rested solely on the future action of God. The nation was to be reconstituted and revived with the regathering of the tribes, and the eschatological expectation of the reunion of north and south. Jeremiah's new covenant would be with the house of Israel and with the house of Judah (Jer. 31:31), while Ezekiel's prophecies spoke of Yahweh himself being the shepherd who would reconstitute his flock (Ezek. 34:12–13, 15) and reunite Israel so that she would no longer be two nations (37:15–23). Within this context of a reconstituted Israel, the eschatological expectation of the ingathering of the Gentiles is presented (note Is. 2:2–4; chs. 60 – 61).

The nation's failure and the concept of a remnant

The nation of Israel was to be holy and to serve the world by being separate. That holiness was provided for with the giving of the Ten Commandments of Exodus 20, together with the Covenant Code (that is, the case law) of chapters 21 – 23, which presuppose the covenant relationship and provide the contours for it. The 'ten words', as they have been called, naturally flow from divine grace and the Lord's redemption of his people. They provided the guidelines within which the relationship between Yahweh and his redeemed would function. Likewise, the building of the tabernacle (Exod. 25 – 31), which follows the ratification of the covenant (Exod. 24), was significant in relation to another of the Lord's goals for his people, namely, that the nation should be a *priestly* kingdom (Exod. 19:6). 'Israel's claim to be a community directed by Yahweh necessitated Israel's worship of Yahweh as her sovereign' (Dumbrell 1994: 47–48).

---

[21] McKnight 1991: 47, cited by Scobie 1992: 288. Note the discussion in ch. 3, 'The second-temple period'.

These merciful provisions were to enable Israel, which was called to be a kingdom of priests and a holy nation, to be different from the nations round about. The latter were opposed to the universal rule of God. The idolatry which characterized them made them a hazard to the covenant life of Israel. Israel was studiously to avoid contact with the nations, except in warfare, so as not to be contaminated by them. Prescriptions such as Deuteronomy 12:30 and 18:9 were aimed at maintaining the purity of the covenant relationship with God (Goldsworthy 1996: 6).

But in spite of all that Yahweh had done for his people, Israel committed apostasy in the incident of the golden calf (Exod. 32), and this was to have profound ramifications in relation to the divine purposes for the nation. Although the Lord graciously renewed the Abrahamic promises to Israel (Exod. 33:1–2), he asserted that his presence would not go forward with Israel to Canaan (v. 3b). Only in response to Moses' intercession does the Lord finally agree to go with Israel (v. 17). After the nation's apostasy in the incident of the golden calf, the future fulfilment of the Sinai covenant will not lie with 'national Israel'. Instead, the expectations of Sinai can be preserved only by an Israel *within* an Israel. And, as Israelite prophecy will later show, the prospects for the fulfilment of the Sinai covenant would be carried, not by the nation with whom the covenant was first made, but by a remnant within it.

As a result, if the covenant promises to Abraham, which envisaged blessing overflowing to all the families of the earth, were to be fulfilled, it was clear that Yahweh himself must bring them to pass. Although his intention was that Israel, by serving the world in holiness, should be the instrument in these gracious purposes, after the sin of the golden calf (Exod. 32 – 34) it became increasingly obvious that national Israel had failed disastrously in its God-given role, and the extension of the covenant blessings to the nations would come through 'an Israel within Israel'. The concept of a remnant within the nation had already begun.

The Davidic kingship and 2 Samuel 7

Critical for an understanding of Yahweh's rule over the nations of the world and the fulfilment of his covenant promises to Abraham is the establishment of the Davidic kingship[22] in 2 Samuel 7. At the beginning

---

[22] Vexed historical questions concerning the origins of kingship in Israel, etc., lie outside the scope of this chapter.

of this important chapter[23] David expresses the desire, now that the Lord had 'given him rest from all his enemies around him' (v. 1), to build a suitable dwelling place for the ark of the covenant. The Lord, however, refuses David's request to build a temple. Instead, Solomon, through whom the Davidic line will continue, has permission to build a house for Yahweh (vv. 12–13), and this he will do when the Promised Land has been fully occupied and complete rest[24] has been given to the nation (vv. 9–11).

Although Yahweh refuses David's request to build a house (i.e. a temple) for the ark of the covenant, he himself promises to build David a house (i.e. a dynasty) and an eternal kingship: 'And I will establish the throne of his kingdom for ever' (v. 13). David's house will be established in perpetuity. But how does this promise line up with the subsequent historical events which led to the dissolution of the Davidic empire? This divine pronouncement stands in contrast to the collapse of the Davidic line at the fall of Jerusalem in 587/586 BC. The answer to this tension appears to be that while the covenantal promises may be withdrawn from individuals of David's line, the line itself will not ultimately fail.[25] Finally, it is Jesus of Nazareth who brings to their consummation the promises given to the house of David.

From this reference to Davidic kingship in 2 Samuel 7 several questions arise in relation to our salvation-historical enquiry into mission in the Old Testament. First, how do the Davidic promises relate to the existing covenant Yahweh has made with Israel? Secondly, what is the connection between David's eternal kingship and the promises of the Abrahamic covenant? And a related question, how does this kingship of 2 Samuel 7 tie in with the Lord's purposes for the human race which began with creation?

<hr/>

[23] For a recent examination of 2 Sam. 7 in the light of a messianic hope, see Satterthwaite 1995: 41–65, esp. 52–56.

[24] Satterthwaite 1995: 54 thinks rather that verses 10–11 are describing 'the continuance of an already existing state of affairs'.

[25] See the discussion in Satterthwaite 1995: 55–56. The narrative of the later years of David's kingship (2 Sam. 8 – 20) suggest that David himself fell short of this ideal. Satterthwaite aptly comments: 'The promise of a dynasty of kings remains in force; but David's own history as king shows an ominous decline which comes close to calling the whole venture into question.' Later prophetic texts (cf. Amos 9:11–15; Is. 11:1–2; Jer. 23:5) also draw a clear distinction between 'an unsatisfactory present' in which 'representatives of David's line did not live up to [the] ideal represented by the figure of David' and 'a glorious future to be inaugurated by a coming descendant of David' (64, 65).

The Davidic kingship and Yahweh's covenant with Israel

The question which immediately presses on us is this: if Yahweh has promised an eternal kingship for the line of David, through which his saving purposes will be established, how does this relate to the existing covenant with Israel? Has the latter been discontinued and is it, therefore, no longer in force? Or are the earlier promises caught up with, perhaps even fulfilled in, the eternal covenant with David? What are the connections, if any, between the two sets of promises?

It needs to be observed that within the context of 2 Samuel 7 the fortunes of David are closely interwoven with the unfolding history of Israel (vv. 6–16). What is more, the promises given to David are *as Israel's representative*. As king in Israel, he embodies and represents the people. The sonship terms previously applied to Israel (Exod. 4:22), are now predicated of David ('I will be his father, and he shall be my son', 7:14), while the language of verses 9–11 (cf. v. 1) indicates that the goal of the exodus, namely, rest in the Promised Land, is to be achieved fully through David. Two additional reasons lead Dumbrell to assert that David as king is the representative carrier of the promises to Israel. The first is that beyond the promises of 2 Samuel 7 the Davidic kingship is linked to the covenant with Israel (esp. Ps. 110:4 which speaks of the priestly nature of Jerusalem, and so of the Davidic kingship). The second reason is that the covenant expectations of Exodus 19:6, that Israel would become a priestly royalty, are embodied in the person of the king. The conclusion, therefore, is: 'Through the occupant of the throne of Israel, [the] Davidic kingship is to reflect the values that the Sinai covenant requires of the nation' (Dumbrell 1994: 71–72).

The Davidic kingship and the promises to Abraham

If the above-mentioned connections with the Sinai covenant may thus be made, then what links, if any, are there between David's eternal kingship and the Abrahamic promises? 2 Samuel 7 (esp. vv. 9–11) contains important allusions to Genesis 12:1–3 which suggest that what God has in store for David is a *reiteration*, if not a *partial fulfilment*, of what was promised to Abraham. So Yahweh says that he will make David's 'name great' (v. 9), and this is probably to be read in the light of the promise of a great name to Abraham (cf. Gen. 12:2). Yahweh adds that he will 'provide a place for my people Israel' (2 Sam. 7:10). The establishment of the Davidic empire 'will set the ideal borders of the Promised Land, which the promise to Abraham had foreshadowed'

(Dumbrell 1994: 70; note Gen. 15:18 with Deut. 11:24 and its reference to Israel's 'place'). Finally, the undertaking that Yahweh will give David 'rest' from all his enemies (v. 11), which is presumably greater than the provisional rest already given (v. 1), is to be understood not simply in terms of the goal of the exodus as rest in the Promised Land, but also in relation to the creation rest to which the exodus rest pointed.

To conclude: the covenant with David looks back to the divine intention for Israel through Sinai. At the same time, this covenant is intimately linked with God's saving purposes for humankind through Abraham, and thus to the reversal of the disastrous consequences of the fall in Genesis 3 – 11. It will be through the Davidic king who functions as Yahweh's vicegerent that the latter's rule over the nations will be exercised. The ultimate fulfiller of this role is Jesus of Nazareth who, as son of David, was son of Abraham, and also Son of God.

Jerusalem in the purposes of God[26]

During the reign of Solomon the fulfilment of various Abrahamic and Davidic promises occurs: the Promised Land comes under Israelite control, Israel has become a great nation, with the 'people of Judah and Israel ... as numerous as the sand on the seashore' (1 Kgs. 4:20), while Solomon completes the building of the temple in Jerusalem, thus fulfilling the expectations of Deuteronomy 12:5–11.

Jerusalem as a world centre

Jerusalem becomes a world centre, with people travelling to the city from all nations to hear Solomon's wise counsel (1 Kgs. 4:34). While many made pilgrimages to the city (10:24), one visit was of particular significance – that of the Queen of Sheba (1 Kgs. 10). She readily acknowledged the distinguished place of the nation of Israel in the world, its significance within the divine plan, and Solomon's privileged position on the throne of Yahweh's people (v. 9). Perhaps as an indication of the world's homage, the Queen of Sheba presents Solomon with an amazing array of gifts (v. 10). This narrative of the queen's visit (10:1–10) has been understood as a paradigm from which the eschatological pilgrimage of the nations to Zion was drawn in later prophecy (Is. 2:2–4; chs. 60 – 62).

---

[26] See McConville 1992: 21–51, together with the literature cited, and note below the treatment of Zion, Israel and the nations in the Psalms. Note also P. W. L. Walker 1996.

The city's eschatological role

One of the key themes of the book of Isaiah is the eschatological role of Jerusalem, and this motif is central to the place of the nations in God's saving purposes.[27] The first half of the prophecy (chs. 1 – 39) opens with the prospect of judgment on Jerusalem and concludes with affirmations of its certainty. In chapter 1, which serves as an introduction to the book, the prophet denounces the city for its apostasy which lies at the heart of the nation's life. Jerusalem must be cleansed and judgment will fall upon her. However, in the eschatological oracle of Isaiah 2:2–4, the assurance is given that once this judgment occurs, Jerusalem, the city of righteousness, will become the divine world centre.

The second half of the prophecy (chs. 40 – 66)[28] moves from the promise of the exiles' return to the appearance of the new Jerusalem which lies at the very heart of God's new creation. Zion will be pivotal to the divine purposes and its role as the city of God means that it will be the centre of the world (Is. 2:2; cf. Ps. 48:1–2), chosen by the Lord as the place of divine government.

The eschatological pilgrimage of the nations

An important strand of Old Testament expectation which is crucial for an understanding of God's saving purposes reaching the ends of the earth is the eschatological ingathering of the Gentiles[29] to Zion (Is. 2:2–4; chs. 60 – 62; cf. Mic. 4:1–5; Pss. 36:8–9; 50:2). Jerusalem is depicted as the centre of the new creation (Is. 35:1–10; 65:17–18). The city is protected by Yahweh himself, for he will dwell among his people through his presence in the temple (Ps. 24:7–10). Zion is to rejoice in her new-found salvation for the Lord is king in her midst (Zeph. 3:14–17). The nations will make their pilgrimage to Jerusalem at the end time, flocking to the banner of the messianic king (Is. 11:10). Zion will have an amazing drawing power (Is. 2:2, 'all nations will *stream* to it'). Ultimately, Yahweh's choice of her (in the light of v. 3,

---

[27] Contrast the view of Martin-Achard (1962: 13) who claims, 'The chief concern of the prophet of the Exile is not the salvation of the Gentiles but the liberation of his own people and its triumphant return to Jerusalem; the heathen are scarcely more than an instrument in the hands of Israel's God.'

[28] Recent Old Testament scholarship has claimed that the role of Jerusalem and her place within the divine plan are themes which bind the prophecy of Isaiah together as a theological unit.

[29] See Rowley 1945: ch. 2; Jeremias 1958: 57–60; Legrand 1980: 20–22; and Scobie 1992: 288–292.

with its mention of 'the house of the God of Jacob'), is in fulfilment of his promises to the patriarchs.

The nations make their journey to Jerusalem at the end time in order to learn about Yahweh and his ways: 'Come, let us go up to the mountain of the LORD ... He will teach us his ways, so that we may walk in his paths' (Is. 2:2–3; cf. Zech. 8:20–23; Mic. 4:1–2). As they come to his chosen city (Is. 60:1), they bring the scattered children of Israel with them (vv. 2–9). In what is an amazing reversal, the nations submit to Israel (Is. 60:14) and, in fulfilment of the Abrahamic promises, stream into the city bringing their wealth (vv. 11–22). The worship and praise of the nations are poured out to Yahweh (Ps. 22:27–31), for they are now joined to him, become his people (Zech. 2:11) and participate in his universal salvation. The admonition of Isaiah 45:22, 'Turn to me and be saved, all you ends of the earth', finds its fulfilment in this eschatological vision of the new age.

Three important features of this eschatological pilgrimage of the nations need to be noted in relation to the question that was raised earlier about Israel's supposed missionary outreach.[30] First, the pilgrimage of the nations is an *eschatological* event. The acceptance of the Gentiles will occur 'in the latter days', or 'in that day', not in the present. From an Old Testament perspective it belongs to God's future. Secondly, the ingathering of the nations is the work of God, not Israel. Sometimes the nations themselves are said to take the initiative,[31] but often it is explicitly stated that God himself gathers the nations (cf. Is. 56:6–7: 'these *will I bring* to my holy mountain'). Although Israel plays a mediating role according to Zechariah 8:20–23, even here the nations are envisaged as coming to seek the Lord. Finally, all these prophetic passages speak of the nations coming to Israel, not Israel going to them. The movement is *centripetal*, not centrifugal. The goal of the eschatological ingathering of the nations is Jerusalem/Mt Zion/the temple, and ultimately God himself.

The restoration of Israel and the new covenant

Several key prophetic books, rather surprisingly, say little about God's salvation reaching the ends of the earth or about the incoming of the

---

[30] Note the summary of Scobie 1992: 291–292.

[31] The Old Testament occasionally speaks of the *spontaneous* coming of the nations (Ps. 68:31; Zech. 8:23). Ultimately, however, this is because of God's initiating activity: 'The nations shall of themselves journey to Israel's God, *as though drawn by a magnet*' (Bavinck 1960: 22, emphasis added).

Gentiles to Mt Zion.[32] This is because their focus of attention is Israel. However, what is envisaged in Jeremiah, Ezekiel and Joel, for example, in relation to the restoration of God's people and the establishment of a new covenant is of considerable importance for our theme of universal salvation.

Jeremiah ministers to a nation in crisis, with the imminent destruction of Jerusalem and the loss of her religious institutions, because the city has defiled itself with the false gods of the nations. But Jeremiah's message is not simply one of doom, for the prophet looks forward to a reconstituted people of God. Central to the so-called 'book of consolation' (Jer. 30 – 33), which speaks of the restoration of Israel's fortunes after the exile, is the prophecy of the new covenant (31:31–34). This covenant with the house of Israel and the house of Judah, which has continuity with the Sinai agreement (cf. v. 33), is *new* because: 1. it is a *temporal* advance in terms of salvation history; 2. it is also a *qualitative* advance since this covenant will be unbreakable: the Lord intends to put his law in the hearts of his people, the new Israel (v. 33). The covenant slogan, 'I will be their God and they shall be my people' (Exod. 6:7; Lev. 26:12; Ezek. 37:27), will continue, but in the new age all members of the covenant will know the Lord, for their sins will be perfectly forgiven without the need of a sacrificial system. Jeremiah's particular concern, then, is for the reconstitution of the new Israel. Only after this has occurred will the Gentiles be incorporated into the new people, as other Old Testament passages make clear (e.g. Is. 2:2–4).

Ezekiel's initial focus (1:1 – 33:21) is on the coming destruction of Jerusalem.[33] The situation changes after the fall of the city, and Ezekiel begins to speak of the restoration of Israel (33:23 – 39:29). In the future age Yahweh himself will be the shepherd who reconstitutes his flock, Israel (34:7–24). He will initiate a new covenant (36:25–27), through which Israel will be cleansed (v. 25) and given a new heart (v. 26) and will render obedience through a new spirit (v. 27). The restoration of Israel is viewed in terms of a resurrection of the nation from the death of exile (37:1–4): in a manner reminiscent of the creation of man in Genesis 2:7, God breathes his Spirit into the dead bodies and effects a national resurrection (vv. 5, 10). Finally, the elaborate temple vision of Ezekiel 40 – 48 'reveals how the

[32] On the prophetic conception of Israel's mission to the nations, note further Oswalt 1991: 85–95, esp. his conclusions on 94–95.
[33] The true locus of God's people has been separated from empirical Jerusalem by Ezekiel when he spells out who are the true meat in the pot (Ezek. 11:3–11).

43

reconstituted people of God will live in the new age' (Dumbrell 1994: 102–108, esp. 108).

In the prophecy of Joel, with its references to the day of the Lord, Israel is subject to divine judgment (Joel 1:1 – 2:11). Yahweh calls on the nation to repent (2:12–17), and then promises to renew the covenant with her (vv. 18–27). The divine judgment which first fell on the household of God is next extended to the whole world, and the nations are judged because of their mistreatment of God's people (3:1– 21). Yet, significantly placed between the two halves of the book, and ultimately of hope to both Israel and the nations, is the famous passage about the outpouring of God's Spirit (2:28–32). This magnificent prophecy envisages the Spirit coming on all the remnant of Israel in the last days, so that all will become partakers of the life-giving Spirit (cf. the last Adam of 1 Cor. 15:45), know the divine mind and tell forth God's word (i.e. 'prophesy'), just as Moses had wished (Num. 11:29). This complete renewal or regeneration of God's people marks the community out as a royal priesthood and a holy nation in the way envisaged at the exodus (Exod. 19:3–6).

Although the expression 'all flesh', upon whom the Spirit will be poured, signifies all Israel in the immediate context, it has overtones that are universal (note the application of 'all flesh' in Gen. 6:12, 13, 17; Num. 18:15; Is. 49:26 [all RSV]), and this is how Peter uses the Joel prophecy to explain the significance of Pentecost (Acts 2). The nations, who are rightly judged because of their treatment of God's people, may yet receive mercy and be beneficiaries of this gracious outpouring of the Spirit (cf. Oswalt 1991: 86).

Jonah and mission?

The book of Jonah has often been regarded in Christian scholarship as one of the high points of the Old Testament's teaching on the theme of mission. As 'a missionary tract', it is believed to establish clearly the obligation which Israel had to go to the nations, and thus is a precursor of the missionary mandate of the New Testament.[34] In our judgment,

---

[34] Bright (1955: 162–163) asserts: 'No sterner attack on smug exclusiveness, no more ringing challenge to Israel to take up her world mission, could be imagined than the little book of Jonah.' He adds that Israel is to embrace 'her task of proclaiming the true God to the nations, however distasteful that may be'. Hedlund (1991: 126), who cites Bright with approval, thinks that Jonah's mission was 'one of the grandest events in redemptive history ... for it announced the calling of the Gentiles in the last days'; while Oswalt (1991: 87) believes the 'book's implication that Israelites have an obligation to bear God's word even to their enemies' is so obvious as to need no comment. Verkuyl (1978:

however, this is to claim too much, even though the book does make its own particular contribution to our understanding of divine salvation reaching the ends of the earth.[35]

The climax of the prophecy and key to its interpretation is Yahweh's question of Jonah, 'Should I not be concerned about that great city?' (4:11). The Lord's willingness to save Nineveh (cf. 4:2) shows that his *ḥeseḏ* ('covenant love') cannot be predicted or confined to Israel. His own rebellious people had on countless occasions experienced the compassion and saving grace of Yahweh, as indeed had Jonah himself when he besought God for mercy and forgiveness (2:1–9). Cannot this same sovereign compassion be extended to foreigners, such as the Assyrians in Nineveh? And were there others in Israel, like Jonah, who were angry that Yahweh's kindness could be shown to such sinners?

Closely tied to this motif of Yahweh's mercy is the response of these Gentiles to his word. In the first chapter the sailors, who are god-fearers, respond to the divine word uttered by the unwilling prophet, and finally confess their faith in the Lord (v. 16). Their fear is first elemental (v. 5), then a fear of the divine messenger (v. 10), and finally a fear of Jonah's God (v. 16). Similarly, in chapter 3 the prophetic announcement of doom causes the pagan inhabitants of Nineveh to repent. Led by the king, the city turns to Yahweh (vv. 5–10), casting itself upon him for mercy (v. 9). His response is immediate.

This prophecy, like some of the psalms noted below, shows that the Lord's kindness is extended to pagan outsiders. His salvation reaches to the ends of the earth, for ultimately his saving concerns are for the world; it is his intention to bless all the families of the earth (Gen. 12:3). Jonah the prophet, however, is not presented as a missionary whose preaching to Nineveh (even if for tragic reasons) is intended to serve as a paradigm for Israel's outreach to the nations.

The ministry of the Servant of Isaiah: Israel and the world

One of the most important figures in the Old Testament whose role and ministry within the divine purposes had reference to both Israel and the

96) speaks of the book being 'so significant for understanding the biblical basis of mission because it treats God's mandate to his people regarding the Gentile peoples and thus serves as the preparatory step to the missionary mandate of the New Testament'. Cf. Kaiser 2000: 65–71.

[35] For a survey of scholarly opinion on the message and purpose of the book of Jonah, see Allen 1976: 188–191 and Stuart 1987: 434–435, together with the literature cited.

45

nations is the Servant of Yahweh. The four 'Servant songs' (42:1–4; 49:1–6; 50:4–9; and 52:13 – 53:12; cf. 61:1–3) delineate his ministry and function, and these contribute significantly to the overall message of Isaiah 40 – 55. Although the Servant's work is in the first instance bound up with the redemption of Jerusalem and Israel's return to the holy city, that work will affect the whole world. This sequence of his ministry, namely, first to Israel which then results in blessing to the nations, suggests not only a pattern similar to the Abrahamic promises but also a partial fulfilment of them (cf. Is. 49:6).

In recent years the focus of scholarly attention has been directed to the identity of the Servant of the Lord, although no consensus has been reached by Old Testament scholars.[36] Our particular concern is the role that the Servant is to fulfil. Ultimately, predictions about the Servant should be compatible with his perceived role and functions.

Introducing the Servant (Is. 42:1–4)

Yahweh's Servant, who is introduced in verse 1, is presented in both royal and prophetic terms (cf. Ps. 89:3–4; 1 Sam. 16:13). Yahweh designates him, equips him and reveals his mission. His manner of working (vv. 2–3) and destiny (v. 4) are set forth, while his mission is twice reiterated (vv. 3–4). Three times the important term *mišpāṭ* ('justice') appears in relation to that mission. What is meant by this key word, and how is the prediction to be understood – as a promise or a threat? Also, in the light of our understanding of *mišpāṭ*, what does verse 4 mean with its statement that in his *tôrâ* the nations 'expect' or *hope* (NIV)? Is this to be understood negatively or positively?

As to the issue of *mišpāṭ* ('justice'), it is noted that in Isaiah 40 – 41 this key term has to do with the Lord's work of creation (40:14, 27) and his sovereignty over the created order. He rules supremely in the processes of history. Further, in this context, *mišpāṭ* ('justice') appears in a trial narrative where Yahweh's case against the nations is established (41:1). Justice also concerns Israel and the Lord's covenant with her. The people's complaint is that their 'cause' (*mišpāṭ*) has been disregarded by their God (40:27). Yahweh's Servant, however, will establish divine justice in relation to the nations (42:1–4), and this will involve his vindicating Israel's special position within the divine purposes (Webb 1996: 171).

Since the verb 'expect' (*yāḥal*) always has a positive nuance when

[36] Note, for example, the interaction with recent scholars by Payne 1995: 3–11, esp. 4–6, and Hugenberger 1995: 105–140.

46

used of Yahweh's work, verse 4 is to be understood positively.[37] The prophet is pronouncing a message of hope for the nations ('In his law the islands will put their hope'). The eschatological ideas expressed are similar to those of Isaiah 2:2–4. Through the Servant's ministry the Lord's rule from Zion will be accomplished, and the city will become a world centre from which the blessings of salvation will flow (see above). Yahweh's 'teaching' (tôrâ) will be dispensed from Jerusalem as he instructs Gentile pilgrims his 'ways' (v. 3).

The Lord's words which immediately follow the first 'Servant song' (vv. 5–9) draw attention to two significant elements in the Servant's ministry: first, the Lord has called him to effect a new covenant for Israel. But, secondly, this covenant has universal ramifications, since the Servant will be not only 'a covenant for the people [i.e. Israel]' but also 'a light for the Gentiles' (v. 6). In other words, what the Servant will achieve through his ministry will affect Israel. But it will also have worldwide ramifications, opening up a new chapter in the Lord's relationships with his people and with the world. The covenant made with Abraham, in which God promised to make of him a great nation and to bless all peoples of the earth through him (Gen. 12:1–3), will be effected through the ministry of the Servant of Yahweh. And this will lead ultimately to new heavens and a new earth (Is. 65:17; 66:22).[38]

The Servant's twofold task: Israel and the world (Is. 49:1–6)

In the second of the 'songs' the nations are summoned to listen to the personal testimony of the Servant. He speaks of his preparation and calling for ministry by Yahweh, which climaxes in his being named 'Israel' (49:1–3). But the nation in exile cannot live up to what it means to be 'Israel', so the Lord must find 'a true and worthy Israel. The Servant is this wondrous new beginning' (Motyer 1993: 386). Yahweh's preparation and commissioning of his Servant is for the purpose of bringing Jacob back to himself and of gathering Israel (v. 5). This involves raising them up from the burden of sin and restoring those alienated from him (v. 6). But this is not all. Yahweh not only reassures him of his success; he also tells him that such a task is far

---

[37] It has been suggested that the prophet anticipated severe judgment on the nations, and that the enforcement of God's tôrâ would be a joyful hope for Israel but a fearful prospect for her enemies, the nations. But see the discussion of the issues by Payne (1995: 8–9), who concludes that the verb rendered 'expect' in some versions should be translated positively since it expresses hope.

[38] The divine 'glory' (cf. vv. 8–9) will be displayed in a new way, surpassing anything that had happened previously. Cf. Webb 1996: 172.

beneath his capacity and dignity. A wider work is, thus, to be included within his calling: 'I will also make you a light for the Gentiles' so that 'you should be[39] my salvation to the ends of the earth'.

The nations, then, who are integral to the Servant's calling and ministry, are urged to recognize him (49:7, 22–23), to render homage to Yahweh, and to bring the exiles of his people to Zion with them as they themselves come in pilgrimage (vv. 12, 18, 22–23).[40] The Servant's work will result in the regathering of Israel to Jerusalem, the rebuilding of the nation and the restoration of the holy city. The Lord will be vindicated in the eyes of the nations (v. 7), and his sovereignty will be established in Zion.

Clearly the Servant's work for Israel will affect the whole world. After her redemption Israel will call other nations to her, and they will come running (55:3–5). In response to Yahweh's invitation to turn to him and be saved (45:14, 22), the nations will bow down before the Lord's people (45:14; cf. 49:23), acknowledging that there is no other God than Yahweh and that he is certainly with them. Even kings and queens will be in attendance on Israel (49:23). Those, however, who oppose the Lord's people and refuse to submit will be consumed (49:26).

The Servant's suffering and death (Is. 52:13 – 53:12)

The fourth 'Servant song'[41] is 'the jewel in the crown of Isaiah's theology, the focal point of his vision'.[42] It provides the key to our understanding of the Servant's ministry, and with it God's plans for his people and for the world. Although forgiveness has already been announced by the prophet, the basis on which it rests has not been explained. Now it is: Yahweh's 'righteous servant will justify many ... he will bear their iniquities' (53:11). This Servant is both priest, who 'sprinkles' the unclean (52:15), and sacrifice ('guilt offering', 53:10), through whose priestly work God's people are cleansed and made fit for priestly service themselves.

Israel, the Lord's people, had been told that they were to be his witnesses (43:10, 12; 44:8). But they were blind and deaf, and

---

[39] For a discussion of this interpretation, rather than the usual rendering, 'that you may bring my salvation to the ends of the earth', see Motyer 1993: 388.

[40] A. Wilson 1986: 275. Note also Davies 1989: 93–120.

[41] The third Servant passage (Is. 50:4–9), which reiterates much of the content of the two preceding 'songs' (42:1–4; 49:1–6), summons the Servant to persevere in spite of opposition and rejection.

[42] So Webb 1996: 209, whose exegesis of this passage is both lucid and full of insight (209–214) and repays careful study.

therefore they did not help others to see or understand (42:18–22). In 53:1–6 these witnesses confess, to their shame, how they had turned away from the Servant and despised him, believing that he had been justly smitten and afflicted by God (vv. 3–4).[43] But how wrong had they been! God had indeed crushed him, but not because he warranted it. Instead, they had deserved those sufferings and that death. The Servant had taken their place. Their peace with God, the healing of their broken relationship with him, was brought about by the Servant's death (v. 5), and they now wish to announce it to the world. Through their witness those who had formerly not heard come to 'see' and 'understand' (52:15).

The Servant's death will not be the end of his career. God adds his 'Amen' to his work by raising and exalting him (53:10–12). After his sacrificial death, the Servant 'will see the light of life', 'be satisfied' with the results of his sacrifice, and bring many into a right relationship with God (v. 11). The Servant's ministry was for pagans (52:13–15) and Israelites (53:1–6), witnesses and hearers, insiders and outsiders. Finally, however, it is for 'only one group: *transgressors, many of them*'.[44] The Servant is the vehicle of God's grace to sinners, and the key to the divine salvation reaching to the ends of the earth. Redeemed Israel witnesses to God's saving power revealed in the suffering, death and exaltation of the Servant. The content of that witness focuses on what Yahweh has achieved through him.

On contextual grounds the consequences of the Servant's death are spelled out in Isaiah 54 – 55. The covenant of peace, the restoration of Zion, the new exodus and the exiles' return will all be achieved by the suffering and death of the Lord's Servant.[45] The significance of his ministry, anticipated in Isaiah 42:1–4, becomes clear. With his death for Israel and thus the restoration of Jerusalem, the new era will be ushered in. The Servant's work will signal the advent of the new age.

The paradox concerning the identity of the Servant will not be fully resolved until the coming of Jesus of Nazareth who is both the expected Messiah (note the Aramaic Targum of Is. 53, where the Servant is called 'messiah') and the one who fulfils Israel's destiny.

---

[43] Although the Servant is identified with Israel in Is. 49:3, the individual references in 52:13 – 53:12 indicate that the role of the Servant will be fulfilled by some future yet unknown person. The 'remnant community, who was meant to be the idealized Servant community upon whom Israel's hopes reposed, has been reduced to one' (Dumbrell 1994: 119). On the rejection of the Servant by his own people, see Watts 1990: 31–59, esp. 53.

[44] Webb 1996: 214 (original emphasis).

[45] Note Dumbrell's detailed arguments in 1994: 121–123.

And Israel's role of world mission, which was forfeited through disobedience, is transferred in the Gospels to Jesus.

The nations within God's plan in the Psalms

The place of the nations within the saving plan of God is a significant issue in the psalter. Much that has already been gleaned about God's redemptive purposes from other Old Testament material is encapsulated in the Psalms,[46] sometimes with special force or particular emphases.

The nations[47] represent the great mass of humankind which is in rebellion against God and which he will judge (Ps. 10:16). Yet they still stand within his plan of grace, for it is the divine intention to bring blessing to the nations of the world.[48] One cannot however, understand, the teaching of the psalter about God's salvation reaching the ends of the earth simply by turning to universalistic texts or isolated references to the nations. Rather, one must begin with Israel as God's people, for although the nations are addressed and invited to turn to the Lord, the invitation is for them to share in the privileges of God's chosen people. As one first turns in Genesis to the covenant made with Abraham in order to learn that all the families of the earth find blessing through him (Gen. 12:1–3), so in the psalter one must begin with Israel, the people of God, in order to understand the place of the nations within the divine saving plan. The election of Israel is not at odds with God's universal mission, but is fundamental to it.[49]

This focus on Israel as God's chosen nation is integrally related to his election of Zion and its place within his purposes.[50] Though previously a Jebusite stronghold, it was conquered by David and then became the city of royal residence (cf. 2 Sam. 5:7). With the entry of the ark into Jerusalem, Zion becomes the permanent centre of the worship of Yahweh in Israel. The enthronement psalms (Pss. 47; 93; 96 – 97; 99) depict Yahweh as king in Zion. The city will not fall to any foe,

---

[46] As with the rest of this exegetical and theological enquiry, we shall examine the psalms in their final canonical form. This will still necessitate taking into account any development in the presentation of 'the nations' in post-exilic psalms, for example.

[47] According to Goldsworthy (1996: 6), '"the nations" in the Old Testament is not purely an ethnic or racial concept. It is the theological significance of the nations that is primarily in view'. *Cf.* Hedlund 1991: 66–72.

[48] *Cf.* Piper 1993: 184–188. On the subject of mission in the psalms, see Senior and Stuhlmueller 1983: 110–138 and Hedlund 1991: 83–92.

[49] So Legrand 1990: 8 and Munro 1996: 1–22, esp. 2–3, to which I am indebted.

[50] See especially Ollenberger 1987; McConville 1992: 21–51, esp. 30–33; and Tan 1997: 23–31, together with the literature cited.

because she is protected by the Lord's presence (Pss. 2; 46; 48; 76).[51] Like the tabernacle and Mt Sinai before it, Zion is holy because of Yahweh's presence. His glory fills the temple, and his holiness radiates from there, sanctifying his temple (5:7; 11:4; 65:4; 68:5; 79:1; 138:2), his anointed king (16:10), his mountain and city (2:6; 3:4; 15:1; 48:1; 87:1; 99:9), his land (78:54) and heaven itself (20:6; 89:5, 7). In fact, the term 'Zion' comes to be applied variously to the sanctuary or temple, the holy mountain, Jerusalem, as well as the nation or a remnant within it. If his people are 'holy' because of his presence in Zion, then Israel is separated from the nations (cf. 78). Salvation for them must involve their coming out of the world to Zion in order to worship the Lord (72:8–11; 102:12–22).

Significantly, the Zion theology of the psalms is covenantal and intimately connected with Yahweh's promises to Abraham, as well as with the Mosaic and Davidic covenants. Psalm 47, an enthronement psalm, celebrates Yahweh's kingship over the whole earth. The psalmist rejoices in the Lord's salvation for Israel. He subdued the nations under his people and rules from Zion. Yet his purpose in choosing Abraham's descendants was to bless the whole earth. According to verse 9, the nations are to have a share in the promises to Abraham: 'The nobles of the nations assemble as the people of the God of Abraham, for the kings of the earth belong to God' (cf. 105:5–11).

In relation to the Mosaic covenant, Psalm 99 connects the Lord who is king in Zion with the God of the exodus and the judges. This psalm demonstrates the continuity of Sinai with Zion (cf. vv. 6–7), as do Psalms 78 and 132, where the choice of David as king is explicitly linked with covenant obedience. Because of the failure of the Davidic line to meet the conditions of the Davidic covenant, the psalmists grapple with the tension between the conditional and eternal aspects of God's promises (cf. 89; 132), a tension which leads to an increasing emphasis on the eschatological nature of God's rule from Zion (see above on 'The Davidic kingship').

A corollary to the notion that Yahweh reigns in Zion is that through his chosen king his rule over the nations is exercised (Ps. 2). The nations will be judged by the way they respond to this Messiah king. Psalm 89, like Psalm 2, greatly exalts the Davidic ruler as king on Zion. The first half of the psalm (vv. 1–37) speaks in glowing, almost extravagant terms about what Yahweh has done for his anointed ruler.

[51] Tan (1997: 27) aptly comments: 'Zion is inviolable only as long as Yahweh dwells in it and not because of some intrinsically sacred character on its part'; cf. Ollenberger 1987: 74.

The second half (vv. 38–52), like a psalm of lament, describes the anguished cries of the psalmist over the loss of Jerusalem. The nations, instead of submitting to the Messiah, are trampling on him.[52]

With the destruction of Jerusalem and the temple, the notion of Zion as the future, eschatological seat from which God's Messiah would rule, comes to the fore. Within the psalter, as elsewhere in the Old Testament, there is an increasing emphasis on the eschatological aspects of God's promises concerning Zion and the nations (cf. Ps. 87). The restoration of Israel, which will come from Zion, will occur first. Yahweh will effect this through his chosen Messiah who will vindicate his people. Salvation for the nations will involve their 'coming in' to worship God in holiness on Mt Zion (72:8–11; 102:12–22), submitting to his rule over them through his Messiah.

Conclusion

We conclude this chapter on mission in the Old Testament by turning to the final paragraph of Isaiah (66:18–24), an eschatological 'vision of staggering proportions' (Motyer 1993: 540), in which God's gracious plan for the world is marvellously presented. The Lord himself is the missionary who gathers and rescues, not simply the dispersed of Israel, but also people from 'all nations', in order that they may see his glory. The goal of mission is the glory of God, that he may be known and honoured for who he really is.

How this purpose is achieved is spelled out in verses 19–21. The Lord 'will set a sign' in the midst of the nations (v. 19),[53] and then (in one of the clearest Old Testament statements on the theme of missionary outreach)[54] he will send 'survivors', that is, the remnant of verses 12–16, to carry out his mission among the nations. The places to which they are sent (to Tarshish, the Libyans, etc.) stand for the farthest outposts of Isaiah's world and thus represent the whole earth. The divine mission will know no boundaries, racial, national or geographic, for it is to extend to all the world. The nations themselves are harvested so that Gentile converts from all peoples are brought to the Lord's holy

---

[52] Note McConville 1992: 31.

[53] This could be a signpost showing the way to those whom the Lord sends, or it could be the sending of the messengers itself. Others have understood the sign in terms of the wondrous birth of vv. 7–8, and interpreted it of 'the whole miraculous complex of events which occurred when Israel was judged and the church was born' (Webb 1996: 250).

[54] Motyer 1993: 541. Westermann (1969: 425) states, 'This is the first sure and certain mention of mission as we today employ the term – the sending of individuals to distant peoples in order to proclaim God's glory among them.'

mountain in Jerusalem and presented to him as holy offerings (v. 20). Both believing Jews and converted Gentiles are amazingly described as 'brothers' in the one family (v. 20), and are united in a new ministry (v. 21; cf. Rom. 15:15–16).

In a final description, which deals with the origin and outcome of God's mission (v. 22), a word of assurance is addressed to believing Israelites, the true children of Abraham in the Old Testament. The promises of the Abrahamic covenant will not fail (cf. v. 22 with Gen. 12:2; 15:5): an enduring *name* and countless *descendants* are guaranteed.[55] These will be perfectly fulfilled in the *new heavens and the new earth*, when all the peoples on earth will offer praise and worship to their creator and redeemer. God is creator and ruler of the universe. His mission is 'simply the outworking of the intentions he had at the beginning, expressed in the blessing he pronounced on the first pair and confirmed in the promises he made to Abraham' (Webb 1996: 251).

[55] Is. 66:24 serves as a reminder that divine judgment on those who curse is no less sure (cf. Gen. 12:3).

Chapter Three

The second-temple period

While the Christian canon itself provides little (if any) information regarding mission in the second-temple period, a survey of this period will prove indispensable, since such a discussion, together with the preceding chapter on mission in the Old Testament, will provide the necessary foundation for the following investigation of mission in the New Testament.

The following questions are particularly relevant. First, was second-temple Judaism, and the Judaism contemporary with Jesus and the early church, a missionary religion?[1] In other words, did Judaism actively set out to make converts to its faith? This seems to be indicated by passages such as Matthew 23:15, where Jesus is quoted as saying: 'Woe to you, teachers of the law and Pharisees, you hypocrites! You travel over land and sea to win a single convert, and when he becomes one, you make him twice as much a son of hell as you are.' If references such as these are taken as evidence that Judaism was a missionary religion, the early church's missionizing could be viewed as having functioned largely within the parameters already established by Judaism. Or was Judaism merely winning proselytes by way of attraction? If so, the Christian missionary movement depicted in the book of Acts or Paul's writings should be considered to be discontinuous with Judaism in significant ways, introducing the (largely) new element of active outreach.

Second, what were the ways by which other religions and philosophical movements in the Graeco-Roman world sought to win followers? The answer to this question will help determine the extent to which Jesus and the early Christians adapted the missionary practices of other movements or whether their outreach was unprecedented and unparalleled in the surrounding world. Since it is the primary interest of the present study to explore degrees of continuity or discontinuity

---

[1] For a discussion of the foundational issue whether or not Old Testament Israel was to engage in mission the way it is understood today, see already 'The question of Israel's "mission" to the nations' in ch. 2 above.

between the missions of Jesus and the early church on the one hand and second-temple Judaism or Graeco-Roman religions on the other, this question will set the parameters for the following treatment.

Mission and second-temple Judaism

The issue of whether or not second-temple Judaism was engaged in mission has recently received considerable attention. The older consensus was represented by scholars such as Harnack and Jeremias, who held that the mission of the early church has been in essential continuity with the missionary efforts of the Jews.[2] This position was subsequently argued forcefully by Georgi.[3] Recently, however, both McKnight (1991) and Goodman (1994), followed by Levinskaya (1996), have challenged the traditional view that second-temple Judaism was a missionary religion.[4] Feldman (1993), on the other hand, continues to maintain that Judaism was engaged in active outreach to the Gentiles, with Paget (1996) taking a mediating position.

McKnight and Goodman in particular have recognized that the

---

[2] Harnack 1972; Jeremias (1958), who begins his discussion with the statement, 'At the time of Jesus' appearance an unparalleled period of missionary activity was in progress in Israel', contending that 'Judaism was the first great missionary religion to make its appearance in the Mediterranean world' (11). In this Jeremias quotes virtually verbatim G. F. Moore (1927: 1:323–324), without, however, noting the latter's highly significant qualification that second-temple Judaism was 'missionary ... with a difference: The Jews did not send out missionaries into the *partes infidelium* expressly to proselyte [sic] among the heathen.' *Cf.* also Kuhn (1954: 161), who calls the first century AD 'the great missionary century of Judaism' (our translation).

[3] Georgi (1986), esp. ch. 2 entitled 'Missionary Activity in New Testament Times', building on Rosen and Bertram (1929) as well as Dalbert (1954); Georgi's argument is accepted by Hahn (1965: 22–23), who nevertheless concludes that 'even though it [second-temple Judaism] may have been a vital movement ... it can hardly be spoken of as "mission"'. *Cf.* also Axenfeld (1904: 78–79), who lists the following as Jewish preparatory elements for Christian mission: the LXX, apologetic-polemical inter-testamental Jewish literature, the offices of apostles, prophets and teachers, the catechization and baptism of proselytes, the forms and times of prayer, the study of Scripture, the form of worship services, and the organization of congregations; and Flusser (1992: 80), who claims that 'the development of Judaism in the intertestamental period is a real *preparatio evangelica* for the coming of Jesus'.

[4] See already Nock (1972: II:929): 'We should be cautious in inferring widespread efforts by Jews to convert Gentiles. Individual Jews did undoubtedly try to "draw men to the Law", but in the main the proselyte was the man who came to the Law, and the duty of the Jew was to commend the Law by his example ... rather than by missionary endeavor'. *Cf.* also Cohen (1992: 21): 'Judaism in the first century B.C.E. and first century C.E., in both the land of Israel and the Diaspora, was not a "missionary religion". Rather it was open to converts and did nothing to raise obstacles in their path, but with a few notable exceptions it also did little or nothing to solicit them.'

outcome of the discussion depends to a significant extent on one's definition of 'mission' in relation to second-temple Judaism.[5] Both argue against a broad definition of the term, urging instead that the expression be limited to a *conscious, deliberate, organized and extensive effort to convert others to one's religion by way of evangelization or proselytization*. Hence the question becomes not merely whether or not the Jewish religion was successful in attracting converts or proselytes – for this is beyond dispute – but whether this was the result of intentional Jewish missionary efforts or not.[6] For it has been argued already on the basis of the term 'proselyte' itself (*prosēlytos*, from *proserchomai*, 'to approach, to come to') that the initiative lay, not with the religious group itself, but with the person interested in joining it, in the present case with Gentiles desiring to join Judaism.[7]

It is important to recognize at the outset that this particular issue is not primarily a *theological* but a *historical* one. The question is not '*Should* Judaism have engaged in mission?' or 'Is a missionary orientation consistent with the essential features of Judaism?' but '*Did* second-temple Judaism in fact engage in mission, narrowly defined?' In interaction with the relevant literature – including intertestamental Jewish 'propaganda' literature (such as the *Letter of Aristeas* or the *Sibylline Oracles*), Josephus (esp. *Against Apion*), Philo and several Graeco-Roman writers, both historical (Tacitus, Suetonius, Dio Cassius) and satirical (Horace, Juvenal) – we will first highlight the pertinent issues and then draw relevant conclusions.

Survey of major issues

First, McKnight has rightly drawn attention to the fallacious logic employed by those who use population statistics as evidence for an

---

[5] In a strangely dated treatment of Jewish proselytism, LaGrand (1999) fails to mention McKnight, Goodman and other recent scholarship on the issue.

[6] Barclay (1996: 408, n. 11) contends that 'the definition of "missionary" partly determines the conclusions drawn'. He himself, however, dissents from the emerging new consensus (317–318, n. 89): 'Goodman (1994) has argued that, before 100 CE at least, there was no concerted Jewish mission to the Gentile world; this may be true (on his definition of "mission"), but it does not gainsay the fact that Gentiles were attracted to Judaism to varying degrees throughout our period and probably aided by Jews in the process.' See also the discussion of Borgen (1996) below.

[7] *Cf.* e.g. Goodman (1994: 86): 'the etymology of the word "proselyte" implies movement by the gentile concerned ... and not a bringing in by the body of the Jews'. *Cf.* also Bosch 1991: 521, n. 2. Schlatter (1906: 69) notes that the synagogue took a passive stance toward Gentiles: 'Missionary work thus is not one of the traits that forms part of the image of a devout person.' Proselytes were received, 'yet always the ones who requested incorporation into the community' (our translations). *Cf.* further Str-B 1:925.

intertestamental Jewish mission.[8] Apart from the fact that demographic estimates vary significantly, the data say nothing about the *cause(s)* for an increase in the Jewish population.[9] A Jewish mission is merely one of several possible inferences. In the ultimate analysis, the available evidence proves inconclusive regarding the causes for Jewish population growth, and certainly inadequate to settle the question of whether the initiative in proselytization lay with the Jews or with Gentile converts.[10]

Second, a certain amount of weight should be given to the lack of information concerning the names of any Jewish missionaries as well as concerning the mode and methods of Jewish outreach.[11] If the Jews were in fact engaged in active evangelism, we know virtually nothing about who carried it out and how.[12] While there is some evidence regarding conversions, it is unclear whether such conversions were in fact the result of intentional missionary activity or not.[13]

Third, it is important to understand the changing dynamics in Jewish history during the millennium prior to Christ's coming. We can do no better than to quote Bedell (1998):

> During the United and Divided Kingdoms, Jews tended to relate
> to the surrounding peoples on the national level, and on this

---

[8] *Cf.* McKnight 1991: 133, n. 20 and forthcoming.

[9] *Cf.* Kasting (1969: 11–13), who contends that the large number of Jews in the diaspora is not necessarily a result of Jewish mission and also notes that the Jews initially settled in the diaspora not for religious but economic or other reasons.

[10] Contra Feldman (1993: 555–556, n. 20), who contends that only proselytism can account for the vast increase in the Jewish population, although he concedes that such is only one possible explanation. But Feldman's treatment suffers from imprecision in the definition of 'mission', when he refers to the fact that 'Judaism ... spread to the entire race of humankind' as evidence for *mission* (297).

[11] McKnight 1991, ch. 3, 'The Methods of Proselytizing', esp. 57; cf. also Sandmel (1969: 22): 'We do not know of even one Jewish missionary who might be mentioned in some analogy to Paul.' Keener (1999: 548) points out that 'Judaism had no central sending agency and hence no "missionaries" in the formal sense' (though he does advocate a 'Jewish concern for Gentile conversions'). Contra Georgi 1986: 83–228.

[12] Note the remarkable admission by Feldman (1993: 289), a strong advocate of Jewish missionary activity in the second-temple period: 'If [Judaism was a missionary religion], how can we explain this fact when we neither know the names of any Jewish missionaries nor possess, as it seems, a single missionary tract?'

[13] This is inadequately acknowledged by Bedell (1998) who lists as 'Evidence of Conversions' Greeks in Antioch (Josephus, *BJ*, 7.45), women in Damascus (Josephus, *B. J.*, 2.559–561) and adherents to the Jewish law in every city in Syria (Jos., *BJ*, 2.463), referring also to Josephus' boast that every city, whether Greek or barbarian, contained those who had taken on the observance of the Jewish law (*Contra Ap.*, 2.282) and forced conversions during the military campaigns of John Hyrcanus I and others (Josephus, *Ant.*, 13.254–258, 318–319, 395–397).

level relations were frequently hostile and militaristic. But with the Assyrian and the Babylonian captivities a new social situation prevailed. Jews now had to learn to live in alien social environments among the idolatrous pagans ... The dynamics of social relationship had changed from an emphasis on the national level to a focus on personal relations. Formerly it had been the Gentile, as the resident alien, who had interacted with Jews on the personal level. The resident alien had been part of a minority and the Jews in the majority, but now the demographics were reversed. Social pressures forced Jews to relate to Gentiles personally in the market and in the forum instead of on the battle-field or as a minority subject people. The resident alien had been under some benign social pressure to convert to Judaism; the pagan masses among which the Jewish Dispersion lived were under no such pressure. New forces must evolve if these were to convert to the God of Israel. The return to the land after the Babylonian captivity did little to reduce personal contact with Gentiles. A large Jewish diaspora continued to live outside of the land of Israel during the second-temple period. Jews within the land continued to have contact with Gentiles, since for much of this period they were a conquered people living in an occupied territory. This increased personal contact with Gentiles led to a range of opinions toward them within second-temple Judaism.

These observations lead us to consider, fourth, the question of the orientation of certain intertestamental Jewish writings.[14] It has been alleged that books such as the *Letter of Aristeas*, certain of the *Sibylline Oracles* (esp. 3), *Joseph and Asenath*, or Josephus' *Against Apion* were written with a Gentile audience in view, to be used as propagandistic tools in the Jewish mission. However, it has recently been recognized that this kind of literature fulfilled, at least in part, the function of helping ethnic Jews to define their own position in the midst of a Gentile environment.[15] As McKnight (1991: 62)

[14] Classic treatments include Dalbert 1954 and Friedländer 1903. See also Schürer 1986: 3:617–700 and Conzelmann 1992.

[15] *Cf.* Kraabel 1994: 71–88. *Cf.* also the seminal article by Tcherikover (1956: 169–193), who is followed by McKnight (1991: 58–59; critique by Feldman 1993: 305–306); Conzelmann (1992: 140) takes exception to Tcherikover's distinction between internal edification and external apologetic and uses the term 'apologetic' for both kinds of writings. *Cf.* further Cohen (1992: 17): 'in recent years scholarship has tended to see Greco-Jewish literature as oriented primarily to Jews and as serving the needs of the

contends, 'we do not have evidence of conversion through literature'.

Fifth, in order to investigate this issue, terms such as 'apologetic' and 'propaganda' on the one hand and 'evangelization' and 'proselytization' on the other must be carefully defined and distinguished. While 'apologetic' may be understood as the defence of one's faith and religious convictions, 'propaganda' involves the literary dissemination of such beliefs. Both constitute indirect means of converting non-adherents of one's religion; 'evangelization' and 'proselytization', on the other hand, represent direct means. Expressions such as 'mission' or 'conversion', likewise, must be properly delimited.[16] For as Bowers contends, not all religious expansion is intentional. Rather, such may occur by natural means in the form of economic, military, cultural, or ideological expansion. Other kinds of non-religious expansion include conquest as well as ordinary processes of social circulation, including trade, immigration, or casual interpenetration of adjacent peoples (Bowers 1980: 318). Moreover, even among deliberate efforts, distinctions must be made. A religious faith may spread by simple means of attraction or by active solicitation. It may be occasional or continuous. And it may be the common tendency of adherents as a whole, be delegated to special agents, or involve individual initiatives unsupported by the general body.

Sixth, it must be acknowledged that second-temple Judaism was by no means monolithic (Kraabel 1992: 9–14). Rigid distinctions between Palestinian and Hellenistic Judaism should in any case be avoided (Hengel 1974). As recent scholarship has conclusively demonstrated, second-temple Judaism evidenced a wide range of orientations that cannot be subsumed under a single heading (Neusner, Green and Frerichs 1987). Sectarians such as the Qumran community were primarily concerned with their own election and predestination (considering themselves to be the last remaining faithful remnant) while remaining utterly indifferent toward a Gentile mission.[17] Jews in Palestine seem to have engaged primarily in discussions of internal

---

Jewish community. Even its apologetic function was intended to persuade not Gentiles but Jews, to show them that loyalty to Judaism did not necessarily mean a denial of their ambient culture.'

[16] See further the discussion below. On definitional matters, see esp. McKnight 1991: 4–7, 49–50; and Goodman 1994: 1–19.

[17] See esp. Schiffman 1997: 153–171. In fact, documents such as the 'War Scroll' actually take pleasure in God's future judgment of the nations (1QM 4:12; 6:5–6; 9:5–9; 11:13–17; 12:11–12; 14:5, 7–8; 15:1–2; 16:1; 17:1; 19:3–4). See also Kuhn 1954: 163–164; McKnight 1991: 38; Hahn 1965: 21; and Bedell 1998.

Jewish affairs, whether national or religious. Jews in the diaspora, on the other hand, by the very nature of their existential situation, had more need and opportunity for dialogue and dealings with the Gentile world (Kuhn 1954: 162–163). Nevertheless, even many diaspora Jews held the Gentiles responsible for bringing destruction on Jerusalem and wished for God's speedy destruction of the nations.[18] Others took a more positive stance.[19] Undue generalizations regarding second-temple Judaism should therefore be avoided.[20]

Seventh, while the issue of whether second-temple Judaism engaged in an active outreach to non-Jews or not is primarily a historical one, this does not alter the fact that important theological issues are tied up with this question. A comparative-religions approach, for instance, might explain the ascendancy of Christianity largely in naturalistic terms, viewing it as the result of the early church's emulation of Jewish patterns of outreach. McKnight's rather rosy picture of second-temple Judaism, on the other hand, concluding that intertestamental Jews generally led holy and righteous lives and sustained positive attitudes towards Gentiles joining their religion, may be due at least in part to the strong pressures exerted in the current cultural and scholarly climate to avoid any hints of racism or discrimination against Jews (McKnight 1991: 29). In the end, the question cannot be dealt with apart from conceptualities such as canon, biblical theology or salvation history. When Paul confronts his Jewish contemporaries by echoing Isaiah's or Ezekiel's denouncements of their fellow-Jews, 'God's name is blasphemed among the Gentiles because of you' (Rom. 2:24; cf. Is. 52:5; Ezek. 36:22), how can this be squared with McKnight's assessment that second-temple Judaism was largely engaging in holy and righteous conduct and sustaining positive attitudes towards the Gentiles? Care must therefore be taken that extracanonical

[18] Bedell (1998) refers to Psalms of Solomon 2:1–2, 19–25; 8:23; 17:1–25; and Jubilees 15:26.

[19] See ibid., who refers to Philo, Decalogue 64; Jos., Ant., 2.152; Sirach 18:13; Wisdom 18:4; Testament of Levi 14:4; Testament of Simeon 7:2. Passages anticipating the salvation of Gentiles in the last time, often in connection with the coming of the Messiah, include 1 Enoch 10:21; 48:4; 90:30–33; 91:14; 4 Ezra 6:26; 2 Baruch 72:1–5; Testament of Levi 2:11; 4:4; Testament of Judah 24:6; 25:5; Testament of Zebulon 9:8; Testament of Asher 7:3; Testament of Benjamin 10:5. References speaking of Gentiles coming to Jerusalem to worship, giving gifts to Israel, include Tobit 13:11; 1 Enoch 53:1; Testament of Benjamin 9:2; 2 Baruch 68:5; Sibylline Oracles 3:702–731,772–775.

[20] See Balch (1998: 22–47), who surveys attitudes toward foreigners in 2 Maccabees, Eupolemus, Esther, Aristeas and Luke-Acts and finds that these writings 'do not promote one normative relationship, but rather a spectrum of possible relationships with foreigners' (46).

intertestamental data be sensitively related to biblical information, and it must be acknowledged that even historical questions have significant theological implications.

Eighth, and here we part ways with another part of McKnight's and Goodman's thesis, it seems unduly restrictive to limit mission in any sense merely to active outreach with the deliberate attempt to evangelize and to convert people to one's religion. While it is useful to distinguish between mission in a narrow and a broad sense, even the making of converts by way of passive attraction may, in a certain sense, be considered to constitute 'mission'.[21] As will be seen further below, this point is crucial. When Peter, for example, in his first epistle depicts the church as emulating Israel's mission (cf. esp. the allusion to Is. 43:20 in 1 Pet. 2:9) and does so primarily in passive terms, it seems arbitrary to exclude this stance from the orbit of 'mission' by limiting such exclusively to an active 'missionary' going out. Rather, believers' corporate witness, whether by way of godly response to suffering or adversity, or through ethical behaviour in their family relationships or at their workplace, may be seen as both a part of, and an indispensable prerequisite for, a more active form of propagation of the Christian faith (cf. also John's Gospel). The concept of mission must not be so truncated as to be reduced solely to an 'active' element while more 'passive' elements are filtered out entirely, with the effect that a full-orbed understanding of mission is hampered.

Ninth, it seems best to reserve the term 'mission' in the present context for a convert-seeking enterprise that is at the root spiritually motivated and pursued on the basis of a theological rationale, be it that of a divine commission, an eschatological hope, or the belief that the unsaved will suffer eternal punishment for their rejection of God. This would exclude from classification as 'mission' those efforts or effects (see points five and eight above) that result in a person's attachment to

---

[21] *Cf.* the helpful discussion by Hahn 1965: 20–21, n. 3. See also Bedell (1998), who identifies the 'basic problem in McKnight's hypothesis' as McKnight's placing 'too much emphasis on intentional effort rather than on results'. But Bedell himself seems to go too far in the opposite direction when he maintains that '[a] believing society may be "missionary" *in its effect* – and therefore participating in "mission" – without sending out missionaries! Accordingly, one may analyze the mission activity in second-temple Judaism by looking at the actual growth accomplished and also the dynamic forces which attracted pagans to faith in Israel's God even without a program of missionaries actually being sent out to evangelize Gentiles.' It is doubtful whether Bedell himself would desire to downplay the importance of a missionary consciousness and intentionality in mission (especially for Jesus and the early as well as contemporary church), as his statements seem to imply. See further the discussion and conclusions below.

one's group, whether the 'missionizing' group remains active or passive, if the primary or predominant content of such association is not found in spiritual conversion. For instance, the Jews doubtless had a significant cultural impact on Graeco-Roman society, such as by the spread of the Jewish week (Schlatter 1906: 70–71), so that Josephus could claim: 'there is not one city, Greek or barbarian ... to which our customs have not spread' (*Ap.* 2.282). Similarly, the philosopher Seneca, one of Emperor Nero's chief advisors, wrote caustically: 'The customs of this accursed race [the Jews] have gained such influence that they are now received throughout the world. The vanquished have given laws to their victors' (*victi victoribus leges dederunt*; quoted by Augustine, *City of God* 6.11). But this indirect cultural influence arguably falls outside the scope of 'mission' in a religious sense of the term. And while it is, of course, difficult to distinguish between spiritual and socio-cultural motives,[22] it is vital to insist on defining 'mission' for our present purposes not merely as a nationalistic or imperialistic enterprise but as a religio-theological one. The practical implication of these considerations is that even if second-temple Judaism should be found to have engaged in passive 'mission', it may in the end be judged not to have engaged in mission, properly defined, if its efforts were primarily nationalistic.[23]

Matthew 23:15

Before sketching out some conclusions, we must briefly consider Matthew 23:15, arguably the verse of Scripture that has had the most impact on the present debate.[24] Traditionally, this passage has been taken as incontrovertible evidence that second-temple Judaism was engaged in active missionary efforts (McKnight 1991: 106–108). But this consensus has been increasingly challenged in the following ways. To begin with, it has been argued that 'travel over land and sea' may constitute a figurative, idiomatic expression denoting extensive effort

[22] Indeed, as Hengel (1974: 307) points out, 'to become a Jew was never simply a religious action; it was always also a political decision: on his conversion the Gentile became a member of the Jewish "ethnos"'.

[23] *Cf.* here Hahn (1965: 24–25), who helpfully urges a distinction between second-temple Judaism's efforts to win over Gentiles and mission 'in the real sense'. He suggests we call the attempt to gain God-fearers 'religious propaganda', and efforts to obtain complete conversions 'the recruiting of proselytes'. Hahn is criticized by Kasting (1969: 30).

[24] The treatment by Bedell (1998), who simply assumes that Matt. 23:15 refers to 'planned and practised proselytization' on part of the Pharisees without wrestling with the complex exegetical issues raised by this passage, is inadequate in this regard, as is LaGrand's (1999: 149–150) reference to Sandmel (1969: 22).

rather than geographical movement (cf. 1 Maccabees 8:23, 32; Josephus, *Ant.* 4.190; 11.53).[25] Also, the point has been made that the term 'proselyte' (RSV) does not necessarily refer to non-Jews but may merely be used in a broad sense to refer to a 'convert'.[26] While Gentile-become-Jew was the term's usual point of reference in the latter part of the first century AD, it had not yet acquired technical force, so that other applications in Matthew's day were still possible.[27] Hence Goodman, followed by Levinskaya, has recently argued that Jesus here merely chides the Pharisees' efforts to convert fellow-Jews to their own particular interpretation of *halakhah*.[28] And in any case, what Jesus here condemns is not Jewish mission as such, but misguided Pharisaic zeal in proselytization, whether of fellow-Jews or non-Jews (McKnight 1991: 107), with the result that these converts become 'twice as much a son of hell' as the Pharisees themselves (Carson 1984: 479). Finally, if Jesus' opponents in Matthew 23:15 are from the conservative school of Rabbi Shammai, the dominant form of Pharisaism in that day, a reference to Gentile proselytization is further rendered improbable by Shammai's well-attested aversion to receiving Gentile proselytes (cf. e.g. *b. Šabbat* 31a).[29] For these and other reasons, the verse should be dethroned from its role as proof text for second-temple Judaism as a missionary religion.

Overall assessment

Was second-temple Judaism a missionary religion? If by 'mission' is meant a conscious, deliberate, extensive effort to convert non-fellow-religionists to one's religion, the available evidence does not sustain such a conclusion. Despite efforts by Feldman and others, we therefore concur with McKnight and Goodman in their essential findings. A

[25] *Cf.* e.g. Kasting (1969: 21): '"To traverse sea and land" should thus not be taken literally; rather, it is a metaphoric expression conveying the extensive propagandistic effort made for the purpose of converting individuals' (our translation).

[26] This is the conclusion of M. Rapinchuk. Carson (1984: 478–479) writes that '"proselyte" ... at this time [the writing of Matthew's Gospel] probably refers to those who have been circumcised and have pledged to submit to the full rigors of Jewish law, including the oral tradition for which the Pharisees were so zealous'. See also the next note.

[27] Regarding the fluidity of the terms 'proselyte' and 'God-fearer', see esp. Lake 1933: 5:85–88; Feldman 1950: 200–208; Wilcox 1981: 102–122; Kraabel 1981: 113–126; and Finn 1985: 75–84. Note also the phrase 'God-fearing proselytes' in Acts 13:43.

[28] Goodman 1994: 69–74, following a suggestion by Munck 1959: 267, and Levinskaya 1996: 36–39. *Cf.* the critique by Jeremias 1958: 18, n. 1.

[29] A strand of anti-Shammaite polemic in the Gospel of Matthew may be traced in the following instances: 5:27–30, 38, 43; 12:9–14; 15:1–2; 19:3; 21:12–13; 23:4, 13, 16–23, 25–26, 29–35. *Cf.* Rapinchuk 1994.

cumulative case construed from isolated, disparate data remains itself fragmentary and inconclusive. We contend therefore that *second-temple Judaism was not a missionary religion*. Moreover, while Jews did allow sympathizers and proselytes to participate in their religious practices to a certain extent, their attitude (at least in Palestine) appeared generally to be guided by national or sectarian Jewish considerations, so that it is doubtful whether much of second-temple Judaism even can be said to have engaged in some form of 'passive' mission. These findings are significant for our evaluation of the mission of the early church, as will be seen further below.

Positively, we may affirm that many Gentiles were attracted to Judaism, particularly in the diaspora, and joined the Jews at their own initiative, be it as proselytes involving circumcision (in the case of males), full submission to the law and probably baptism, or as sympathizers or God-fearers.[30] The pervasive Jewish presence in the Graeco-Roman world, which included synagogue worship, an ethical life-style and monotheism, markedly set the Jews apart from their largely immoral pagan surroundings. The Jewish way of life proved attractive to many Gentiles, who chose to join Judaism, albeit not usually as a result of a direct Jewish mission. This is not to say that individual Jews refrained entirely from engaging in evangelistic dialogue or the use of propagandistic elements in their literature. Nor does it deny that Jews were often tolerant, even receptive, towards Gentile proselytes. But it disavows the notion that Judaism *as a whole* should be characterized as a missionary religion, with missionary outreach constituting a core tenet of second-temple Judaism which Jews generally held and regularly practised.[31]

As Kasting correctly notes, Jewish attitudes toward Gentiles in the second-temple period were generally torn between two extremes: universalism and exclusivity, attraction and rejection, openness and separation (Kasting 1969: 32). McKnight likewise detects concurrent

[30] The questions of whether or not circumcision was in every instance a requirement for a Gentile proselyte and whether or not the categories of 'proselyte' and 'God-fearer' were technical and fixed continue to be subjects of debate (though an affirmative answer would appear to be suggested by the evidence from the Aphrodisias inscription which lists Gentile God-fearers [*theosebeis*] as synagogue patrons separate from Jews and proselytes; cf. Levinskaya 1996: chs. 4 – 7, esp. 4 and 7). But these matters do not materially affect our broad general conclusions here.

[31] *Cf.* Conzelmann (1992: 134): '[The Jews] carried on a propaganda campaign and attempted to win converts from the Gentiles. But mission was not a *conditio sine qua non* of their existence. The church, on the other hand, could only exist as a missionary institution.'

dispositions of integration and resistance in second-temple Judaism.[32] While the Jews recoiled from unnecessary contact with Gentiles because of their idolatry, low ethical and moral standards and ceremonial uncleanness (cf. e.g. Acts 10:28), Gentiles were allowed some participation in Jewish religion.[33] Jews, in turn, participated in Gentile society.[34] At the same time, Israelites travelling in Gentile countries were in a very difficult position, which would have rendered the task of Jewish missionaries exceedingly difficult (Schürer 1979: 2:84). In fact, Juvenal alleged that certain Jews would show the way only to co-religionists and would direct only the circumcised to a well (*Sat.* 14.103–104).

Flusser, finally, contends that Jews and Gentiles in Palestine largely went their separate ways. While Judaism and paganism existed side by side, Jews were careful to keep their distance from idolatry and pagan customs. Thus a quasi-segregation of Jews and pagans prevailed in New Testament times (Flusser 1987: 1065–1100). As Flusser states categorically, 'As a rule, proselytes and "God-fearers" were welcome by the Jews and regarded very highly, but there is in Palestine no active propaganda to further the cause of proselytism. This was one of the points in which the ancient Judaism of the Land of Israel differed from that of the hellenistic Diaspora and from Christianity' (Flusser 1987: 1095). Moreover, there is considerable evidence for Jewish indifference towards pagan conversion and for Jewish preoccupation with internal affairs. As Goodman remarks: 'it was extremely unusual for any Jew in the first century CE to view the encouragement of Gentiles to convert to Judaism as a praiseworthy act ... In the diaspora Jews were not much concerned whether particular outsiders joined them or not.'[35] Many diaspora Jews lived in pagan surroundings but led their own separate lives, religiously as well as socially. They were people with their own ancestral laws who felt no imperative impulse to make religious propaganda, being convinced that paganism, as an

---

[32] McKnight lists the following integrating tendencies: universalism, Gentile participation in Judaism, citizenship, Hellenistic education, intermarriage, assimilation and apostasy. Resistance tendencies include separation, temple circumscription, warnings of idolatry, prohibition of intermarriage, revolting against reforms and vindictive judgment scenes (1991: 11–29).

[33] *Cf.* Josephus, *BJ* 7.45; Acts 13:16, 26, 43, 50; 17:4, 17. Gentiles' participation in Jewish temple worship in Jerusalem was not limited to proselytes but involved, according to the custom of the day, even Gentiles who wished in no way to make a confession of faith in the 'Jewish superstition'. *Cf.* Schürer 1979: 2:309–313.

[34] For a general survey of intertestamental Jewish attitudes toward Gentiles, see J. M. Scott 1995: 335–356; cf. also McKnight 1991: 11–48.

[35] Goodman 1989: 176–177, quoted in Kraabel 1994: 78.

ungodly phenomenon, would disappear at the end of time (Flusser 1987: 1095–1096).

Moreover, even where Jews *were* engaged in efforts to reach out to Gentiles, their motivation was largely apologetic or nationalistic.[36] Often, the aim was mere 'naturalization' rather than spiritual conversion.[37] This stands in marked contrast to the Old Testament notion, given expression already in the Abrahamic promise, that in Abraham's seed all the nations of the earth would be blessed (Gen. 12:1–3). It also falls short of the future expectation of the full inclusion of Gentiles in the orbit of God's salvation which is vividly portrayed in apocalyptic portions of Old Testament prophecy.[38] If anything, the latter notion would actually have *prevented* intertestamental Jews from active outreach to Gentiles, since the ingathering of Gentiles was generally considered to be God's own eschatological prerogative (cf. e.g. *4 Ezra* or *2 Baruch*). Consequently, any Jewish effort at evangelizing Gentiles would have been considered to constitute a usurpation of Yahweh's sovereign salvation-historical authority.[39]

Jews therefore generally refrained from seeking to hasten the coming of the eschaton, being largely preoccupied with their own internal religious and national affairs. So-called intertestamental Jewish propaganda literature, to be sure, occasionally includes a general apologetic for the Jewish faith, but this is too vague and general to be taken as evidence for specific, concrete and concerted Jewish missionary efforts.[40] True, Jewish exclusiveness was already surmounted by the prophetic idea of God as the God of all the nations, especially in Isaiah,

[36] This is inadequately recognized by Keener (1999: 548), who points to wide scholarly recognition of a 'Jewish concern for Gentile conversions' – but for what reason? And to what end?

[37] *Cf.* Hahn 1965: 24; and J. M. Scott 1995: 342. *Cf.* also McKnight (1991: 47): 'proselytization is resocialization or nationalization'.

[38] *Cf.* Hahn (1965: 23): 'there is no question here of a real mission – nowhere is any claim made to a special divine commission – nor does the Old Testament eschatological basis of the conversion of the Gentiles play a decisive part'. *Cf.* also Jeremias 1958; Kuhn 1954: 163.

[39] See already the discussion of 'The eschatological pilgrimage of the nations' in ch. 2 above. See further McKnight (1991: 74), who contends that it may be inferred from the pervasive Jewish belief that an act of God would lead to mass conversions of Gentiles in the eschaton that the Jews were not presently engaged in missionary activity. Contra Kasting 1969: 31.

[40] *Cf.* Schürer (1986: 3:617–700), who distinguishes between Jewish intertestamental literature intended to attract converts (*Sibylline Oracles*) and apologetic or general propaganda literature about Jewish ethics and theology (*Letter of Aristeas*). He views Jewish intertestamental writings written under Gentile pseudonyms in terms of a more general encouragement towards the acceptance of Jewish attitudes, contending that missionary literature would be unlikely to succeed in a Gentile guise.

where Israel is summoned to proclaim God to the nations (42:1–4; 49:1–6) and to become a light to the Gentiles (42:6; 49:6). Yet the prophet's prediction that the Gentiles will also be accepted by God (56:1–8) should not be taken to imply that Israel in fact rose to the challenge. More often than not, passages such as Isaiah 49:6 were interpreted merely in Jewish nationalistic terms (*Sibylline Oracles* 3.195; Rom. 2:19–20), and the conversion sought was towards the viewpoints of Judaism in general or towards a certain Jewish sect in particular.

Implications for mission in the New Testament

For these reasons it must be concluded that Jesus and the early church did not merely build upon Jewish precedent but significantly advanced the notion of mission.[41] This is not to deny that the presence of Jewish synagogues all over the Graeco-Roman world greatly aided particularly Paul's and the early church's missionary efforts (Georgi 1986: 84–92; Kasting 1969: 19). Nor is it to deny several other ways in which Judaism had a preparatory role for the early church's mission. Indeed, the largely positive witness provided by the Jews' ethical life-style, as well as their adherence to monotheism, could not fail to pave the way for such efforts (even though the latter was, of course, as later in the case of Christianity, viewed as atheism by the Graeco-Roman world). Thus we concur with Hengel (1974: 169) that Judaism 'represented an ethical monotheism grounded in the doctrine of creation, to which the missionary preaching of the early church could attach itself'.

Thus mission represents a significant element of discontinuity between Judaism and Christianity. How may this striking difference be explained? How is it, for instance, that Isaiah's visionary statement regarding the Servant of the Lord, 'I will also make you a light for the Gentiles, that you may bring my salvation to the ends of the earth' (Is. 49:6), was appropriated and realized not by second-temple Judaism but by Jesus (Luke 2:32), Paul (Acts 13:47) and the early church? Is Hengel (1974: 309) correct when he finds the power source of the Christian mission in the 'incomparable vitality and dynamism of the Jewish people', who engaged 'in a world-wide mission which was likewise without analogy, and then in the new force which burst the

[41] Contra Harnack (1972: 15): 'To the Jewish mission which preceded it, the Christian mission was indebted [in many ways] ... The amount of this debt is so large, that one might venture to claim the *Christian mission as a continuation of the Jewish propaganda*' (emphasis ours). But see Kraabel (1994: 85): 'without a Jewish mission it will be necessary to find another explanation for the early, energetic and pervasive mission of the new religion [*i.e.* Christianity]'.

framework of a nationalistic legalism which had grown too narrow with its prophetic and eschatological appeal: the primitive Christianity which grew out of Judaism'?

We do not think so. For as Hengel (1974: 313) himself notes, 'A universal missionary consciousness could not really develop freely in the face of this elemental impulse towards national self-preservation.' Rather, the answer to the irresistible spread of Christianity arguably lies in Jesus' own messianic consciousness, issuing, among other things, in his commission to disciple the nations (Matt. 28:19–20; cf. Acts 1:8), and in the conviction of the early church that the eschaton, including Yahweh's ingathering of the Gentiles, had already begun *in Jesus*. The early Christians, in turn, understood themselves to serve as God's agents, bringing his salvation 'to the ends of the earth'. When therefore Feldman contends that Acts everywhere assumes the validity of the early church's mission to the Gentiles because of the antecedent Gentile mission established by the Jews (Feldman 1993: 324), it must be responded that, to the contrary, Acts clearly indicates the early church's reluctance to engage in such a mission, which was overcome by the seminal vision given by God to Peter prior to the conversion of Cornelius (Acts 10).

Moreover, as will be argued in our treatment of mission in Mark and Matthew below, Jesus himself confined his active outreach to the Jews (even though he allowed Gentiles to approach him at their own initiative). Arguably, if Judaism had already engaged in an extensive outreach to Gentiles, the reluctance on the part of Jesus and the early church to do likewise appears entirely incongruous. But if our conclusion regarding second-temple Judaism's reluctance to seek Gentile converts is correct, surely Jesus would have operated in concordance with the stance adopted by contemporary Judaism. Moreover, since Jesus' stance in this regard is arguably indicative of God's will at that particular stage of salvation history, second-temple Judaism's primarily passive stance towards a Gentile mission should not be construed as necessarily sinful or contrary to God's will. Rather, it is found to cohere with the divine injunction for Israel to function as a mediatorial 'priestly kingdom' (Exod. 19:6; cf. 1 Pet. 2:5) and as an outpost of divine revelation in the surrounding pagan world.[42] In God's plan, the large-scale ingathering of Gentiles into the orbit of salvation belonged to the eschaton. It was to be inaugurated by the Isaianic Servant of the Lord, Jesus (cf. e.g. John 12, esp. 37–41), and to be

---

[42] Jonah's mission to Nineveh (which consisted primarily of a proclamation of divine judgment) is no real exception. See the section on Jonah in ch. 2 of this volume.

implemented by the Spirit-directed new messianic community.

Mission and Graeco-Roman religion and philosophy

If second-temple Judaism did not provide the early Christians with a paradigm for its mission, what about Graeco-Roman philosophies or religions? Did Jesus and the early church follow the pattern of itinerant Cynic-Stoic philosophers in propagating their beliefs? Before turning to a discussion of mission in the New Testament, we must briefly address this question. The issue here is not whether Graeco-Roman religions featured itinerant preachers or engaged in propagandistic efforts – they did.[43] Conquering nations, whether Egyptians, Assyrians, Chaldeans, Persians, Greeks, or Romans, all took the opportunity to introduce vassal states to their respective pantheons while frequently tolerating local religions (Gressmann 1924: 10). The spread of imperial religion was part of the extension of political power.[44] Gressmann (1924: 23–24) even mentions 'beggar monks' who, according to the pattern of the Greek mythological figure of Attis, traversed the entire earth, initiating converts into mysteries, speaking of their own experiences, and singing songs of the divine Mother.

The question rather is whether these propagandistic efforts functioned in any way as paradigms for the missions of Jesus and the early church. But despite the best efforts of the fellows of the 'Jesus Seminar' and others, the notion that Jesus self-consciously emulated Cynic-Stoic or other Graeco-Roman patterns of persuasion in his mission has failed to garner broad support in general scholarship, and for good reason.[45] Ultimately, the New Testament data reveal that Jesus' messianic self-

[43] *Cf.* esp. Georgi 1986: 83–228. Georgi's treatment, however, is marred by fallacious logic: he compares Cynic-Stoic wandering preachers to Jewish propagandists; asserts that 'the popular philosophers should be regarded as the models for preaching and missionary activity in late antiquity' (100); concedes the scarcity of evidence for Jewish itinerant teachers in the pre-Talmudic period (100–101); argues that Paul and early Christians were so successful because they could build on established models (101); and thus believes to have established that Paul and the early Christians operated in conscious reference to pagan patterns of propagation! *Cf.* also Liefeld (1967); but note the critique by Bowers (1980: 321, n. 8), who rightly notes that the evidence visibly fails to support Liefeld's attempt to fit the Rabbis into the mould of the wandering preacher, in so far as patterns of movement affect the question.

[44] An infamous example of an attempted 'conversion' of a nation by force is Antiochus IV Epiphanes. *Cf.* Gressmann 1924: 17.

[45] See recently Eddy (1996: 449–469), who points particularly to the problem of dating and concurs with H. D. Betz 'that to presume a Cynic presence in the Galilee of Jesus' day is little more than "fanciful conjecture"' (467).

consciousness and mission are rooted primarily in Old Testament conceptualities, not in Graeco-Roman ones.[46] The fact that Jesus limited his mission to a fairly small territory in Palestine already constitutes presumptive evidence against the view that he took his cues to any significant extent from Graeco-Roman itinerant philosophers. More likely, he adopted certain contemporary rabbinic practices, albeit frequently with modification (cf. e.g. John 15:16; Köstenberger 1998c; Riesner 1991: 197). The same observation applies to the early church, which sought to emulate Jesus and to comply with her risen Lord's commission.

For these reasons it is not necessary here to provide a more detailed discussion of practices adopted by Graeco-Roman philosophers in the propagation of their beliefs. While Paul may have accommodated himself at times to such practices, such as in the case of his appearance at the Athenian Areopagus (cf. Acts 17:16–34), neither Jesus nor the early Christians looked in any significant degree to Graeco-Roman religion or philosophy in their search for paradigms for their mission.

Conclusion

We conclude therefore that the essential mission of the early church can be explained neither by recourse to second-temple Judaism nor to Graeco-Roman itinerant preaching and propaganda. The mission of the early Christians was unique. It was rooted in Jesus' appropriation of Old Testament messianic prophecy and his inauguration of Old Testament eschatological expectations regarding the inclusion of the Gentiles into the orbit of God's salvation, and it was carried out in fulfilment of his commission to disciple the nations and to extend the good news of salvation and forgiveness of sins to the ends of the earth.

---

[46] Contra Georgi (1986: 174), who claims to 'have been able to establish a determining influence of Hellenistic-Jewish Apologetics on the development of the early church's mission'; Schüssler Fiorenza (1976: 2): 'Jews as well as Christians appealed to the Greco-Roman world and used the means and methods of hellenistic religious propaganda ... The appropriation of such missionary-propagandistic forms was necessary if Judaism as well as Christianity were to succeed in the face of competition from other religions.'

Chapter Four

Mark

At a first glance, Mark's Gospel seems to have little to offer on mission. The prominence of discipleship failure, together with the absence of a final commissioning, appear to suggest to many that Mark is not interested in this subject.[1] The shift from the study of the actual contents of Mark to an exploration of the community behind the Gospel has further narrowed the scope of recent investigation.[2] Nevertheless, a vocal minority maintains that mission is a serious concern for Mark. Here it is particularly the instances where Jesus is shown ministering to Gentiles that have led some to argue that Mark's Gospel features Jesus as embarking on a 'Gentile mission'.[3]

Thus the spectrum of interpretive opinion reaches from those who find 'no mission' in Mark to those who find mission to be a significant theme in this Gospel. What are we therefore to conclude? In order to adjudicate between these claims, we will first trace the narrative flow of Mark's Gospel giving particular attention to references to mission. The ensuing discussion will explore the most pertinent issues arising from Mark's Gospel concerning mission. It will become evident that Mark's treatment of mission lies somewhere between the two positions sketched above. Mission turns out to be a significant concern for this evangelist, yet the mission to the Gentiles is essentially placed at a future time from the perspective of Jesus' earthly ministry.

---

[1] For example, the otherwise excellent entry by Guelich (1992: 512–525) does not mention mission at all. Neither do most commentaries or monographs on Mark. For a curious effort to excise mission from Mark's Gospel, see also Kilpatrick (1955: 145–158), who contends that 'universalism is absent from Mark' (157). Cf. also Harnack (1924: I:45, n. 2), arguing that Mark 'excluded the missionary question altogether'.

[2] But see now the devastating critique of such approaches by Bauckham 1997. Cf. Kato 1986: 194–195.

[3] Gill 1991: 35–41; Hahn 1965: 111–120; Kato 1986; Rhoads 1995: 340–355; Senior and Stuhlmueller 1983: 211–232; and Stock 1982: 130–144. Cf. also the relevant discussions in Schnabel 1994: 37–58; Martin 1993: 219–226, who devotes eight pages of his conclusion to Mark's missionary interest; and Telford 1985: 15, 23, who notes among Mark's primary concerns an interest in Gentiles and the Gentile mission.

Introduction: the character of Mark's Gospel (Mark 1:1–14)

Mark tells us a story, a 'Gospel',[4] about Jesus.[5] Possibly patterned after the blueprint of Petrine preaching,[6] the work's major thrust is the demonstration that *Jesus is the Son of God* (1:1).[7] This is where the narrative strands converge. Persons as diverse as God (who refers to Jesus as his 'beloved son' at Jesus' baptism and the transfiguration; 1:11; 9:7); demons (1:25; 3:11–12; 5:7); Jesus himself (12:6; 14:61); and the Roman centurion (15:39) concur that Jesus is the Son of God. In support of this claim, Mark's Roman audience is treated to a dazzling display of Jesus' miracle-working power which attests to his authority over the realms of nature, sickness and death, and even the supernatural (4:35 – 5:43).[8]

But as with the other evangelists, the primary problem confronting Mark is to account for Jesus' crucifixion. Why should anyone believe in a miracle-working messianic pretender who ended up being crucified as a common criminal? In response to this objection, Mark writes 'an apology for the cross', contending that it is precisely as the Crucified that Jesus proves himself to be the messianic king[9] and the Son of God (Gundry 1993).[10] To be sure, Jesus' true identity remains a mystery to his first followers for most of his public ministry. In fact, no-one in the earthly realm truly understands who Jesus is. For his real identity can be grasped only in light of the cross (Kato 1986: 195).

---

[4] 1:1; cf. 1:14, 15; 8:35; 10:29; 13:10; 14:9.

[5] In what follows, Markan priority is tentatively assumed, but little rests on this assumption. On the setting and purpose of Mark's Gospel with a view towards mission, see also J. F. Williams 1998: 137–141.

[6] Cf. esp. Peter's sermon in Acts 10:34–43 (Guelich 1992: 513).

[7] Commonly Mark is divided into three major sections, the introduction (1:1–14), Jesus' ministry in Galilee (1:15 – 8:26), and the way to Jesus' passion (8:27 – 16:8), with the second and the third unit being subdivided into three further sections: 1:16 – 8:26 into 1:16 – 3:12, 3:13 – 5:43, and 6:1 – 8:26; and 8:27 – 16:8 into 8:27 – 10:52, 11 – 13, and 14 – 16. We will use the above outline in the following treatment, except that we will break up the second section not at 3:12 and 5:43 but at 6:29 on the basis of Mark's presentation of Jesus' mission in and around Galilee. For a lucid discussion of the structure of Mark, see Guelich 1992: 516–517.

[8] Cf. Gundry 1993: 237; Guelich 1989: 261–263.

[9] 'Kingdom of God' (*basileia tou theou*): 1:15; 4:11, 26, 30; 9:1, 47; 10:14, 15, 23, 24, 25; 12:34; 14:25; 15:43; Jesus as king (*basileus*): 15:2, 9, 12, 18, 26, 32.

[10] Mark shares this concern with John: see esp. John 12:30–36.

Jesus' ministry in Galilee (Mark 1:15 – 6:29)

After having rooted Jesus' mission in the ministry of John the Baptist (1:2–3), the evangelist shows how Jesus begins to call and train a select group of followers for their missionary task. In Mark's account of Jesus' activities in Galilee,[11] Jesus' preaching and healing ministry is held up as the pattern for his disciples to emulate.[12] As the narrative progresses, Jesus draws his followers more and more fully into his own messianic mission: he calls them away from their natural vocation to follow him (1:16–20; 2:13–17), chooses the twelve 'to be with him' (3:13–19),[13] and, at the climax of the first part of Mark's Gospel, sends them on a mission (6:6b–13).[14]

Early in his ministry, Jesus dissociates himself from blood ties and affirms new forms of kinship.[15] He redefines who his true mother and brothers are (3:31–35) and is rejected in his home town of Nazareth (6:1–6a). The important principle of access on the basis of spiritual rather than ethnic distinctives paves the way for the future extension of the gospel to non-Jews (Senior and Stuhlmueller 1983: 222). It also demonstrates the nature of true discipleship: following Jesus involves conflict, rejection by one's own, even the bearing of one's 'cross'.[16] By distancing himself from his own family, Jesus models in his own life a stance towards kingdom membership that the disciples are to emulate in their relationships with one another and in their mission.[17]

---

[11] Note the *inclusio* of 1:14 and 6:29 (cf. 9:11–13).

[12] Cf. e.g. 1:14–15, 21–28, and 34 with 6:12–13. Cf. Stock 1982: 137–138, who further contends that Mark is a missionary document in the sense that it narrates Jesus' training of 'missionaries' (144).

[13] Donahue (1983: 10) contends that the major importance of the texts referring to the twelve in Mark is the strong missionary dimension of the narratives in which they appear. According to Donahue, Mark thereby roots the missionary orientation of his community in the period of its origin. Cf. also Pesch (1980: I:48–69, 205–267), followed by Senior and Stuhlmueller (1983: 227), for whom the Gospel of Mark is primarily a *Missionsbuch*.

[14] Note the link word *proskaleitai* in 3:13 and 6:7. As W. L. Lane (1974: 133) notes, '*Being with Jesus* qualified the Twelve to bear witness to him and to participate in his distinctive ministry of proclamation and the overthrow of demonic power ... The promise of a future ministry is fulfilled initially in the mission of the Twelve to the Galilean villages (ch. 6:7–13), but finds its wider significance in the apostolic mission after the resurrection.'

[15] Cf. also the Synoptic parallels and John 2:1–11; 7:1–9.

[16] Cranfield 1959: 282: 'the disciple must be ready to face martyrdom'. Cf. 8:34: *aratō ton stauron autou*; literally required of Simon of Cyrene, 15:21: *arei ton stauron autou*.

[17] Cf. J. F. Williams (1998: 146): 'Following a Messiah who came to die on a cross involves sacrifice, suffering, and service.'

Withdrawals from Galilee (Mark 6:30 – 8:26)

Already in 3:6, the reader is told of the Pharisees' plot with the Herodians to kill Jesus.[18] While this rejection of Jesus by the official representatives of Judaism does not cause him to forsake his mission to the Jews, it does give him increased exposure to Gentiles (Telford 1985: 23; Hahn 1965: 113). This includes Jesus' healing of the Gerasene demoniac in 5:1–20, his encounter with the Syrophoenician woman in 7:24–30, and his feeding of the multitude in 8:1–10, which is reminiscent of Elisha's miraculous feeding of Gentiles in 2 Kings 4:42–44.[19] Nevertheless, when Jesus, for instance, restores the Gerasene demoniac to sanity, he does not invite the healed Gentile to join his messianic mission but sends him home to tell his own people what has happened to him.[20]

In his account of the sending of the twelve, Mark, unlike Matthew (10:5–6), had not explicitly limited their mission to Israel (cf. 6:6b–13).[21] Nevertheless, Jesus' ministry in the first part of the Gospel is primarily devoted to the Jews (cf. esp. 7:26a). After Herod's mistaken identification of Jesus as the resurrected John the Baptist (6:14–29), mounting opposition to Jesus causes him to withdraw from Galilee, first to the region of Tyre and Sidon north of Galilee (7:24–30), then to the Decapolis east of Galilee (7:31 – 8:12), and finally to the far north in Caesarea Philippi (8:27 – 9:32). While Mark duly notes the disciples' obduracy,[22] at the same time he portrays their increased

[18] Cf. also 12:13 in relation to 6:14–29 and Jesus' warning in 8:15, as well as Matt. 22:16.

[19] Cf. Kato 1986: 191. Note also that Luke, while generally following Mark rather closely at this stage, omits the material found in Mark 6:45 (or 7:1) to 8:26, an omission that is all the more striking since the Gentile mission, which also represents one of Luke's most significant concerns, appears to be the overruling theme of this unit (Persson 1980: 44–49).

[20] Cf. 5:1–20; par. Matt. 8:28–34; Luke 8:26–39. Cf. Schnabel 1994: 51–52, apparently following Kato 1986: 59. Schnabel may, however, overstate the significance of this pericope for Jesus' alleged 'Gentile mission'. Contrary to this author's contention that 'God's grace is *now freely available to non-Jews as well*, while retaining the salvation-historical privilege of Israel' (53; emphasis added), the evangelist actually seems to focus on Jesus' reluctance to heal rather than on his eagerness to extend salvation 'freely' to Gentiles 'now'.

[21] On both points, cf. Hahn (1965: 119), who notes the following parallelism: rejection of Jesus in his home town / more far-reaching mission (ch. 6); rejection of Jesus by Israel / proclamation of gospel in the whole world (ch. 13).

[22] Cf. e.g. 3:5; 4:41, 6:45–52; 7:18; 8:14–21, 32–33; 9:10, 18, 28, 32; 10:35–45; 16:8; note esp. 6:52 and 8:17–21, where discipleship failure is magnified by the disciples' lack of understanding despite the *repetition* of Jesus' feeding miracle. See on this Markan motif esp. W. L. Lane (1974), who notes in 'the juxtaposition of rejection and

involvement in Jesus' mission.[23]

Also, the primarily Jewish context of Jesus is gradually broken up, not merely by the indictment of the Jews according to Isaiah's prophecy,[24] by Jesus' increasingly frequent withdrawals from Galilee, and by his declaration of all food as clean in 7:19,[25] but particularly by the incident with the Gentile Syrophoenician woman, who wants Jesus to exorcize a demon from her daughter but who is initially rebuffed by Jesus.[26] This device, of course, is aimed at eliciting the acknowledgment that Jesus' coming was directed to the Jews *first*.[27] Moreover, the woman's *acceptance* of the Jews' salvation-historical primacy becomes the *condition* for Jesus' help (Kato 1986: 190).

Final ministry in Galilee, Judea and Perea (Mark 8:27 – 10:52)

Subsequent to Peter's confession of Jesus as the Christ,[28] which occasions a thrice-repeated pattern of passion prediction, discipleship failure and instruction regarding true discipleship,[29] the 'messianic

---

mission a pattern confirmed in the rejection of Jesus by the nation, climaxed by crucifixion and resurrection, which created the apostolic mission' (205).

[23] Thus, at the occasion of the feeding of the five thousand, Jesus gives bread *to the disciples* in order for them to pass it on to the crowd (6:41). Some see in the two feeding stories of Mark 6:30–44 and 8:1–10 a reference to the respective missions to the Jews and Gentiles. See Farrer 1951: ch. 13; Boobyer 1953: 80–87; and the discussion in Hahn 1965: 113–114, n. 6. The frequent use of 'bread' terminoloy (*artos* and related terms) in Mark's entire Gospel and particularly in chs. 6 – 8 is noted by Gill 1991: 37 (cf. 2:26; 3:20; 5:43; 6:8, 37, 38, 41, 44, 52; 7:2, 5, 27; 8:4, 5, 6, 14, 16, 17, 19; 14:22).

[24] Cf. the reference to Is. 29:13 in Mark 7:6–7.

[25] Cf. Acts 10:19–16; 11:5–10; Rom. 14:13–23.

[26] 7:24–30; par. Matt. 15:21–28. The treatment of the present passage by W. L. Lane (1974: 260–264) repays careful study. See also the helpful narrative analysis by Swartley 1997: 16–22.

[27] Cf. later 13:9–10; see also the Matthean parallel in 15:24, which includes the much stronger statement that Jesus was sent *only* to lost sheep of the house of Israel, in direct equivalence to Matt. 10:6: *ta probata ta apolōlota oikou Israēl*. The distinction in 7:27 between 'children' and 'dogs' alludes to the division between Jews and Gentiles in ancient society. The term *prōton* ('first') is unique to Mark (cf. Matt. 15:26) and implies a *deuteron* ('second'; cf. Martin 1993: 222; Hahn 1965: 74–75, 113; Jeremias 1958: 29). Hahn contrasts the *heilsgeschichtliche prōton* in 7:27a with the eschatological *prōton* in 13:10.

[28] Cf. 8:29–30. Kato (1986: 190) intriguingly notes that the 'messianic secret' continues to be upheld, since the salvation-historical distinction between Jews and Gentiles continues to exist, but that Jesus' messianic identity none the less cannot be hidden from the Gentiles.

[29] Cf. 8:27 – 9:1; 9:30–41; 10:32–45. As W. L. Lane notes, 'The central importance of

secret' is gradually lifted, at least for the disciples.[30] Nevertheless, as long as the disciples fail to understand the inner dynamics of the cross, they do not yet recognize their mission, since this mission is contingent upon the disciples' following of Jesus in the way of the cross (cf. 8:34; Senior and Stuhlmueller 1983: 226).

Jesus ministers in Galilee until 8:26 and does not leave it permanently until 10:1.[31] The entire section of 8:27 to 10:52 is cast as a journey from Caesarea Philippi to Jerusalem.[32] Intriguingly, Mark limits instances of gospel proclamation entirely to Galilee.[33] The only two references to the preaching of the gospel in the Jerusalem section of Mark refer to the *future* proclamation of the good news to the Gentiles.[34] Moreover, a future meeting between Jesus and the disciples is intimated in 14:28 and 16:7, which further directs the reader's attention to Galilee.[35]

From the triumphal entry to the Olivet discourse (Mark 11 – 13)

Following Jesus' entry into Jerusalem (11:1–11), Mark uses scenes surrounding the Jewish temple to draw attention to the marked shift that would ensue as a result of Jesus' ministry and his rejection by the Jews (Donahue 1973: 137; Juel 1977: 212).[36] Thus Mark refers to the temple as a house of prayer *for all the nations*,[37] indicating that the particularism of Jewish worship had come to an end and that the temple

---

Peter's confession in the Marcan structure is confirmed by the sharp change of tone and orientation which it introduces' (1974: 288–289). Gundry (1993: 425) speaks of an 'outburst of predictive energy [that] will carry through the rest of the gospel and add an important element to Mark's apology for the Cross'.

[30] Cf. 1:34, 44–45; 3:12; 5:43; 7:36–37; 8:26, 29–30; 9:9.

[31] On the Markan Galilee motif, see Boobyer 1952–53: 340–348; Van Canghe 1972: 59–72.

[32] Cf. 9:30, 33; 10:1, 17, 32, 46, 52. On the 'way' or 'journey' motif in Mark, see Kelber 1974: 67–85; Pesch 1980: 1:59–60.

[33] Cf. 1:14, 38–39, 45; 3:14; 5:20; 6:12; 7:36.

[34] Cf. 13:10; 14:9. See Van Canghe 1972: 59–72.

[35] Some have seen in this a geographical symbolism that features Galilee as the centre of gospel proclamation, perhaps even with the two sides of the Sea of Galilee symbolizing Jesus' ministry to both Jews and Gentiles. Cf. Senior and Stuhlmueller 1983: 218–219; Kelber 1974: 45–62; Hahn 1965: 112–114.

[36] Cf. also the tearing of the temple curtain in the hour of Jesus' death, immediately followed by the climax of Mark's story, the centurion's confession (cf. 15:38–39; Hahn 1965: 117).

[37] Cf. the quotation of Is. 56:7 in Mark 11:17; the phrase 'for all the nations' is absent from the parallels in Matt. 21:13 and Luke 19:46.

would soon be replaced by an eschatological 'house of prayer'.[38] The cursing of the fig tree, with accompanying lessons regarding its significance (11:12–14, 20–26; 13:28–31), likewise draws attention to the rejection of the Jews as a result of their rejection of Jesus as Messiah.[39] The climax is reached in the historical allegory of the tenants of the vineyard (12:1–12), where Jesus declares that God's vineyard would be taken away from the Jews and be given *to others* (cf. 12:9).[40] These 'others' come into view particularly during Jesus' eschatological discourse in chapter 13, which is once again occasioned by a scene at the temple. Here Jesus, after predicting the destruction of the temple, informs his disciples that the glorious coming of the Son of Man would be preceded by the preaching of the gospel to *all the nations*.[41] Thus 'Mark in effect identifies the community's activity between Jesus' own ministry and the cataclysmic end of the world as a time of universal proclamation and witness' (Senior and Stuhlmueller 1983: 224).

Jesus' passion and resurrection (Mark 14 – 16)

The last major section of Mark's Gospel begins with accounts of the anointing and the institution of the Lord's Supper.[42] This intimate scene is contrasted with the harsh reality of Jesus' trial before the Sanhedrin (14:53–65). At the high point of the Jewish trial, Jesus responds to the

---

[38] Cf. Martin 1993: 224–225; Stock 1982: 142; Donahue 1973: 114; Senior and Stuhlmueller 1983: 223.

[39] W. L. Lane (1974: 402) calls Jesus' cursing of the fig tree 'a prophetic sign warning of God's judicial action against the nation ... equivalent in function to Ch. 12:9' (see discussion below).

[40] As W. L. Lane (1974: 419) notes, 'The sacred trust of the chosen people will be transferred to the new Israel of God.'

[41] Cf. 13:9–10, 26; cf. also 14:9, which harks back to 1:39 (Kato 1986: 191–193). Regarding 13:10, compare Acts 1:8; 22:21; the Matthean parallel is at a different part in the discourse (cf. 24:14). The different wording in Mark 13:10 and 14:9 suggests that 13:10 does not distinguish between Gentiles and Jews but rather refers to all people, as does 14:9 (13:10: *kai eis panta ta ethnē prōton dei kērychthēnai to euangelion;* 14:9: *ean kērychthēi to euangelion eis holon ton kosmon; cf.* 11:17: *Ho oikos mou oikos proseuchēs klēthēsetai pasin tois ethnesin;* cf. Hahn 1965: 119, n. 2; Kato 1986: 3. Kilpatrick's effort to reinterpret this passage with the effect of diminishing Mark's concern for mission has been almost universally rejected (cf. Martin 1993: 224; Hahn 1965: 71, 112; Jeremias 1958: 23, n. 5). Jeremias (1958: 22–23) argues unpersuasively that the reference in 13:10 does not refer to a proclamation of the gospel to all the world by human beings in the time prior to the parousia but by God's angel on the last day. Jeremias also appears to believe that Mark misunderstood the import of the original saying.

[42] Cf. 14:12–26, with the phrase *hyper pollōn* in 14:24 echoing *anti pollōn* in 10:45, a possible allusion to the Gentiles; cf. Is. 53:12.

high priest's question of whether he is the Christ, the Son of the Blessed One (cf. John 20:30–31), in the affirmative.[43] In contrast, Jesus refrains from answering Pilate's question of whether he is the king of the Jews, presumably owing to the term's political overtones (15:2). Thus the reader is led to understand that Jesus is the Messiah in terms of Jewish Old Testament expectations but not a king in Roman political terms (cf. John 18:36).

Finally, at the climax of Mark's Gospel, the Roman centurion exclaims at the foot of the cross, 'Surely this man was the Son of God' (15:39), indicating that now the messianic secret has been lifted even for the (Roman) Gentiles, so that the missionary power of Jesus' suffering and death has been extended also to non-Jews.[44] If there is a genuinely Markan equivalent to the Matthean 'Great Commission', the centurion's confession would certainly qualify. Indeed, the fact that it is not a Jew but a Gentile who confesses Jesus at the end of Mark is highly significant for the Gospel's narrative thrust (Kato 1986: 193).

At the same time, it is certainly no coincidence that a christological confession by a Gentile (cf. Peter's 'Jewish' confession in 8:29)[45] is not issued until *after* Jesus' death. If 16:8 is indeed the original ending of Mark's Gospel,[46] the account concludes on a note of fearfulness on the part of Jesus' followers, a state of affairs that may resemble the situation of Christians in Rome at the time of writing.[47] The abrupt

[43] 14:61–62; cf. 13:26. Jesus' response is couched in terms of Ps. 110:1 and Dan. 7:13.

[44] Cf. esp. Kiddle 1934: 45–50; see also Stock 1982: 142 and 1978: 289–301, and the overview by Kato (1986: 8–11).

[45] As W. L. Lane (1974: 576) contends, 'the centurion's words constitute an appropriate complement to the affirmation of Peter that Jesus is the Messiah in Ch. 8:29 and the triumphant climax to the Gospel in terms of the programmatic confession of Jesus in Ch. 1:1'.

[46] Cf. Petersen 1980: 151–166; Meye 1969: 33–43; Boomershine 1981: 225–239. J. F. Williams (1998: 146–150) discusses at some length 'The Missing Post-Resurrection Commission' in Mark on the assumption that 16:8 constitutes the original ending. He theorizes that the lack of a closing 'Great Commission' in Mark redirects the Gospel's emphasis to Jesus' pre-resurrection commissions; stresses Jesus' absence in the present rather than his helping presence (cf. Matt. 28:20), thus highlighting the importance of his second coming; and de-emphasizes the involvement of the Spirit (but cf. Mark 13:11), thus portraying the disciples as weak, powerless and persecuted rather than Spirit-empowered as in Luke-Acts. For J. F. Williams, 'The teaching of Mark's Gospel on mission can serve as a corrective to an unrealistic optimism' (150). However, it is unclear to what extent Mark and his original readers would have been aware of such a 'missing post-resurrection commission', especially if Mark was the first to write his Gospel.

[47] Cf. esp. Lincoln (1989: 283–300), who reads Mark 16:7–8 as a promise–failure juxtaposition that would have encouraged the Gospel's readers to persevere despite failure and disobedience, since the promise of 16:7 was fulfilled despite the disciples' failure.

ending[48] leaves open for the reader how Jesus' announcement that he would meet the disciples in Galilee will be fulfilled (cf. 14:28; 16:7; Stein 1973–74: 445–452).[49]

Mark's use of the Old Testament and mission

It is sometimes believed that, in contrast to Matthew, Mark had little interest in grounding Jesus' mission in the Old Testament owing to his writing for a Graeco-Roman audience. If so, this would set Mark (and perhaps Luke) significantly apart from Matthew's presentation, not only of Jesus' mission, but also of that of his followers. But is this stereotype borne out by closer analysis? As it turns out, the opposite is true. For while Mark's grounding of Jesus' mission in Old Testament conceptualities is not as thorough and methodical as that of Matthew, it is nevertheless demonstrable and sustained. In fact, the following theme clusters are firmly rooted in the Old Testament:

1. the ministry of John the Baptist;[50]
2. Jesus' rejection by the Jews;[51]
3. Jesus' confrontation with the Jewish leaders on topics such as the temple,[52] the Law,[53] and Jesus' Davidic sonship;[54]
4. Jesus' sufferings and cross-death;[55] and
5. the second coming.[56]

As this survey makes clear, Mark's presentation of Jesus' mission is set self-consciously in an Old Testament framework, which decisively

---

[48] On the appropriateness of the ending of Mark within its own literary and theological framework, see W. L. Lane 1974: 591–592.

[49] On discipleship failure and women in Mark's Gospel see especially Malbon 1983: 29–48.

[50] Cf. 1:2–3, quoting Is. 40:3; Mal. 3:1; cf. also the extended account of the Baptist's end in 6:14–29, and 9:11–12 alluding to Mal. 4:5–6.

[51] Cf. 4:12, quoting Is. 6:9–10 (cf. 8:18); 7:6–7, quoting Is. 29:13 (LXX); 12:1, 10–11, quoting Is. 5:1–2 and Ps. 118:22–23.

[52] 11:17, quoting Is. 56:7 and Jer. 7:11.

[53] Cf. 2:23–28 on picking heads of grain on the Sabbath (alluding to 1 Sam. 21:1–6 and 2 Sam. 15:35); 7:10; 10:19; 12:19, 26, dealing with the fourth and other commandments (cf. Exod. 3:2, 6, 15, 16; 20:12; Deut. 5:17; 25:5); 10:4–8, dealing with divorce (cf. Deut. 24:1, 3; Gen. 1:27; 2:24).

[54] 12:36, quoting Ps. 110:1; cf. 14:62; 16:19.

[55] Cf. 9:12 (alluding to Ps. 22 and Is. 53:3; cf. 10:45; 14:60–61; 15:4–5); 14:34 (alluding to Pss. 42:5, 11; 43:5). Substantiated from the Old Testament are further: 1. Judas' betrayal (14:18, quoting Ps. 41:9); 2. the scattering of Jesus' followers (14:27, 50, alluding to Zech. 13:7); 3. the soldiers' casting of lots for Jesus' garments (15:24, citing Ps. 22:18); and 4. the sponge of vinegar (15:36, quoting Ps. 69:21).

[56] 13:14, 19, 24–26, quoting or referring to Dan. 7:13–14; 9:27; 11:31; 12:1, 11, and other Old Testament apocalyptic passages.

invalidates efforts to understand Mark's Gospel primarily in terms of the 'divine man' motif or other Graeco-Roman conceptualities. While Mark does not refer to God's promises to Abraham, a theme that enjoys considerable prominence in other portions of the New Testament, he incorporates virtually all the major *testimonia* of the early church.[57] The evangelist draws particularly on the Psalms' portrayal of the circumstances surrounding the Messiah's death and Isaiah's depiction of the Jewish rejection of the Messiah. Perhaps the most dominant Old Testament motif underlying Mark's presentation of Jesus' mission is the Isaianic Servant of the Lord:[58]

Subject	Mark	Isaiah
1. The forerunner	1:2–3	40:3
2. Rejection of message	4:12; 7:6–7; 12:1, 10–11	6:9–10; 29:13; 5:1–2
3. Suffering	9:12; 14:60–61; 15:4–5	53:3; 53:7
4. All nations	11:17	56:7

R. E. Watts (1995) has recently suggested that Mark's opening Exodus-Malachi-Isaiah citation and his prologue are intended to evoke the pattern of the Isaianic 'new exodus'. Hence Mark's portrayal of Jesus' exorcisms and healings corresponds to Yahweh's deliverance of the exiles, while Jesus' entry into Jerusalem ought to reflect Yahweh's triumphal arrival but results instead in his rejection and death. Since John, the new Elijah, is not heard, Yahweh's coming in Jesus results in judgment. Just as Israel failed to heed Isaiah's message, Israel's leadership rejected Jesus, and even the response of his own disciples is characterized by obduracy and misunderstanding. If Watts is correct, Mark's presentation operates within the Old Testament framework of the expectation of a 'new exodus' by a faithful remnant of God's people.[59] Mark's simultaneous presentation of Jesus' mission as directed towards Israel and as attracting Gentiles who participate in the fruit of his coming indeed breathes the spirit of Isaiah 40 – 66.

---

[57] Cf. Pss. 2:7; 22; 41; 42; 69; 110:2; Is. 6:9–10; 29:13; 40:3; and 53. See the classic treatment of Dodd 1952, esp. 28–60.

[58] See 2. – 4. above. See already the extended discussion of 'The ministry of the Servant of Isaiah – Israel and the World' in ch. 2.

[59] Cf. the treatment of the 'new exodus' in ch. 2 above.

Mission in Mark: an appraisal

The preceding survey of Mark's narrative with particular attention to relevant mission passages and a proper appreciation of the Old Testament antecedents of the evangelist's theology make it possible for us to draw some observations regarding mission in Mark.

First, it is readily apparent that Mark unequivocally presents *Jesus' mission* as the core mission of his Gospel, with *the cross* functioning as the *focal point*, not merely for discipleship, but also for mission (e.g. 14:9).

Second, *Jesus' followers* are presented both as *strugglers* on the way to apprehending the full significance of Jesus' identity and mission and as drafted into Jesus' mission as *partners* in ministry on whom the task of future gospel proclamation rests. One notices a counter-movement in Mark's presentation of Jesus and the disciples: while Jesus is increasingly revealed as the Son of God who had been sent to inaugurate God's kingdom, the disciples are progressively shown in their failure to understand the true significance of Jesus' mission. How would the gospel be spread now that the women had fled the tomb in fear? Mark does not elaborate (but see 13:9–11).

This, third, raises the question of whether, speaking from the vantage point of Jesus' earthly ministry, *the Gentile mission* is for Mark already a present reality or merely a future prospect. In the above survey, Mark's presentation was found to respect important salvation-historical boundaries. Jesus' ministry still primarily focuses on the Jews, while his contact with Gentiles provides an eschatological foretaste of a fully fledged Gentile mission which remains to be accomplished at a later stage (cf. 7:27a). When Jesus does minister to Gentiles, it is usually not Jesus but the Gentile who takes the initiative (cf. esp. 7:24–30), while Jesus, sometimes with apparent reluctance, agrees to help.[60] Thus Mark presents Jesus as envisioning *the proclamation of the gospel to the Gentiles as part of the eschaton* which spans the time signalled by the imminent destruction of the temple to the glorious coming of the Son of Man (cf. 13:10).[61] It is in the period subsequent to Jesus' death that the

---

[60] Cf. esp. Loader (1996: 45–61), who argues that Jesus' encounters with the leper (1:40–45), the woman with the flow of blood (5:25–34) and the Syrophoenician woman (7:24–30) in Mark show Jesus as conservative regarding 'boundary crossing'. Loader points out that each of these pericopes shows Jesus to be sensitive regarding purity boundaries and yet prepared to cross such boundaries after initial reluctance.

[61] Contra N. T. Wright (1996: 339–368), who argues that Mark 13 speaks, not of Christ's return, but of the destruction of the temple itself. While ingenious, Wright's

gospel will be preached in all the world (cf. 14:9). This does not mean that Mark is uninterested in implications for the Gentile mission from Jesus' earthly ministry. It does mean, however, that Mark draws out these implications without violating the historical perspective of Jesus' earthly ministry.[62]

Fourth, in a related point, it is therefore demonstrably fallacious to read Mark's entire Gospel in terms of his alleged concern for the Gentile mission (Kato 1986). To give but three examples: 1. one of the major instances where Jesus ministers to a Gentile, his encounter with the Syrophoenician woman, is carefully qualified by the statement regarding the *Jews' primacy in salvation history*; 2. the reference to Isaiah 56:7 in 11:17 is *eschatologically* constrained; and 3. both 13:10 and 14:9 refer to the church's *future* (not present) universal gospel proclamation. Thus Martin's contention that Mark, by narrative material (7:24–30), Old Testament allusion (11:17; cf. Is. 56:7), and Jesus' own sayings (13:10; 14:9), 'places Jesus' universalistic appeal in the forefront' (1993: 225), must be set in the context of Jeremias' observation (1958, passim) that Mark, together with the other evangelists,[63] portrays Jesus as limiting his earthly ministry to Israel.[64]

Fifth, the contention that Mark's focus on Jesus' ministry *in Galilee*

---

contention that much of the New Testament revolves around 'the story of how Israel's long exile was finally coming to its close' (367) too often has to subvert the overt reading of New Testament texts to make his case. On a different note, Luke, strikingly, omits reference to three of Mark's most significant mission passages: Mark 7:24–30; the reference to 'all the nations' in the quotation of Is. 56:7 in Mark 11:17; and 13:10 (Schnabel 1994: 46–47).

[62] Cf. Schlatter (1999 [1922]: 69): 'Jesus does not embark on a mission to the Gentiles: the apostles do.' Dunn (1990: 320) claims that Mark 13:10 is 'about as clear an example of an interpretative addition in the light of a changed perspective as we could expect to find in the Synoptic tradition'. To the contrary, it must be maintained that Jesus' vision of the ingathering of the Gentiles is grounded firmly in Old Testament prophetic passages (e.g. Is. 11:10, cited in Rom. 15:12; Is. 49:6) that envision such an ingathering for the eschaton in fulfilment of the Abrahamic promise (so rightly D. Wenham 1993: 699).

[63] Cf. esp. Matt. 10:5–6; John 10:16; 12:20–26.

[64] However, Jeremias overstates his case when he denies that Jesus ever went beyond the boundaries of the Jewish population. For Mark does occasionally provide instances of Jesus' ministry to Gentiles (Alt 1951: 51–72). Yet this does not (as Jeremias seems to fear) furnish proof of an active, intentional missionary effort on Jesus' part to reach the Gentile world. Increasing Jewish antagonism rather necessitated Jesus' occasional withdrawals which allowed him to come into contact with a certain number of Gentiles, albeit generally not at Jesus' own initiative (contra Wefald 1995: 3–26, who seeks to demonstrate two fully fledged missions in Mark, one to the Jews and one to the Gentiles).

indicates an emphasis on Gentiles does not stand closer scrutiny.[65] To begin with, Galilee should not be equated with ministry to Gentiles,[66] since Galilee had a significant Jewish population. Moreover, Mark does not always present Galilee in a positive light. Galilee is also cast as the place where Jesus is rejected (6:1–6) and where he, in the context of his (uninitiated) ministry to a Gentile, asserts the salvation-historical primacy of the Jews (7:27a).[67]

Sixth, the primary aim of Jesus' 'mission' to the Gentiles (if it is appropriate to use this term at all) appears to be the manifestation of his messianic presence and the attraction of individual followers. While Jesus' overt attention was directed to the Jews, Gentiles, too, were drawn to Jesus, albeit 'from afar' (cf. 8:3; Gill 1991: 39). The pattern of Jesus' mission thus bears a striking resemblance to that of Old Testament Israel which was called to be a mediatorial kingdom to the surrounding nations (cf. Exod. 19:6). Only *subsequent* to the cross and the resurrection was the gospel to be preached to all the nations (cf. Luke 24:46–47).[68]

Thus, seventh, the command for the first disciples to 'go' and disciple the nations (Matt. 28:19–20) marks a decisive point of discontinuity between the church's future task and the stance taken by both Israel and Jesus, neither of whom actually 'went' to missionize the Gentile world.[69] At the same time, Jesus, as in many other aspects of his ministry, is able to combine in his mission a concern for both Jews and Gentiles by limiting his direct ministry to the Jews while allowing the Gentiles to be drawn to him as well. Ingeniously, this enables him *both* to be true to the salvation-historical constraints of the divine economy of redemption *and* to provide an eschatological foretaste of God's desire to make salvation available to *all* people. Nevertheless, Mark does not even hint at a church that transcends Jewish–Gentile boundaries. This reveals both Mark's respect for the historical constraints of Jesus' mission and the limited degree to which Jesus himself elaborated

[65] See esp. Kelber and Senior and Stuhlmueller; and the helpful summary by Kato (1986: 4–8).

[66] Cf. e.g. 1:39 where Jesus is said to have preached in *synagogues* all over Galilee.

[67] 'Over-realized eschatological readings' of Mark's Gospel with regard to Jesus' alleged 'Gentile mission' appear to be a result of the frequent practice of reading Mark's own Gentile horizon back into the historical setting of Jesus' ministry.

[68] This pattern was still in place in Jesus' day through the network of Jewish synagogues whose presence attracted numerous Gentile proselytes and God-fearers without direct efforts at proselytization on the part of the Jews. See the chapter on mission in the intertestamental period above.

[69] See further the chapters on mission in the intertestamental period (above) and on mission in Matthew (below).

on the implications of his own mission for the further development of his messianic community.

Conclusion

Is Mark therefore a *Missionsbuch*? Yes, in the sense that Mark shares the concern, pervading the entire New Testament, for preaching the good news of Jesus Christ to the entire world.[70] No, in the sense that Jesus' disciples, far from being a potent missionary force during Jesus' earthly ministry, are consistently shown to fail in their efforts to understand the true nature of Jesus' identity, the meaning of the cross and the thrust of his mission. No, furthermore, because Mark's focus on Jesus' mission to the Jews places the Gentile mission still in the future, even though pericopes such as the one featuring the Syrophoenician woman provide instances where Jesus indeed ministered to Gentile individuals. The claim, however, that Mark portrays Jesus as fully and unreservedly embarking on a Gentile mission as part of his earthly ministry goes beyond the evidence. Jesus rather appears to follow the pattern of Old Testament Israel, still practised by the Jewish synagogue in Jesus' own day, whose presence was to attract the surrounding nations to her God without going out of her way to reach them.

---

[70] Cf. 11:17; 13:10; 14:9. As is noted by Senior (1984: 63–81), 'the question of the community's mission to the nations brings balance to the concentration of some biblical scholars on inner-community questions'. For a helpful discussion of implications for mission from Mark's Gospel, see Gill 1991: 40–41. This author notes, among other things, that mission begins and ends with Jesus; that mission is the crown of discipleship (thus mission can only result from true discipleship which entails an understanding of Jesus' person, the significance of his cross-work and the purpose of his mission); that mission is not to be bound by social, cultural and economic boundaries; and that mission is to be concerned for all aspects of existence, including the personal, social, economic and political domains of life.

Chapter Five

Matthew

The Gospel of Matthew provides a crucial contribution to a biblical theology of mission. Framed by references to Jesus, the son of Abraham, and the 'Great Commission', this Gospel furnished the (Antiochian?) church of the latter part of the first century with a solid theological foundation for its mission to the Gentiles and still stands as a reminder of the church's unfinished task to disciple the nations. How is it that in this Jewish Gospel, designed as it is to present Jesus as the Messiah fulfilling Old Testament predictions and typologies, we find a consistent, growing stream of references to the Gentile mission?[1] And how are we to explain the limitation of Jesus' and the disciples' mission to Israel in the earlier parts of the Gospel (10:5–6; 15:24) in light of the references to a universal mission of the church in the later sections of Matthew (24:14; 28:16–20)?[2]

As in the case of Mark, we will follow the narrative flow of Matthew, with special attention given to relevant mission passages.[3] In particular, we will seek to demonstrate that Jesus' final commission to his followers in 28:16–20 provides the unifying climax of the entire Gospel's teaching on mission that is anticipated in many ways throughout Matthew's narrative.[4] As one recent writer points out, 'This carefully crafted climax brings together several major strands of the

---

[1] Hagner (1993: lxvii) calls the tension between particularism and universalism the 'major puzzle' in the Gospel of Matthew. Blomberg (1992: 26) considers this cluster of motifs 'the most foundational or overarching theme of the book' (26).

[2] For helpful surveys of scholarship on the issue, see Legrand 1964: 87–104, 190–207; Sundkler 1937: 1–38; and S. G. Wilson 1973: 1–28. See also the comments by Schlatter 1999 [1922]: 80–81; and the interesting suggestion by Tan 1997: 239–240.

[3] For a helpful general overview, see Schnabel 1994: 37–58.

[4] Cf. Frankemölle 1982: 110–111: 'The universalism does not merely catch the reader by surprise at the very end but rather accompanies him from the first verse of the Gospel' (AJK's translation). See also Michel 1983: 35: '*Matt. 28:18–20 is the key to the understanding of the whole book*' (original emphasis); Brooks 1981: 2: 'the concluding *pericope* (xxviii 16–20) has controlled the entire design of the Gospel of Matthew'; and Carson 1984: 36: 'the closing pericope (28:16–20) is ... the climax toward which the entire Gospel moves'.

story, including: mountain as a locus of christological significance; the manner and meaning of the risen Jesus' appearance; the disciples' obedience, worship and doubt; Jesus' claim to reception of divine authority; making disciples as a universal commission; baptism in the triadic name as ritual initiation into the community; the centrality of Jesus' *entolai* for the community; and the promise of his risen, continuous presence with his commissioned disciples.'[5] The chapter concludes with a discussion of some general theological implications from mission in Matthew's Gospel.

Genealogy, infancy narrative and early Galilean ministry: Jesus the representative 'son' (Matt. 1 – 4)

Matthew, in adaptation of Mark's 'Roman' Gospel for a (predominantly) Jewish audience,[6] introduces his account with a genealogy that presents Jesus Christ as the son of David and the son of Abraham.[7] This characterization reminds the reader of God's promise to Abraham that in his seed 'all the families of the earth' would be blessed (Gen. 12:1–3).[8] It also conjures up memories of God's promise

[5] See Kupp 1996: 201, who further claims, with reference to works by Lohmeyer (1945) and Michel (1950), that 'the last pericope of Matthew contains *in nuce* the essence of the Gospel; it provides the "abstract" for Matthew's "dissertation", but more, it is, in rhetorical and theological terms, both a digest and *telos* of the work'.

[6] In the following discussion, we will tentatively proceed on the basis of the hypothesis that Matthew used Mark in the composition of his Gospel. But little in the argument of this chapter rests on this view.

[7] See already the discussion of 'The Davidic kingship and the promises to Abraham' in ch. 2 above. Cf. further Bornkamm 1971: 225–227 and LaGrand 1999: 170–177. Some also note the inclusion of four Gentile women (Tamar, Rahab, Ruth, Bathsheba) in Matthew's genealogy as evidence for this evangelist's interest in Gentiles, but it is doubtful whether Matthew includes these women in his genealogy *because they are Gentiles*. If so, how would this fit with Mary, the fifth woman included (so correctly Sim 1995: 22–23)? It is more likely that the women are featured to highlight the unusual circumstances that led to their incorporation in Jesus' ancestry: seduction, prostitution, kinsman-redemption, adultery – and a virgin birth! Cf. R. E. Brown (1977: 71–74), who does, however, allow Gentile inclusion as a secondary purpose; and Hagner 1993: 10. See further Freed (1987: 3–19), who adds the observation that Matthew may here seek to defend Jesus against the Jewish charge that he was the illegitimate son of Mary and thus disqualified from being 'son of David'. In response, the evangelist 1. points to the fact that God has worked through unusual circumstances in salvation history before; 2. shows how Joseph's initial reluctance was overcome by divine revelation; and 3. presents the virgin birth as the fulfilment of Old Testament prophecy (Is. 7:14).

[8] Note the reiteration of this promise in Gen. 18:18; 22:18; 26:4: *panta ta ethnē*; and see Carson's comment (1984: 62) that 'with this allusion to Abraham [Gen. 22:18], Matthew is preparing his readers for the final words of this offspring from Abraham –

to David that his line would inherit an 'eternal kingdom' (2 Sam. 7:13, 16).[9] Jesus, the paradigmatic, representative 'son', is therefore both the channel of blessing for the nations and the eternal, enthroned Davidic ruler (cf. also 2:5–6, quoting Mic. 5:2).[10] Jesus, the Saviour (1:21), is also Immanuel, 'God with us' (1:23), a truth reaffirmed at the very end of Matthew's Gospel, where Jesus promises his followers that he will be with them 'always, even to the end of the age' (28:20).[11]

While magi from the East (Gentiles), 'representing heathen thought and life' (LaGrand 1999: 180), come to pay homage to the child Jesus, Herod the king persecutes him (2:1–18).[12] Matthew interprets Jesus' flight to Egypt in terms of 'son' typology: like God's 'son' of old, Israel, Jesus experienced deliverance from his land of temporary exile (Rapinchuk 1996). But unlike Israel, whose faithless wilderness generation died without seeing the land God promised, Jesus, while tempted to pervert his calling as the 'Son of God', remains faithful to his call (4:1–11; cf. Exod. 4:22–23).[13] Jesus' settlement in Nazareth of

the commission to make disciples of "all nations" (28:19)'. Contra Gundry (1994: 13), who, after acknowledging that the 'substitute may also imply that Jesus is Abraham's seed, a blessing to all nations in fulfillment of God's promise', comments, 'Since elsewhere Matthew will show little interest in Abraham, however, he may have intended his readers to understand David rather than Jesus as the son of Abraham.'

[9]See the discussion of 'The Davidic kingship and 2 Samuel 7' in ch. 2 above. Interestingly, the recognition of Jesus as 'son of David' comes in Matthew primarily from blind people and Gentiles (Blomberg 1992: 162–163, with reference to Gibbs 1963–64: 446–464). Milton (1962: 176) detects a chiasm between Matthew's genealogy focusing on Abraham and David and the conclusion of the Gospel.

[10] Later references to Jesus as 'Son of David' in Matthew's Gospel are: 9:27; 12:23; 15:22; 20:30–31; 21:9, 15; 22:42, 45. As Blomberg (1992: 53), Carson (1984: 69–70) and others point out, at the heart of Matthew's genealogy is a device called *gematria*, in which the ancient Hebrew numerical equivalent of the name 'David' (i.e.. fourteen) is used to highlight Jesus' identity as David's 'son' (but see the cautious assessments by Hagner 1993: 7; Keener 1999: 74).

[11] So e.g. Blomberg 1992: 433–434; Gundry 1994: 597. On the Matthean 'presence motif', see esp. Kupp 1996.

[12] See the discussion in LeGrand 1999: 177–180. Carson (1984: 83) likens the magi to the men of Nineveh who 'will rise up in judgment and condemn those who, despite their privilege of much greater light, did not receive the promised Messiah and bow to his reign (12:41–42)'. Gundry (1994: 26) remarks that 'the coming of the magi previews the entrance of disciples from all nations into the circle of those who acknowledge Jesus as the king of the Jews and worship him as God'.

[13] Cf. Carson, Moo and Morris 1992: 84. Carson (1984: 112) draws attention to the parallels with historic Israel in the Matthean temptation narrative, noting both the 'combination of royal kingship and suffering servanthood attested at his [Jesus'] baptism and essential to his mission' and the 'twin themes of kingly authority and submission ... as the complementary poles of the life and self-revelation of Immanuel: "God with us"' (114). The mount of temptation is the first of several mountains featured

Galilee, originally prompted by fear of Archelaus' rule over Judea subsequent to Herod's reign (2:22–23) and reaffirmed at the beginning of Jesus' ministry (4:12–16), likewise is taken to fulfil Old Testament prophecy: in Jesus, a light had dawned for the people in darkness, even in 'Galilee of the Gentiles' (4:15, quoting Is. 9:1–2; cf. Is. 42:6).[14]

Thus even prior to the onset of Jesus' public ministry, Matthew has presented him both as the vicarious representative of Israel's destiny and as a light unto the Gentiles who will save 'his' people from their sins (1:21; cf. 26:28: 'for many').[15] And when Jesus' ministry begins, its impact quickly spreads beyond Jewish territory to Syria and the Decapolis (4:24–25). The Pharisees and Sadducees, on the other hand, are excoriated by John the Baptist for wrongly presuming upon their relationship with Abraham. God can raise up children for Abraham 'from these stones', and the axe is already at the root of the trees (3:7–10).

The Sermon on the Mount: the arrival of God's kingdom (Matt. 5 – 7)

Another instance of Jesus' reenactment of Old Testament history is the Sermon on the Mount (5 – 7), the first of five major discourses in Matthew and reminiscent of God's giving of the Law through Moses at Mt Sinai (Allison 1993: 111–118; Gundry 1994: 65–66).[16] At the heart

---

in this Gospel; see further the discussion under 'Transfiguration' below.

[14] To see this, as Gundry (1994: 59) does, as 'a prefiguring of worldwide evangelism', is perhaps a bit overblown. Better is his subsequent comment that 'Though Jesus will minister in Galilee mainly to Jews, this description ["Galilee of the Gentiles"] makes that ministry prefigure his disciples' wider mission to Gentiles' (60). See also Hagner (1993: 73), who appropriately remarks that 'Matthew does not refer to a mission of Jesus to the Gentiles, but Matthew's readers may well have seen in these words a foreshadowing of what would occur after the resurrection (28:19; cf. 24:14).'

[15] While 'his people' in 1:21 may appear to refer to Israel (cf. 2:6: 'my people Israel'), it becomes clear in retrospect that *laos* is here broader than Israel, including the Gentiles as well. Contra Luz 1989: 121.

[16] The question of the role of the Law in Matthew's Gospel is exceedingly complex and cannot be broached in the present context (for a thorough survey of the issue, without necessarily endorsing the conclusions drawn, see Stanton 1985: 1934–37; a briefer, still helpful overview is provided in Carson 1984: 29–31). Suffice it to say that the mission motif in Matthew can be comfortably accommodated within the framework proposed by Meier (1976): 'when the new age breaks in at the death-resurrection of Jesus (the culmination of the fulfilment of all prophecy), the latter will fall in favour of the prophetic, eschatological fulfilment of the Law which Jesus brings' (summarized by Stanton 1985: 1936–37). See also Carson (1984: 146), 'the precise form of the Mosaic law may change with the crucial redemptive events to which it points. For that which

of Jesus' message is the arrival of God's kingdom and the righteousness required of those who would receive it (cf. esp. 5:3–12, 20; 6:33). Jesus' followers are 'the salt of the earth' and 'the light of the world' (cf. 4:16, quoting Is. 9:2); they are to let their light so shine before others that they see their good works and glorify their heavenly Father (5:13–16). Jesus is even-handed in his criticism of both Jews and Gentiles: the prayers of the former group are hypocritical, while those of the latter are wordy (6:5–7).[17] Jesus' disciples, by contrast, are to utter prayers to their heavenly Father that are unhypocritical and to the point, so that his will may be done 'on earth as it is in heaven' (*hōs en ouranō kai epi gēs*). This phrase anticipates Matthew's character-ization of Jesus as the one to whom all authority is given 'in heaven and on earth' at the end of his Gospel (28:19: *en ouranō kai epi gēs*). By implication, Jesus functions as the Father's plenipotentiary in pursuit of the latter's salvation-historical programme. Notably, Jesus' authority in Matthew pertains particularly to his teaching and his word (cf. 7:28–29; 28:20). Nevertheless, the *inclusio* of 4:23–25 and 9:35, framing chapters 5 – 7 and 8 – 9 respectively, points to the unity of Jesus' word and work.

The mission of the twelve: 'to the lost sheep of Israel' (Matt. 10)[18]

Structurally, by delaying John the Baptist's enquiry regarding Jesus' messianic ministry until *after* the missionary discourse in chapter 10, Matthew connects the missions of Jesus and the disciples (cf. also 10:5–6 and 15:24; Frankemölle 1982: 126). This is further accentuated by the transitional pericope of 9:36–38, which links Jesus' compassion

---

prophesies is in some sense taken up in and transcended by the fulfillment of the prophecy'; and Jeremias (1971: 141–151, 205–208).

[17] Other 'anti-Gentile' statements in Matthew include 5:46–47 (even Gentiles love those who love them); 6:31–32 (Gentiles concern themselves with mundane matters); 18:15–17 (unrepentant church member to be treated like a Gentile or tax-collector); and 20:24–28 (Gentile rulers lord it over others). Cf. Sim 1995: 25–30.

[18] For a (partial and not entirely unbiased) survey of the history of scholarship on the Matthean mission discourse, see Park 1995: 9–31. See esp. Park's discussion of McKnight (1986), whose redaction-critical study assigns to Matthew a date of around AD 85 and views the mission discourse as a Matthean attempt at polemicizing 'against the Pharisees as the false leaders of Israel' (376). McKnight's historical-critical assumptions, however, render him unduly sceptical regarding the authenticity of the material and cause him to pay inadequate attention to larger theological questions. On the basic literary, historical and theological questions surrounding Matt. 10, see also Carson 1984: 240–243.

for the crowds who are 'like sheep without a shepherd' (an allusion to Num. 27:17) with his exhortation to his followers to 'ask the Lord of the harvest to send out workers into his harvest field' (cf. *m. 'Abot* 2:15).[19] Reference has already been made to the apparent tension between the restriction of Jesus' and the disciples' mission to 'the lost sheep of the house of Israel' (10:5–6 and 15:24: unique to Matthew) and the universal command to 'disciple all the nations' at the end of the Gospel (28:19).[20] However, it is not necessary to interpret these two sets of passages as reflecting different traditions found in the 'Matthean community'.[21] This is suggested by the fact that the discourse expresses the expectation of the bearing of future witness, not merely in Jewish synagogues, but also to Gentiles (10:18: Matthew adds *kai tois ethnesin* to Mark 13:9).[22] The movement rather proceeds along salvation-

---

[19] Hagner (1993: 260–262) notes the sense of eschatological urgency, accentuated further by the contrast between the multitudes to be reached and the scarcity of workers. For a similar piece of instruction, including 'harvest' imagery, see John 4:34–38; see also the Lukan parallel (10:2) at the occasion of the instruction of the seventy(-two). As Gundry (1994: 181) notes, the 'Lord of the harvest' is Jesus himself (10:5; cf. 13:37–43), who is here likened to 'one who hires workers and sends them to the field', in the present instance the 'mission field'. The term 'worker' recurs in 10:10, which suggests that the twelve were to be the answer to their own prayers for 'workers for the harvest'.

[20] See the general sketch by Blomberg (1992: 26), who proposes to resolve this tension by pointing to the pattern adopted by Paul throughout the book of Acts (13:46; 18:6; 19:9) and articulated in his epistles (Rom. 1:16), i.e. going to the Jews first and then also to the Gentiles. By analogy, Blomberg 'sees Jesus as going first to the Jews and then also to the Gentiles. God's chosen people get first chance to respond to the gospel, but then Jesus and his disciples must expand their horizons to encompass all the earth' (Carson's solution is similar: 1984: 23). But the analogy from Paul's life should not be so facilely applied to Jesus retroactively. Rather, salvation-historically, the line should be drawn between *Jesus going to the Jews* and *his disciples* (but not also Jesus, other than proleptically) *going beyond the Jews also to the Gentiles* after the sending of the Spirit at Pentecost (see e.g. John 10:16 where Jesus speaks of his bringing in of yet 'other sheep', i.e. the Gentiles, through the agency of his disciples *as still in the future* from his pre-crucifixion vantage point).

[21] Contra S. Brown 1977: 21–32 and 1980: 193–221. For a helpful categorization of attempted resolutions, see Frankemölle (1982: 100–103): 1. both words are from Jesus, characteristic of different stages of ministry, with the second superseding the first (Jeremias, Lohmeyer, Meinertz, Schlatter, Vögtle, Zahn); 2. both words originate with the early church, reacting to two stages of its missionary activity (Bornkamm, Bultmann, Käsemann, Strecker, Trilling, J. Weiss); 3. the first is a word of Jesus, the second of the early church (Goppelt, Harnack, Kümmel, Manson); 4. the two words reflect two competing groups in 'Matthean community' (Barth, Bornkamm, Hahn, Strecker, Trilling). A somewhat different view has recently been proposed by Park (1995: 140), who assigns the first word to 'pre-Matthean tradition' (though not originating with Jesus himself), because 'it ıs very unlikely that Mt would have composed a saying ... which directly contradicts his view on mission'. However, Park's position depends on the highly speculative theory of plural recensions of Q.

[22] So, rightly, Carson 1984: 241.

historical lines, portraying a dynamic that is well corroborated by the other Gospels and Acts: Jesus, the Jewish Messiah, offers the kingdom to Israel; Israel rejects Jesus, issuing in his crucifixion; the kingdom is offered universally to all those who believe in Jesus the Messiah, Jew and Gentile alike.[23]

The message of the twelve[24] to Israel, then, is that 'the kingdom of heaven is near' (10:7), in continuity with the preaching of both John the Baptist (3:2) and Jesus (4:17).[25] Their mode of travel must be 'unencumbered, relying on hospitality and God's providence' (10:9–10).[26] Pervading the Matthean mission discourse are references to the prospect of rejection of the gospel message (10:11–16, cf. 40–42), issuing in persecution of the messengers (10:17–20, 23–33) and division even among a person's own family (10:21–22, 34–39). Even such division, however, is shown to fulfil Old Testament Scripture (10:35–36, par. Luke 12:53, citing Mic. 7:6). Also pervasive is the principle of the close identification of Jesus' messengers with their sender, Jesus, as they embark on their mission. In keeping with the Jewish concept of the šāliaḥ (messenger), a man's agent was considered to be like the man himself (m. Ber. 5:5).[27] For better or worse, then, Jesus' emissaries have thrown in their lot with their master: if people welcome him and his message, they will also receive his followers; if people reject Jesus, his followers will likewise be rejected (10:11–14, 40–42). Thus following Jesus entails radical discipleship. Anyone who would be his disciple must forsake all other ties and loyalties in favour of unreserved, committed allegiance to Jesus (10:37; cf. 4:22; 8:21; 12:46–50)[28] and take up his cross (10:38–

[23] Cf. Hagner (1993: 271), who appropriately speaks of 'a salvation-history perspective, which sees a clear distinction between the time of Jesus' earthly ministry and the time following the resurrection and thus a movement from particularism to universalism'. Carson (1984: 146), citing Meier 1976, similarly speaks of 'the centrality of the death and resurrection of Jesus as the pivotal event in Matthew's presentation of salvation history. Before its Jesus' disciples are restricted to Israel (10:5–6); after it they are to go everywhere.'

[24] Called 'disciples' (mathētai) in v. 1 and 'apostles' (apostoloi) in v. 2, the twelve are mentioned again in v. 5; 11:1; 20:17; 26:14, 20, 47 (cf. 19:28). The term apostolos (Gk. for Heb. šāliaḥ, 'messenger') appropriately appears only here in Matthew and is thus reserved for Jesus' twelve disciples. The number twelve unmistakably suggests a parallel with the twelve tribes of Israel (cf. 19:28).

[25] See also the 'kingdom parables' in chs. 13 and 18 and the additional parables in chs. 21, 22 and 25.

[26] Carson 1984: 245; see also Keener 1999: 317–319.

[27] For a discussion of the ancient background, see Keener 1999: 313–315.

[28] The demand is phrased in even more categorical terms in Luke: 'If anyone comes to me and does not hate his father and mother, his wife and children, his brothers and

39; cf. 16:24–26).[29] Even so, there is no need for fear (10:26–31). Should Jesus' followers get arrested, the 'Spirit of your Father' (cf. 28:19) will speak through the disciples (10:19–20). The mission discourse ends with Jesus promising eternal rewards to those who are faithful in accomplishing the mission mandate (10:40–42; cf. 10:32–33; 16:27; 19:27–30).

Jesus' ministry to Gentiles in Galilee and the regions beyond (Matt. 8:1 – 16:12)

Even during his earthly ministry, Jesus exceptionally ministers to Gentiles in response to their believing request, though he never takes the initiative. What is more, sometimes he seems to take positive steps to avoid ministry to Gentiles (esp. 10:5–6; 15:24, 26). An example of Jesus' exceptional ministry to Gentiles is his healing of the centurion's servant in Capernaum, in the course of which he commends the centurion's faith as greater than that of 'anyone in Israel' (8:10). The healing also prompts Jesus' utterance, 'I say to you that many will come from the east and the west, and will take their places at the feast with Abraham, Isaac, and Jacob in the kingdom of heaven. But the subjects of the kingdom will be thrown outside into the darkness' (8:11–12). According to Matthew, Jesus therefore clearly foresees the Gentiles' full future participation in God's promise to Abraham.[30] Notably, Matthew strikes a note of judgment on Israel even more strongly than the Lukan parallel (13:28).

This is similar to the Parable of the Wicked Tenants in 21:33–46, where Matthew adds to Mark 12:1–2 the statement that 'the kingdom of God will be taken away from you and given to a people who will produce its fruit' (21:43).[31] Indeed, God's judgment on Tyre and Sidon, even Sodom, will be more tolerable than that on Korazin and Capernaum (11:20–24). And the men of Nineveh and the Queen of the South will condemn the unbelief of Jesus' contemporaries (12:41–42).

---

sisters – yes, even his own life – he cannot be my disciple' (14:26). As Matthew's wording makes clear, however, what Jesus calls for is not literal hate of one's family but a refusal to love one's natural associations *more* than Jesus (Matt. 10:37).

[29] As Gundry (1994: 200) rightly notes, 'Matthew's context makes the disciple's cross stand for persecution to the point of martyrdom.'

[30] So Jeremias 1958: 55–63. Contra Allison 1989: 158–170; Davies and Allison 1991: 2:26–31, who claim that the many from east and west are not Gentiles but diaspora Jews.

[31] See the discussion of this passage below.

In a subtle christological typology, Jesus is presented as a 'greater Jonah' who, after three days and three nights in the depths of the earth, will go and preach salvation to the Gentiles (12:39–41). Not all Gentiles welcome Jesus, however. In the country of the Gadarenes, Jesus, after healing two demoniacs, is urged by the whole city to depart from their region, a clear indication of the rejection of Jesus' ministry by this Gentile community (8:34; Sim 1995: 23).

In a very telling fashion, and in import not unlike Luke's quotation of Isaiah 62:1–2 in Luke 4:18–19, Matthew inserts a lengthy quotation of Isaiah 42:1–4 between his account of the Pharisees' criticism of Jesus' behaviour on the Sabbath (12:1–14) and their charge that he does his works by the power of Beelzebub (12:22–30). 'Thus he interprets Jesus' healing ministry, not so much in terms of "Son of God" or even royal "Son of David" christology, but in terms of Yahweh's Suffering Servant' (Carson 1984: 285). What is particularly striking is the prominence given to the Gentiles in this Isaianic passage. Matthew thereby seeks to draw attention to the fact that Jesus' ministry fulfilled the prediction of Isaiah's Servant song that 'he will proclaim justice to the Gentiles' (12:18) and 'in his name the Gentiles will hope' (12:21, NRSV).[32] 'It is remarkable how Matthew is able to intertwine the parallel themes of God's providential work in the sending of the Messiah; the fulfillment of OT prophecy in the arrival of Jesus; and the mission of Jesus being simultaneously received by the Gentiles and repudiated by Israel' (Keathley 1997: 19).

Often overlooked is the fact that not merely Luke, but also Matthew portrays Jesus as concerned about those of low status in society. Matthew, however, uses such people, in particular children, to illustrate the nature of God's kingdom revealed through Christ. In 11:25–27, a passage that in turn anticipates 28:16–20, Jesus is portrayed as saying, 'I praise you, Father, Lord of heaven and earth, because you have hidden these things from the wise and learned, and revealed them to little children ... All things have been committed to me by my Father. No-one knows the Son except the Father, and no-one knows the Father except the Son and those to whom the Son chooses to reveal him.' In many other pericopes, Jesus uses little children to teach lessons about the kingdom.[33] Discipleship, including a person's need to grow in faith, is one of the major themes of Matthew, constituting an indispensable prerequisite for mission. Once again, these themes culminate in 28:16–

[32] See already the discussion of 'The ministry of the Servant of Isaiah – Israel and the world', and here especially 'Introducing the Servant (Is. 42:1–4)' in ch. 2 above.
[33] Cf. 10:42; 18:2–6, 10, 14; 19:14–15; 21:14–16. Cf. Arias 1991: 416–418.

20. This draws attention to the fact that discipleship *entails* mission and without it remains incomplete. While not necessarily involving cross-cultural ministry, the kind of discipleship mandated by Jesus involves a commitment to 'seek first God's kingdom and his righteousness' (6:33) as well as service to one's fellow-man, including the teaching of others to obey Jesus' commandments as the disciple does himself (28:20).

The disciples' own need for growing in faith is the point of the pericope of Jesus' walking on the water. When Peter expresses his desire to follow Jesus' example, he is encouraged to step out in faith and walk on the water just like Jesus did. But after a few steps, Peter looks at the wind and begins to sink. 'You of little faith, why did you doubt?' Jesus chides Peter (14:31). In this instance, it is clear that 'doubt' does not imply complete unbelief, but merely lack of adequate faith, leading to a hesitant, tentative approach.[34] This is significant for an understanding of the Gospel's final pericope in 28:16–20, the only other passage in the New Testament where the same Greek word for 'doubt' (*distazō*) is used. As will be argued further below, when it is said there that the disciples worship Jesus but doubt, this may be taken to connote a certain amount of reluctance towards Jesus that the latter assuages by reassuring his followers of his authority and continued presence. After further controversy with the Pharisees and scribes, Jesus, while withdrawing into the region of Tyre and Sidon (15:21–28; cf. 11:20–24) encounters a Canaanite woman.[35] In a pericope reminiscent of the healing of the centurion's servant in 8:5–13, Jesus yields to the woman's request for healing on behalf of her demon-possessed daughter, but not until she has acknowledged Israel's salvation-historical privilege (15:24–27; cf. John 4:22).[36] As in the case of the

[34] Cf. Hagner (1995: 885) following I. P. Ellis (1967–68: 574–580), who notes that the evangelist had available *apistein* for 'disbelieve' and *aporein* for 'be perplexed'. However, neither word is ever used by Matthew (though the noun *apistia* and the adjective *apistos* appear in 13:58 and 17:17 respectively). Ellis documents the meaning of hesitation or indecision for *distazō* in Plato and Aristotle. See also the discussion in Carson 1984: 593–594.

[35] The account is also featured in Mark 7:24–30 (though, puzzlingly, not in Luke, despite his interest in Gentiles). On the Matthean reworking of the material, see Hagner 1995: 439–440.

[36] Beare (1981: 341–342) calls Jesus' statements at this occasion 'brutal', 'offensive', 'insolent', 'embarrassing', 'atrocious' and 'chauvinistic'. All he can hope for is that these statements are a later 'retrojection into the life of Jesus'. France (1989: 234), on the other hand, takes strong exception, calling Beare's comments 'remarkably hostile', noting that 'The whole story is one which, if read with wooden literalism, gives good reason to complain of the "chauvinistic" attitude it displays, but which, if read within total literary context and with a due openness to a dialogue conducted not so much by sober propositions as by verbal fencing, fits well into Matthew's theology of Jesus as the

centurion, Jesus commends the woman for her great faith (15:28).[37]

Jesus' ministry to his disciples: the formation of Jesus' community and the Matthean mountain motif (Matt. 16:13 – 20:34)

But scattered ministry to individual Gentiles is merely incidental at this point in Jesus' ministry. The major share of his ministry is devoted to the training of Jesus' (Jewish) disciples, particularly the twelve. At a pivotal point in Matthew's Gospel, Peter, speaking for Jesus' inner circle, confesses Jesus to be 'the Christ, the Son of the living God' (16:16), eliciting Jesus' prediction, and promise, that 'on this rock' he will build his (messianic) community (*ekklēsia*).[38] Notably, in the only other occurrence of the term *ekklēsia* in the Gospel (18:17–20), Jesus assures his followers that where two or three are gathered in his name, there he will be in their midst (18:20: *ekei eimi en mesō autōn*). This anticipates Jesus' promise at the end of Matthew that, as his followers disciple the nations, he will be with them (28:20: *egō meth' hymōn eimi*). How Jesus' community will be built is likewise further developed in the Gospel's final pericope: this will be accomplished by the messianic community's discipling of the nations, which involves the building of communities by way of baptism and instruction in Jesus' teachings (28:18–20). It is also possible that a thread of predictions of the glorious coming of the Son of Man finds its culmination in the risen Lord's final commission to his followers.[39]

An anticipation of Jesus' future glory is given to the inner circle of Jesus' inner circle on the Mount of Transfiguration (17:1–8; Carson 1984: 383–387).[40] The Mount of Transfiguration is one of seven

---

Messiah of Israel – *and* of all those who respond in faith'.

[37] Gundry (1994: 314) detects in Matthew's version of this account a heightening of the obstacles to the woman's faith for dramatic effect. Rather than implying a bias against Gentiles on Matthew's part, Gundry suggests, this 'casts the faith of that Gentile in all the better light and by this means justifies a mission to Gentiles now that Jewish officialdom has rejected Jesus'. See also the excellent discussion in Hagner 1995: 440–442.

[38] This pattern of passion predictions (of which this is the first; though see allusions to Jesus' death in 9:15; 10:38; and 12:40) is already a familiar feature of Mark's Gospel: see discussion there. Later passion predictions in Matthew include 17:22–23 (cf. 17:12b) and 20:17–19. See also the discussion in Carson 1984: 375–377.

[39] Cf. 16:27–28; 26:64; cf. also the allusion to Dan. 7:14 in 28:19.

[40] Gundry (1994: 342–345) sees in the transfiguration another instance of Matthew's casting Jesus as the 'new and greater Moses'.

mountains featured in Matthew's Gospel which include:
1. the mountain of temptation (4:8–10);
2. the mountain of teaching on God's kingdom (5 – 7);
3. the mountain of prayer (14:23);
4. the mountain of ministry (15:29–38);
5. the mountain of transfiguration (17:1–8);
6. the mountain of private instruction regarding the end (24 – 25);
7. the mountain of commission (28:16–20).[41]

It is possible to detect in this arrangement a chiastic structure, with the 'mountain of ministry' at the centre (4) and with three pairs of two mountains respectively forming corresponding elements:
- the mountains of temptation (1) and commission (7);
- the mountains of teaching on God's kingdom (2) and private instruction regarding the end (6);
- the mountains of prayer (3) and transfiguration (5).

If this observation is correct, the Matthean mountain motif highlights, among other things (but cf. already Old Testament precedents such as Mt Sinai or Mt Zion; see further below), the correspondence between Jesus' temptation to pursue his calling as the Son of God in worldly terms (cf. also 16:21–28 and 27:40) and his comprehensive authority subsequent to his vindication and exaltation as the risen Son who issues the 'Great Commission' (Donaldson 1985: 188–189). This also allows the various strands of the 'son' (particularly 'Son of God') motif in Matthew to converge in the final pericope (Kingsbury 1974: 573–584).

Jesus' final parables and discourses and the passion narrative: increasing references to a universal mission and geographical symbolism (Matt. 21 – 27)

Nearing the end of the Gospel, one finds increasing references to the eschatological implications of Jesus' death, especially in terms of mission. The Parable of the Wicked Tenants includes the statement that 'the kingdom of God will be taken away from you [Israel] and given to a people who will produce its fruit' [the Gentiles] (21:43).[42] As Carson

---

[41] On the Matthean mountain motif, see esp. Donaldson 1985, esp. 87–190. Note also the discussion of Mt Zion under the heading 'The nations within God's plan in the Psalms' in ch. 2 above.

[42] Overman 1996 (esp. 303–304; see also 1990), following Saldarini 1994, claims that 'nation' in 21:43 refers, not to the Gentiles, but to a group other than the leaders of Israel, that is, the 'Matthean community'. But this is to substitute social reconstruction

rightly points out, strictly speaking this does not refer to 'transferring the locus of the people of God from Jews to Gentiles, though it may hint at this insofar as that locus now extends far beyond the authority of the Jewish rulers; instead, it speaks of the ending of the role the Jewish religious leaders played in mediating God's authority' (1984: 454). The Parable of the Wedding Banquet, likewise, speaks of the unworthiness of those invited to the wedding feast (Israel), which leads to the invitation of others (22:8–10). In Jesus' final eschatological discourse, the preaching of the 'gospel of the kingdom' (24:14)[43] for a witness *to all the nations* will precede the end (cf. Mark 13:10; Thompson 1971: 18–27).[44]

The universal preaching of the gospel is also anticipated in Jesus' pronouncement at the occasion of his anointing, 'Truly I say to you, wherever this gospel is preached in the whole world, what this woman has done shall also be spoken of in memory of her' (26:13, NASB). An instance of the opposite procedure is 21:13, where Matthew omits the final phrase from Jesus' statement, uttered at the occasion of his cleansing of the temple, 'My house shall be called a house of prayer *for all the nations*' (quoting Is. 56:7; cf. Mark 11:17, NRSV).[45] The phrase 'all the nations' (*panta ta ethnē*) is, however, found in 24:9, 14; 25:32; and 28:19, in each of these instances referring to the nations *including Israel* (see also 21:43).[46] This phrase links Jesus' mission thrust as

for the salvation-historical substructure of Matthean theology. For interpretations of this parable along salvation-historical lines, see Carson 1984: 450–454; Hagner 1995: 615–624.

[43] Earlier instances of this term are 4:23 and 9:35; cf. also 13:19 (NRSV): 'word of the kingdom' and 26:13: 'this gospel'.

[44] Amazingly, Park 1995: 7 *assumes* at the very outset of his study that the universal mission spoken of in 24:14, 25:32, and 28:19 is not reflective of Jesus' own vision but rather represents the creation of the evangelist Matthew ('his idea', 191). According to Park, at this stage the Matthean community 'has already outgrown the notion of the exclusive Jewish mission and is now beginning to open the door to the gentiles'; 'This universalism is Matthew's own development' drawn from the notion of the Abrahamic promise in Gen. 12:1–3. But this is highly implausible historically, since the book of Acts shows the early Christians already engaged in the Gentile mission much earlier than the composition of Matthew's Gospel. Moreover, Park fails to take account of passages such as Acts 1:8, which clearly attribute this universal vision to Jesus himself.

[45] See already the discussion of 'The nations within God's plan in the Psalms' in ch. 2 above.

[46] Contrast with this the occurrences of the phrase 'the nations' with reference to the Gentiles in 4:15; 6:32; 10:5, 18; 12:18, 21; and 20:19, 25. See esp. Meier 1977b: 94–102 and the summary discussion in Carson 1984: 596; contra Hare and Harrington 1975: 359–369, R. Walker 1967: 111–112, and Lange 1973: 302–305. Scholars favouring the inclusion of the Jews among the term 'all the nations' in 28:19 include Bosch, Donaldson, Frankemölle, Hagner, Hahn, Hill, Hubbard, Meier, Michel, O'Brien, Senior and Stuhlmueller, Strecker and Trilling.

traced in Matthew's Gospel (see already 1:1 and below on 28:18–20) with God's promise to Abraham that all the nations would be blessed through him (Gen. 12:3; note *panta ta ethnē* in Gen. 18:18; 22:18, LXX). Towards the end of the Gospel, likewise, the expectation is nurtured that, just as Jesus' base for his ministry was Galilee (4:12–16; cf. 2:22–23), Galilee would be the place for Jesus' commissioning of his disciples for ministry (cf. 26:32; 28:7, 16; Carson 1984: 116).

This favourable attitude towards Galilee stands in marked contrast with Matthew's focus on the inimical reaction of Israel and Jerusalem to Jesus.[47] From chapter 10 onward, one observes a distinct and rising note of hostility towards Jesus. While the crowds continue to grow, there is no indication that Israel as a whole accepts her Messiah. A telling series of events occurs in chapters 12 – 14 when the Pharisees plot to kill Jesus (12:14) and accuse him of healing by the power of Beelzebub (12:24); a sign is demanded (12:38); his home town of Nazareth takes offence at Jesus (13:57); and John the Baptist is beheaded (14:1–12). In response, Jesus delivers a series of scorching denunciations against Israel (11:20–24; 12:31–32, 39–42; 16:1–4), culminating in a blistering attack on Israel's leadership in chapter 23. Israel's repudiation of Jesus is complete when Barabbas is chosen over Jesus and the nation accepts the consequences of their action (27:21–25).[48] This is further underscored by Matthew's switch from *ochlos/ochloi* ('crowd[s]') in 27:15, 20, 24 to *laos* ('nation'), a term frequently employed by Matthew with reference to Israel (e.g. 2:6, citing Mic. 5:2), in 27:25 to seal Israel's culpability.

In terms of geographical symbolism, Matthew, by employing the pilgrimage motif in his narration of Jesus' journey from Galilee to Jerusalem in four stages (16:21; 17:22–27; 19:1; 21:1 – 23:39), casts the entire story of 16:21 – 23:39 as the return of the exiled king to confront the city of the throne of his forefather David. This dramatic presentation highlights the scandalous nature of Israel's response to her Messiah. By dethroning the holy city and the old-covenant community from their place of pre-eminence in salvation history, Matthew draws attention to the fact that Jesus' gospel of the kingdom radically undercuts Jewish presumptions of God's partial favour. The import of Jesus' mission, according to Matthew, is rather that a universal gospel

---

[47] On Jerusalem, see already the discussion entitled 'Jerusalem in the purposes of God' in ch. 2 above. For some of the material in the next two paragraphs, we are indebted to Keathley 1997: 20–21 and Verseput 1994: 105–121.

[48] See further Kingsbury 1973: 50–52 as to how the repudiation of Jesus by Israel signals an extension of the mission to the Gentiles.

is preached to all the nations transcending ethnic boundaries.

This reality comes into even sharper focus in the Matthean passion narrative. At the occasion of Jesus' death, Pontius Pilate, the Roman procurator, unsuccessfully seeks to shift blame for Jesus' crucifixion on to the Jews (27:24), while the nation accepts full responsibility for Jesus' death (27:25).[49] Nevertheless, the fact that Jesus, the Jewish Messiah, 'the king of the Jews',[50] was 'handed over into the hands of the Gentiles' fulfilled Old Testament prophecy. The blasphemous treatment of Jesus by the Roman soldiers preparing him for crucifixion indicates that Matthew's Gospel does not have a 'Gentile bias'.[51] Regarding the Jews, Matthew, in material unique to him, seeks to counter a rumour that Jesus' disciples stole his body, in an effort to discredit reports of Jesus' resurrection (27:62–66; 28:11–15).[52] In this obduracy, the Jewish people are confirmed 'to this [Matthew's] day' (28:15). Thus the Gospel presents both certain Gentiles and Jews as hardened toward Jesus and his messianic claims. A core group of followers, the twelve, which is composed of Jews, is the nucleus through whom Jesus intends to build his messianic community by way of his followers' discipling of the nations.

Jesus' resurrection and the 'Great Commission' (Matt. 28)

This leads us to a treatment of the final pericope, the famous 'Great Commission' passage (28:16–20).[53] The previous discussion has

---

[49] On 27:25, see esp. McKnight 1993: 55–79, esp. 72, n. 64. McKnight rightly asserts that the passage 'speaks as much of the suspension of national privilege and the extension of the gospel to the Gentiles as it does of Jewish guilt'. Cf. also Fitzmyer 1965: 670–671. Contra Cargal 1991:101–112.

[50] 27:11, 29, 37, 42; cf. 21:5, quoting Zech. 9:9.

[51] 27:27–31; cf. 20:19. Cf. recently Sim (1995: 19–48), who, however, interprets his findings not in relation to Jesus but with reference to the Matthean community. According to Sim, the 'anti-Gentile' statements found in Matthew's Gospel are evidence that the Matthean community took steps to distance itself from its Gentile neighbours in response to persecution following the first Jewish war against Rome. But the exact opposite seems to be demonstrable. Rather than portraying the post-AD 70 church as reverting back to the initial mission to the Jews, Matthew's Gospel shows how Jesus engaged in a mission to the Jews that, after his exaltation, was broadened to include the Gentiles.

[52] This may, by way of *inclusio*, mirror Matthew's defence of Jesus' Davidic provenance at the onset of his Gospel against Jewish charges of the illegitimacy of Jesus' birth (see Freed 1987: 3–19).

[53] Regarding the plethora of treatments of Matthew's 'Great Commission', see the detailed bibliography in Hagner 1995: 878–880, plus now also Keener 1999: 715–721.

already indicated that this passage is intricately interwoven with the Gospel as a whole,[54] a fact that confirms the impression that the pericope was composed (or at least thoroughly reworked) by the evangelist rather than merely having been taken from traditional material.[55] Some significance rests on the genre of this section. Rather than dealing with this issue in terms of competing, mutually exclusive options, we may detect elements of enthronement, covenant renewal and commissioning (O'Brien 1976: 66–71). In an echo of Daniel 7:14, Jesus is portrayed as the exalted eschatological ruler of the world's kingdoms (enthronement);[56] by assuring the disciples of his continuing presence, Jesus reaffirms his covenant with them (covenant renewal); and, reminiscent of Old Testament commissioning narratives, Jesus issues to his followers his final charge (commissioning).[57] In the end, it is not any particular genre, or even a combination of these, that accurately describes Matthew's final pericope. The evangelist rather brings his own Gospel to his own intended conclusion.[58]

By omitting reference to the name of the mountain in Galilee ('into Galilee' echoes 26:32; 28:7, 10) where the event took place and by providing no description of Jesus' external appearance, Matthew focuses attention on Jesus' words uttered on this occasion.[59] Before

---

Apart from the sources listed above, see esp. Bornkamm, Barth and Held 1963: 131–137.

[54] Cf., apart from references previously quoted, also Brooks 1981: 2–18; Scaer 1991: 245–266.

[55] Cf. Kingsbury 1974: 573–574; Schlatter 1948: 801: 'the ending of the first Gospel [is] ... written by Mt.'; Kilpatrick 1946: 48–49; and Bosch (1991: 57), who calls this the 'most Matthean' pericope in the entire Gospel. Contra Bornkamm, Hahn, Michel and Strecker. See also LaGrand (1999: 235–247), whose chapter on the 'Great Commission' is given almost entirely to a discussion and defence of the passage's authenticity.

[56] This is the view of Bornkamm, Barth and Held (1963: 133–134); Meier (1977a: 413) (with reference to previous publications); Michel (1983: 36); and others. Donaldson (1985: 181–188) contends that many important features of Dan. 7:13–14 are missing in Matt. 28:16–20: the coming on the clouds of heaven, the terms *basileia*, *doxa*, and the term 'Son of Man' itself. He prefers to view the mountain setting, the terms *edothē*, *exousia*, and 'Son' christology as pointers to a background of a Zion eschatology.

[57] Note, however, that this commissioning is given to a group rather than to individuals as in Old Testament narratives.

[58] Cf. Bosch (1983: 222): 'we have here a pericope which is *sui generis* and eludes the labels of form criticism'; Meier (1977a: 424): 'no form-critical category yet proposed fits Matt 28:16–20 ... the pericope is so *sui generis* ... that it defies the labels of form criticism' (but see the qualifications by Carson 1984: 592).

[59] The authenticity of the event is highly probable, contra Barth (1961: 57), who claims that the event is recounted, not in the style of history but, like the creation story, in the style of historical saga.

focusing on Jesus' words, we may briefly discuss the response Jesus encountered on the part of his disciples: 'When they saw him, they worshipped him; but they (or: some) doubted' (28:17, NRSV). The instance of 'doubt' in 14:31 has indicated that, for Matthew, doubt did not necessarily amount to unbelief; it rather indicated people's wavering or lack of resolve.[60] Together with the fact that the Greek plural article *hoi* is usually used by Matthew in the sense of 'they' rather than 'some',[61] the emphasis here appears to be on the disciples' lack of resolve (Bauer 1988: 110; Hagner 1995: 884–885). This interpretation coheres well with the fact that Jesus' final charge concludes with a strong assurance that he would be with his followers until the end of the age as they carried out his commission.[62]

'All authority has been given to me in heaven and on earth' (28:18, NASB): the divine passive 'has been given' (*Edothē*) indicates that it is *the Father* who gave Jesus all authority.[63] What kind of authority has the Father given to Jesus? All we are told is that Jesus' authority is comprehensive (*pasa*). In fact, 'all' dominates the entire 'Great Commission' passage: Jesus has 'all authority' (v. 18); his followers are to go and make disciples of 'all nations' (v. 19); and Jesus will be with them 'always' (lit. 'all the days'; v. 20).[64] In the present instance, the authority spoken of pertains to his mission, to be carried out through the disciples as his emissaries, on the basis of his word.[65] The image in mind here may be that of a victorious military general who assures his followers of his unlimited authority (Borgen 1996: 59–60).

On this basis, Jesus' disciples are to 'go and make disciples': the aorist participle 'go' (*poreuthentes*) modifies the aorist imperative

---

[60] See the treatment of 14:31 above.

[61] Cf. 2:5; 4:20, 22; 14:17, 33; 15:34; 16:7, 14; 20:5, 31; 21:25; 22:19; 26:15, 67; 27:4, 21, 23; 28:15.

[62] Cf. 28:20: *synteleia tou aiōnos*; cf. 13:39–40, 49; 24:3.

[63] McNicol (1989: 37) plausibly suggests that Matt. 28:18–20, the last unit in Matthew, echoes 2 Chr. 36:22–23, the last unit in the Hebrew Bible. LaGrand (1999: 238), referring to Barth 1961: 56, considers Matt. 28:18b 'the decisive fulfillment of 10.23'. Note also the tie-in with the temptation narrative in Matt. 4:9 ('"All this I will give you," Satan said, "if you will bow down and worship me"'; par. Luke. 4:6: 'I will give you all their authority and splendour, for it has been given to me'). At the beginning of his ministry, Jesus had resisted the devil's temptation and gone the way of the cross. At this climactic high point in Matthew's Gospel, subsequent to the resurrection, Jesus proclaims that he has in fact been given 'all authority' – but now the giver is God, and the authority has been legitimately obtained (cf. Gundry 1994: 595; Keener 1999: 716, who also cites France 1985: 413).

[64] This is noted by Carson 1984: 594 et al.

[65] Though it is of course true that all of God's authority is mediated through the risen Christ this side of his resurrection and ascension.

'make disciples' (*mathēteusate*) as an auxiliary reinforcing the action of the main verb.[66] The making of disciples (the term occurs elsewhere only in 13:52; 27:57; and Acts 14:21) entails the bringing of a person into the relationship of student to teacher in order to take the teacher's yoke upon himself and learn from him (11:29). In effect, successful disciple-making therefore presupposes the committed discipleship of the disciple-makers themselves.[67] Moreover, in the context of Matthew's Gospel, pursuing the road of discipleship 'means above all to follow after righteousness as articulated in the teaching of Jesus'.[68]

Perhaps the most striking element of the present command, however, is the fact that Jesus' followers are called not merely to disciple *individuals*, but entire *nations*, indeed, *all* nations. This vision is as startling as it is grand.[69] Apart from Jesus' promise of his continuing presence with his own, it would surely have to be judged hopelessly ambitious and beyond reach. As already argued, 'all the nations' includes Israel.[70] Nevertheless, the primary focus in the present context may well be said to lie on the evangelization of the (Gentile) nations other than Israel.[71] The two present participles 'baptizing' (*baptizontes*)

---

[66] The closest Matthean parallels featuring the aorist participle of *poreuomai* plus an aorist imperative are 2:8 ('go and search'); 9:13 ('go and learn'); 11:4 ('go and report'); 17:27 ('go and throw'); and 28:7 ('go and tell'). In each case, the weight of the phrase rests, not on 'go' (though a mild imperatival force extends to this term as well), but on the subsequent imperatival expression (Luke adds several additional examples: 7:22 = Matt. 11:4; Luke 13:32; 14:10; 17:14; and 22:8; the occurrence of the construction – not elsewhere featured in Mark – in Mark 16:15 suggests an assimilation to Matt. 28:19). Likewise, what is stressed in 28:19 (contrary to popular notions) is not going, but the making of disciples (though the latter may well imply the former). Compare with this the use of the *imperative* of *poreuomai* plus a second imperative in 28:10 ('go and tell'), where proportionately more weight may rest on the going itself; and the use of the *present* participle of *poreuomai* plus an imperative in Matthew 10:7 ('as you go'), where the participial force may receive greater emphasis (the contention by Culver [1968: 243–253] that we are simply to make disciples 'as we go' rather than going somewhere for the express purpose of making converts is unduly extreme; see the proper qualifications registered by Carson 1984: 595). See on these matters esp. Rogers 1973: 258–267; cf. Donaldson 1985: 184 and O'Brien 1976: 72–73.

[67] As Carson puts it, all of Jesus' disciples are 'to make others what they themselves are – disciples of Jesus Christ' (1984: 596).

[68] Hagner 1995: 887, referring to Kvalbein 1988: 48–53.

[69] Keener (1999: 719) calls it a 'drastic innovation'.

[70] See the helpful summary discussion by Carson (1984: 596), complete with a critique of the 'church growth movement'. Contra Park (1995: 190), who claims that the 'Kingdom is not simply *expanded* to accommodate the gentiles but is *transferred* from the Jews to the Gentiles (21:43)' (emphasis original).

[71] So rightly Keener (1999: 719), who also notes that the present commission extends beyond the boundaries set in the commissioning of the twelve in ch. 10.

and 'teaching' (*didaskontes*) specify the characteristic mode[72] of making disciples, whereby baptism and instruction are to be construed in complementary terms.[73] In both cases, further qualifiers are given.

Baptism is to be administered in (*eis*) the name (singular) of the Father and the Son and the Holy Spirit, the most straightforward trinitarian formula in the entire New Testament.[74] In light of the fact that the early church is shown to have baptized in the name of Jesus Christ (Acts 2:38; 10:48) or 'the Lord Jesus' (Acts 8:16; 19:5) and Paul refers merely to baptism in the name of Christ (Gal. 3:27; Rom. 6:3), the question arises whether this formulation reflects later baptismal practice. If Matthew was written prior to AD 70,[75] however, there is hardly enough time for a trinitarian practice of baptism to evolve. It appears more likely that the early church felt no contradiction between Jesus' command to baptize in the name of the Father, the Son and the Holy Spirit, and its practice of baptizing in the name of Jesus, since the latter implied the former (Riggenbach 1903).

Regarding teaching, the disciples are enjoined to teach others 'to obey everything I have commanded you' (28:20a; cf. Deut. 4:1; 6:1). This brings into play the entire body of Jesus' teaching presented in the course of Matthew's Gospel (cf. esp. 5:17–20; 7:21–27), similar to the way in which the disciples' commissioning in John 20:21 rests on the Fourth Gospel's sending christology. Moreover, the present charge makes clear that mission entails the nurturing of converts into the full obedience of faith, not merely the proclamation of the gospel.[76] This was perhaps most admirably carried out by the apostle Paul, whose

---

[72] Though not the means: see Carson 1984: 597.

[73] As Carson aptly notes, 'The NT can scarcely conceive of a disciple who is not baptized or is not instructed' (1984: 597). Hagner (1995: 887) notes that the mention of baptism here comes somewhat as a surprise, since baptism is mentioned earlier in Matthew only in ch. 3 (and 21:25) with reference to John the Baptist, and we know nothing about Matthew's view of Christian baptism.

[74] As Blomberg (1992: 432) points out (with reference to Mounce 1985: 277), 'Jesus has already spoken of God as his Father (Matt 11:27; 24:36), of himself as the Son (11:27; 16:27; 24:36), and of blasphemy against God's work in himself as against the Spirit (12:28) ... "That Jesus should gather together into summary form his own references ... in his final charge to the disciples seems quite natural"' (cf. the positive assessment by Keener 1999: 717). Neither Blomberg nor Carson 1984: 598 (followed by Hagner 1995: 888; see also Osborne 1976 and 1978), however, thinks it likely that the present phrase preserves Jesus' *ipsissima verba*.

[75] While most commentators favour a post- AD 70 date for Matthew's Gospel (see survey chart in Davies and Allison 1988: 127-128 and the authors' own conclusion on 138), a date prior to AD 70 is not without its advocates (e.g. Carson, Ellis, Gundry, Maier, Meinertz, Moule, Reicke and Robinson). For a summary of the discussion and a defence of a pre- AD 70 date, see Carson, Moo and Morris 1992: 76–79.

[76] See already the expression 'make disciples' (*mathēteuō*) in v. 19.

ambition it was to 'present everyone perfect in Christ' (Col. 1:28). Finally, as the church disciples the nations, it is assured of its risen Lord's continued spiritual presence until his bodily return: 'And surely I will be with you always, to the very end of the age' (28:20b; cf. Deut. 31:6).[77]

Mission in Matthew: some theological soundings

Matthew 28:16–20 marks the culmination and fulfilment of Jesus' mission: the fulfilment of Israel's destiny as the representative, paradigmatic Son, with the result that God's blessings to the nations, promised to Abraham, unrealized through Israel (despite Exod. 19:6), would be fulfilled through Jesus in the mission of his followers,[78] which nevertheless remains his own mission.[79] Jesus thus has become the eschatological replacement of Israel as God's locus of blessing for the nations (cf. John. 15). He is the replacement of Mt Zion, God's holy mountain, to which the nations would come in the last days (Donaldson 1985: 183–186). He also is the agent of God's restorative programme focused on Zion (Tan 1997). This alleviates the tension between the restrictive statements of chapters 10 and 15 and the universal affirmations in chapters 24 and 28: Israel is subsumed under the 'nations' of chapter 28, and chapters 10 and 15 merely affirm the salvation-historical primacy of Israel prior to Jesus' death and resurrection.

During Jesus' earthly ministry, one already finds indications that he will also attract people beyond the boundaries of Israel, albeit not at his own initiative. Jesus is shown to exercise salvation-historical restraint and to wait for the period subsequent to his own death when he would reveal himself to the disciples as the risen Messiah to whom the nations are now to be summoned by the proclamation of the gospel (J. J. Scott Jr 1990: 161–169). In the following pattern, Matthew concurs with the other evangelists: Jesus' commission to Israel – rejection by Israel – judgment on Israel – opening of the kingdom to the Gentiles, with the

---

[77] Hagner (1995: 888) also notes the parallel in Hag. 1:13 and a series of Old Testament passages that promise the presence of Yahweh with his people: Gen. 28:15; Exod. 3:12; Josh. 1:5, 9; Is. 41:10.

[78] See the important recent study by LaGrand (1999).

[79] Cf. 28:20b; cf. also John 14:12; Acts 1:1. Beale (1997: 28–29) ties in the Great Commission with his proposed 'new creation' motif as the centre of New Testament theology. Where Adam, Noah and Israel failed, Christ succeeded as the Last Adam and true Israel. He 'subdued' and conquered for God as his vicegerent, and thus is in a position to authorize the church to go on its mission to the ends of the earth.

goal of forming communities of Christian disciples (Frankemölle 1982: 112–113). By conceiving of mission in terms of discipleship rather than mere gospel proclamation, and by conceiving of discipleship in terms of righteous living rather than mere believing, Matthew appears to share a certain degree of affinity with the Petrine concept of mission.[80]

Similar to John's Gospel, Matthew presents Jesus' mission from two vantage points: his earthly mission ('God with us', 1:23), which is devoted to his gathering of an embryonic *ekklēsia* (16:18; cf. 18:20: 'in their midst', NASB), initially climaxes in his rejection by Israel issuing in his crucifixion, yet is superseded by his resurrection and commissioning of his followers; and the mission of the exalted Jesus who promised his disciples to be with them 'always, even to the end of the age' (28:20b, NASB).[81] The movement from the first to the second stage of Jesus' mission therefore involves no relinquishing of Jesus' pre-eminent role, but rather merely represents a transposition on to a higher plane of activity and salvation-historical realization.[82]

Conclusion

In conclusion, how was the 'Great Commission' intended to function among the original recipients of Matthew's Gospel? Perhaps it was designed to further reinforce the notion (or correct any misperceptions) that the Gentile mission in which the early church engaged (after some hesitation) was rooted in a command of the risen Lord Jesus Christ himself. The reference to Jesus' all-encompassing authority, the charge to disciple *all* the nations by baptizing and teaching them, and the assurance of Christ's presence until the parousia would strengthen and undergird further missionary work.[83]

As Hagner (1993: lxx) suggests, Matthew's original readers were in a position between their Jewish brothers and sisters on the one hand and Gentile Christians on the other, 'wanting to reach back for continuity with the old and at the same time to reach forward to the new work God

[80] Cf. ch. 9 on mission in the General Epistles, particularly 1 Peter.

[81] The phrase 'end of the age' is also found in 13:39–40, 49; 24:3. Note that Jesus' missionary vision encompassed both a temporal component ('to the end of the age', Matt. 28:20b) and a spatial, geographical dimension ('to the ends of the earth', Acts 1:8).

[82] For a discussion of the relationship between the missions of Jesus and the church in the Gospel of Matthew, see Powell 1994: 77–89, esp. 78–79.

[83] Note the suggestion by Gundry (1994: 9) that Matthew wrote his Gospel 'to keep persecution of the church from stymieing evangelism'. 'Wherever the church ... loses its vision of worldwide evangelism', Gundry writes, 'there the Gospel of Matthew speaks with power and pertinence' (10).

was doing in the largely gentile church'. The particularist sayings preserved in Matthew, then, were to reassure Jewish believers of God's faithfulness to his covenant people, stressing 'the continuity of God's salvific promises and the actuality of their fulfillment in the first instance to Israel, as the Scriptures promised'.

At the same time, however, Matthew's Gospel serves as a reminder that the Jewish nation as a whole rejected the Messiah. Only a righteous remnant, vis-à-vis the religious establishment of Pharisaic Judaism, remained to form the nucleus of the new messianic community that consisted of followers of the Messiah irrespective of ethnic identity. Perhaps Hagner is right when he finds the audience of Matthew's Gospel 'struggling to define and defend a Jewish Christianity to the Jews, on the one hand, and to realize their identity with gentile Christians, on the other' (1993: lxxi).[84]

To be sure, Jesus and his followers and Israel stand in painful tension in Matthew.[85] Jesus is presented as superior interpreter of the Law (7:28–29) who scathingly denounces the scribes and Pharisees (23:32–33) and predicts Jewish persecution of the church (10:17; 23:34). What may be perceived as 'anti-Judaism' (though not anti-Semitism), however, in fact provides salvation-historical justification for the reconstitution of the messianic community as a new entity distinct from ethnic Israel, legitimizing a mission that reaches out to Jews and Gentiles alike with a message of repentance and faith in Jesus the Messiah in light of the imminence of God's kingdom.

Finally, together with 10:23 and 24:14, the concluding commission of 28:16–20 also places the Christian mission firmly within an eschatological framework: mission is the church's primary task between Christ's first coming and his return. The striking open-endedness of the commissioning scene, similar to the open-endedness of the book of Acts, is pregnant with anticipation and potential.[86] The eleven, as representatives of later generations of believers, are to

[84] Hagner's masterful description of the tension between particularism and universalism in Matthew's Gospel and his thoughtful discussion of the life-setting of Matthew's community (1993: lxv–lxxi) are well worth pondering.

[85] See esp. 4:23; 7:29; 9:35; 10:17; 12:9–10; 13:54; 23:34; 28:15.

[86] Cf. Hahn (1980: 30) with reference to Bornkamm (1970: 290): 'This means at the same time that the pericope remains "entirely open-ended concerning the present" and must in no way be understood as a "farewell discourse"' (our translation). See also Carson (1984: 599), who notes that while previously in Matthew's Gospel narrative units starting with an account of Jesus' ministry always concluded with a block of Jesus' teaching, in the present instance the Gospel ends with the expectation of continued mission and teaching, but now *on the part of his disciples*: 'In this sense the Gospel of Matthew is not a closed book till the consummation.'

embark on their mission, at the command and on the basis of the authority of the exalted Christ, the eschatological ruler, the Son of God.[87]

---

[87] For an interesting recent historical study related to the history of interpretation of the 'Great Commission', see Friesen 1998.

Chapter Six

Luke-Acts

In the Gospel of Luke and its sequel, the book of Acts, the theme of mission is of profound importance. So significant is this motif that Luke's two-volume work 'may be the clearest presentation of the church's universal mission in all of the New Testament'.[1] The Gospel tells the story of Jesus and his salvation; Acts traces the movement of that salvation to Israel and the Gentiles. The first volume begins with a summary of what had been promised to Israel and indicates how these promises are now to be fulfilled. It thus sets the stage for the beginning of Acts – the regathering of Israel and her role as a light to the nations (cf. Dumbrell 1994: 207).

As in the case of Mark and Matthew, we will follow the narrative flow[2] of Luke, giving special attention to the relevant mission passages within their salvation-historical context.

Luke's prologue (Luke 1:1–4)

Luke's stated purpose in his prologue, 'so that you [Theophilus] may know the certainty (*asphaleia*) of the things you have been taught' (v. 4), applies to both his Gospel and Acts.[3] Luke's broad purpose is the edification of believers, and he accomplishes this by recounting how God's plan, which had come to fulfilment in Jesus, had continued to unfold in the history of the early church. This was effected through the Spirit-empowered witness to Jesus, undertaken by his apostles at the

---

[1] Senior and Stuhlmueller 1983: 255. Green (1992: 23) comments, 'Mission is central to both Lukan volumes'; the author displays 'a strategic concern' with the relationship between Jesus' own mission in the Gospel and that of the early Christian movement in the Acts of the Apostles.

[2] That is, a cumulative account of the story that unfolds as the narrative is read from the beginning.

[3] Although there is some dispute over this, it is best to treat the prologue as an introduction to the twofold work, not least because of the reference back to the first volume in the prologue of Acts (1:1). The statement of purpose in the prologue of Luke applies equally to the Gospel and to Acts. *Cf.* Fitzmyer 1981: 9 and Witherington 1998: 4–9, together with the literature cited.

command of Jesus (cf. Acts 1:1–8). The corollary is that the mission and message of Jesus' apostles are true.

The infancy narratives (Luke 1 – 2)

The infancy narratives of Luke 1 – 2, which have been described as an 'overture' and 'introduction' orienting the reader to God's work of salvation,[4] function as a prologue to both the Gospel and the book of Acts. These narratives not only introduce many of the key themes in Luke's two-volume work; they also establish continuity with the Old Testament, survey what will happen in the course of Luke-Acts and provide a framework of interpretation for the subsequent events.[5]

God had previously acted in the history of his people, Israel. Now, according to the canticles of Luke 1 – 2, he is about to intervene once more on their behalf: Israel's hopes for a Saviour of David's line who will reign for ever (Luke 1:30–35) are about to be realized, so fulfilling the expectations of 2 Samuel 7:12–13.

Through the birth of Jesus, according to the Song of Mary (Luke 1:46–55), God will restore Israel (v. 54), thus fulfilling his promises to Abraham and his descendants (v. 55). The Song of Zechariah (Luke 1:67–79), which expands on the significance of the births of John the Baptist and Jesus, praises God for having visited and redeemed his people in the sending of his Son (v. 68). John's role is that of a forerunner, the prophet of the Most High (vv. 76–79), whose task is to prepare Israel to meet her Messiah and to accept him (1:17, 76–77; Franklin 1975: 84). Jesus, the Son of the Most High, is the Messiah of the house of David. He is the mighty Saviour who will repeat the triumphs of the exodus in fulfilment of the Abrahamic promises (vv. 71–73). The purpose of the Messiah's deliverance of his people is that they may serve God 'in holiness and righteousness' (vv. 74–75), in other words, that Israel may fulfil her divine calling from of old (cf. Exod. 19:5–6). The salvation which the Davidic king brings is not a political deliverance or the physical restoration of Israel, but the forgiveness of sins that enables God's people to serve him 'without fear' (vv. 74, 77; Carroll 1988: 46).

Not all historical Israel, however, is truly God's people. The Israel which is the recipient of the divine promises has been redefined. God's mercy extends to those who *fear* him, he has lifted up the *humble* and

[4] Bock 1994: 68. He suggests that these chapters serve 'as a theological overview of the work of God'.
[5] For a detailed examination of the infancy narratives including their function within Luke-Acts, see Bock 1994: 68–258.

filled the *hungry* with good things; but he has scattered the proud, brought down the rulers and sent the rich away empty (vv. 50–54). The Abrahamic promises are fulfilled not in national Israel, but in those who fear him.

The climax of the infancy narratives is the Song of Simeon (2:29–32),[6] where for the first time in the Gospel Jesus' saving work is explicitly related to the Gentiles (v. 32; cf. v. 31). Simeon is looking for 'the consolation of Israel' (v. 25; cf. Is. 40:1; 49:13), and this is described in terms of the salvation that God has prepared 'in the presence of all peoples' (NRSV), that is, before the whole world[7] (vv. 30–31). This salvation comes with Jesus' birth: Simeon's taking of the child in his arms is 'intended to picture the arrival of [the] messianic hope for Israel'.[8] The one who brings this salvation and personifies it is revealed to Simeon as the Lord's Messiah (v. 26) who fulfils the role of Yahweh's Servant (v. 32; cf. Is. 42:6; 49:6–9). His advent is in accordance with the Abrahamic promises. This salvation is for the glory[9] of God's chosen people, Israel (v. 32), even though not all in Israel will accept the consolation Jesus brings. His ministry will lead to division, described as 'the falling and rising of many' (v. 34). At the same time, the divine salvation, brought by Yahweh's Servant, is 'a light for revelation to the Gentiles' (v. 32; Is. 49:6).[10] Having witnessed it (v. 31) Gentiles will also experience it. Thus, 'God's plan of

[6] The basic themes of all the hymns are reiterated within the narrative of vv. 25–35. In addition, Jesus is here linked with the Servant's hope of Is. 40 – 66, and the universal scope of his work is specifically introduced for the first time. *Cf.* Hahn 1965: 129.

[7] The rendering of *pantōn tōn laōn* as 'all peoples' (NRSV) is preferable to 'all people' (NIV). The expression refers not simply to Israel but to both Israel and the Gentiles, suggesting the note of universalism in Luke for the first time (Farris 1985: 148). The parallelism of v. 32 with its mention of the Gentiles (*ethnōn*), together with the Old Testament background to 'peoples', indicates a universal reference. For the moment, Simeon speaks of the preparation of this salvation in the sight of all (v. 31); the following verse will make it clear that all racial groups will *participate* in this salvation.

[8] Bock 1994: 241. In seeing Jesus Simeon sees God's salvation, since he is at the centre of that salvation. Contra Franklin 1975: 120–121.

[9] Most commentators understand 'light' and 'glory' as parallel, and both in apposition to 'your salvation' (v. 30). On this view, salvation is a light to Gentiles and glory to Israel. On the other hand, it is syntactically possible to take 'revelation' and 'glory' as parallel and in apposition to 'light', which refers back to salvation. On this interpretation, salvation is light for all people, in particular it is revelation for Gentiles and glory for Israel. Although there is Old Testament support for the second view (Is. 60:1–3), and it is consistent with Luke 1:78–79 and Acts 26:22–23, the first view is slightly preferable, given the background in Is. 49:6 (note the detailed discussion in Bock 1994: 244, who prefers the second interpretation).

[10] On Luke's presentation of Jesus as the fulfilment of the Servant of Isaiah, see recently T. S. Moore 1997a: 47–60. Note the discussion of this motif in ch. 2 of this volume.

salvation for Israel and her world will not fail'; it 'will redound to Israel's glory' (Dumbrell 1994: 209).

The infancy narratives which function as a prologue to Luke-Acts show that the promise of Israel's restoration is fulfilled in Jesus, who is the consummation of Old Testament hopes.[11] In him God has confirmed his earlier promises and brought the nation's history to a climax. The salvation which he brings has its roots in Israel's history: in Abraham, the exodus, David and the Servant of Isaiah. Through the Saviour's birth the promises by which Israel would be a blessing to the world are being brought to fruition.

The preparation for Jesus' ministry (Luke 3:1 – 4:15)

Although Jesus' earthly ministry was restricted to Israel,[12] Luke signals that the Saviour's coming will have worldwide repercussions. His apparently insignificant birth is set against the backdrop of Augustus' imperial rule and that of Quirinius, his governor (Luke 2:1), while John the Baptist's and Jesus' ministries are deliberately located within the context of universal history (Luke 3:1–2). This is not simply for conventional historiographical reasons, but is particularly because 'the word of God' that comes to the forerunner John (v. 2) has significance for 'all mankind' who soon 'will see God's salvation' (v. 6).[13] By specifically underscoring this universalist motif at the beginning of his Gospel and again at the conclusion of Acts (note 'God's salvation' in 28:28), Luke shows it to be a unifying theme which ties together his two volumes. God's intention to save men and women from all nations is the purple thread that runs through Luke-Acts from beginning to end.[14]

Jesus' baptism (Luke 3:21–22) marks the point of preparation for his ministry. He receives divine confirmation that he is the Davidic Messiah (Ps. 2:7) and the Servant of Isaiah (Is. 42:1), who is anointed by the Spirit and whose task is to cleanse and restore Israel (Turner 1996a: 211).

[11] Jesus is set forth as God's final action for Israel in these narratives (Franklin 1975: 81).
[12] Significantly, the particularist statements in Matthew (15:24: 'I was sent only to the lost sheep of Israel'; note also 10:6, 23) do not appear in Luke.
[13] Only Luke, who does it deliberately so as to emphasize the universality of salvation, adds the last clause from Is. 40:5, 'and all mankind will see God's salvation'. See Turner 1996a: 170; cf. S. G. Wilson 1973: 38–39; Senior and Stuhlmueller 1983: 260; and Penney 1997: 23, 36–37. Franklin (1975: 139) comments: 'In the beginnings of the story [of Jesus] the final significance of the whole event is foreshadowed.'
[14] So Tannehill (1986: 40), who comments: 'The end of the work reminds us of the divine purpose which was disclosed at the beginning and which remains central throughout.' Cf. Hahn 1965: 129.

Immediately following the baptism Luke records Jesus' genealogy (3:23–38). Both its content and position before the commencement of his ministry serve to highlight the scope of Jesus' concern for all humanity.[15] A key feature of the genealogy is that it goes beyond Abraham to Adam (contrast Matt. 1:1–17). Jesus is identified with *all people*, not simply with the nation of Israel as the chosen Son, since he is 'the son of *Adam*, the Son of God' (v. 38). This universal perspective – in other words, Jesus' relationship with all humanity as their representative – fits hand in glove with Luke's emphasis on salvation reaching to the ends of the earth (Acts 10:34–43; 17:22–31).

In the temptation narrative (Luke 4:1–13) Jesus as God's Son, that is, Israel's Messiah, replays the story of Israel's experience in the wilderness, in what amounts to a 'new exodus'. Tempted by hunger, Jesus (unlike Israel) depends wholly on God for sustenance (cf. Deut. 8:3). He rejects the temptation to worship the devil in exchange for all the kingdoms of the world (Deut. 6:13; contrast Israel, Deut. 9:12) and, unlike Israel, God's Son refuses to put the Lord God to the test (Deut. 6:16). 'As the messianic king and Son of God (2 Sam. 7.14; Ps. 2.7; 89.27; 4QFlor), Jesus represents the nation and fulfills the task of eschatological Israel in the wilderness'.[16] Israel's restoration has begun through the victory of God's Son over the devil.

Jesus in the synagogue at Nazareth (Luke 4:16–30)

According to Luke the basic and foundational mission is that of Jesus who has been sent by God.[17] This emerges clearly in the 'programmatic' statement of Luke 4:16–30,[18] where Jesus speaks of his anointing by the Holy Spirit (at his baptism, 3:22–23) and declares the purpose of his being sent. This is the first episode of his public ministry reported in any detail, which exemplifies what Jesus proclaimed in synagogues throughout his mission and spells out in summary form the nature of his ministry. Verses 16–30 are closely tied with the preceding material, beginning with 3:21 in relation to Jesus' baptism, his identification as God's Son and the Servant of Isaiah, and his anointing

[15] Bock 1994: 360. Note Marshall's comment: 'Jesus has his place in the human race created by God' (1978a: 161).

[16] Strauss 1995: 215–216; Turner 1996a: 205.

[17] See O'Brien 1999a: 203–214. The language of mission is used of God sending messengers to Israel (Luke 20:9–12) which culminates in the sending of Jesus (v. 13).

[18] Note the treatments of this paragraph in Tannehill 1986: 60–73; Nolland 1989: 188–203; Green 1992: 24–33; Bock 1994: 394–421; Menzies 1994: 145–156 (who speaks of vv. 16–30 as 'the cornerstone of Luke's entire theological program', 145); Turner 1996a: 213–266; and Penney 1997: 42–45.

115

with the Spirit for the fulfilment of his mission (vv. 21–22). Later summaries of Jesus' ministry (cf. 7:21–22; Acts 10:38) refer back to this account of the nature of his mission (4:18–19), while the future outreach to Gentiles (vv. 25–27) and the Jews' rejection of Jesus (vv. 28–30), to name but two important motifs, are foreshadowed in this programmatic section.[19]

The centrepiece of the passage is the reference to Isaiah 61:1–2 (cf. 58:6) in verses 18–19 where Jesus speaks of his anointing by the Holy Spirit (at his baptism, 3:22–23) and the purpose of his mission.[20]

> 'The Spirit of the Lord is on me,
>   because he anointed me
>   to preach good news to the poor.
> He has sent me to proclaim freedom for the prisoners,
>   and recovery of sight for the blind,
>   to release the oppressed,
> to proclaim the year of the Lord's favour.'

Jesus is the Spirit-anointed prophet who announces the new era of salvation which he brings to pass as the anointed Messiah (Is. 61:1–2; 58:6). The nature of his mission is marked out by four infinitival expressions, three of which involve preaching: 'to *preach good news* to the poor', 'to *proclaim* freedom for the prisoners and recovery of sight for the blind', 'to *release* the oppressed' and 'to *proclaim* the year of the Lord's favour'. The first is fundamental to Jesus' task and is apparently amplified[21] by the following three.[22] Jesus is conscious that he has been commissioned and sent by God for his mission, which is essentially to 'preach good news' (*euangelizomai*) or to 'proclaim'

[19] 'As Luke has told the story, the ministry of Jesus in Nazareth serves a central role in the Gospel as a whole' (Green 1992: 26).

[20] For other passages in which Jesus indicates the purpose for which he came, see Luke 5:32; 12:49–53; 19:10.

[21] Tannehill 1986: 62–63. Green (1992: 27) suggests that the threefold repetition of 'me' closely links the anointing, the mission and the speaker, while the three clauses with the verbs in the infinitive ('to proclaim ...', 'to send ...' and 'to proclaim ...') together interpret what is meant by 'to preach good news to the poor' (*cf.* Green 1994: 73). (Turner 1996a: 250) considers that Jesus' mission is 'largely a unified one', since all but the last clause involve 'a different Isaianic metaphor for Israel's low estate, and all five concern her impending release from such a state'.

[22] The former term, to 'preach good news' (*euangelizomai*), is used repeatedly in summaries of Jesus' activity, and indicates that he is continually doing what he was sent to do (4:43; 7:22; 8:1; 16:16; 20:1). The same verb is picked up and used of the proclamation of the gospel by Jesus' apostles and other disciples (*cf.* Luke 9:6; Acts 8:4, 12, 25, 35, 40; 11:20; *etc.*).

(*kēryssō*), and it has 'release' (*aphesis*) as its goal, a 'release' which throughout the rest of Luke-Acts signifies 'the forgiveness of sins'[23] and 'deliverance' from bondage to Satan (4:31–37; Green 1994: 73).

The 'poor' to whom the good news is announced are not to be understood narrowly of the economically destitute, as most recent scholars have suggested;[24] rather the term refers more generally to 'the dispossessed, the excluded' who were forced to depend upon God. Within the wider canonical context of the Old Testament, for example in the Psalms, the 'poor' refers to the socially deprived, those in great need, arising from suffering or persecution, as well as literal poverty.[25] The 'poor' can also describe Israel over against the nations that oppress her (Ps. 9; cf. 68:10). In Isaiah the term is extended metaphorically to designate the great need into which Israel had fallen because of the exile: the 'poor' are the afflicted ones, those returning from captivity (49:13). According to chapter 61 the 'poor' designates the eschatological community, the suffering exiles or faithful in Israel who have been spiritually oppressed.[26] It is to these poor and oppressed in Israel that Jesus comes announcing the gospel of the kingdom.

As the eschatological prophet Jesus announces the ultimate Jubilee: he comes 'to proclaim the year of the Lord's favour' (4:19; Lev. 25:8–10). Already the language of liberation has been used in this composite Isaianic quotation: 'to proclaim *release* to the captives' (Is. 61:1), and 'to *release* the oppressed' (Is. 58:6). By ending his reading in the middle of Isaiah's sentence and omitting any reference to 'the day of vengeance of our God', Jesus presents his mission in terms of hope. The ultimate time of God's vengeance has not yet arrived (even though there are implications of a future judgment; cf. 4:24–27). Jesus' coming is the dawn of the new age, but it is not a call to fulfil literally the legal requirements of the Jubilee. Rather, in his announcement the Jubilee is a picture of total forgiveness and salvation just as it had become in Isaiah 61.[27]

When Jesus claimed that this Old Testament Scripture had 'today'

[23] Luke 1:77; 3:3; 24:47; Acts 2:38; 5:31; 10:43; 13:38; 26:18.
[24] Note the survey of the lengthy scholarly discussion as to who are 'the poor', together with further bibliographical details, in Green 1994: 60–65.
[25] Pss. 22:24; 34:6; 35:10; 86:1; 88:15; Seccombe 1982: 26–28.
[26] Seccombe 1982: 36–39; *cf.* Turner 1996a: 250–251.
[27] Luke does not take up the distinctive Jubilee language or ideas in his writings (*e.g.* 'year of Jubilee release', Lev. 25:10, 11, 13, *etc.*), while his use of the key term 'liberty' or 'release' (*aphesis*) is interpreted in terms of 'the forgiveness of sins'; Tannehill 1986: 67–68; Turner 1996a: 244; *cf.* Dumbrell 1994: 211–212. Turner thinks that Luke has rather presented this material as part of 'a more general New Exodus soteriology'.

been fulfilled in his ministry, the initial response of the people of Nazareth to 'his gracious words' (v. 22) was positive. But he did not meet their preconceived expectations, and because he was unwilling to perform signs in their midst (as he had done in Capernaum), he experienced the violent rejection which prophets can expect in their homeland (Luke 4:22–23, 28–29). This is the first of many rejections Jesus encountered from 'his own people'. The good news which he proclaimed was from the beginning shadowed by a conflict that would persist to the end of Acts.

Jesus' response to the rejection at Nazareth was to recall the actions of Elijah (1 Kgs. 17 – 18) and Elisha (2 Kgs. 5)[28] who, at a time of severe famine and covenant unfaithfulness in Israel, performed miracles among Gentiles outside the Promised Land (vv. 25–27). Although the point is not explicit, the emphasis on Elijah's and Elisha's ministry among Gentiles foreshadows the Gentile mission in Acts.[29] Here is a major group towards which the mission is moving. Given the larger Lukan perspective of the redefinition of Israel and God's salvation reaching to the ends of the earth, with its early adumbrations of Gentiles being included within the divine saving purposes (2:30–32; 3:6), the mention of the rejection at Nazareth is not surprising. Later, in Acts 10:36–38, when the mission of God begins to spread to the Gentiles, the Nazareth scene will be recalled. Ultimately, the proclamation of 'the year of the Lord's favour' will be understood as a proclamation to people of every nation (Tannehill 1986: 72). And for Israel the implication is clear: those closest to Jesus may miss out on God's blessing, while others who are far away may receive it.

Jesus and the centurion's faith (Luke 7:1–10)

Jesus' healing of the centurion's servant (Luke 7:1–10), which is his first encounter with a Gentile recorded in Luke's Gospel, foreshadows the expansion of his ministry to the nations, an expansion already

[28] The acts of Jesus in Luke's Gospel bear close resemblances to those of Elisha (Luke 7:1–10; cf. 2 Kgs. 5) and Elijah (Luke 7:11–16; cf. 1 Kgs. 17:17–24). After Jesus restores the life of the widow's son (Luke 7:14–15), the people claim he is a great prophet (v. 16), and this links with Luke 4:25–26. Cf. Johnson 1977: 98.

[29] So S. G. Wilson 1973: 40–41, who notes that the 'main reason, in the immediate context, for the inclusion of vv. 25–27 is that they give Old Testament precedents for performing miracles among strangers'. But the deeper meaning of vv. 25–27 is that they are prophetic of the inclusion of the Gentiles. Note the treatment of Tannehill 1986: 70–73; cf. Senior and Stuhlmueller 1983: 260, 'In this inaugural scene, Luke manages to preview the ultimate consequences of Jesus' own ministry'; Nolland 1989: 203; Penney 1997: 14; and Larkin 1998: 164–65.

anticipated in 4:25–27. Of fundamental significance to the narrative is Jesus' climactic statement, addressed to the multitudes,[30] about this God-fearer: 'I tell you, I have not found such great faith even in Israel' (v. 9). This Gentile, who recognized his own unworthiness, believed in Jesus' authority and the power of his word over physical illness at a distance. Our Lord's willingness to heal the centurion's servant shows that the extent of his mission was not particularist or limited to Jews, but was implicitly universal – to Jew and Gentile alike.

Jesus' sending of the twelve (Luke 9:1–6)

If the foundational mission, according to Luke, is Jesus' being sent by God, then the sending of the twelve is an integral part of Jesus' own mission. From a larger group of disciples Jesus chose and commissioned twelve 'apostles' (*apostoloi*, Luke 6:12–15). He now shares his power and authority with them,[31] and sends (*apostellō*) them on their mission (9:1–2),[32] which involves them also in preaching the rule of God and healing the sick (v. 2). This ministry has in view the reconstitution of Israel (6:13; 22:30),[33] a goal already anticipated in the birth narratives (see above). Significantly, Luke's description of the twelve's mission (cf. vv. 2, 6) is reminiscent of his portrayal of Jesus' mission and message which was developed in the light of the Isaiah quotation in 4:18–19.

The twelve are to depend on God as they journey, recognizing the urgency of their message. They are to take no extra provisions, relying instead on those who respond to supply their basic needs. Since they are an integral part of Jesus' mission to God's people, Israel, the twelve can expect the sort of opposition that he faced; some of the towns they visit will not welcome them (9:5).

The mission instructions to the twelve are paralleled, even extended, in the mission charge to the seventy-two (10:1–24), while the greater mission announced in 24:46–49 will lead to an even more extensive ministry of proclamation.

---

[30] Note the close parallels between this narrative and the Cornelius narrative in Acts 10:1 – 11:18.

[31] 'Jesus testifies to their authority as God's representatives' (Bock 1994: 818).

[32] A mission which, in fact, marks the end of Jesus' Galilean ministry.

[33] On the significance of the number 'twelve' in Luke's narrative, see Jervell 1972: 75–112.

Jesus' sending of the seventy(-two) (Luke 10:1–24)[34]

Likewise, the sending of the seventy-two is intimately connected with Jesus' mission. As part of the travel narrative (9:51 – 19:28), the discourse grounds their mission 'in Jesus' own mission of suffering and death'.[35] These unnamed disciples prepare the Lord's approach to Jerusalem: they are sent (lit.) 'before his face' (10:1), an expression that specifically recalls the beginning of the travel narrative when Jesus set his face steadfastly to go to Jerusalem (9:51–52). Like John the Baptist (1:17, 76; 3:4; 7:27), they are 'messengers' (*angeloi*), sent to prepare the way of the *Lord* as they travel 'to every town and place where he was about to go' (10:1).

The mission of the seventy-two is to Israel.[36] As royal heralds who are sent on Jesus' mission (v. 3), they have the same twofold task: to proclaim a message of national emergency[37] and to heal.[38] Their journey with Jesus to Jerusalem will mark the final call to Israel to

[34] It is difficult to come to any final decision regarding the number of disciples sent out by Jesus – seventy or seventy-two. Both numbers are represented in the Jewish tradition of the table of nations (Gen. 10), which makes the textual problem of Luke 10:1 difficult to solve. Further, although it is not certain whether the seventy or seventy-two points back to Gen. 10, the clear table of nations allusion in Acts 2 suggests the mission of the seventy(-two) is intended to anticipate the mission in Acts (note the detailed treatment of Luke's geographical perspective by J. M. Scott [1994: 483–544]). Dumbrell (1994: 19), however, has recently argued, against his earlier interpretation, that because the mission in Luke 10 is to Israel, a reference to the seventy Jewish elders of Num. 11 is more plausible. Penney (1997: 51–52) favours both! On the textual question, see Metzger 1994: 150–151 and Bock 1996: 1014–1016.

[35] Matson 1996: 33. The regular mention of journeying in 9:51 – 19:28 and the repeated references to rejection, death and resurrection (Luke 12:49–50; 13:33–34; 16:31; 17:25; 18:31), which give a sense of narrative movement, suggest that the mission of the seventy-two stands under the shadow of the cross. *Cf.* Tannehill 1986: 232.

[36] Egelkraut 1976: 147–148 and S. G. Wilson 1973: 45–47; Wilson acknowledges that 'in the immediate context the mission of the Seventy is clearly to Israel'. However, he does admit that 'Luke may well have had one eye on the later mission of the Church'. Note the full discussion of Matson (1996: 31–36), who has not, however, given sufficient attention to the salvation-historical dimension of this mission in its Lukan context.

[37] Both the dangers (v. 3) and the urgency of their task ('do not greet anyone on the road', v. 4) are stressed.

[38] Because the seventy-two are involved in Jesus' own mission they are commissioned and sent (*apostellō*) by him (v. 3) with the same twofold task: to declare the kingdom's coming and to heal (v. 9). Their healings are signs of the inbreaking of the kingdom (*cf.* 11:14–23).

repent and submit to her King (v. 9; Dumbrell 1994: 18–19). Their official declaration, 'Peace [*i.e.* salvation] to this house' (vv. 5–6), is an indication that the final messenger, Jesus himself, is present. To reject the message of the kingdom is to have no part in the eschatological people of God (vv. 10–11).

During the ministry of the seventy-two the kingdom powerfully advances: demons have been subject to Jesus' name, and Satan has fallen from heaven (vv. 17–18). The time of eschatological fulfilment has come. But a division has occurred within Israel (v. 21): the official representatives ('the wise and learned') have been bypassed for they have not responded to the inbreaking of the kingdom, while the disciples ('the little children') have been given God's revelation. Jesus rejoices not over the success of the mission as such, but because of their incorporation into the new people of God (vv. 20–21).

There are hints in the narrative of Luke 10 that this mission to Israel anticipates[39] and prepares the reader for the universal mission in the book of Acts. These include the reference to 'seventy-two' disciples, which may call to mind the seventy-two nations of the world in Genesis 10 (which are specifically in view in Acts 2), and their being sent into the harvest field to gather God's people against the threat of judgment (Luke 10:1, 3) which anticipates strategic points in the narrative of Acts (Matson 1996: 35–36). In both missions the message's expansion is under God's control, since he is the Lord of the harvest (10:2). The acceptance or rejection of the mission, a prominent motif in Jesus' missionary discourse (10:8, 10), is a key theme in Acts, while the instructions to the missionaries about shaking the dust off their feet as a consequence of their rejection by Israel (vv. 10–12) anticipate incidents in the ministry of Paul and Barnabas (cf. Acts 13:46–51).

Gentiles participate in the messianic banquet (Luke 13:28–30; 14:23–24)

Two Lukan parables envisage Gentiles being invited to share in God's salvation. On his journey to Jerusalem, Jesus was asked about the number of those who would be saved (Luke 13:23). His response (the parable of the closed door: 13:24–30) was to urge his hearers to 'make

---

[39] Many recent writers, with varying degrees of conviction, have drawn attention to this supposed foreshadowing of the Gentile mission in Acts: see, for example, Dumbrell 1994: 214; Penney 1997: 51; and Green 1997a: 411. Note the full discussions of Tannehill 1986: 232–37 (who refers to 'the points of contact' between the mission depicted in Luke 10 and the universal mission in Acts) and Matson 1996: 31–36.

every effort to enter through the narrow door' (v. 24). This was a compelling word for Israel to repent and be saved during the time of Jesus' gracious ministry. To reject his urgent warning would lead to exclusion from the kingdom. Israel would forfeit her privileges and in her place Gentiles would share in God's salvation. In a profound reversal, the nations ('those who are last') will enter into the blessing of Israel's ('the first') inheritance (v. 30).

In the parable of the great feast (14:15–24) the subject of participating in the future kingdom of God is addressed (cf. v. 15). Many were invited to the banquet but refused with ridiculous and insulting excuses (vv. 18–20). The master then summoned the poor and outcasts of Israel to participate in his supper (v. 21). Even with their acceptance there was still room. An invitation was sent outside the city to Gentiles to attend the great banquet so that the master's house would be full (vv. 22–23). Israel's leadership refused God's gracious invitation. They rejected the ministry of Jesus and his representatives and, as a result, are rejected by God. Gentiles, who would not have been expected to attend, gladly respond to the opportunity of sharing in the great messianic feast (Nolland 1993a: 759). For them the anticipated banquet of the 'kingdom of God' has become a present reality (Turner 1996a: 319). The parable redefines membership of the kingdom, and by offering it to outsiders Jesus challenges the privileged and powerful (Dumbrell 1994: 215). Gentiles are placed on an equal footing with Jews in the messianic age.[40]

The rejection of Jesus by Jerusalem: his passion and death (Luke 19 – 23)

Jesus draws near to Jerusalem, enters the city and is acclaimed by his disciples as Messiah, but is opposed by the Pharisees (Luke 19:37–40). He weeps over Jerusalem because the city will not acknowledge her Messiah, and so will be destroyed (vv. 41–44).[41] In his confrontation with the authorities he tells them the parable of the tenants (20:9–19), which prefigures their rejection of him and God's giving of the vineyard to others (v. 16).

Jesus' ministry now comes to its climax. It is a time of eschatological

---

[40] Senior and Stuhlmueller 1983: 153. For a different interpretation, see Braun 1995: passim, who argues that Luke 14 is 'a skilfully crafted rhetorical unit in which Jesus presents an argument for Luke's vision of a Christian society' (Braun's summary).

[41] On the rejection of Jesus by Jerusalem and the reasons for the city's judgment, see especially P. W. L. Walker 1996: 69–80.

crisis when Satan's activity reaches its peak (Luke 22:3, 31, 53). There is, however, no doubt about the outcome of this conflict – the defeat of Satan (cf. 10:18). At the last supper, a Passover meal, Jesus' body is given for his disciples, the representatives of the twelve tribes of Israel (22:14–22). The blood of the new covenant is poured out for them. There is a divine purpose in Jesus going to his death. What is written in Scripture about him finds its fulfilment (cf. Is. 53); he is numbered with the transgressors. Jesus dies in Jerusalem, rejected as Messiah and Son of Man on earth, but vindicated in heaven.

The Lukan Great Commission (Luke 24:44–49)

After his burial, resurrection and post-resurrection appearances which confirm the reality of his resurrection (24:1–43), Jesus commissions his disciples and proclaims that through his saving work the way is now open for the forgiveness of sins to be proclaimed from Jerusalem to all the nations. This commission forms the climax of the risen Lord's revelation to his disciples. Along with the triumphant ascension (vv. 50–53), it concludes Jesus' history and prepares for the transition to Acts.

The paragraph is a major development within the story and reveals how God's purposes are being realized.[42] Bosch claims that Jesus' words quoted in verses 46–49, 'reflect, in a nutshell, Luke's entire understanding of the Christian mission'.[43] The following elements are especially significant:

1. At the centre of God's saving plan is the person of Jesus the Messiah, and in him the Old Testament Scriptures have been fulfilled.[44] His death and resurrection are the climactic events of history. Just as God's mission in sending Jesus (to Israel) was central and foundational during his earthly ministry, so too after his death and resurrection, with the way now open for repentance and the forgiveness of sins to be proclaimed in his name to all the nations (Luke 24:47), this sending of Jesus is still the essential mission.

[42] The story in Acts will unfold as described in Jesus' preview in vv. 47–49. See Tannehill 1986: 194–298, who shows in some detail how Luke unifies the narrative by interlacing elements of Luke 24:47–49 at major transition points in his second volume.

[43] Bosch 1991: 91. Senior and Stuhlmueller 1983: 256 refer to this paragraph as 'the keynote of Luke's mission theology'.

[44] On the motif of fulfilment in Luke-Acts note Peterson 1993: 83–104, esp. 85–86, 93 (together with the bibliography cited); cf. Bock 1996: 1936–37. The Old Testament canon as a whole is in view here, and a global understanding of it is necessary to comprehend Jesus' place within the eschatological purposes of God.

2. His universal mission will be effected by his disciples as witnesses *after* he returns to the Father (v. 44). There have been strong hints and anticipations throughout the earthly ministry of Jesus that his saving work will have worldwide repercussions, benefiting the nations as well as Israel (Luke 2:31–32), since it is God's intention that all flesh shall see his salvation (3:6). However, Jesus did not inaugurate a full-blown universal mission during the course of his earthly ministry. His own mission, together with that of the twelve and the seventy-two, was to Israel.

3. The disciples' task is one of proclamation (*kēryssō*),[45] the content of which Jesus summarized from the Old Testament in three clauses:[46] namely, that 'the Christ will suffer (*pathein*)' (v. 46), that he will 'rise (*anastēnai*) from the dead on the third day' (v. 46), and that 'repentance and forgiveness of sins will be preached (*kērychthēnai*) in his name[47] to all the nations, beginning at Jerusalem' (v. 47). Thus the disciples will bear witness to the necessity of the Messiah's suffering and entering into his glory (24:26). The third essential element in their apostolic announcement is a call for repentance with a view to the forgiveness of sins.[48] This too had been anticipated in the Old Testament and Jesus opened the disciples' minds to understand its salvation-historical significance.[49] It follows that this universal mission has its immediate basis in minds that have been opened to understand the Scriptures.[50] Having witnessed and understood God's plan, the disciples are now commissioned to go forth and proclaim it (Osborne 1984: 130–131).

[45] No mention is made of healing, exorcism, or 'signs and wonders' ministries (Larkin 1998: 22).

[46] The expression 'This is what is written' is followed by three coordinate infinitives which refer to the Messiah's suffering (*pathein*, 'to suffer'), his resurrection (*anastēnai*, 'to rise') and the proclamation (*kērychthēnai*, 'to be preached') in Jesus' name. These are fundamental steps in the realization of God's purposes in Scripture (Tannehill 1986: 294; *cf.* S. G. Wilson 1973: 47).

[47] That is, under his authority. In the Old Testament the equivalent phrase referred to the authority of Yahweh – an authority that has now been transferred to Jesus. In Acts the 'name' of Jesus is repeatedly mentioned as the disciples 'witness' and fulfil their commission through the powerful authority of the risen and glorified Lord (Acts 2:38; 3:6, 16; 4:7, 10, 12, 17–18; *etc.*).

[48] Syntactically the infinitive *kērychthēnai* ('to be preached') is coordinate and parallel with the previous infinitives.

[49] As in v. 46, Luke's language is general and Jesus specifies no particular Old Testament texts. However, Acts 13:47 (Is. 49:6) and 15:15–18 (Amos 9:11, 12) provide some clues as to the identity of these scriptures (see below). Note especially the chapter on 'Mission in the Old Testament'.

[50] What the disciples could not understand before Jesus' death and resurrection now becomes clear (*cf.* Luke 24:25, 27, 32).

4. The repentance to which the disciples are to call men and women –
this is Luke's summary term in Acts for the response to the apostolic
gospel (2:38; 3:19; 5:31; 8:22; 11:18, *etc.*) – signifies the turning away
from sin and rebellion against God. It is a reorientation, a change in
thinking that results in turning to God in faith. The 'forgiveness'
(*aphesis*) of sins, which summarizes the salvation[51] blessings, is now
mentioned for the first time in Luke after its application to the missions
of John (1:17; 3:3)[52] and Jesus (4:18). This expression serves to
'connect the inaugural portrait of Jesus' message and mission to the
message and mission He now gave the disciples' (Moore 1997a: 52).
As the disciples proclaimed the forgiveness of sins they were
continuing Jesus' Servant ministry (Is. 61:1–2). Their basic message of
24:47 was not new, but the story of salvation has developed since the
earlier mention of forgiveness (*aphesis*) in the ministries of John and
Jesus: now the summons to repent for the forgiveness of sins is
announced in Jesus' name, it is grounded in his death and resurrection
and is to be universal.[53]

5. The scope of this authoritative proclamation in Jesus' name is
described by the pregnant expression 'to all nations (*eis panta ta
ethnē*)' (v. 47). This phrase occurs in significant Old Testament
contexts that speak of all Gentiles participating in God's eschatological
salvation.[54] It appears in the threefold restatement of the Abrahamic
covenant in Genesis 18:18; 22:18; and 26:4, where 'all the nations'[55]
will participate in the covenantal blessings, and in the extensive
Isaianic usage, which envisages 'all the nations' streaming into Jerusalem in the last days (Is. 2:2; 66:18–20), to participate in the
eschatological banquet (25:6–7) and to worship God (56:7; 61:11).[56]
Gentile participation in salvation, according to Isaiah, is inseparably
linked with the mission of the Servant to the nations (cf. Is. 52:10–12

[51] In Luke-Acts 'salvation' is frequently described in terms of the forgiveness of sins
and the consequent gift of the Holy Spirit (*cf.* Acts 2:21 with v. 38).
[52] It has been suggested that Luke 3:3 and 24:47 form a kind of inclusion because of
the connection of *metanoia* ('repentance') and *aphesis* ('forgiveness') in both verses
(T. S. Moore 1997a: 51).
[53] Note Tannehill 1986: 296 and Nolland 1993b: 1221.
[54] There are other contexts besides those that speak of salvation in which 'all the
nations' turns up: *e.g.* in warnings of the destruction of Israel's enemies (Is. 29:8; 34:2),
in statements about Yahweh's power over the nations (Is. 40:17) and the power of
Israel's enemies (Is. 14:12; 36:20); so T. S. Moore 1997a: 52.
[55] 'All the nations' (*panta ta ethnē*) appears as the equivalent of 'all the families of the
earth' (Gen. 12:3); see 'Mission in the Old Testament'.
[56] Note also Pss. 71:11, 17; 85:9; 116:1; Jer. 3:17; Dan. 7:14; Amos 9:12; Hag. 2:7.
So T. S. Moore 1997a: 52.

with 52:13 – 53:12; cf. 61:11 with v. 1; see above). In the Lukan commission there is a probable connection between 'all the nations' and Isaiah's reference to the 'light for the Gentiles' (Is. 42:6; 49:6; 51:4). This is confirmed by the parallel commission in Acts 1:8, as well as 13:47, and 26:23.[57] Luke's description of the extent of the disciples' mission (24:47) can be understood in relation to the scope of the Abrahamic promises (Gen. 12:3), and the work of the Servant who is 'a light for the Gentiles' (Is. 49:6) and whose salvation extends to 'all the nations'.[58]

6. The disciples' mission begins at Jerusalem because, in the first instance, it is the mission of the Servant to Israel,[59] and then through a restored Israel to the ends of the earth. The holy city, with its unparalleled position in salvation history, is not only the focus of opposition to and rejection of Jesus, and the place where he suffers, dies (Luke 9:51; 13:33; 18:31), rises again and appears (24:1–11, 36–49). It is also the all-important starting point for the gospel mission to Israel and then to all nations. Three features of Jesus' commission lead to this conclusion:

a. The expression 'beginning at Jerusalem' alludes to the restored Zion of Isaiah, from which the word of the Lord will go forth (Is. 2:3), bringing justice and peace for all the nations.[60]

b. Jesus' affirmation to 'the twelve', 'You shall be my witnesses', is to be understood in the light of Isaiah 43:8–13; 44:6–8 where the Servant of the Lord, Israel, is to testify to his saving acts on behalf of his people.[61] The 'twelve', who are Jesus' witnesses, take up the task of

---

[57] In Acts 1:8, the phrase 'to the ends of the earth', which is drawn from Is. 49:6, replaces 'to all the nations'. At 13:47 Paul and Barnabas quote Is. 49:6 as the Lord's command to them (similar language from Isaiah appears in Luke 2:30–32 and 3:6; see above). According to Acts 26:23, Paul's proclamation of 'light' is 'both to the people [of Israel] and to the Gentiles'. The scope of his ministry matches that of the Servant who is sent to both Jews and Gentiles (Is. 49:6). See Tannehill 1986: 297.

[58] Understanding 'all the nations' in this sense runs counter to Larkin (1998: 169), who thinks that 'Taken literally, it points to a target audience of all cultures, ethnic groups including the Jews, a truly comprehensive universal mission'. Similarly, T. S. Moore (1997a: 53) comments that 'Luke gave no indication that the mission was to be for the nations/Gentiles to the exclusion of the Jews. Rather, the mission was to all the nations, including the Jewish people.'

[59] Bosch 1991: 94. He adds, 'The risen Lord has entrusted the *Gentile* mission to the apostles (Lk. 24:47; Acts 1:8); they execute this mission by turning, first, to the *Jews*!' (95). And as Hengel (1983: 59) comments, 'Anyone who wanted to address all Israel had to do so in Jerusalem.'

[60] Penney 1997: 56, following Neuberger. As to why the movement of Gentiles to Jerusalem envisaged in the Old Testament is now replaced by the gospel going out from Jerusalem, see below.

[61] T. S. Moore 1997a: 53–55. He adds that Luke 24:48 'verbally recalls Isaiah 43:10,

the Servant and testify to God's saving acts in Jesus' death and resurrection ('these things', v. 48). They represent a restored Israel that will now minister to Israel (cf. Is. 49:3, 6).

. c. The instruction to the apostles to wait in Jerusalem until they have been clothed with power from on high (v. 49) evokes the language of Isaiah 32:15 with its hopes for the refreshment and restoration of Israel. The mission given to the disciples to fulfil is that of the prophetic 'servant' of Isaiah 49:6. They will receive the Spirit as a 'prophetic empowering to extend this message and its benefits to Israel and beyond'.[62] This endowment is specifically to enable them to proclaim the good news (cf. Acts 1:8; 2:11).

The Gospel of Luke reaches its climax with the ascension (24:50–53). At the conclusion of the book we return to its beginning, and are back in the temple praising God (v. 53; cf. 1:5–25). Now, however, for the first time worship is offered to Jesus (v. 52). Jesus' ascension (cf. 9:51) has been accomplished via the cross. Not until the very end of the Gospel does his journey end. Paradoxically, Israel's hopes have been achieved; the redemption of Israel has been provided (24:21), and the stage is now set for the advance of the gospel to all the nations.[63]

The prologue to Acts (1:1–11)

The Acts of the Apostles is a narrative of missionary expansion which commences with a small group of Jesus' disciples in Jerusalem and extends across significant ethnic, religious and geographical boundaries to end in Rome where Paul preaches the gospel of the risen Christ to Jew and Gentile alike (Rosner 1998: 216). Luke records the progress of the gospel in Acts, as evidenced in its acceptance by Jew and Gentile, a 'progressive expansion' which is introduced in Acts 1:8 (Barrett 1994: 49), and then confirmed in summary statements throughout the rest of the book.[64] If the first volume begins with a summary of what had been promised to Israel and indicates how these promises are now to be

---

12; and 44:8, and in so doing picks up the Isaianic background in which Israel, God's servant, is summoned to testify of God's saving acts on behalf of His people'. Other scholars who have recognized the Isaianic background of 'you are witnesses' in Luke 24:48 and Acts 1:8 include Dodd (1952), and more recently Johnson (1990: 347); Evans and Sanders (1993: 205); Turner (1996a: 300–301); and Penney (1997: 57–58).

[62] Turner 1996a: 343, 301; see further on Acts 1:8. Cf. Marshall 1978a: 106; Menzies 1994: 199.

[63] Luke's Gospel ends poised for the witness theme to begin. The narrative is ready for the next stage in the divine purposes: the proclamation of forgiveness.

[64] Acts 2:47; 6:7; 9:31; 12:24; 16:5; 19:20; 28:30–31.

fulfilled, then it sets the stage for the beginning of Acts – the regathering of Israel and her mission as a light to the nations.

The opening verses of Acts show close literary connections[65] with the Gospel of Luke, as well as extensive conceptual and verbal parallels with Luke 24,[66] and these emphasize the continuity between Luke's two volumes (Talbert 1974: 60). Several of these parallels, including the coming of the Holy Spirit upon the disciples, the designation of the twelve as 'witnesses', and parallel expressions about the extent of their witness are central to our theme of God's salvation reaching the ends of the earth.[67] The scope of Luke's Gospel is summarized in verses 1–2, before Luke goes on to the next stage of the story. The first volume tells us what Jesus began to do and teach; Acts now recounts the continuing work of Jesus through his witnesses empowered by the Holy Spirit (v. 1).[68] 'Jesus' ministry on earth, exercised personally and publicly, was followed by his ministry from heaven, exercised through his Holy Spirit by his apostles.'[69]

During the period of forty days before his ascension Jesus appeared to his disciples, showed them that he was alive – thereby confirming them as his successors – and spoke with them about 'the kingdom (*basileia*) of God' (v. 3). This expression which summarizes the content of Jesus' post-resurrection teaching stresses the continuity with

---

[65] The literary unity of Luke-Acts has been strongly advocated, for example, by Brawley (1990: 86–106) on the grounds that 1. both works are dedicated to Theophilus; 2. Acts 1:1–2 summarizes the Gospel; 3. Acts repeats themes and literary patterns found in the Gospel; and, 4. the narrative schema in Luke forms a bridge into Acts. See also the treatments of Talbert (1974: 58–61); and Marshall (1993: 163–182); the latter interacts with recent literature.

[66] So T. S. Moore (1997b: 394), following Zehnle 1971: 98–99; Talbert 1974: 58–61; Menzies 1994: 168–172; and Soards 1994: 196–197. Note also Tannehill 1990: 10–20 and Rosner 1998: 3. Barrett (1994: 61), who regards vv. 1–14 as the prologue of Acts, considers that most of the material in these verses is mentioned in some form in Luke 24, if not earlier in the Gospel, and it is best to see this whole section as a recapitulation, with some additional elements, before Peter's first speech in Acts 1:15–22. Note also the treatments in Dumbrell 1994: 219; Satterthwaite 1993: 353–354; and Witherington 1998: 105.

[67] Senior and Stuhlmueller (1983: 269) go a step further and claim that 'the scope, structure and content of Acts are dominated by the question of the universal mission'.

[68] In the expression *hōn ērchato ho Iēsous poiein te kai didaskein*, the auxiliary 'began' (*ērchato*) is emphatic and should be given its full weight ('all that Jesus *began* to do and teach', so NIV), rather than being taken as an auxiliary (= 'all that Jesus did and taught', so Haenchen 1971; NRSV). Accordingly, Acts contains an account of the continuing work of Jesus. Note the syntactical discussions in Bruce 1990b: 98; Marshall 1980: 56; Longenecker 1981: 253; and Barrett 1994: 66–67. For a different view, see Haenchen 1971: 137.

[69] Stott 1990: 32. Hengel (1986: 59) rightly observes: 'In reality, the whole double work covers the one history of Jesus Christ.'

his message in the Gospel.[70] Four of the eight references to God's kingdom in Acts have a framing function for the book as a whole (1:3, 6; 28:23, 31), and most occurrences of the phrase turn up in summary statements of the apostolic preaching. The missionary message which the disciples proclaim is 'the good news of the kingdom of God and the name of Jesus Christ' (8:12; 28:23, 31). The close link between Jesus' name and the kingdom draws attention to the significance of Jesus' reign within the divine rule. They are not two separate topics but one, for God's rule is established in the world through the reign of his Messiah, Jesus.

After teaching his apostles about 'the kingdom of God' Jesus urged them to remain in Jerusalem until they were baptized with the Holy Spirit (vv. 3–4). Their question which followed, 'Lord, are you at this time going to restore the kingdom to Israel?' (v. 6), is apparently an enquiry about the manner of this restoration as well as its timing, and is not misguided by nationalistic expectations, as many suppose.[71] When told of the Spirit's coming, the disciples, in line with prophetic eschatology, would naturally have in mind the last days (Joel 2:28–32) and the messianic cleansing or restoration of Zion.[72] Is this the time when Jerusalem will become the world city to which the Gentiles will journey?

Jesus' response to the disciples' question comes in two parts. First (v. 7), he does not deny the expectation of the 'restoration'. However, they cannot know the times or dates, and he corrects any suggestion that it will come immediately (see Acts 3:20–21). In the second part of his answer (v. 8), Jesus assures his disciples that the Holy Spirit will come upon them, and that they will be his witnesses in Jerusalem, in all Judea and Samaria, and to the ends of the earth. 'In Luke 24 the disciples were invited to see Jesus' work of redemption by looking *back* to his crucifixion, now they are invited to look *forwards* to their mission "to the ends of the earth". The "redemption" of Israel is a twofold entity –

---

[70] Tannehill 1990: 14; Palmer 1993: 63.

[71] For a succinct discussion of a number of related issues, see Penney 1997: 69–74. Bolt (1998: 197) regards the disciples' question as still being too narrowly nationalistic, ignoring the expansiveness of Israel's hopes erected by the prophets, but Jervell (1984: 98) thinks the disciples' question is hardly to be construed as a nationalistic misunderstanding. Turner (1996a: 294–302) rightly considers the question of Acts 1:6 to have been prompted by Jesus' teaching about 'the kingdom of God'. It 'is quite appropriate [that] the disciples should think (a) the kingdom will soon be restored *to* Israel, and (b) that *Jesus* will accomplish this' (299; original emphasis). Turner connects the promise of the Spirit with salvation, a salvation that is concerned with Zion/Jerusalem's restoration which will then spread to the nations (298).

[72] So Tiede 1986: 278 and Dumbrell 1994: 220.

inaugurated through Jesus' death and resurrection, but implemented through the disciples' mission' (P. W. L. Walker 1996: 96). There are clear Old Testament antecedents linking the restoration of Israel with witness to the nations, notably in a restoration context of Isaiah where the ministry of the Servant is to Israel (Is. 43:1–7; 49:6) and this, in turn, benefits the nations (43:8–12).[73]

The significance of Acts 1:8[74] in the narrative structure of Acts can hardly be overstated, while its relationship to our theme of God's universal salvation is recognized by all. Verse 8 has been regarded as the 'Table of Contents' of Acts, with the apostolic witness spreading from Jerusalem (chs. 1 – 7), to Judea and Samaria (chs. 8 – 12), to 'the ends of the earth' (chs. 13 – 28). This, however, has to be qualified, for although the references to Jerusalem, Judea and Samaria correspond roughly to the development in Acts 2 – 9, some significant omissions occur if the whole expression is interpreted simply in *geographical* terms. Important steps in the progress of the mission beyond Samaria are ignored. There is no reference to the spread of the gospel to Antioch, Asia Minor or Greece, although each of these is significant in Acts (Tannehill 1990: 17). Nor is there any reference to Rome if, as we believe, it should not be identified with 'the ends of the earth'.[75]

Accordingly, the stages of the witness are to be interpreted *ethnically* and *theologically*, as well as geographically. The first stage is Jerusalem, where Jesus finished his work and where Israel was to be restored in the remnant of Jews who believed in him as Messiah. The second stage is Judea-Samaria – the two places are linked with a single article in the Greek of verse 8 – referring to the area of the ancient kingdoms of Judah and Israel.[76] This fulfils the ancient promises of the

---

[73] Turner (1996a: 300–301) contends that Acts 1:8 reiterates the hope of Israel's restoration in its three allusions to Isaiah: 1. mention of the Spirit's coming (*cf.* Luke 24:49) rests on Is. 32:15 (LXX 'until the Spirit from high comes upon you') which is about the new-exodus restoration and the transformation of Israel's 'wilderness' estate; 2. 'you shall be my witnesses' takes up Is. 43:10–12 where restored Israel, God's Servant, is given this commission; and 3. the task of bearing witness to Jesus 'to the ends of the earth' picks up the closing line of Is. 49:6. According to Turner, all three allusions point to Israel's restoration.

[74] The verse should be read in the light of Luke 24:47–49 (T. S. Moore 1997b: 394). There are conceptual and verbal parallels between the two passages, including the coming of the promise/Holy Spirit upon the disciples, the designation of the disciples as witnesses, and the parallel expressions of the extent of the mission, namely, 'to all the nations' and 'to the ends of the earth'.

[75] The movement 'to the ends of the earth' points beyond Paul's arrival in Rome at the end of the book (T. S. Moore 1997b: 398; *cf.* Tannehill 1990: 18 and Hengel 1995: 35). See the footnote below.

[76] The Greek has *pasē tē Ioudaia kai Samareia* ('[in] all Judea-Samaria').

restoration of the *whole* house of Israel under one king (*e.g.* Ezek. 37:15–22). Finally, the apostolic witness will extend to 'the ends of the earth', a key expression which comes from Isaiah 49:6 (see the direct quote in Acts 13:47) and indicates that God intends his salvation should reach all peoples. Geographically, the phrase denotes the end of the world in a general sense. Ethnically, it refers to the Gentile world.[77] If the gospel is for the Jew first, then it is also for the Gentile (Rom. 1:16–17). Worldwide witness thus appears at the beginning and end of the Acts (1:8; 28:28–31). And the closing words of Luke's second volume are deliberately open-ended. 'The ends of the earth are never reached in Acts. The mission goal is never completed. It remains open ...'[78]

Pentecost and the gift of the Spirit (Acts 2:1–41)

The long-awaited day of Pentecost arrives (Shepherd 1994: 159–160). For Luke this day is of profound importance, signifying a decisive moment in the outworking of God's saving plan. The outpouring of the Spirit is clinching evidence that the last days have arrived (Num. 11:29; Is. 32:15; 44:3; Ezek. 36:27). The language of fulfilment is used (v. 1),[79] first, because the prophecy of Joel 2:28–32 has been wonderfully fulfilled in the Spirit's coming and, secondly, because his arrival has been anticipated by prophecies of John the Baptist and Jesus (Luke 3:16; 24:49; Acts 1:4–5, 8).[80] Peter's sermon which interprets the significance of the Spirit's coming locates Pentecost 'in the last days' (Acts 2:17).[81]

---

[77] To 'the ends of the earth' has this significance in Is. 49:6, for it is conceptually parallel to 'a light to the nations'. The parallel in Luke 24:47 leads to the same conclusion (see above), as does Acts 13:47, where Is. 49:6 is cited by Paul as a justification for his pattern of preaching to the Jews first and then of turning to the Gentiles. For a detailed discussion, see T. S. Moore 1997b: 389–399; *cf.* S. G. Wilson 1973: 94; Best 1984: 3; Tannehill 1990: 17; Rosner 1998: 217–219; and note Brawley 1990: 43, 105.

[78] So Polhill 1992: 62, cited by Penney 1997: 73.

[79] The scene is introduced with an unusual phrase, lit. 'When the day of Pentecost was being fulfilled' (*symplērousthai*), which closely resembles Luke 9:51. Penney (1997: 78), following Tannehill (1990: 26–27), thinks the phrase 'heightens the sense of an imminent eschatological fulfilment of Old Testament prophecy'.

[80] So Tannehill 1990: 26–27. Witherington (1998: 130), who claims it is a 'critical event which sets in motion all that follows', then adds: 'Without the coming of the Spirit there would be no prophecy, no preaching, no mission, no conversions, and no worldwide Christian movement.'

[81] The replacement of 'after these things' (*meta tauta*, Joel 2:28, LXX) by 'in the last days' (*en tais eschatais hēmerais*) identifies the gift as the eschatological promise of the

Pentecost was originally the festival of firstfruits (Lev. 23:19–22) that was celebrated seven weeks after Passover at the time of the wheat harvest. It came to be regarded in second-temple Judaism as the day when the law was given on Mt Sinai,[82] and drew a large number of pilgrims from abroad. Those gathered for Pentecost in Acts 2 included not only all Jews dwelling in Jerusalem (v. 14), but also representatives from every land of the dispersion ('God-fearing Jews from every nation under heaven', v. 5) – in other words, 'all Israel' (v. 36) was present.

The Holy Spirit comes upon the whole group of 120 disciples (v. 4),[83] although Luke highlights the gift of the Spirit to the twelve for their role as witnesses[84] (Acts 2:32; cf. 1:8; Luke 24:48–49; Is. 43:8–13; 44:6–8).[85] The election of Matthias to replace Judas (Acts 1:15–26) had meant there was now a full complement to the twelve. They are the nucleus of a restored and reconstituted Israel (cf. Luke 22:28–30) whose witness to the whole nation is about to begin in Jerusalem. With the coming of the Spirit, they are involved in taking up the task of the Isaianic Servant (as Jesus' words in Luke 24:48 had implied; cf. Acts 13:47) who ministers representatively to the whole nation, that is, to 'Jews from every nation under heaven' (Acts 2:5), and 'all the house of Israel' (v. 36, RSV).

Peter's sermon in Acts 2:14–39, which explains the significance of the Pentecost event and is central to Acts,[86] spells out the content[87] of

---

Spirit (Turner 1996a: 270).

[82] Sinai and Pentecost are connected in several intertestamental texts (*Jubilees* 1:1, 5; 6:1–21; 15:1–24). For a full discussion, see Turner 1996a: 280–289.

[83] The recent approach of Bolt (1998: 199) is different. He understands Acts 2 to narrate the arrival of the Spirit on the witnesses (*cf.* 1:4, 8), who he thinks are not only the focus of attention in Acts 1 but also the probable subject of 2:1.

[84] This is not to suggest, however, that the coming of the Spirit was a prophetic empowering simply for mission or witness (*cf.* Stronstad 1984: 51–52; Menzies 1994: 168–175). Luke's account in Acts 2 *alone* shows that the giving of the Spirit is for salvation (vv. 38–39), and for transformed lives in the community (vv. 42–47) that are given to worship, prayer, praise, adherence to apostolic teaching and the sharing of one's possessions. Note the critique of Turner 1996a: chs. 12, 13; and 1996b: 42–43, 46–48.

[85] According to Turner (1996b: 46–47), this is because the 'expansion of the witness is a major plot in Acts, and the twelve (especially Peter) are the leaders in this'.

[86] Turner (1996a: 267) suggests that Peter's explanation of the Pentecost event in Acts 2:14–39 has perhaps greater claim than Luke 4:16–30 to be called 'the programmatic' text of Luke-Acts. He adds: 'What gives the Pentecost speech its central place is not simply what is said explicitly about the Spirit, but the way what is said here is reintegrated with other cardinal aspects of Luke's theology.' Green (1992: 33–34) thinks that Acts 2:1–41 is of central significance for four reasons: 1. the way in which the event that is 'narrated and interpreted in this passage has been anticipated throughout the Lukan story' (esp. the pronounced activity of the Holy Spirit [Luke 1:15, 35, 41, *etc.*;

the disciples' witness[88] 'in Jerusalem' (cf. 1:8). This coming of the Spirit is associated with the gift of prophecy (according to vv. 17–18 all will receive the prophetic Spirit), and Peter interprets the event in terms of Joel 2:28–32 where God had promised to pour out his Spirit on 'all flesh', that is, on 'all Israel'. The apostle moves from the Joel passage with its mention of people calling upon the name of the Lord to be saved (v. 21), to focus first on Jesus' crucifixion (vv. 22–23), then God's raising him from the dead and exalting him to be Lord and Messiah (vv. 33–36). After his exaltation Jesus poured out the promised Holy Spirit. The apostle also picks up the prophetic promise of salvation to all who call upon the name of the Lord (Joel 2:32; Acts 2:21) and urges his hearers to call upon the Lord *Jesus* by repenting and being baptized in his name for the forgiveness of sins (cf. Luke 24:47). They will receive the gift of the Spirit, since the promise is for them and their children (v. 39). Peter's witness then is to the whole house of Israel to hear and appropriate this message of renewal and eschatological blessing. His sermon moves from the coming of the Spirit upon the 120, and especially the twelve as witnesses (cf. v. 32), to the promise of the Spirit for the hearers who will experience salvation.

We have underscored the point that those gathered in Jerusalem for Pentecost were devout Jews who represented 'all Israel' (2:5, 36; cf. v. 14). Peter's testimony was given to the people of God. Yet there are clear hints in the narrative of Acts 2 that the coming of the Spirit on a renewed and cleansed Israel will ultimately point forward to universal blessing (as the prophetic writings had foreshadowed: *e.g.* Is. 42:6; 49:6):

1. The presence of Jews 'from every nation under heaven' (v. 5), while referring to those of the dispersion, is nevertheless thought to

---

Luke 3:16; 11:13; 24:49]) which builds up to the outpouring of the Spirit in Acts 2:1–4. 2. While Pentecost is a non-repeatable event, 'the outpouring of the Spirit at Pentecost serves a paradigmatic function elsewhere in the Acts of the Apostles'; *cf.* 10:44, 47; 11:1–3, 17. 3. The number of parallels between Jesus' inaugural sermon at Nazareth in Luke 4:16–30 and the Pentecost narrative point to the latter's significance in the context of Acts. 4. Acts 2 'sets the agenda for the mission of Jesus' followers in the book as a whole' (*cf.* vv. 35–41). *Cf.* Peterson 1993: 97.

[87] Trites (1977: 142) aptly remarks: 'The content of the apostolic testimony is most fully revealed in the speeches of Acts, particularly those in chapters 2, 3, 5, 10 and 13.'

[88] They testify to Jesus' death, resurrection and the forgiveness of sins (each of which is explained according to the Scriptures; note Luke 24:46–47). This threefold focus is reiterated throughout the sermons in Acts, especially those to Jews (3:14, 15, 19; 10:39, 40, 43; 11:18; *cf.* 17:30; 26:18, 20).

SALVATION TO THE ENDS OF THE EARTH

'anticipate' what will occur worldwide.[89] The devout visitors to Jerusalem are considered by Luke to be representatives of the various lands from which they had come, and of the local dialects of those lands.[90]

2. The list of nations in verses 9–12, which amplifies verse 5, shows a marked similarity to the Jewish table of nations tradition based on Genesis 10, and which is present in partial form in Isaiah 66:18–19, where Yahweh promises to 'gather all nations and tongues'.[91]

3. The expression 'all flesh', which in Joel has Israel as its immediate focus, is given a universal twist when Peter speaks of the forgiveness of sins and the gift of the Spirit being 'for all who are far off' (v. 39).[92] This is not inconsistent, however, with a broader focus in the Joel passage, namely, that 'all flesh' hints at something wider than Israel (see below).

4. The enthronement of Jesus as Lord and Christ implies a role towards the nations. Psalm 110:1–2 (Acts 2:34–35) indicates that the 'Lord' has taken his seat to await the overthrow of his enemies, while Psalm 2, which also indicates that the nations will be defeated by Christ, declares that an amnesty is available for those who submit to the Son (cf. Bolt 1998: 200). Because Jesus the Davidic Messiah is the Lord upon whose name men and women should now call to be saved (Acts 2:21, 34–36; Joel 2:32, 36–39), forgiveness is available to all through him.

5. Luke's accounts of subsequent bestowals of the Spirit throughout Acts deliberately pick up the 'programmatic' language of chapter 2, and show that Pentecost is only a partial realization of the Joel promise to '*all* flesh'.[93] In the subsequent narratives of Acts, the response of

[89] Tannehill (1990: 28) thinks that the presence of Jews 'from every nation under heaven' introduces a 'symbolic dimension' into the narrative that suggests 'first that it is the goal of the gospel to address all Israel, scattered throughout the world, and second that it must also address the gentile inhabitants of the lands from which these Jews come'. *Cf.* Menzies 1994: 176–177.

[90] Bruce 1988: 55. Dumbrell (1994: 223) speaks of 'the world being universally affected by the Pentecost event' because Jews from every nation are 'represented and what has happened now to Israel is a paradigm for the Spirit of prophecy to descend in these last days "on all people" (v. 17)'.

[91] Scott 1994: 527–530 and Penney 1997: 82.

[92] The words 'for you and your children and for all who are far off', have rightly been understood as an allusion to the Abrahamic covenant, recalling especially Gen. 17:7–10 ('you and your descendants after you'), with the last phrase, 'all who are far off', pointing to the nations who will find blessing through Abraham's descendants (Gen. 22:18; *cf.* 12:3); so Penney 1997: 91.

[93] Note the following expressions which echo Acts 2: 'the gift of God' (8:20) given to the Samaritans; the comparisons to Pentecost in 10:46–47; 11:15, 17 and the Spirit as

134

new groups to the word of God brings similar outpourings of the Spirit and shows a progressive movement of the realization of Joel's promise to *all*: the Samaritans (Acts 8:14–17), the Gentiles (10:44–48; 11:15–18) and the disciples of the Baptist (19:1–7). These so-called 'mini-Pentecosts' occur at crucial stages of the missionary expansion. Pentecost is a non-repeatable event, but 'the outpouring of the Spirit ... [on this occasion] serves a paradigmatic function elsewhere in the Acts of the Apostles' (Green 1992: 33–34).

Finally, although the account of Pentecost ends at verse 41, it must be read in conjunction with the first of Luke's summaries in Acts, namely, 2:42–47.[94] Here the picture is drawn of the Jerusalem community – the remnant of Israel, restored and given new life by the exalted Christ through the Holy Spirit. This congregation, whose members demonstrate wholehearted care for one another (vv. 44–45), is characterized by devotion to the apostolic teaching, the fellowship, the breaking of bread and prayer (v. 42). As 'the little flock' to whom the Father was pleased to give the kingdom (Luke 12:32), this community models what Israel of old should have been (Exod. 19:5–6). Not only do they meet together with glad, sincere hearts and praise God; they also enjoy the favour of 'all the people (*laos*)', and daily the Lord adds to their number other Israelites who were being saved. This restored community is presented by Luke as a model for God's purposes *for the world*.

The pilgrimage of the Gentiles to Jerusalem?

It is clear from the narratives of Acts 1 – 2 that for Luke Jerusalem is 'the all-important starting-point for the gospel'. However, it is not 'its final goal'.[95] The risen Lord's commission to the apostles is as follows: 'You will be my witnesses in Jerusalem ... and to the ends of the earth' (1:8). Jerusalem's position within salvation history is unparalleled (an emphasis we have already observed throughout the Old Testament), for the city is the source of the gospel message for the whole world. But the word of the Lord is no longer tied to the holy city; it must go out from Jerusalem. Moreover, although the narrative of Acts frequently

---

God's gift for the Gentiles (10:45; 11:17); and the contrast between the baptism of John and baptism in the Holy Spirit in 19:1–7, found in 1:5; and 11:16. *Cf.* Tannehill 1990: 30–31; and Dumbrell 1994: 223.

[94] On the significance of these Lukan summaries in relation to the 'Progress of the Word', see Rosner 1998: 215–233.

[95] P. W. L. Walker 1996: 81 (note esp. 81–94, to which we are indebted).

returns to Jerusalem, the ultimate goal is the progress of the gospel 'to the ends of the earth'.

This *centrifugal* focus on the word of the Lord going forth from Jerusalem is rather unexpected given that the eschatological pilgrimage of the nations to Zion, the ingathering of the Gentiles, was a *centripetal* movement which kept Jerusalem at the centre of the divine purposes (see ch. 2). Now with the risen Lord's commission to the disciples that movement is reversed. There is, however, biblical justification for this centrifugal focus. Isaiah's prophecy states that 'the Law will go out from Zion, the word of the LORD from Jerusalem' (2:3). Although Luke does not cite this verse explicitly, the ongoing powerful advance of the word of God is a central theme of Acts which may have its antecedents in this Old Testament prophecy (cf. Is. 55:11). As we have seen, Isaiah clearly had an important influence on Luke-Acts, 'not least because of its charter for universal mission in Isaiah 49:6 (Acts 13:47; cf. 1:8)' (P. W. L. Walker 1996: 83).

Two related factors may explain this change of orientation: first, the Old Testament pilgrimage of the nations to Jerusalem, in which Gentiles journeyed with Jews to the Holy City, especially the temple, was in order to meet with God who dwelt there (cf. Zech. 8:23, 'In those days ten men from all languages and nations will take firm hold of one Jew by the edge of his robe and say, "Let us go with you, because we have heard that God is with you"'). Now, however, as the early witnesses bear testimony to the death and resurrection of Jesus and proclaim the forgiveness of sins in his name to all the nations, so God *sends* Jesus his servant to them, to bring blessing to 'all the families of the earth', not only to Israel but also to the Gentiles (Acts 3:13, 25–26). By believing the word of the gospel, men and women from the nations receive the risen Lord Jesus whom God has sent to them. The expectations of meeting with God himself, the key purpose for the pilgrimage of the Gentiles, are fulfilled in this way.[96] A similar point is made in relation to temple language. The Old Testament looked forward to the time of eschatological peace when Israel and the nations would be united in one cult at Zion (Is. 2:4; Mic. 4:3). The early church understood itself in terms of the renewed temple of eschatological fulfilment.[97] Although the imagery is somewhat flexible,

[96] Dumbrell (1994: 221) claims that the missionary activity of a restored Israel which goes out in mission is 'a departure from the centripetal program of the Old Testament, [that] was necessitated by national Israel's end as the geographical center for divine revelation'. On the rejection by and judgment of Jerusalem, see P. W. L. Walker 1996: 89–94.
[97] Note the discussion and bibliography details of Bauckham 1995: 442–448.

believers are the stones of which the temple is constructed (1 Pet. 2:5). Jesus Christ is the foundation (1 Cor. 3:11) or the cornerstone/keystone (Eph. 2:20; 1 Pet. 2:4, 6–7, alluding to Is. 28:16; Ps. 118:22). According to the Fourth Gospel, Jesus himself is the temple (John 2:19–22). Gentile believers have become integral parts of this new building, not by journeying to Jerusalem, but through their union with Christ. They too, along with Jewish Christians, are being built as living stones (1 Pet. 2:5) into this heavenly temple, the place where God dwells by his Spirit (Eph. 2:22).

Witness in Jerusalem (Acts 3:1 – 8:1)

God's promises to Abraham and the fathers are an important theme which runs through Luke-Acts (cf. Luke 1:55, 73; Acts 3:25). Consistent with these promises, which are foundational to God's redemptive plan (cf. Gen. 12:1–3),[98] salvation is offered to 'the Jew first, then to the Greek'. Accordingly, throughout Acts 3:1 – 8:1 the disciples' witness to Jesus is given in Jerusalem (cf. Acts 1:8). Peter's sermon, after the miracle at the temple gate (3:1–10), emphasizes the Abrahamic origins of the gospel.[99] In fulfilment of the covenant promises made to Abraham, God has sent (*apostellō*) the risen Jesus, his Servant (v. 13; cf. Is. 53:12), to bring blessing to 'all the families of the earth', in the *first* instance to Israel (the 'heirs of the prophets and the covenant'), *then* to the Gentiles (vv. 25–26).

Moreover, God's sending of Jesus, which is 'the most basic mission' in Luke-Acts, is carried out 'by his chosen witnesses who are equipped with ... and endorsed by his Spirit'.[100] Through listening to the testimony of the apostles (in this instance, the sermon of Peter), Israel can hear Jesus, the prophet like Moses, addressing them (vv. 20, 22). Even those responsible for his death (vv. 13–15) may share in these covenantal blessings, if they turn from their wicked ways (vv. 19, 26).

Israel's opportunity for true repentance, however, is not unlimited. God will *send* the Christ again, when he will restore all things (v.

Following others, Bauckham claims that the image of the Christian community as the temple is so common in early Christian literature that it 'very plausibly goes back to early Palestinian Christianity' (444).

[98] Note ch. 2, 'Mission in the Old Testament'.

[99] On the significance of the Abrahamic promises in Acts 3, see Tannehill 1990: 55–57; Dumbrell 1994: 225–227; and Penney 1997: 91–94; *cf.* Brawley 1994: 252–268.

[100] Bolt 1998: 195. See Luke 24:49; Acts 1:4–5, 8; 2:17–21, 33; 5:32.

21),[101] and only those who repent before his second coming will experience forgiveness and refreshing (vv. 13–15, 17, 19). Anyone who does not listen to Jesus, the Servant and end-time prophet like Moses, 'will be completely cut off' (vv. 21, 23).

The witness of Peter and John 'in Jerusalem' to the powerful *name* of Jesus, by which a crippled beggar had been healed (3:6, 16; 4:7, 10; cf. v. 30), encountered significant and determined opposition from the Jewish leadership (4:1–22; 5:17–42). This came to a head in the persecution and death of Stephen (6:1 – 8:3). It marked the turning point in the ministry to national Israel, and led to a break with Judaism.[102] Surprisingly, the narrative begins by underscoring the ongoing growth of the number of the disciples: in Jerusalem they 'increased rapidly', and even 'a large number of priests became obedient to the faith' (an *inclusio*, 6:1, 7). The Sanhedrin's determined resistance did not stop the gospel's remarkable progress. Luke presents the picture of the powerful appeal of the word of God and the rapid growth of the church in Jerusalem since Pentecost (Rosner 1998: 226).

The gospel spreads to Judea and Samaria (Acts 8:4–40)

The immediate aftermath of the stoning of Stephen was a campaign of repression by the Jerusalem authorities, apparently directed against the whole church (cf. Gal. 1:22–23), although the Hellenists seem to have been the principal targets. They were scattered from Jerusalem and carried the gospel to the neighbouring regions of *Judea and Samaria*, the second division of Acts 1:8. God used the persecution that was the immediate cause of the Hellenists' departure to Samaria (8:4), and even beyond (11:19–24), to effect his purposes of salvation.[103] The tragic irony was that the attempts of the Sanhedrin to stop the spread of the word of God, which were carried to such extreme lengths in the stoning of Stephen, resulted in the word spreading in Judea, Samaria and

---

[101] The times of refreshing for Israel and her world which began with the death and resurrection of Jesus, together with the apostolic mission, will continue until the full restoration takes place with the return of Jesus (Dumbrell 1994: 226–227). There is a 'now' and 'not yet' tension between the restoration in Acts 1:6 and that of 3:21. Peter invites his hearers to experience in Jesus 'the times of refreshing' while they await a more universal restoration. Israel's response, like the later Gentile mission, is a precursor to the final restoration anticipated in Acts 3:21. See the discussion of P. W. L. Walker 1996: 94–102; *cf.* Stenschke 1998: 141.

[102] Tannehill (1990: 80) refers to it as the 'climax of the conflict in Jerusalem'. *Cf.* Neudorfer 1998: 280; and Rosner 1998: 226, following Dollar 1993: 123.

[103] Note esp. Rapske 1998: 235–256.

Antioch (Tannehill 1990: 101).

This advance of the gospel in Judea and Samaria[104] was carried out, not by the apostles who remained in Jerusalem, but by Philip (8:5), who was one of those scattered by the Jewish authorities (v. 4). Unlike the twelve and Paul, who were witnesses, Philip was an evangelist who proclaimed 'the good news of the kingdom of God' (8:12). His ministry of preaching and healing is described in ways that underscore its continuity with the mission of Jesus and his apostles.[105] Thus, Jesus' commission in Judea and Samaria, the second stage of Acts 1:8, was accomplished through a new instrument of God, Philip the evangelist.[106]

Although we might have expected to be given an account of the missionary travels of the twelve apostles, generally this does not appear in Acts (though note 8:14–25). Instead, Luke sees them as closely linked with the city of Jerusalem, a connection that persists throughout the narrative. As the nucleus of the restored Israel, they are pre-eminently witnesses to Israel 'in Jerusalem', from which centre the word of the Lord will sound forth, as the Old Testament prophecies had anticipated (*e.g.* Is. 2:1–4; Mic. 4:1–5).[107] Fundamentally theirs was a stationary rather than a missionary role (Clark 1998: 180). To be a witness was not necessarily the same as being a missionary.

When the apostles in Jerusalem heard about Philip's effective ministry, they sent Peter and John (8:14) down to Samaria. The Spirit came upon the Samaritans after prayer and the laying on of the apostles' hands; hence, the incident has been called 'the Samaritan Pentecost'. This delayed imparting of the Holy Spirit (which Luke

---

[104] Philip's Samaritan mission is linked geographically with his work along the coastal plain of Judea (8:26–40).

[105] A summary of Philip's ministry is mentioned directly in 8:4–8, 12–13 (*cf.* the treatment of Spencer 1992: 32–53). Those scattered from Jerusalem, including Philip, appear as the proclaimers of 'the word' (8:4). More specifically, Philip is presented as an evangelist (21:8) who 'proclaimed Christ' (8:5; *cf.* Luke 4:8, 19, 44; 8:1; 9:2), 'preached the good news of the kingdom of God' (8:12; see Luke 4:18, 43; 9:6; Acts 5:42) and the 'name' of Jesus (8:12; *cf.* Acts 4:17–18; 5:28, 40). His preaching was also accompanied by signs: he exorcized 'evil spirits' (Acts 8:7) and healed the paralysed and lame (v. 7). As a result there was great joy (vv. 7–8).

[106] Philip also features in a second incident which is concerned with the missionary expansion of the church. In addition to 'preaching the Christ' to the Samaritans, Philip is led by the Spirit to 'preach Jesus' to a God-fearing pilgrim who not only represented a foreign nation but who, being a eunuch, was debarred from membership of the congregation of Israel (Deut. 23:1). He was, however, 'a worshipper of God' and should be regarded as an 'exile of Israel' (Is. 56:8) rather than as a Gentile. The admission of Gentiles to faith comes in Acts 10.

[107] Clark 1998: 176, following Fitzmyer.

indicates was unusual: 'the Spirit had *not yet come* upon any of them', v. 16) is connected with the fact that here was a significant advance in the programme outlined by Jesus in Acts 1:8. The point was not that the Spirit could be received only through the laying on of the apostles' hands (cf. 10:44 and 19:6). Rather, God had given a clear and impressive endorsement to both the apostles and the Samaritans themselves that he had included them in salvation through Jesus, thereby fulfilling his ancient promises to restore the whole house of Israel under one king (*e.g.* Ezek. 37:15–19). Through the coming of the Spirit the old division between north and south had been healed. The Samaritans were incorporated into the new people of God, the messianic community (8:14–25),[108] and this was recognized by the apostles.[109]

Paul's conversion and commission (Acts 9:1–31)

The conversion and calling of Saul of Tarsus marked a significant advance in the preaching of the gospel and the mission of Jesus to the Gentile world. Luke clearly attached great importance to this event and wished to impress it unforgettably on his readers.[110] So he used the simple but effective method of repetition, recounting the story three times in Acts (chs. 9, 22, 26) – once in the third person and twice on Paul's lips.[111]

The account in Acts 9 opens with the picture of Saul '*still* breathing

---

[108] Similarly, in 10:44–48 the coming of the Spirit was a visible sign that God wished to include the Gentiles in the salvation that Jesus brings (see also 11:15–18). Those who have clearly received the Spirit, whether Samaritans or Gentiles, cannot be rejected even if they belong to alienated groups.

[109] Clark (1998: 176) notes that the apostles legitimize the new development in the expanding mission (8:14; *cf.* 9:26–28; 11:1, 18; 15:5–6, 22–23). 'The crucial new developments in the growth of the early church are validated by the men who form the nucleus of the restored people of God.'

[110] Most scholars note this point. Towner (1998: 418) observes that since the progress of the Christian mission is central to Luke's concerns, 'the role of Paul in opening up the whole world to the gospel is crucial to the Lukan narrative'. *Cf.* Witherington 1998: 303; and Hansen 1998: 322, who suggests that Luke repeats the conversion story twice in the defence speeches (22:4–16; 26:12–18) 'to emphasise that Paul's witness to the resurrection was commissioned and empowered by the risen Lord Jesus'. Each of the three narratives is shaped to suit a different purpose. On the cumulative effects of the three accounts note Hansen 1998: 322–324 and his interaction with Hedrick 1981: 415–432.

[111] Jervell (1998: 278–279, 288) observes that while Luke reports the calling of other apostles, including Peter and the twelve, he mentions Paul's conversion and calling three times. The particular significance of this lies in Paul's mission. On p. 279, however, Jervell presses the point too far when he claims that only Paul, according to Luke, fulfils the commission of Jesus in Acts 1:8 (see above).

out murderous threats against the Lord's disciples' (v. 1). Even after the death of Stephen (cf. 8:3) and the expulsion of the Hellenistic Christians from Jerusalem, Saul intended to continue the persecution in places outside the Sanhedrin's immediate jurisdiction. He approached Damascus with the High Priest's commission to arrest 'any who belonged to the way' with the intention of bringing them back as prisoners to Jerusalem (vv. 1–2). But Saul was stopped in his tracks. Confronted by the risen and exalted Lord Jesus, and questioned why he was persecuting him, he was converted and commissioned to bear witness to the Gentiles (vv. 4–19).[112] Luke stresses the unprecedented nature of Paul's turnaround and the genuineness of his conversion.[113]

Of particular significance for our theme of mission in Luke-Acts are the following:[114] first, Paul is a chosen vessel to bear Christ's name to the Gentiles as well as to the people of Israel (9:15; 22:15). Both the comprehensive scope of his commission (it is to *all*) and its special focus (to *Gentiles*)[115] are in view. His calling as an apostle to the Gentiles is part and parcel of the divine plan of salvation (22:14), and this is why his ministry is said, on occasion, to stand under divine constraint (*dei*, 19:21; 23:11).

Secondly, Paul's role is parallel to that of the other apostles.[116] Like the twelve he was '*appointed* [*procheirotoneō* is used of the twelve at 10:41] to know God's will' (or 'plan', 22:14, Squires 1993: 2), while his bearing 'witness to all' and being sent to the Gentiles (22:21) parallel the description of the twelve apostles as Jesus' 'witnesses to the people of Israel' (13:31). Paul fulfils the commission given to the apostles (1:8), for he preaches in Jerusalem, and in all Judea and to the Gentiles (26:20). Like the twelve, he bears witness to the same three scriptural elements of Jesus' commission in Luke 24:46–48, namely, the Messiah's suffering, his resurrection and the announcement of repentance for the forgiveness of sins to all the nations (26:22–23).

---

[112] Tannehill (1990: 121) comments: 'Thus the one who is called to be a light of the nations and to open the eyes of Jews and Gentiles has encountered the Messiah in light and is himself a healed blind man, forced by the Messiah's light to recognize his own blindness and to receive sight through him' (*cf.* Gaventa 1986: 62, 85).

[113] Barrett (1994: 422) aptly remarks: 'This was a radical change of religious direction, and it was accompanied by as radical a change of action: the active persecutor became an even more active preacher and evangelist. If such radical changes do not amount to conversion it is hard to know what would do so.'

[114] We shall draw on material from each of the three conversion narratives, recognizing that each is shaped to suit a particular purpose.

[115] The position of 'Gentiles' first in the narrative (v. 15) is emphatic and indicates 'a new development' (Tannehill 1990: 121).

[116] Note esp. Clark 1998: 188–189.

Accordingly, Paul's message, like that of the twelve, is described as
'the word of God' or 'the word of the Lord' (13:44–49; 14:3; 15:35–
36; 18:11), even 'the whole counsel of God' (20:27, RSV), and as such
it makes its dynamic progress throughout the world (cf. Rosner 1998:
215–233). Paul too will suffer for the sake of the Lord Jesus' name
(9:15–16; cf. 5:40–41), since he, like the twelve, follows in the steps of
the suffering Servant.

Thirdly, Paul continues the mission of Jesus by fulfilling the ministry
of the Servant. We have already seen that the mission on which Jesus
has been sent by the Father (cf. Acts 3:20, 26) is effected by his
witnesses bearing testimony to Israel (2:21; 13:31; cf. 10:36–39) and to
the Gentiles, and this includes Paul's apostolic witness (9:15; 22:14–
15; 26:16). He 'shares in carrying out the task assigned by Christ to the
apostles',[117] a work which is explicitly identified with the role of
Yahweh's Servant (Acts 13:47, citing Is. 49:6). As he continues Jesus'
mission, the resurrected one proclaims light *in and through him* to the
nations (26:23).

At the end of the first account of Paul's conversion the section of
Acts closes with a summary statement of the spread of the gospel
beyond Jerusalem into Judea, Galilee and Samaria (9:31): peace results
because the persecution following Stephen's death has ceased, and
growth occurs through the surprising power of the word to find new
opportunities in spite of resistance.

Cornelius and the Gentiles (Acts 10:1 – 11:18)

With the word of the Lord steadily bearing fruit and increasing, the time
had come for the gospel to cross the barrier that separated Jews from
Gentiles and to be presented directly to the latter. Events moved to a new
stage as God prepared for their entry into his people. The length of this
account of Cornelius and the Gentiles (sixty-six verses in all) and the way
it is told twice indicate its very great importance to Luke in the context of
Acts.[118] The passage stands in a strategic position within the book: it constitutes the climax to its first half as well as to Peter's apostolic ministry,
and signals a fundamental turning point in Luke's narrative of the spread
of the gospel to 'the ends of the earth' (1:8).[119]

[117] O'Toole 1978: 82, cited by Clark 1998: 189.
[118] So most writers. Reference to the incident twice more in the narrative of Acts
(15:7–11, 13–21) underscores its profound significance. Note particularly Matson 1996:
91; and Witherington (1998: 365), who speaks of it as 'the most crucial drama yet
recorded in the book of Acts'.
[119] Green 1997b: 243. *Cf.* Witherup 1993: 45–66 and Matson 1996: 92.

Four issues receive special emphasis in Luke's presentation of the material: first, the early church resisted the idea of Gentiles being evangelized directly or accepted into the Christian fellowship without first becoming Jewish proselytes (cf. 10:14, 28; 11:2–3, 8). With the apostolic testimony at Pentecost to Jesus as Lord and Christ, and the mighty outpouring of the Spirit, the universal movement had begun (Acts 2). What started with the twelve in Jerusalem continued throughout Judea and Samaria and was moving towards the ends of the earth (1:8). Yet the apostles have to be 'sold' on the Gentile mission, which is extraordinary given Jesus' commission to them to bear witness to 'the ends of the earth' (1:8; cf. Luke. 24:47) and their experience of Pentecost.[120] Peter was reluctant to go to the Gentiles, visiting Cornelius and his Gentile friends only after he had been constrained by divine revelation (10:9–16). His preaching of the gospel in the home of those who were 'uncircumcised' aroused great alarm among believers in Jerusalem who later took him to task for his conduct (11:1–3).[121]

Secondly, it was God himself who introduced Gentiles into the church and miraculously showed his approval (cf. 10:3, 11–16, 19–20, 22, 30–33, 44–46; 11:5–10, 13, 15–18).[122] The divine initiative and action are patently clear throughout the narrative: by means of divine visions and revelations to Cornelius and Peter, through God's preparing the hearts of the Gentiles to hear the gospel, and by his pouring out the Holy Spirit upon them, cleansing their hearts by faith and granting them repentance unto life. God's Holy Spirit, who confirmed the word of the gospel, declared by his manifest presence that these Gentiles were truly God's children.[123] 'The Holy Spirit's coming upon Cornelius and the others in a manner strictly comparable to Pentecost is the final and most compelling indication of the new divine initiative (Acts 10:44–46; 11:15)' (Rapske 1998: 241).

[120] Peter's sermon at Pentecost refers to God pouring out his Spirit on 'all flesh' (2:17, NRSV), and this directly recalls the universal promise of Luke 3:6. Yet the apostle had not grasped the radical implications of these words.
[121] On this opposition to the Gentile mission, see Rapske 1998: 239–242. The two-fold nature of the criticism was that Peter entered into the house of the uncircumcised and ate with them (11:3), actions that were anathema to any self-respecting Jew. (On the subject of table fellowship, see Blue 1998: 473–497, esp. 490–494.) Rapske comments that Peter's preaching of the gospel to the Gentile Cornelius and his household was 'at once momentous and deeply troublesome to the early church' (239). His proclamation was 'not a "freelance" operation but fully apostolic', and he was 'not simply led, but "driven", to acknowledge and embrace the unfolding plan of God' (240).
[122] Marshall 1980: 181; so most writers, including Green 1998: 92.
[123] The circumcised believers from Joppa were seized with amazement when they saw that 'the gift of the Holy Spirit had been poured out *even* on the Gentiles' (vv. 45–46, emphasis added).

Thirdly, it was Peter, the leader of the Jerusalem apostles, rather than Paul, whom God used as the human instrument to open the door to the Gentiles (cf. 10:23, 34–43, 47–48; 11:15–17). Peter's speech to Cornelius is described as 'the message God *sent* to the people of Israel telling the good news of peace through Jesus Christ' (10:36), in other words, what was promised in Isaiah 52:7. According to the prophet, Jerusalem's coming redemption would be displayed 'in the sight of all the nations, and all the ends of the earth will see the salvation of our God' (52:10). With Cornelius' conversion, 'what was promised by the prophet and picked up by the programmatic Acts 1:8, begins to unfold further'.[124] Since Jesus is truly 'Lord of all' (v. 36), then the conversion of the Gentiles is a necessary consequence. Luke is concerned to make clear the connection between the salvation of Israel and the Gentile mission, and what better way to do this than by showing that God used Peter, the leader of the Jerusalem apostles, to initiate Jesus' mission to the Gentiles through his apostolic testimony. Peter has already borne witness to Israel in Jerusalem, he was involved in the coming of the Spirit upon the Samaritans, and is now God's chosen witness to open the door of faith to the Gentiles (cf. 1:8). The twelve, then, continue the ministry of the Lord's Servant which had to do with Israel's redemption, on the one hand, and divine salvation reaching the ends of the earth, on the other (Is. 49:6).

Fourthly, the Jerusalem church subsequently accepted the Gentiles' conversion to Jesus the Messiah without insisting that they come via the Jewish route. Although called to account for his actions in the house of Cornelius (11:2–3), Peter explained to the Jewish believers[125] in Jerusalem how God had prepared him with the vision of clean and unclean animals, then led him to Cornelius' house where he and his Gentile friends gladly heard the message of salvation. For Peter and the others, however, the dramatic coming of the Holy Spirit on all who heard the apostolic message was decisive confirmation that God had graciously cleansed the hearts of the Gentiles and accepted them. The apostle realized that the words of the risen Christ to him and his fellow-disciples (1:5) which had been fulfilled at Pentecost were fulfilled anew here. When the Jerusalem believers heard Peter's account, they had no further objections but praised God, acknowledging that he had 'even

---

[124] Bolt 1998: 204; *cf.* Bayer 1998: 268.

[125] They shared the same perspective towards Gentiles and entry into their houses as Peter did (10:14, 28); so Matson 1996: 119. Tannehill (1990: 144) observes: 'The audience is led through the same sequence of events so that they can appreciate and share Peter's new insight.'

granted the Gentiles repentance unto life' (11:18).[126]

The Cornelius episode was not simply an exceptional situation, but had paradigmatic and normative significance: it was to '*the* Gentiles', that is, 'as a class of people, not to Cornelius and his friends alone', that God has given this repentance.[127] Significantly, when Peter later rehearsed this story before the Jerusalem Council (15:7–11), he did not just recount a personal experience, but drew emphatic theological conclusions from the incident in order to justify Paul's work among the Gentiles generally. The incident is 'for Luke the test-case par excellence for the admission of Gentiles into the Church' (S. G. Wilson 1973: 177).

The spread of the gospel to Antioch (Acts 11:19–30)

A significant breakthrough of the gospel occurred at Antioch, the third largest city of the Roman empire, which culminated in the initiation of the Gentile mission led by Paul and Barnabas. The Greek-speaking Jewish Christians who had been forced to leave Jerusalem at the time of Stephen's death (8:1, 4) were scattered northwards as far as Antioch. They spread the gospel as they went and in Antioch continued their mission to Jews (11:19). Some from Cyprus and Cyrene, however, went to Antioch and began to share the good news with Greek-speaking Gentiles (v. 20). The activity of these unnamed evangelists[128] had the approval of God so that many believed and were converted (v. 21). This incident began a new chapter, in one sense the most important, in the history of the Christian mission.[129] The door which was opened to the Gentiles at Caesarea by Peter was even more widely opened at

---

[126] Marshall (1980: 197) points out that 'Luke compares the experience of the Gentiles, not to those of the first Jews' converts in the temple courts on Pentecost, but to the very experience of the original inner circle of Jesus' followers. Thus, their full equality is made evident.' *Cf.* Witherington 1998: 364.

[127] Witherington 1998: 364, n. 149, following Barrett 1994: 543. Throughout Peter's account (esp. vv. 10–11) 'there is a constant shifting between Cornelius in particular and the Gentiles in general, such that the former is clearly representative of the latter (10:34, 45; 11:17–18)' (S. G. Wilson 1983: 72; *cf.* Tannehill 1990: 184–185; Matson 1996: 125; and Blue 1998: 493).

[128] Bruce (1988: 225) describes them as 'daring spirits ... [who] took a momentous step forward'. The arrival of the gospel in Antioch was 'not the result of a mission organized by the Jerusalem church. Nor ... [was] it caused by the conversion of Cornelius' (Tannehill 1990: 146; *cf.* Schnabel 1997: 757).

[129] Fernando (1998: 347) aptly remarks that 'the scattering by the persecution in connection with Stephen was indeed the scattering of the seed of the gospel in God's plan'.

Antioch by unnamed Hellenistic Jewish Christians.

The church at Antioch grew rapidly. It then went through a period of rapid growth (v. 24) similar to the initial growth of the Jerusalem church. The same language is used to describe it, since references to people being added, or to the Lord adding to the church, form a repeated theme in the narrative of the early Jerusalem church (cf. 2:41,47; 5:14). The believers at Antioch demonstrated the same concern for their fellows as did the church in Jerusalem, though they freely shared with their fellow-disciples in Judea (vv. 29–30).

Paul's first missionary journey (Acts 13:1 – 14:28)

From Acts 13 on, Paul, rather than Peter, moves to 'centre stage and mission is the central theme' of the narrative (Squires 1998a: 610). The commissioning of verses 1–3 introduces an important new episode[130] that will lead to Paul's programmatic speech in Pisidian Antioch (13:16–41) and the momentous announcement that he and Barnabas are turning to the Gentiles (13:44–48). Luke follows Paul's journeys and shows how he fulfils his divine commission (9:15). The Holy Spirit makes it known that Paul has been marked out[131] for a particular 'work', the content of which is clarified throughout chapters 13 and 14. The description of the mission, which is highlighted as a fresh beginning, parallels several key features of the beginnings of Jesus' mission and that of the apostles.[132] In this way the account underscores

---

[130] From 13:1 to 21:17, the third section of Acts. This details Paul's activities and those of his co-workers in Asia Minor and the Aegean sea, with special interest in the 'turning to the Gentiles' which Paul had boldly announced in 13:46 (cf. 18:6); so Squires 1998b: 611.

[131] The Holy Spirit's initiative is emphatically stressed first by the fact of the command, 'the Holy Spirit said' (v. 2), secondly by its content, 'Set apart for me' (v. 2 emphasis added), and finally through the narrative which states that Barnabas and Paul were 'sent on their way (ekpempō) by the Holy Spirit' (v. 4). Luke is probably suggesting that the communication of the Holy Spirit came by prophetic utterance.

[132] Tannehill (1990: 160–161) draws attention to the following parallels between the three missions: 1. a major statement at the beginning of Jesus' mission (Luke 4:18–21) and the apostles' (Acts 2:14–40), as well as Paul's (13:13–52); 2. the three speeches contain or lead to a Scripture quotation which interprets the mission that is beginning (Luke 4:18–19; Acts 2:17–21; 13:47); 3. the inclusion of the Gentiles in God's salvation plan is mentioned (Luke 4:25–28; Acts 2:39; 3:25–26; 13:45–48); 4. the beginnings of the missions present the key characters as workers of wonders and signs (Luke 4:32; Acts 2:43; 13:12), presumably as evidence of the Lord's confirmation of his message of grace (cf. Acts 14:3); 5. a scene follows in which a lame man is healed shortly after the announcement of the mission (Luke 5:17–26; Acts 3:1–10; 14:8–10).

the fundamental points that there are *not three distinct missions, but the one mission of God* who has sent his Son Jesus as the missionary *par excellence* and in whose mission the twelve apostles and Paul participate as 'witnesses'. In fact, Paul plays 'a key role in the fulfillment of a mission that begins with John the Baptist and Jesus and stretches on beyond the apostles and Paul into the future' (Tannehill 1990: 159). In other words, his vital mission work with its remarkable scope is part of the larger plan of God.

Paul's sermon in Pisidian Antioch, which is recorded by Luke in some detail, is presented as the pattern of how the gospel was planted in the cities of Asia and beyond.[133] This message[134] shows the type of preaching appropriate to essentially *Jewish audiences*, especially in its use of the Old Testament as the basis on which to expound the gospel.[135] Paul begins by rehearsing God's dealings with his people Israel from the exodus to the reign of David. To the recital of the acts of God in the past, Paul adds a recital of God's more recent mighty acts. He moves from the ministry and witness of John the Baptist to the death and resurrection of Jesus. In Jesus, God's faithful love promised to David was embodied (Is. 55:3). Once again the apostolic testimony contains the threefold scriptural content: the death (vv. 27–29) and resurrection (vv. 32–37) of Jesus, as well as the forgiveness of sins, that is, a justification which comes simply through believing in Jesus (vv. 38–39), is now announced to them as the fulfilment of God's promise to the fathers (v. 32). A warning based on Habakkuk 1:5 is uttered, urging the synagogue audience not to be contemptuous of the message sent to them (vv. 26, 41). A week later, however, this becomes a reality: the Jews reject 'this word of salvation'.[136] So Paul boldly declares that since they judge themselves unworthy of eternal life,[137] he

[133] The speech provides a model of what was said on many occasions. Later summaries hark back to elements of this sermon.
[134] It is summarized as 'the grace of God' (13:43; *cf.* 14:3), and is called the 'word of God' (13:46; *cf.* 13:5, 7), 'the word of the Lord' (13:44, 48, 49), the 'message of salvation' (v. 26) or 'consolation' (v. 15). Six times in the narrative context and twice on Paul's lips our attention is focused on the powerful word of the Lord – a major theme of Luke-Acts – as preached by Jesus and his witnesses.
[135] As with Jesus' announcement in Nazareth and Peter's Pentecost speech, Paul declares that the word of salvation has been sent first to the synagogue audience, that is, the children of Abraham and God-fearing Gentiles (13:26). Note once again that the language of mission is conjoined with the notion of witness: here it is the 'word' that has been *sent* (*exapostellō*) via Paul's apostolic witness.
[136] Because the Jews reject the 'word of God' (v. 46), their response is tantamount to blasphemy (*cf.* Barrett 1994: 655).
[137] This is Paul's theological evaluation of the Jews' rejection of the message (*cf.* vv. 40–41).

SALVATION TO THE ENDS OF THE EARTH

is going to the Gentiles (v. 46), and he cites Isaiah 49:6 as a command of the Lord in support.

Elsewhere in Luke-Acts this text from the second Servant song (Is. 49:1–6) refers to Jesus as Yahweh's Servant: he is 'a light for revelation to the Gentiles' (Luke 2:32).[138] Now, however, the Old Testament passage is applied to Paul (and Barnabas). But in what sense? Usually this has been taken to mean that the Servant is a corporate figure,[139] of which Paul and Barnabas are members, and that they are continuing the Servant's ministry. Without necessarily denying this corporate dimension, however, verse 47 could be understood as signifying that Paul is a light for the Gentiles because of the Christ whom he preaches. The double use of the light imagery is important because of the apostle's role of making known to the Jews of Pisidian Antioch this 'light for the Gentiles' and the 'means of salvation to the ends of the earth'. 'Paul is a light of the Gentiles only in virtue of the Christ whom he preaches; Christ is a light to the Gentiles as he is preached to them by his servants'.[140] Paul recalls the Lord's command (*i.e.* Is. 49:6) which was addressed to him by the risen Jesus on the Damascus road (cf. 9:15; 22:15; 26:16–18). Through the apostolic 'word of salvation' Christ has been sent to the people of Israel (13:26). But, according to Isaiah 49:6, Christ, the Servant, has a mission to the Gentiles as well. Since that mission is effected by those who bear witness to God's word, when the Jews oppose it 'the proclaimers simply move to the alternative mission field' (Bolt 1998: 207).

Paul's momentous assertion about turning to the nations does not indicate that he would never preach to the Jews again, much less that he would leave them to their fate, in order to devote his complete attention to the Gentiles. Luke makes it clear[141] that after leaving Antioch the apostle continues to follow the pattern of 'to the Jew first' and preaches repeatedly to them in the synagogues (18:4–6, 19; 19:8). Moreover, the

---

[138] In the narrative of Acts Jesus' identity as the Servant of Yahweh is made clear (Acts 3:13, 26; 4:27, 30). He is explicitly identified as the one to whom the Isaianic Servant Songs point (Acts 8:32–35); *cf.* Pao 1998: 107.

[139] Recently Pao (1998: 102–109) has suggested that the use of Is. 49:6 here in Acts 13:47 signifies a shift in the development of the early Christian movement. It points to the 'establishment of the identity of the people of God' (107) in contrast to the ethnic nation of Israel. This new people, which fulfils what is envisaged by 'the Isaianic New Exodus', includes Gentiles within it.

[140] So Barrett 1994: 658, who is followed by Fitzmyer 1998: 521; *cf.* Bolt 1998: 206–207. Fitzmyer claims that this makes sense of the singular 'you' (*se*), of whom the Isaiah passage speaks, as well as the application to Paul and Barnabas who speak as 'we' or 'us' (v. 47).

[141] So correctly Barrett 1994: 656–657 and Fitzmyer 1998: 521.

same 'decisive' turning point occurs on two further occasions (18:6; 28:28).

Nor does the apostle's announcement indicate a new principle that Gentiles are offered the word of God only because of Jewish rejection, as though they were a kind of afterthought or second choice. From the birth narratives Luke understands that God intends to bring salvation to all peoples (2:30–32; 3:6). An inclusive mission was entrusted by the risen Messiah to his apostles (Luke. 24:47; Acts 1:8), while Paul is specifically commissioned to go to the Gentiles (9:15; 22:15; 26:16–18), and he has evangelized them before this point in the narrative (11:25–26). Salvation for the Gentiles is firmly rooted in Scripture (13:47).

The Jews were not abandoned. Their rejection of the gospel 'provided the occasion but not the cause'[142] for the mission to the Gentiles. It was already commanded in the Old Testament (v. 47). So Paul made his direct appeal to Gentiles, over the heads of the synagogue Jews, so to speak. God had his chosen among them, and the task of bringing that salvation 'to the ends of the earth' through the preaching of the gospel about Jesus was given to *the apostle to the Gentiles and his associates.*

The conclusion of this first missionary journey was that God had done mighty things through his witnesses (15:4, 12). He had opened 'the door of faith to the Gentiles' (14:27), and a great step had been taken towards the completion of the programme of Acts 1:8.

The Council of Jerusalem (Acts 15:1–35)

The dramatic advance of the gospel in central Asia Minor, which resulted in a large influx of Gentiles into the church, was put at serious risk by Jewish believers from Judea who demanded that Gentile Christians must be circumcised in order to be saved (15:1). This caused a major dispute which led the church at Antioch to send Paul and Barnabas as official representatives to Jerusalem[143] to thrash out the issue.

The dispute was resolved at the Jerusalem Council by 'three speeches that together present a single persuasive interpretation of God's

---

[142] Barrett 1994: 656; *cf.* Pao (1998: 104), who speaks, however, of the rejection of the Jews as not 'the cause', but 'the force behind the move to the Gentiles' and 'signifies the beginning of a period when the Gentiles will become the majority'.

[143] Up to this point the Jerusalem church, no doubt because of its place within the saving purposes of God, exercised oversight of the developing Christian mission, particularly to Gentiles (*cf.* Bauckham 1995: 450–451).

purpose' (Tannehill 1990: 184). First, Peter speaks out unambiguously
in the interests of gospel liberty (vv. 7–9), recounting how ten years
earlier God had accepted Cornelius and the Gentiles and cleansed their
hearts by his Holy Spirit when they believed 'the word of the gospel'
(v. 7). Gentiles are saved through the grace of the Lord Jesus just as
Jews are (v. 11). Peter's reference to the Holy Spirit's legitimization of
the Gentiles silences the opposition (vv. 8, 12). Secondly, Paul and
Barnabas support his argument by referring to the miraculous signs
which attended their own Gentile mission (v. 12; cf. 14:3). Finally, in
what is the high point of the chapter (vv. 13–21), James asserts that
God has taken to himself a people (*laos*), from the Gentiles who now
belong to him as Israel does. By using the term *laos*, which was
normally applied to Israel, James links the new people, the Gentiles, to
Israel. Believing Gentiles now have a share in Israel's hope. James's
argument has prophetic warrant (v. 15):[144] combining Amos 9:11–12
with allusions to three other prophetic passages (Hos. 3:5; Is. 45:21;
Jer. 12:15–16), he associates 'the eschatological conversion of the
Gentile nations with the restoration of the Temple in the messianic age'
(Bauckham 1995: 455). From Amos 9 it is established that Gentiles are
included in the eschatological people of God as Gentiles without
having to become Jews.[145] The messianic temple (that is, David's fallen
tent) is to be understood as the Christian community. The expression
'all the nations over whom my name has been invoked' (which literally
renders the Hebrew of Amos 9:12) is equivalent to the covenant term in
which the nation Israel is called 'my treasured possession' (*s^egullâ*).[146]
Both the Hebrew and the LXX of Amos 9:12 predict 'the extension of
Israel's covenant status and privileges to the Gentile nations'
(Bauckham 1995: 457).

Thus in Acts 15:16–18 the Gentile mission is viewed as the fulfilment

[144] For an important examination of the Jerusalem Council and particularly the
significance of James's speech, see Bauckham 1995: 415–480, esp. 450–462, and 1996:
154–184.

[145] Bauckham (1995: 457–458) points out that other Old Testament texts indicate that
the temple of the messianic age is the place where the Gentiles would come into God's
presence (Ps. 96:7–8; Is. 2:2–3; 25:6; 56:6–7; 66:23; Jer. 3:17; Mic. 4:1–2; Zech.
14:16). Moreover, other prophecies anticipate that the Gentile nations will become, like
Israel, God's own people (Zech. 2:11; *cf.* Is. 19:25). Many of these could be taken to
mean that Gentiles would be proselytes. But Amos 9:11–12 states that the nations *as
Gentile nations* belong to Yahweh (his name has been invoked over them). This text
makes the point more clearly than any other that 'in the new Temple of the messianic
age, the Christian community, they could do so as Gentiles' (Bauckham 1995: 458).

[146] An expression that was used in the Old Testament of private property held by
royalty (Eccles. 2:8) or David's own personal treasure over which he alone had control
(1 Chr. 29:3).

of this promise: the fallen fortunes of the house of David are restored by the raising up of Jesus as the Messiah of David's line, who extends his sovereignty over the nations through the Gentile mission, so that people everywhere are now seeking the true God and are being called by his name through faith. The apostolic council recognized the Gentiles, apart from the law, as full heirs of salvation and as members of the people of God.[147]

Regarding the practical question of fellowship between Jewish and Gentile Christians, the latter were urged, without compromising their Christian liberty, to respect their Jewish brothers' scruples by abstaining 'from food polluted by idols, from sexual immorality, from the meat of strangled animals and from blood' (v. 20). Without necessarily solving all future problems of relationships between Jewish and Gentile Christians, this way of living by the Gentile believers would make fellowship with more conservative Jewish believers possible.

Luke's account of this momentous incident in Acts 15 has been described as 'the most crucial chapter in the whole book', since it is positioned both 'structurally and theologically at the very heart' of Acts.[148] The chapter describes the turning point of Luke's story. The threat to the expansion of the gospel to Gentiles is not only dealt with, but is turned around so that the Christian mission now extends to western Asia and Europe (15:36 – 19:41). After the council the Jerusalem church is hardly mentioned in Acts. Once the decision has been made, there is no further mention of the Jerusalem apostles (apart from 16:4), and the focus of the book is on the irresistible progress of the gospel to 'the ends of the earth' through Paul.

Paul's universal mission and testimony (Acts 15:36 – 20:38)

After his account of this critical episode in the history of the early church (15:1–35) Luke begins the second half of his story in Acts by highlighting Paul's universal witness, particularly his testimony to the Gentiles in the eastern Mediterranean world and the beginning of his mission beyond Asia. During this period Paul, consistent with the divine salvation-historical plan, continues his pattern of bearing witness to the Jews first and then to the Gentiles (18:4–6, 19; cf. 19:8). The

[147] S. G. Wilson 1973: 231; Dumbrell 1994: 231.
[148] So Witherington 1998: 439, who follows Marshall 1980: 242. Note recently, Barrett 1998: 709–710; Fernando 1998: 414; and Fitzmyer 1998: 538.

progress of the word 'concerns primarily geographical boundaries rather than ethnic or relational ones' (Rosner 1998: 228).

In his second missionary journey, which begins and ends in Antioch (15:36 – 18:22), Paul is involved in a campaign in Macedonia and Achaia which includes the advance of the gospel in Philippi, Thessalonica, Berea, Athens and Corinth. Paul's missionary preaching to Gentile audiences[149] concentrates on the proclamation of repentance and forgiveness which flows from the resurrection (cf. 14:15; 17:18). To the Athenians he explains that the resurrection was proof to all of Jesus' appointment as judge on the final day, and that as a consequence all people everywhere are to repent (17:30–31).

Paul's third missionary journey (18:23 – 20:38) is based in the important commercial and political centre of Asia, the city of Ephesus. Paul's extended stay from the late summer of AD 52 until the spring or early summer of AD 55 in Ephesus turned out to be one of the most important phases in his apostolic career. The planting of the gospel in the province of Asia during those years was carried out so effectively that for centuries these churches were the most influential in the world.[150]

Paul's arrest and imprisonment (Acts 21 – 28)

At the conclusion of his third missionary journey Paul visits Jerusalem, where he is arrested (21:1–40) and accused of teaching apostasy to Jews of the dispersion as well as being a revolutionary.[151] Against the former charge he claims to be a Pharisee who is faithful to the law and customs of the Jewish people. In fact, the accusation against his orthodoxy is easily rebutted. Luke portrays Paul as an exemplary Jew who takes a vow (Acts 18:18), is purified (21:26), and apologizes for speaking against the high priest (23:5). Against the latter charge Paul is a Roman citizen who is completely innocent under Roman law of all the accusations brought against him. This trial section of Acts 21 – 28 is intimately connected with the mission section of chapters 13 – 20. 'If Paul were rejected on the basis of his apostasy from Jewish law and his guilt under Roman law, then his Gentile mission and the Gentile church planted by that mission would be seriously undermined.'[152]

[149] See the detailed treatment of Hansen 1998: 307–317.

[150] For the claim, not wholly convincing, that Paul's extended stays in Corinth and Ephesus reflect a development in his mission practice, see Towner 1998: 417–436.

[151] See the insightful examination of Paul's defence speeches (Acts 21 – 28) by Hansen 1998: 317–324, to which we are indebted.

[152] So Hansen 1998: 320, following Jervell (1972: 174), who adds: 'if the greatest

Luke makes the point repeatedly that Paul was accused for his belief in the resurrection: 'I am a Pharisee, the son of a Pharisee. I stand on trial because of my hope in the resurrection of the dead' (23:6; 24:21; 26:6; 28:20). The real nature of the Jews' objection, however, was his proclamation of the resurrection of Christ (Hansen 1998: 321–323). In his defence speeches Paul witnesses to the fact that the resurrection of Jesus fulfils the promises to Israel, that it was prophesied in the Old Testament (cf. 24:14–15), and was part of the Davidic messianic promise (13:33) (Dumbrell 1994: 231). Twice Paul's conversion story is repeated in these speeches (22:4–16; 26:12–18; cf. 9:1–31) to underscore the fact that his witness to the resurrection was commissioned and empowered by the risen Lord Jesus. In recounting the words of Christ in Acts 26:16–18, Paul claims to have had a similar experience to the prophets of Israel when they were commissioned by Yahweh (cf. Is. 6:9; Jer. 1:10; Dan. 10:11). Paul is sent to be the Lord's servant and witness to the Gentiles (Acts 26:16–17). His task is to open the eyes of the blind – the purpose of Jesus' mission (Luke 4:18; 7:22) – the goal of which is deliverance from darkness to light and from Satan to God, the forgiveness of sins, and an inheritance with all those sanctified by faith in Christ (v. 18). All of this is intimately connected with the purpose of Jesus' coming. Jesus' mission is effected in and through the witness and ministry of Paul, a point we have observed earlier in relation to the twelve apostles continuing the mission of Jesus. Christ was raised from the dead 'to proclaim light to his own people and to the Gentiles' (26:23). 'Not only was Paul's mission a continuation of the mission of Jesus because Paul did the work of Christ, but also because Christ did his work through Paul'.[153]

The conclusion: an open-ended mission to Jews and Gentiles (Acts 28:17–31)

The narrative structure of Acts gives special emphasis to this concluding paragraph of Luke's second volume (Acts 28:17–31), with its final episode (vv. 17–28) and closing section (vv. 29–31), both of which are highly significant for our theme of mission. The Jewish focus of verses

---

segment of the Christian church stems from a Jewish apostate, then the church is not the restored Israel and likewise has no right to appeal to Israel's salvation'.

[153] Hansen 1998: 323–324, following O'Toole (1978: 119), who adds: 'Paul preaches to the Gentiles; the resurrected Christ has from the Father a mission which Paul performs. What Paul does can be predicated of Christ. So, the resurrected Christ cannot only be said to be in heaven; he is with and in Paul proclaiming light.'

17–28 is both remarkable and important, while the closing section highlights the unending progress of the word of God. Accordingly, the main emphasis of this climactic paragraph is an open-ended mission to Jews and Gentiles. The manifesto of Acts 1:8 is not completed with the arrival of Paul in Rome, while the witness 'to the ends of the earth' represents a target not reached in Acts.[154]

Several major issues of this crucial paragraph need to be examined:

First, its pointed *Jewish focus*. Since chapter 19:21 the reader of Acts has been looking forward to Paul's arrival in Rome (cf. 23:11; 25:11–12, 21; 26:32; 27:24).[155] Once he reaches the capital, he meets with the Jews[156] (rather than with Christians[157] or Gentiles for whom he has apostolic responsibility), and explains to them the message of the kingdom of God (v. 23). This climactic ministry to the Jews of Rome is remarkable and suggests that the issues related to the encounter are vital[158] for the mission to Israel. Paul's loyalty to Israel, the fact that his mission is not anti-Jewish and that he is on trial for 'the hope of Israel', that is, the hope of the resurrection (vv. 17–20), capture the goodwill of his audience so that he is able to address them about the kingdom of God and Jesus' place within it (v. 23). There is, however, a mixed response to his exposition of the gospel. Some Jews are 'persuaded' while others are not (vv. 24–25). A division results, and in response Paul cites (vv. 26–27) the well-known text of Isaiah 6:9–10, telling his audience that 'God's salvation has been sent to the Gentiles, and they will listen!' (v. 28).

The presumed shift from Israel to the Gentiles has been interpreted by some as evidence of God's final judgment on his people, and an indication that the Jews were never intended recipients of his salvation.[159] But against this negative evaluation the following need to be noted: 1. In neither Acts 13:46 nor 18:6, where the issue of Jewish

---

[154] Rosner 1998: 230–231; against Fitzmyer (1998: 788), who thinks Luke has depicted Paul journeying 'to the ends of the earth' (1:8) in Rome.

[155] Dumbrell (1994: 232) thinks that 'Paul's arrival in Rome caps his role as God's chosen instrument to testify before Gentiles and kings and the people of Israel'.

[156] 'This journey brings Paul not simply to Rome, but to the Jews of Rome' (H. J. Hauser, cited by Palmer 1993: 62). The terminology employed includes 'the Jews' (of Rome), 'the [Jewish] people', 'the ancestral customs', 'Jerusalem' (v. 17), 'my nation' (v. 19), 'Israel' (v. 20), 'the law of Moses and the prophets' (v. 23), and the quotation of Is. 6:9–10 in vv. 26–27.

[157] Paul was not the first to bring the gospel to Rome; there were already Christians in the capital prior to his arrival (28:15–16).

[158] So Tannehill 1990: 344 and Barrett 1998: 1236–1237. Palmer (1993: 62) points out that the three separate occasions in Acts 28:17–28 are 'closely linked to form a single episode'.

[159] So Parsons 1987: 169; Tyson 1992: 176–178; and Sanders 1987: 80.

rejection of the gospel is in view, are the Jews abandoned (see above). From chapters 13 – 28 a minority of Jews – albeit a significant one – has been converted through the gospel, while the majority has rejected it. The citation in Acts 28 reflects this same two-fold response: a *righteous remnant* has gladly welcomed the announcement of Jesus and the kingdom, but the rest, who refused to believe, received this prophetic word of judgment. Isaiah 6 did not signal a total rejection of Israel by God in Isaiah's day, nor does its citation by Paul point to a divine rejection of all Jews during his ministry. 2. Paul's response in verse 28 is 'not a program for all future missionary efforts' (Witherington 1998: 804). It does not signify that he is *now* turning to the Gentiles, simply that 'this salvation of God has already been sent'[160] to them. In fact, this third statement (cf. 13:46; 18:6) is the only one of the three in which Paul does *not* say explicitly that he is *turning* from the Jews to the Gentiles. Perhaps it is mentioned in this final speech as a spur to the Roman Jews (cf. Rom. 11:11–12, where 'salvation has come to the Gentiles to make Israel envious'). 3. The movement of the apostolic witness in Acts (from Jerusalem through all Judea and Samaria to the ends of the earth; 1:8) does not signify that one form of particularism (Jews alone) has been replaced by another (Gentiles alone) (Rosner 1998: 228). According to verse 30, Paul 'welcomed *all* who came to him' in the capital, that is, both Jews and Gentiles, and he continued to proclaim the same message about Jesus and the kingdom to both after this encounter with the Jewish leaders (cf. v. 23 with v. 31). His challenge to the Jewish audience remains open. Although the great tragedy was that the majority of Jews continued to respond negatively to the message of Jesus and the kingdom, 'Luke does not compound this tragedy by suggesting at the end of his work that God had rejected them as well, or that the gospel should no longer be offered to all' (Witherington 1998: 806).

Secondly, the *mission to the Gentiles*. The final episode of Acts is not a justification of the mission to the Gentiles. This has already occurred in Acts 10 – 11, and was recognized at the Council of Jerusalem in chapter 15. Acts 28:17–31, then, is not a defence of the Gentile mission addressed to Jews in Rome. Luke has already made it plain that God's sending of his Son is for both Jews and Gentiles. This was indicated in the programmatic statement of Simeon (Luke 2:30–32), announced in Luke 3:6 as God's plan (that 'all mankind will see [his] salvation') and, as we have shown, reiterated throughout Luke's two-volume work.

[160] He does not say that this salvation 'will now – from this time – be sent' to the Gentiles (Barrett 1998: 1236; *cf.* Palmer 1993: 68).

Thirdly, the *significance of the ending of Acts*. Luke's ending to Acts has been a puzzle to many, if not a disappointment, and there is no agreement as to what the passage signifies.[161] Although this may not be all that can be said on the subject, Witherington's contention is valid: 'that the book's ending makes much better sense if Acts is some sort of historical work, meant to chronicle not the life and death of Paul but the rise and spread of the gospel and of the social and religious movement to which that gospel gave birth' (1998: 807).

The last verse of Acts (v. 31) is something of a summary statement about Paul's activities during his house arrest in Rome, as well as throughout his missionary work. That ministry of proclamation and teaching, with its focus on the kingdom of God and the place of the Lord Jesus, was effected by Paul without internal constraint or external hindrance. Witherington's comment is worth quoting in full:

> Luke's main concern is to leave the reader a reminder about the unstoppable word of God, which no obstacle – not shipwreck, not poisonous snakes, not Roman authorities – could hinder from reaching the heart of the Empire, and the hearts of those who dwelled there. It was a universal message that was proclaimed, and yet it was from the start of Acts to its conclusion the same story over and over again about the coming of the kingdom and of Jesus (cf. Acts 1:6–8 and 28:31). It was a message that asserted that God in the end was sovereign, and that God was faithful to both his word and his people.[162]

According to Rosner, several lines of evidence point 'to a deliberately open-ended ending of Acts that functions to portray the ongoing progress of the word'.[163] This motif of the advance of the word

---

[161] Questions such as 'Why does not Luke tell us what happened to Paul?' and 'What is the literary function of the ending of Acts?' are just two questions that have been raised. For recent discussions, see Brosend 1996: 348–362; Witherington 1998: 807–812; and Rosner 1998: 229–233.

[162] Witherington 1998: 815–816; cf. Barrett 1998: 1235, 1246.

[163] Rosner 1998: 232 (cf. 229–233). These lines of evidence are: 1. The plan of Acts 1:8 is not completed with the arrival of the gospel in Rome. 2. Acts 28:30–31 belongs to a series of texts that 'may be described as progress reports in which certain deeds and consequent growth are recounted. The function of these verses ... was to act as transitions from one period of witness to the next' (231). 3. Luke's silence about the result of Paul's trial is similar to endings in Graeco-Roman poetry and historiography (*e.g.* Homer and Herodotus). *Cf.* Marguerat 1993: 89. 4. Good endings like that of Acts include circularity (the reign of God in 1:3, 6, and Jesus' commission, 1:8, are recalled), parallels (the hope of Israel and turning to the Gentiles: 23:6; 24:15; 13:46; 18:5–6; *etc.*) and incompletion (about Paul's future and the witness to the end of the earth).

is both widespread and central to the purpose of the book. It is anticipated in Luke's Gospel, presented in Acts 1:1–11, confirmed throughout by means of progress reports, and closely linked with other main theological themes of Acts (*e.g.* the plan of God, salvation, witness, the Holy Spirit). However, the progress of the gospel is not to be understood in a triumphalistic sense. Acts does not simply chronicle a continuous advance; Luke shows that rejection and persecution pervade the book throughout. And if there is any advance it is due to God's mighty working – he has planned, initiated, guided and supported it.

Finally, the open-ended conclusion of the book seeks to draw the readers in to identify with the powerful advance of the gospel of salvation, and to include them in the continuing task of spreading this word.[164] The apostolic testimony did not reach the ends of the earth with Paul's arrival in Rome. This open-endedness is a reminder of an unfinished task and encouragement to all of us as readers to be committed to the ongoing *missio Dei*.

Concluding remarks

We have seen in the Gospel of Luke and its sequel, the book of Acts, that the theme of mission is of great importance, so much so that it may be the clearest presentation of this motif in the whole of the New Testament. Luke's Gospel tells the story of Jesus and his salvation, while the book of Acts traces the movement of that salvation to the Gentiles.

The infancy narratives (Luke 1 – 2), which function as a prologue to Luke-Acts, indicate that Israel's hope for a Saviour of David's line are about to be realized (1:30–35; cf. 2 Sam. 7:12–13). Through the birth of Jesus God will restore Israel and fulfil his promises to Abraham and his descendants (Gen. 12:1–3). These promises, however, are fulfilled not in national Israel, but in those who fear God (1:50–55). The Lord's Messiah fills the role of the Servant of the Lord (2:32; 4:18–19; cf. Is. 42:6; 49:6–9; 61:1–2).

During Jesus' earthly ministry the foundational mission, according to the Gospel of Luke, is his own sending by God to Israel (Luke 4:18–19). He is the Spirit-anointed prophet and Messiah who announces the new era of salvation that he is currently bringing to pass (cf. Is. 58:6; 61:1–2). Essentially, his mission is to 'preach good news' with 'release' as its goal, a release which throughout the rest of Luke-Acts is

---

[164] Darr (1992: 53) contends that the 'text is designed to persuade the readers to become believing witnesses'. *Cf.* Rosner 1998: 232.

first and foremost 'the forgiveness of sins', that is, a picture of total forgiveness and salvation, which it had become in Isaiah 61. The 'poor' to whom the good news is announced are 'the dispossessed, the excluded', who were forced to depend on God. According to Isaiah 61, the 'poor' designates the eschatological community, the suffering exiles or faithful in Israel who have been spiritually oppressed. It is to these poor and oppressed that Jesus comes announcing the gospel of the kingdom.

First the twelve, then the seventy-two, are intimately involved with Jesus in his mission and play a key role. They are sent by the one who has himself been sent from God. Jesus did not embark on a universal mission during the course of his earthly ministry, although there are hints and anticipations throughout Luke's Gospel[165] that his saving work will have worldwide repercussions.

Just as God's mission in sending Jesus (to Israel) was central and foundational during his earthly ministry, so too after his death and resurrection, with the way now open for repentance and the forgiveness of sins to be proclaimed in his name to all the nations (Luke 24:47), this sending of Jesus is still the essential mission. There is now, however, a major development within the story as to how God's saving purposes for Israel and the nations are to be realized. Jesus' universal mission, which is grounded in his death and resurrection (v. 46), is to be effected through his disciples as witnesses after he returns to the Father (v. 49; cf. Acts 1:8, 22; 2:32; *etc.*). They have been chosen by him and are to be equipped and endorsed by the Holy Spirit for this task. Their testimony, which focuses on three scriptural necessities, namely, the suffering and death of the Messiah (Luke 24:46), his rising from the dead (v. 46), and the call to repentance with a view to the forgiveness of sins (v. 47), is to be given 'in Jerusalem, and in all Judea and Samaria, and to the ends of the earth' (Acts 1:8). Acts, then, recounts the continuing work of Jesus, that is, what he continued 'to do and to teach' (cf. 1:1) by his Spirit through his apostles.

With this testimony to Jesus as Lord and Christ, and the mighty outpouring of the Spirit at Pentecost, a Jewish festival, the universal movement has begun (Acts 2). Although it will encounter opposition, even rejection, it is unstoppable. What started with the twelve in Jerusalem continues throughout Judea and Samaria and moves towards the ends of the earth (in accordance with Acts 1:8). Luke's account

---

[165] Apart from the birth narratives and Luke 4:25–27, as we have seen, there are hints in the narrative of Luke 10 that the mission of the seventy-two to Israel anticipates and prepares the reader for the universal mission in the book of Acts.

traces the progress of the gospel from Jerusalem, the centre from which the word of the Lord sounds forth. As the story progresses, Paul too is commissioned as a 'witness' and *sent* to carry Jesus' name to the Gentiles, their kings and the people of Israel, a task that would involve him in suffering (9:6, 15–16; 22:17–21; 26:15–23).

Events with major significance for the mission recorded in the book of Acts include Pentecost and the gift of the Spirit (Acts 2), Stephen's martyrdom (ch. 7), the spread of the gospel to Judea and Samaria (8:4–40), Paul's conversion and commission (9:1–31), Cornelius and the Gentiles (10:1 – 11:18), Paul's first missionary journey (13:1 – 14:28) and the Council of Jerusalem (15:1–35). The last has been depicted as 'the most crucial chapter in the whole book', since it describes the turning point in Luke's story. The threat to the expansion of the gospel to the Gentiles is turned around so that the Christian mission now extends to Western Asia and Europe. Paul's universal mission and testimony begin the second half of Luke's story in Acts: his universal witness (15:36 – 20:38) is highlighted and this finally leads to his arrest and imprisonment (chs. 21 – 28). The conclusion of Luke's second volume describes an open-ended mission to Jews and Gentiles (28:17–31). This reminds readers of an unfinished task and the urgency of being identified with the ongoing advance of the gospel of salvation.

Chapter Seven

Paul

Paul's uniqueness as a missionary in the ancient world

At both the popular and scholarly levels Paul has had a special fascination for missionaries, whether in relation to his conversion, his methods and strategies, or his success. Over the years sermons have been preached about this missionary and countless writings have been produced in relation to his significance for the Christian mission.

There are very good reasons for this focus of attention on his missionary activity. According to Martin Hengel, 'the success of the earliest Christian mission ... was unique in the ancient world'. And with specific reference to Paul, Hengel adds: his 'mission [was] an unprecedented happening, in terms both of the history of religion in antiquity and of later church history ... With Paul, for the first time we find the specific aim of engaging in missionary activity throughout the world' (Hengel 1983: 48, 49, 52). As a result, what he did 'has remained unparallelled over the subsequent 1900 years'. C. H. H. Scobie makes a similar point: 'The importance of Paul for the subsequent missionary expansion of the Church can scarcely be overemphasized. By his own extraordinary missionary activity concentrated into a relatively few years and by the theology worked out in his letters Paul laid the foundations for the later expansion in both practice and theory.'[1]

The significance of his encounter with the risen Christ

How, then, are we to explain this profound, even unprecedented, influence? We must begin with the most decisive event in Paul's life, namely, his confrontation with the risen Christ on the Damascus road.

---

[1] Scobie 1984: 47. He adds: 'What Paul preached and practised was a universal mission. Clearly Paul sees himself playing the major role in proclaiming the Gospel throughout the whole *oikoumenē*' (48).

In this revelation of God's Son through the gospel there was a personal disclosure of Jesus Christ to Paul, a present revelation by God which anticipated the glorious unveiling on the final day: Christ was revealed to Paul in the form in which he will come at the end time. Paul saw Christ as the risen and exalted one in his glory (Gal. 1:11–12). From this time on the course of his life was set. Although scholars disagree as to how Paul's encounter should be understood, it is best to regard it as *both* a conversion *and* a calling.[2] The former term signifies 'a radical change of thought, outlook, commitments and practice, which involves either an overt or a subconscious break with one's past identity', while the latter refers to 'a summons to a new career or a particular pursuit'.[3]

The term 'conversion' is appropriate to describe the confrontation with the risen Christ, for it led to a dramatic 'paradigm shift' in Paul's thinking.[4] He came to understand that Jesus is at the centre of God's saving purposes, and that he is Israel's Messiah, the Son of God and Lord of all (Longenecker 1997b: 18–42). Also, Paul's conversion was the event that decisively shaped his eschatology: he now knew of 'God's personal saving intervention in the world that was accomplished through his Son and by his Spirit, which marks the end of the old world and the beginning of the new age'.[5] If Jesus was the crucified and exalted Messiah, then the divine curse was 'for us' since it was God's purpose that 'in Christ Jesus the blessing of Abraham might come to the Gentiles' (Gal. 3:13–14). Christ had brought the law to an end as a way of salvation. Paul's zeal for the law[6] and for righteousness based on it had led him to the gravest sin of opposing God and his Messiah.

---

[2] Stendahl (1976: 7–23) claims that Paul's Damascus road encounter was not really a conversion at all, according to traditional definitions of conversion. He did not change religions nor did he suffer from an inner experience of guilt or despair. His experience is best understood as a call to be the apostle to the Gentiles. Some advocates of the 'new perspective' on Paul have agreed with Stendahl's emphasis even if there have been differences regarding the details.

[3] R. Longenecker 1997a: xiii. Other terms, discussed by Longenecker, that have been used to describe the Damascus road event are *transformation* ('a new perception and a marked change in form or appearance, but not necessarily a break with the past') and *alternation* ('a shift in perspective and practice, but without any distancing from one's past'). See also the treatment by Corley 1997: 15, following Gaventa 1986: 1–13.

[4] Corley (1997: 16) suggests that there are four models, albeit with some overlap, which are an index to current thinking about the impact of Paul's conversion on his theology: soteriological (Dupont, Wilckens, Stuhlmacher), christological (Menoud, Hays, Wright), missiological (Munck, Sanders, Dunn) and doxological (Kim, Segal, Newman).

[5] Marshall 1997: 60. Note his important article (1997: 43–61) on the significance of Paul's conversion for his eschatology.

[6] Note the recent essay by Westerholm on 'Paul's Reevaluation of the Mosaic Law' after the Damascus road encounter (1997: 147–165).

He now knew that justification is by God's grace alone, for he, the ungodly, had been justified through God's sheer mercy. His teaching on justification by grace alone and through faith alone was due to the insights regarding the law, human existence and a person's relation to God which arose out of his Damascus encounter. It was out of his personal experience of God's forgiveness and reconciliation on the Damascus road that Paul developed the imagery of reconciliation to interpret God's saving work in Christ (Kim 1997: 102–124).

At the same time, Paul understands his encounter with the risen Christ in terms of a personal calling. God 'was pleased to reveal his Son in me', he declares, 'so that I might preach him among the Gentiles' (Gal. 1:15–16). His call to the Gentile mission was 'a specific individual assignment, which he grounds not in a common experience in Christ but in a unique personal experience which set him apart'.[7] If Paul's encounter with the resurrected Jesus in glory had revolutionary theological implications for the unconverted Pharisee and led to a significant reorientation in relation to Christ, his cross and the law, and thus to a new understanding of salvation, then his encounter on the Damascus road also included a special commission to the Gentile mission.[8]

This is not to suggest that when he was converted Paul grasped everything about his calling to be a missionary or the nature of his worldwide mission. In affirming that his commissioning to the Gentiles was an essential ingredient in the Damascus-road revelation, we do not deny that his convictions about this calling grew or that he came to a deeper understanding of the magnitude of his missionary task. No doubt Paul reflected further on the Old Testament Scriptures in relation to his mission within the purposes of God. But the main lines of this commission to the Gentiles and its place within God's redemptive plan were set when he was confronted by the risen Christ in that life-changing encounter.[9]

[7] Bowers 1993: 612–613; also Dunn 1987: 251–266 and Donaldson 1997a: 62–84 (for his treatment of the origin of Paul's Gentile mission). Donaldson claims that 'a mission among the Gentiles was by no means a necessary outcome of the kind of conversion experienced by Paul' (63). This is worked out in greater detail in Donaldson 1997b.

[8] Bowers (1993: 613), who adds: 'Once this duality of Paul's initial experience is acknowledged, the contours both of his missionary career and of his theological development can be appropriately clarified.'

[9] There is significant difference of opinion as to whether Paul's commissioning had the Gentiles in view from the very beginning, or whether the significance of the Damascus road christophany came to him later or emerged in his thinking over a period of time. 1. Donaldson (1997a: 64) contends: 'we do not know whether a concern for

Further, because of the centrality of the Gentile mission to his life and thought, we cannot rightly understand Paul's theology until his perspective on mission has been integrated into the larger interpretation of his theology.[10] Yet Paul's theology and mission do not simply relate to each other as 'theory' to 'practice'. It is not as though his mission is the practical outworking of his theology. Rather, his mission is 'integrally related to his identity and thought', and his theology is a missionary theology.[11]

Paul's mission within the purposes of God

A cursory glance at Paul's letters quickly reveals that the apostle understood his missionary activity to Gentiles within the context of an Old Testament expectation in which the Gentile nations would on the final day partake of God's ultimate blessings to Israel. He recognized that his mission was part of a larger whole, namely, 'the Divinely superintended eschatological ingathering of the nations of Old Testament expectation' (Bowers 1976: 172).

Old Testament texts of a universalistic kind were frequently used by Paul, particularly in relation to his apostolic ministry of the gospel with its missionary outreach. Through the preaching of the gospel, God was bringing to himself a new people comprising not only Jews but also

---

Gentiles was present from the outset as part of his conversion experience itself, or whether it emerged only gradually, perhaps in response to subsequent experience'. 2. Riesner (1998: 235–237, esp. 236), suggests it is 'possible that *the initiation* of the mission to the Gentiles represents a realization that emerged for the apostle only sometime later from this Christophany' (emphasis added). Chae (1997: 302–307), in part as a reaction to S. Kim's statement that '[Paul's] gospel and apostleship are grounded *solely* in the Christophany on the Damascus road and that he understands himself solely in the light of it', contends that by 'the time he writes the letters (especially Galatians and Romans) Paul is fully aware of God's call for him to be [the] apostle to the Gentiles, and thus he is keenly conscious of his apostolic obligation' (306). Chae thinks that the risen Christ 'called Paul on the Damascus road; then he progressively unfolded the content of his call ... and Paul's understanding of his task and capacity as apostle to the Gentiles was accordingly developed'. 3. We have argued elsewhere, particularly on the basis of Gal. 1:11–12, 15–16, that 'Paul's commission to the Gentiles was part of, indeed an essential ingredient of, the revelation on the Damascus road ... that Paul should preach Christ among the Gentiles – was part of the revelation itself' (O'Brien 1995: 22–25, esp. 23–24; so also recently Dunn 1998: 178).

[10] Chae (1997: 289) concludes from his study of Romans that there is an undeniable link between Paul's self-understanding as the apostle to the Gentiles and what he has written, *i.e.* his theology, in the letter.

[11] Hultgren 1985: 125, 145. *Cf.* Hengel (1983: 53), who states: 'This calling forms the basis of his whole theology'; and Dunn 1987: 265.

Gentiles, and this was in fulfilment of Hosea 2:23 and 1:10 (in Rom. 9:25-26). The rapid progress of the Gentile mission over against the slow response among Jews fulfilled the prophetic words of Isaiah 54:1, 'Sing, O barren woman, you who never bore ... because more are the children of the desolate woman than of her who has a husband' (quoted in Gal. 4:27). Paul's own outreach to those who had never heard the gospel was a fulfilment of Old Testament expectation (Is. 52:15 in Rom. 15:21), while he claims in an extended argument at Galatians 3 and Romans 4 that the Abrahamic promise, 'in you shall all the nations be blessed' (Gen. 12:3), is now being fulfilled as Gentiles turn to Christ. The presence of Gentiles along with Jews within the one worshipping community was both a confirmation of the promises given to the patriarchs and the occasion for Gentiles to glorify God for his mercy (Rom. 15:1-13); the Old Testament quotations strung together in verses 9-12 show that in Christ God had opened up his covenant promises to Gentiles.

What is true generally is also confirmed specifically by particular passages that speak of Paul's missionary commission in God's salvation-historical plan (Gal. 1; Eph. 3) and Romans 15:14-33 where he throws light on his understanding of his mission and its place within the saving purposes of God.

Old Testament prophetic-call language and Paul's apostolic self-consciousness (Gal. 1)

It has generally been recognized by New Testament scholarship that Paul formulates his calling as an apostle to the Gentiles in language drawn from the Old Testament prophets, notably the Isaianic Servant of the Lord and apparently Jeremiah (Gal. 1:15, 'God ... has set me apart before I was born', NRSV; cf. Is. 49:5; Jer. 1:5). This is sometimes understood as signifying that Paul has aligned himself with these Old Testament figures in redemptive history in which God renews his will for the salvation of Gentiles. While it is agreed that Paul's understanding of his calling is closely linked with the theology of election and calling in Isaiah, some doubts have been expressed as to whether he is drawing upon the language of Jeremiah.

But the analogy with Jeremiah reflects Paul's apostolic self-consciousness,[12] while his allusion to Isaiah suggests that he was

[12] Paul echoes the language of Jeremiah in Gal. 1:15-16, since the prophet's experiences are akin to Paul's 'apostolic self-consciousness'. Jeremiah knew that his call from Yahweh had been a true experience and that his message was God's sure word to Israel. But how could he prove that he was a true prophet who stood in the council of the

chosen by God to continue the work of the Servant of Yahweh.[13] The Servant knew that he had been set apart by Yahweh from birth (Is. 49:1, 5). This choice from the beginning had a positive ministry to Gentiles in view: 'I will give you as a light to the nations, that my salvation may reach to the end of the earth' (v. 6). Further, the Servant's ministry was wholly dependent on Yahweh's calling of him (v. 1). Paul's description in Galatians 1:15–16 highlights each of these three elements: choice from birth, calling and a ministry to Gentiles.

In drawing on this Isaianic language Paul is not suggesting that he was the new servant of the Lord.[14] Rather, his mission arises from and, in a sense, is a continuance of that of the Servant who had been set apart by the Lord from birth with a specific ministry to Gentiles in view. Other references to the Isaianic Servant of the Lord in Paul's letters suggest that the apostle saw his missionary role as intimately related to this salvation-historical figure.[15]

Paul's stewardship and the divine mystery (Eph. 3)

In Ephesians 3:1–13 Paul makes it clear that his missionary calling to preach the gospel to Gentiles is integral to God's redemptive plan. This point emerges, not through the apostle's language echoing that of the

---

Lord and had heard his word (Jer. 23:18–22) when the false prophets had not? The validity of Jeremiah's commission was bound up with the truthfulness of the Lord's message. Similarly, the validity of Paul's commission was also questioned. Attempts were made to undermine his apostolic standing in the eyes of his Galatian converts. In the final analysis Paul's commission and the gospel he preached were inextricably linked. To denigrate one was to despise the other. Paul, like Jeremiah, had 'stood in the council of the Lord', that is, he had received both his gospel and his commission to preach it from the risen and exalted Lord Jesus. *Cf.* Fung 1988: 63–64.

[13] Riesner (1998: 236–237) contends that Gal. 1:15 is 'formulated with unmistakable reference to Isa. 49:1'. He adds that 'Paul understood his own conversion as a prophetic calling analogous to that of the Deutero-Isaianic Servant of God ... In the Old Testament, the most unequivocal statements of hope concerning the Gentile world appear in the second part of the book of Isaiah' (Is. 45:20–22; 51:4–5; 56:1–8), especially in connection with the Servant of Yahweh (Is. 42:1, 3–4, 6; 49:1, 6, 22). Note also Sandnes 1991: 48–70.

[14] Wagner (1998: 222) rejects the view that Paul conceived of himself 'as the Servant of Isaiah 52:13 – 53:12'. Rather, Paul 'finds himself playing the crucial part of a *herald* who announces the good news, the word of Christ' (original emphasis).

[15] On the wider use of the Servant language in relation to Paul's ministry, see Radl 1986: 144–149. In connection with earlier debates note also the discussion of Bowers 1976: 137–143. Concerning the more general but profound influence of Isaiah on Paul's conception of his apostolic ministry (esp. in Romans), see Wagner 1997: 72. He claims that 'Paul has carried on a sustained and careful reading of large sections of the book through the lens of his own situation as an apostle and missionary' (note also his 1999 thesis).

Old Testament as in Galatians 1, but because of his relationship with the mystery and its administration (vv. 2–4, 8–9). The broad sweep of God's salvation-historical plan is in view when the term 'mystery' is used in 3:1–13 (as read in the light of 1:3–14), while important features of its content are emphasized in verse 6. Gentiles are recipients of the divine promise to Abraham (Gen. 12:1–3); they are fellow-heirs because they are heirs of God and fellow-heirs with Christ (Rom. 8:17). Old Testament promises regarding the divine indwelling through God's Spirit also find their fulfilment in these Gentiles who are partakers of the promised Holy Spirit in Christ Jesus (Eph. 1:13; 2:18; 4:30). These promises come to fruition through the gospel which Paul preaches.

The grand design of God's salvation-historical plan was that 'now, through the church, the manifold wisdom of God should be made known to the rulers and authorities in the heavenly realms' (3:10). A new multi-racial community was 'taking concrete shape before people's eyes' (Stott 1979: 123), and in it the wisdom of God was being displayed. The resulting new humanity of Jews and Gentiles as fellow-members of the body of Christ was 'to serve throughout the universe as an object-lesson of the wisdom of God'.[16] The presence of the *church itself* is the manifestation of the hidden secret. 'The establishment of the Church, which is the working out of the divine mystery, is the tangible evidence of this [hidden secret]'.[17]

The Old Testament prophets had already looked forward to the day when Gentiles along with Israelites would be embraced within the sphere of divine blessing. How this would come about – by incorporation of both Jews and Gentiles into the body of Christ – had not been made known. *This* had remained a mystery until the time of its fulfilment and Paul, as the apostle to the Gentiles and first steward of this mystery, had the privilege of unfolding its wonder. His missionary commission included two elements: 1. the preaching of the unsearchable riches of Christ (3:8), and 2. an integral feature of that proclamation: the bringing to light for all to see how this hidden purpose of God was being put into effect (v. 9). As he engaged in this task the divine promises were being fulfilled and awaiting their consummation.

[16] Bruce 1961: 320. Bockmuehl (1990: 203) comments: 'as the visible evidence of the mystery of Gentile incorporation into the Messianic community ... [the church] is well suited to serve as a manifestation of God's inscrutable saving wisdom to the hitherto ignorant angelic powers'.

[17] Brown 1968: 60. So also many commentators.

The effects of Paul's mission and salvation history (Rom. 15:14–33)

In this highly significant passage the apostle gives a brief overview of his missionary career – from its beginning to the present, a period of more than twenty years – and describes its amazing effects. At this important turning point, the conclusion of his missionary activity in the east, Paul offers a number of significant clues about his previous ministry and his hopes for the future. He employs a number of salvation-historical motifs to describe a missionary activity which involved the proclamation of the gospel that led to the establishment of settled congregations, and all of this was set within an eschatological frame of reference in which divine blessing has come to the Gentiles in fulfilment of Old Testament expectation.[18] These motifs are expressed in cultic terms, exodus phraseology, Isaianic Servant language (52:13 – 53:12) and geographic terminology.

Cultic language

With a concentration on Old Testament cultic terminology that is quite remarkable, Paul refers first to the content of that ministry to which he was called (he is a *leitourgos*), as 'the priestly duty (*hierourgounta*) of proclaiming the gospel of God', and then to the purpose of this commissioning – and thus of his whole missionary career – as '*so that* the Gentiles might become an offering (*prosphora*) acceptable (*euprosdektos*) to God, sanctified (*hēgiasmenē*) by the Holy Spirit' (Rom. 15:16).

But the apostle did not think of his own ministry as involving literal cultic activity. His carefully chosen language does bring 'home the continuity between his ministry and the whole revelation of Israel'. Yet even 'more striking' is the way Paul 'transforms and transcends all that had hitherto been bound up in that cultic language. By applying it to his own noncultic ministry of preaching the gospel he confirms that for him the cultic barrier between sacred and secular has been broken through and left behind' (Dunn 1988b: 867). The sacrificial language has been transformed – not simply 'spiritualized' – because of its eschatological fulfilment. The 'day of salvation', the acceptable time (*dektos*, 2 Cor. 6:2), has come and is present in the gospel which Paul, the missionary, proclaims.

---

[18] Bowers 1976: 15; *cf.* also Robinson 1974: 231–245.

Exodus terminology

As he writes about the means by which this ministry was being fulfilled, the apostle employs a significant expression: 'signs and wonders' (*sēmeia kai terata*, Rom. 15:19, NRSV). This is a rare combination in the Pauline letters (cf. 2 Cor. 12:12; 2 Thess. 2:9), which is here employed positively in a way that seems designed to recall its Old Testament equivalent. 'Signs and wonders' was a traditional way of speaking of the exodus miracles;[19] they are the events by which God redeemed his people from Egypt and brought them to the Promised Land.[20]

The expression regularly designates events surrounding the great redemptive acts of God: they are also associated in the Old Testament with true prophecy (Is. 8:18; 20:3), and in the New Testament with the works of Jesus (cf. John 20:29–31; Acts 2:19, 22) and the ministry of the apostles, including Paul, together with those closely associated with them (Acts 2:43; 5:12; 14:3; 15:12; cf. Heb. 2:3–4). Here in Romans 15:19 Paul asserts that his ministry to the nations, through which Christ has effectively borne testimony, stands within this salvation-historical framework. Indeed, his work as a missionary to the Gentiles (*ethn$* appears three times in this context)[21] is one of those very redemptive acts of God.

By mentioning 'signs and wonders' Paul is not simply affirming that he has the *marks of a true apostle* as God's special envoy to the nations, though this was undoubtedly correct. After all, Christ through his Spirit has been powerfully at work through him. He is at the same time asserting that Christ's working through him is part and parcel of God's redemptive activity, associated with 'signs and wonders'. This activity has been effected through Moses at the exodus, the prophets, the saving ministry of Jesus and the apostles whose ministry was particularly to Jews. Paul's missionary calling and work among the nations stand within a salvation-historical framework – especially related to the exodus – with which the purposes of God for the saving of both Jew and Gentile are closely bound.

[19] Exod. 7:3, 9; 11:9–10; Deut. 4:34; 6:22; *etc*. For further references see Stolz 1972: 125–144; Woodhouse 1987: 17–35; and Dunn 1988b: 862–863.

[20] So Woodhouse (1987: 22), who concludes: 'in the Bible the "significant wonders" – the wonders that matter for faith – are the events surrounding the great redemptive acts of God' (27).

[21] Verses 16 (twice), and 18; *cf.* vv. 12, 27.

Servant language

At verse 21, in support of his pioneer policy of preaching the gospel where Christ has not been named, Paul quotes from the fourth Servant song (Is. 52:15, LXX) and refers to the effects of the Servant's ministry on many nations (*ethnē*) and kings.

> 'Those who were not told about him will see,
> and those who have not heard will understand.'

This prophetic word was the basis for Paul's ambition to preach Christ in a pioneer situation, that is, where Gentiles had not been told about this Servant or his ministry on their behalf. The apostle found this promise to be reliable for, as he pursued his ambition, people from many nations (*ethnē*) in the eastern Mediterranean, did begin to *see* and to *understand* that the Servant's vicarious work of redemption was for them.

In applying this Old Testament text to his own missionary activity, Paul believed that he was carrying on the work of the Servant of Yahweh, even if he did not explicitly identify himself with this figure. Wagner appropriately remarks: 'Paul's mission, then, is nothing less than the outworking of Christ's own mission'.[22] We have already seen that he interpreted his missionary calling in terms of the Servant's commission (Gal. 1:15–16; cf. Rom. 1:1) and understood his role to be that of continuing the Servant's mission by taking the light of the gospel 'to the nations' (Is. 49:6). Here Paul's *pioneer policy* has Old Testament endorsement in relation to the work of that same salvation-historical figure.

The geographic dimension to Paul's mission

The apostle saw a particular pattern in his missionary efforts which could be expressed within a geographical frame of reference. He claims to have fulfilled the gospel 'from Jerusalem all the way round to Illyricum' (v. 19). The opening phrase 'from Jerusalem' is puzzling. Paul began his Christian preaching in Damascus and the surrounding area of Arabia (Acts 9:19–25), while his more extended work as a missionary to the Gentiles started when he was based in Antioch (Acts 13:1–3). We do not know of any important ministry in the Jerusalem area. Although he may have had an occasion in mind, such as his vision in the temple relating to his call to preach to the Gentiles (Acts 22:19–

[22] Wagner 1998: 198. Note his treatment of this important passage (195–202).

170

21), or the time in Jerusalem when he was given the right hand of fellowship for his work among Gentiles (Gal. 2:9), these are unlikely. In order to overcome the difficulty, both geographical references have been regarded as exclusive rather than inclusive (that is, 'not including Jerusalem or Illyricum'). Accordingly, it is taken to mean that he had preached from the boundary of Jerusalem to the boundary of Illyricum.[23] 'He is stating the limits of his preaching, so far, not claiming to have preached in both.'[24]

It is preferable, however, to understand this reference within a salvation-historical perspective: Jerusalem was the starting point of the whole Christian mission (Luke 24:47; Acts 1:8, and Paul's strong emphasis on the priority of the Jew in hearing the gospel: cf. the 'first' in Rom. 1:16, *etc.*), because it was from Jerusalem that the gospel went forth. The reference to Jerusalem, then, helps us to realize that Paul is not writing exclusively of his own work. Instead, he is setting it within the overlapping context of a universal gospel mission.[25] On this view, which makes good sense in the context, behind Romans 15:19 stands a salvation-historical concept of mission.

Paul's description continues: 'and in a sweep round to Illyricum'. The words, 'in a sweep round' (*kyklō*, lit. 'in a circle'), are normally taken as referring to a broad arc or portion of a circle extending from Jerusalem to Illyricum.[26] We have no other evidence that Paul pushed as far north as Illyricum in his missionary work, but since the area did border on Macedonia it is just possible that he did. If, however, the preposition 'to' is used exclusively rather than inclusively and means 'up to' (rather than 'into'), then the phrase may simply be a reference to the northern limitation of Paul's Macedonian mission.[27] Illyricum

[23] So Käsemann 1980: 394; Wilckens 1982: 119–120; and Hultgren 1985: 131.

[24] Morris 1988: 514. *Cf.* Zeller 1976: 227, who argues that Paul is thinking of his own ministry, rather than more generally of the gospel's expansion (as in Col. 1:5–6).

[25] Bowers (1976: 20) comments that Jerusalem was 'the proper originating point of every advance for the gospel in [Paul's] day, because all missionary progress of the period was, both from a historical and from a theological point of view, necessarily "from Jerusalem"'. *Cf.* Riesner 1998: 263. J. M. Scott (1995: 136–138) thinks that the geographical movement 'from Jerusalem ... to Illyricum' refers to Paul's own apostolic ministry. By this expression, according to Scott, Paul emphasizes 'the centrality of Jerusalem to his mission rather than to describe the path that he took to Illyricum' (138).

[26] Rather than a circle round about Jerusalem itself (as J. M. Scott 1995: 138 claims). So BAGD 456–457 and many commentators.

[27] One wonders whether Paul saw his work not simply as an arc but as the top half of a circle which presupposed that others were engaged in the lower half (through Egypt, Alexandria and North Africa). *Cf.* Dunn 1988b: 864. Knox (1964: 11) suggests that Paul may have hoped he might encircle 'the whole Mediterranean world' within his lifetime. Note Hultgren 1985: 132–133.

would then signify the limit of the apostle's missionary endeavours. What does emerge from this geographical reference is that Paul's journeys were not 'sporadic, random skirmishes into gentile lands' (Hultgren 1985: 133; cf. 2 Cor. 1:17; 2:12).

The apostle may have found support in the Old Testament for the geographic breadth of his mission, particularly in Isaiah 66:19 which provides a 'geographic description within the context of eschatological hope for the Gentiles'.[28] He seems to have regarded this text as being fulfilled, in part at least, through his own missionary activity, and traces of this Old Testament passage apparently lie behind Romans 15:16–24. As the 'apostle to the Gentiles' Paul understood himself to be an eschatological emissary to the nations (like those of Is. 66:19). He too was a *survivor* sent (Is. 66:19; cf. Rom. 5:9; cf. 8:24) to those who had not heard of Yahweh's salvation. The place names mentioned in Isaiah 66:18–20 include those nations that are the particular focus of Paul's mission in Romans 15. This Old Testament passage is to be taken as a promise that God will gather 'all nations and tongues' to Jerusalem (66:18, 20). The scope of verse 19, which proceeds in a north-westerly arc to the far west, is broader than the more limited range of Paul's mission in Romans 15. He did not go to all the nations listed; nevertheless the apostle to the Gentiles 'would surely have viewed himself as *part* of the eschatological missionary enterprise to the *ethnē* portrayed in Isa 66:19'.[29] His work, then, is part of a larger whole in which God will gather ' all nations and tongues', not simply a few.

God had called him to a priestly service that involved the proclamation of the gospel to the Gentiles, 'so that [they] might become an offering acceptable to God, sanctified by the Holy Spirit' (15:16). This 'offering' was the Gentiles themselves, which is further amplified and explained in the following expressions about the collection for the poor saints of Jerusalem. As the apostle journeyed to Jerusalem with the gifts provided by the Gentiles, he was also in their representatives 'bringing the Gentiles into the eschatological Jerusalem

---

[28] Riesner 1998: 245. *Cf.* Aus 1979: 232–262. Hays (1989: 162) aptly comments: 'Isaiah offers the clearest expression in the Old Testament of a universalistic, eschatological vision in which the restoration of Israel in Zion is accompanied by an ingathering of Gentiles to worship the Lord' (cited by J. M. Scott 1995: 146).

[29] J. M. Scott (1995: 136–149, esp. 146), who understands Is. 66:19 as part of the table of nations traditions (of Gen. 10) of which Rom. 15 also partakes. Note also his evaluation of Riesner (145–147).

as an offering of the end time'.[30] Their gifts were a concrete expression of the Gentiles themselves.[31]

The gospel Paul preached

Out of a considerable number of statements made by the apostle about the gospel he preached we focus our attention especially on Romans 1 and 3.

Paul's total commitment to the gospel (Rom. 1)

Set apart for the gospel of God (v. 1)

The opening verse of Romans draws attention to Paul's involvement in the gospel. Here he introduces himself as 'a servant of Jesus Christ, called to be an apostle, and *set apart for the gospel of God*' (*eis euangelion theou*). If one is speaking about the *eschatological basis* of Paul's separation, then it was grounded in a *past* event, the personal revelation of the resurrected and exalted Lord Jesus to him, rather than a future one, such as an imminent parousia. As one who is set apart for the gospel, Paul is called to preach it. He serves the gospel 'by an authoritative and normative proclamation of it' (Cranfield 1975: 53). From the time of his conversion onwards Paul's commitment to the gospel was the dominant and determinative focus of his whole life. D. Moo rightly observes: 'Paul is claiming that his life is totally dedicated to God's act of salvation in Christ – a dedication that involves both his own belief in, and obedience to, that message as well as his apostolic proclamation of it' (Moo 1996: 43). 'Gospel' (*euangelion*) here has a verbal nuance to it (as a noun of agency): it is the *act of preaching the gospel* that is in view. However, this is not all that is implied by the term, for the following relative clause draws attention to its content, namely, that 'which God promised beforehand through his prophets in the Holy Scriptures' (v. 2). 'The content of the message and its proclamation are not two distinct meanings of the word *euangelion*,

---

[30] Riesner 1998: 250, together with further references. Note also Pedersen's detailed arguments (1985: 47–67).

[31] According to Old Testament prophecy the temple at Jerusalem was to be the place where all nations at the end time would come to worship and pray to the living God (see ch. 2). According to Eph. 2:21–22 the temple imagery is to be understood in fulfilment of these promises. Now, through Christ, Gentiles have been brought near to God, and along with believing Jews they have become the new temple, the place where God's presence dwells. *Cf.* O'Brien 1999b: 219–220.

only two sides of one concept'.[32]

Serving God wholeheartedly in the gospel of his Son (v. 9)

Paul's *total* involvement in the gospel of God's Son is to the fore in verse 9, where he makes an important statement about his rendering spiritual service in its proclamation. Using the verb *latreuō* ('I serve'), which was employed exclusively of religious service in the LXX[33] and was determinative of the New Testament occurrences where it has no reference to human relations, Paul speaks of his active service to God. He was wholly committed to this service ('in my spirit'), and the sphere of his ministry was 'in the gospel of his Son'. Once again *euangelion* is used as a noun of agency, meaning 'the proclamation of the gospel', and it is equivalent to the verb *euangelizomai* ('to preach the gospel'). Further, as a deliberate contrast to the typically cultic worship of the Jews, Paul's ongoing proclamation was 'a religious act comparable with the praise offered in conjunction with the sacrificial ritual of the tabernacle or temple ... it is clear from what follows in the context that *gospel preaching* was the focus and goal of all his activity (cf. 1:11–15)' (Peterson 1992: 180).

Eager to preach the gospel in Rome (vv. 15–16)

At the conclusion of his introductory thanksgiving paragraph (vv. 8–17), Paul speaks of his great eagerness to preach the gospel in Rome (v. 15). He knows that he is a debtor to all the Gentiles. In a solemn affirmation he states that he is *under obligation* to those who are 'barbarians' (NRSV) no less than to those who are 'Greeks', to the wise as well as to the foolish (v. 14). In fact, Paul was obligated to Christ who had died for him. But a debt to Christ was transformed 'into a debt to those whom Christ wished to bring to salvation'. Thus, 'obligation to him who died produces obligation to those for whom he died'.[34] Paul's readiness to preach the gospel knew no limits. Further, this eagerness to preach the gospel in Rome is because he is 'not ashamed of the gospel' (v. 16). This apparently weak and foolish message, the content of which centres on Jesus Christ, mediates the almighty power of God that

[32] Molland 1934: 48. *Cf.* Schütz 1975: 40. On the background to Paul's use of *euangelion*, see the Appendix below, p. 271.

[33] Either to Israel's God or to the gods of the nations. It could describe the cultic service of Israel as a whole, and on occasion conveyed 'the idea of fidelity and devotion to God as lord and master in the broadest possible terms' (Peterson 1992: 179–180; *cf.* Deut. 10:12–13; Josh. 24:14–24). However, the terminology was mostly applied in the specific sense of honouring God by ritual observance (*cf.* Exod. 3:12; 2 Sam. 15:8).

[34] Minear 1971: 102–110, esp. 104.

leads to salvation. Paul's confidence lies not in his circumstances but in God who has commissioned him as his accredited apostle and who works mightily through the gospel (cf. Rom. 9:33; 10:1; 1 Cor. 1:27; 2:3; 2 Cor. 10:8; Phil. 1:20).

The Old Testament warrant, content, purpose and saving power of Paul's gospel (Rom. 1)

Promised beforehand in the Old Testament Scriptures (vv. 1–2)

The gospel to which Paul has been set apart and is wholly committed is *God's* gospel – not in the sense that it is the message which speaks about him (*i.e.* an objective genitive), though this is true theologically. Rather, it is his gospel in that he is the source and authority of the message ('of God' is a genitive of origin). He is the one who has acted to bring salvation, to preserve his justice and to work out his purposes in history.

Paul describes this divine proclamation further, and asserts that the gospel promises were 'through [God's] prophets in the holy scriptures'. This expression stresses not only that the Old Testament writings are the *place* where these promises are to be found; it also *anchors the gospel in salvation history*. The Old Testament Scriptures contain the divine promises of the gospel; moreover, they reveal the unfolding purposes of God in significant events of that gospel which are announced, effected and divinely interpreted (*e.g.* the call of Abraham, the exodus from Egypt and that from Babylon). God preserved in these holy writings both the announcements and the unfolding execution of his plan of salvation. At this point in Paul's opening no attempt is made to specify whether any particular scriptures of the Old Testament are in view. Later in his thematic reference (1:16–17) and more detailed exposition (10:14–21; cf. 15:19–20) where he uses *gospel* terminology, the apostle focuses on material from Habakkuk (2:4) and Isaiah (52:7; 53:1; 65:1–2).

The content of the gospel: Jesus Christ, Son of David and risen Son of God (vv. 3–4)

Next a succinct summary of the gospel's content is set forth: it is the message concerning God's Son, who is the seed of David, Messiah and Lord. This important accumulation of titles is a reminder that Paul's gospel cannot be understood apart from the person of Jesus Christ, who by his resurrection has inaugurated the new age of salvation. This highly significant, though compressed, christological statement takes us to the heart of the gospel.

By means of two lines in antithetic parallelism, in which the 'flesh–spirit' contrast of Paul's salvation-historical framework appears, the apostle makes two affirmations about the Son of God: 1. In Jesus' earthly life he was the seed of David, the Messiah (v. 3). He fulfils the prophetic hopes of the people of Israel for the age to come (the promise to David that his seed would have an eternal reign, 2 Sam. 7:12–16, became a particular focus of messianic expectation in the Old Testament: cf. Is. 11; Jer. 23:5–6; 33:14–18; Ezek. 34:23–31; 37:24–28). As such he goes to his death. 2. By virtue of his resurrection Jesus is appointed as Son of God in power (v. 4). With this mighty event the inauguration of the new age has begun. His resurrection fulfils the words of Psalm 2:7, which speak of the coronation of the Davidic king, and in this new stage of God's plan Jesus rules as the powerful, life-giving Son of God. He has become the ruling heir of the nations of Psalm 2:8 (Garlington 1991: 236), and is mightily active to bring salvation to all who believe (cf. 1:16).[35]

Thus, at the centre of the apostolic gospel is the unique Son of God, the mediator of salvation between God and man, who was in his earthly life the seed of David, the Messiah. By his resurrection he has become the powerful Son of God – Jesus Christ, our Lord.

The purpose of the gospel: the risen Christ's rule over the new people of God (v. 5)

The purpose of Paul's missionary commission, as well as that of his apostolic gospel, is 'to bring about the obedience of faith among all the Gentiles[36] for the sake of the name of Christ' (v. 5). The expression 'the obedience of faith (*eis hypakoēn pisteōs*)' is of considerable importance, for it appears again at 16:26 as part of the letter's concluding doxology, and thus forms an *inclusio* with 1:5.[37] This

---

[35] Hurtado (1988: 93–99) interprets Rom. 1:1–4, along with a number of other passages (1 Thess. 1:9–10; 1 Cor. 15:20–28; Phil. 2:5–11; 1 Cor. 8:1–6), as evidence of 'the earliest christological conviction ... that the risen Jesus had been made God's chief agent' (95).

[36] Although the term *ethnē* could mean 'nations' in a strictly geographical sense, this would run 'contrary to the semantic focus of the term in Paul when it is used of the sphere of his apostolic work. Paul's call was not so much to minister in many different nations as it was to minister to Gentiles in distinction from Jews' (Moo 1996: 53).

[37] In both references 'the obedience of faith' is an eschatological reality: it stands in direct relation to 'the prophetic scriptures' and such a response by Gentiles is the purpose for which the revelation of the mystery looked (16:25–26). Note also Rom. 15:18, where the goal of Paul's calling as a missionary is spelled out in terms of the closely related notion: '*for* the obedience of the Gentiles' (emphasis added).

programmatic verse[38] draws attention to the purpose, sphere and person
on whose behalf the totality of Paul's missionary endeavours were
being pursued. 'God is *now* bringing his purposes to pass in salvation
history through Paul's gospel, i.e. the preaching of Jesus Christ
[16:25]' (Garlington 1990: 205, original emphasis). As the apostle
proclaims this authoritative message, 'Jesus, the king of Israel, takes
the nations in captive obedience to himself' (Gen. 49:10; Ps. 2:8–9).
The gospel thus preached is the means 'by which the risen Christ in the
fullness of time asserts his rule over the new people of God'
(Garlington 1990: 203).

The saving power of the gospel (1:16–17; 3:21–26)

Romans 1:16–17. In the thematic statement of Romans the saving
power of the gospel to everyone who believes is forcefully
underscored. Paul shifts the focus from his own ministry (v. 16a), the
very essence of which has been the gospel (vv. 1, 9, 15), to what the
gospel achieves (vv. 16b–17). The ground or reason (*gar*) for his not
being ashamed to confess the gospel is that this apparently weak and
foolish message, the content of which centres on Jesus Christ, mediates
the almighty power of God that leads to salvation. It is not that the
gospel simply speaks about divine power; *it is God's power* leading to
deliverance on the last day.[39]

Here, as elsewhere in his letters, Paul has humanity's relations with
God in view when he uses the 'salvation' word group (*sōzō* and
sōtēria). The terms have primarily an eschatological reference (1 Cor.
5:5; cf. Rom. 5:9–10; 13:11; 1 Cor. 3:15; Phil. 1:28; 2:12; 1 Thess.
5:8–9; 2 Thess. 2:13). Negatively, they speak of a deliverance from
God's wrath in the final judgment (Rom. 5:9) and, positively, of the
reinstatement in that glory of God which was lost through sin (Rom.
8:30). While salvation is usually spoken of in future tenses, Paul can
use a past tense in connection with it (Eph. 2:5, 8; cf. Rom. 8:24), since
the decisive act of God by which the believer's final salvation is
secured has already been accomplished.

The saving power of the gospel needs to be understood in the light of
humanity's dreadful predicament outside of Christ (Rom. 1:18–32).
The world comprising both Jews and Gentiles stands under judgment,
'for the wrath of God is revealed from heaven against all ungodliness

[38] Garlington 1990: 201; 1991: 233–253.
[39] This notion that the message is an effective power (*cf.* 1 Cor. 1:18) is to be
understood in the light of such Old Testament passages concerning the divine word as
Gen. 1:3, 6, *etc.*; Ps. 147:15; Is. 40:8b; 55:10–11; and Jer. 23:29.

and wickedness' of men and women who suppress the truth (v. 18). Whether we follow the traditional view that Paul is describing an ongoing process in which the wrath of God is revealed in the events of human experience, or a revelation of holy anger that occurs in the preaching of the gospel (K. Barth and C. E. B. Cranfield), it is clear that humankind outside of Christ and his gospel lies under divine judgment. In the light of this, the mighty salvation of God by which men and women are delivered from this judgment stands out all the more clearly as being truly glorious.

Paul explains that the gospel is God's saving power to everyone who believes *because* (*gar*) in it there is a revelation of the righteousness of God (*dikaiosynē theou*). The apostle is stating that 'the gospel in some way actually makes manifest, or brings into existence, "the righteousness of God"'.[40] This takes place in the ongoing preaching of the gospel. The passive voice points to the fact that God is the one at work: it is he who brings into existence his righteousness. He is causing his righteousness to be experienced, by Gentiles and Jews who believe.[41] And with special reference to Gentiles, 'Paul's experience of evangelizing ... [them] gives him firm confidence that in the gospel as the power of God to salvation such early converts are being given to see the righteousness of God actually happening, taking effect in their own conversion'.[42] That continuing revelation of God's righteousness 'through the proclamation of the Law-free gospel is bound up with the consummation of his purpose in history' (S. K. Williams 1980: 256).

Romans 3:21–26. The righteousness of God in the gospel that is announced in the thematic statement of 1:16–17 is elaborated in 3:21–26. These verses provide a careful restatement of the former as Paul explains how God's righteousness empowers the gospel to effect salvation for sinful human beings: the saving righteousness of God has

---

[40] Moo 1996: 69. The verb 'reveal' (*apokalyptō*) here denotes the 'uncovering' of God's saving plan, as it unfolds in human history (*cf.* Rom. 2:5; 8:18, 19; 1 Cor. 1:7; Gal. 1:16; 3:23; 2 Thess. 1:7; 2:3, 6, 8).

[41] In spite of lively, diverse and even heated theological debate, no scholarly consensus has been reached as to the meaning of 'the righteousness of God' in Paul – either generally or specifically in this passage. *Dikaiosynē theou* has been taken to refer to 1. *a status given by God* (with *theou* as a genitive of source ['righteousness *from* God'], or an objective genitive ['righteousness that is valid before God']); 2. *an activity of God* (*theou* is a subjective genitive); or 3. *God's justice* or *his faithfulness* – to his covenant with Israel, or to his creation as a whole (*theou* is a possessive genitive), or some combination of these. For recent interactions with the scholarly literature, see S. K. Williams 1980: 241–290; Seifrid 1992: 211–219; Seifrid 2000; Moo 1996: 70–90; and Schreiner 1998: 62–74.

[42] Dunn 1988a: 48. For a recent discussion of the significance of 'from faith to faith', see Schreiner 1998: 71–73.

178

been revealed in Jesus Christ and his atoning death.

A momentous event has just taken place. God has *now* decisively intervened in the human predicament and it has been radically transformed because of his saving act in Jesus Christ (vv. 21–22). A mighty transition from the old era of sin's domination to the new era of salvation has occurred, a transition effected in history at the cross and in the lives of men and women at conversion. God's righteousness 'has been manifested' in this unfolding stage of his saving plan and independently of the Mosaic covenant, though the Old Testament anticipated and paved the way for the new era of fulfilment (v. 21). It is through the faithfulness of Christ, that is, his faithful obedience to death on the cross, that God has manifested his righteousness (v. 22) and opened up the way for all peoples to participate. The universal outreach of God's saving purposes and action is emphasized in the expression 'to all who believe'.

Men and women are justified freely by God's grace at great cost, namely, through the redemption that is in Christ Jesus (v. 24). Paul unfolds the nature and means of this redemption by declaring that God set forth Jesus as a mercy-seat (*hilastērion*; v. 25).[43] Through his sacrificial death on the cross the divine answer to the disastrous human predicament is provided: God's wrath revealed against men and women in their ungodliness and wickedness (1:18) is now turned aside and sin is forgiven. God has therefore shown himself to be just, for, although he had passed over previous sins, he has not compromised his goodness and mercy, since it had been his intention all along to deal with sins decisively and finally through the cross (v. 26c). At the same time, God demonstrates his righteousness even as he justifies sinful men and women who have faith in Jesus. He acquits the guilty, whether they are Jew or Gentile, on the basis of Christ's death. Salvation becomes effective for everyone who believes, both Jew and Gentile. God's covenant promises to Abraham are revealed in this authoritative announcement and find their fulfilment. Gentiles along with Jews become children of Abraham.

Fulfilling the aims of his missionary apostleship: the content of Paul's ministry

At significant points in his letters Paul spells out the goals of his apostleship (1 Cor. 9:19–23; Rom. 1:5; 15:15–16), describing these

[43] So recently Schreiner 1998: 191–194 and Bailey 1999.

aims in a variety of ways. He writes of making himself a slave to everyone 'to win as many as possible', and then explains this in terms of his seeking by all possible means to 'save some' (1 Cor. 9:19, 22). In Romans the overarching goal of his missionary commission is to bring about the obedience of faith among all the Gentiles for the sake of the name of Christ (1:5). Later in the same letter he uses Old Testament cultic language to speak of his priestly duty of proclaiming the gospel of God, the goal of which was 'so that the Gentiles might become an offering acceptable to God, sanctified by the Holy Spirit' (15:16).

But what tasks were included within the scope of Paul's missionary calling as he endeavoured to accomplish these goals? What kinds of activities did he engage in as he sought to fulfil his divine calling as the apostle to the Gentiles? Some have claimed that Paul was *simply* a primary evangelist who chose not to build on anyone else's foundation (Rom. 15:20; cf. 1 Cor. 3:10), but wished to go *only* where the gospel needed to be preached for the first time.

Certainly Paul was engaged in primary evangelism. Whether he speaks of it in terms of the task assigned to him (1 Cor. 1:17), his main line of action in a mission setting (Gal. 4:13), or what he would like to do in the future (2 Cor. 10:16), the apostle clearly regarded primary evangelism as integral to his mission. That he 'perceives his role as initiatory in nature is apparent as well in the specific metaphors he applies to his vocation',[44] namely, planting (1 Cor. 3:6–9; 9:7, 10, 11), laying foundations (Rom. 15:20; 1 Cor. 3:10), giving birth (1 Cor. 4:15; Philem. 10) and betrothing (2 Cor. 11:2).

But the apostle not only proclaimed the gospel and, under God, converted men and women. He also founded churches as a necessary element in his missionary task. Conversion to Christ meant incorporation into him, and thus membership within a Christian community. The apostle's letters are addressed to such churches. Indeed, the existence of these congregations Paul regards as an authentication of his apostleship (1 Cor. 9:2; 2 Cor. 3:1–3; cf. Bowers 1987: 187–188). From his *practice* of residential missions (at Corinth and Ephesus) and nurture of churches (1 Thess. 2:10–12), from his *priorities* (1 Thess. 2:17 – 3:13; 2 Cor. 2:12–13; 10:13–16), and from his *description of his assignment* (Rom. 1:1–15; 15:14–16; Eph. 3:8–9; Col. 1:24 – 2:7) in relation to admonition and teaching believers to bring them to full maturity in Christ, it is clear that *the nurture of*

---

[44] Bowers (1987: 186), to whose insightful paper (185–198) we are indebted; *cf.* Howell 1998: 70–73.

emerging churches is understood by Paul to be 'an integral feature of his missionary task'.[45]

This conclusion about the wide-ranging content of Paul's ministry is supported by four key passages, several of which describe the aims of his missionary commission to the Gentiles, as outlined below.

Winning as many as possible (1 Cor. 9:19–23)

Here Paul expresses the stance which characterized his whole missionary career. Five times he employs the well-known missionary term *kerdainō* indicating that he aims to 'gain' or 'win' the many, that is, Jews, those under the law, those not under law and weak Christians (vv. 19–22), while in the general sentence of verse 22 he uses the more common synonym *sōzō* ('save'). Although the verb to 'win' has been taken to refer to Paul's goal of *converting* 'as many as possible' (v. 19), including Jews and Gentiles (vv. 20–21), it cannot refer only to their conversion, since in verse 22 he speaks of his aim of winning 'the weak', a designation which should be understood of Christians (rather than non-Christians; cf. Rom. 5:6) whose consciences trouble them about matters which are not in themselves wrong (cf. 1 Cor. 8). Paul's goal of winning Jews, Gentiles and weak Christians has to do with their full maturity in Christ and thus signifies *winning them completely*. To win Gentiles has to do with his ultimate purpose for them, namely, their being brought to perfection in Christ on the final day. Nothing short of this will fulfil Paul's ambitions for them. Similarly, his goal of winning 'weak' Christians has to do with their full maturity and blamelessness at the second coming. On this interpretation *kerdainō* has a consistent meaning throughout the paragraph.

Further, the parallel verb to 'save' (v. 22), which usually has a future orientation in Paul's letters, is best understood as meaning to 'save from the coming wrath on the final day', and so to 'save [completely]', not simply to 'convert'. 'Win' or 'save' then speaks not only of the initial activity whereby a person comes to faith, but of the whole process by which a Jew, a Gentile or a weak Christian is converted and brought to glory. This understanding of the apostle's words harmonizes with his statements elsewhere in which he anticipates his converts being his joy and crown as they stand fast on the final day, demonstrating that he has not run in vain in his ministry (2 Cor. 1:14; Gal. 2:2; Phil. 2:16; 4:1; 1 Thess. 2:19).

---

[45] Bowers 1987: 188–197, esp. 197; note also Howell 1998: 73–76.

The 'obedience of faith' (Rom. 1:5)

In this important phrase, which occurs within a description of Paul's missionary commission (see above), the key terms 'faith' and 'obedience' appear. Many regard them as equivalents.[46] But while there is obviously a close relationship between the two concepts, with similar assertions being made about each in Romans,[47] they are not identical. Perhaps the best rendering of the original is 'faith's obedience' (or 'believing obedience', with 'of faith' [*pisteōs*] being an adjectival genitive).[48]

Nevertheless, the immediate context of Romans 1:5,[49] the flow of the argument in chapters 1 – 8,[50] together with other instances in Paul's letters of the language of obedience which refer to Christian behaviour, all indicate that the apostle has in view the believer's total response to the gospel, not simply his or her initial conversion. The phrase 'captures the full dimension of Paul's apostolic task, a task that was not confined to initial evangelization but that included also the building up and firm establishment of churches' (Moo 1996: 53). This notion of a total response accords well with the parallel expression of 15:18, 'the obedience of the Gentiles' (NRSV), which focuses not simply on the nations coming to faith or their acceptance of the gospel, but on their initial response *and* constancy in Christian conduct as well.

Preaching the gospel to Christians in Rome (Rom. 1:15–16)

Paul writes of his enthusiasm to preach the gospel *in the city* of Rome and its environs, where there were undoubtedly many non-Christians.

---

[46] So that 'of faith' (*pisteōs*) is treated as a genitive of apposition. Commentators who make the identification between the two nouns include Barrett, Calvin, Cranfield, Käsemann, Murray, Ridderbos, Sanday and Headlam, Schlier and Wilckens.

[47] Rom. 1:8 with 16:19; 10:16a with 16b; 11:23 with 30, 31; 1:5 with 15:18.

[48] This preserves the apparently deliberate ambiguity of the original that denotes 'an obedience which consists in faith and an obedience which finds its source in faith' (Garlington 1990: 224).

[49] Paul includes the Roman Christians in 1:6 within the scope of his apostolic commission to promote 'the obedience of faith' – and they were already believers. His earnest desire to impart some spiritual gift so that his and their *faith* might be mutually strengthened (vv. 11–12) can be understood only of the advance of those already committed to Christ, while the 'harvest' (*karpos*) he wishes to reap among them probably has to do with their progress in the faith as well as the conversion of other Gentiles in the surrounding area. Similarly, his obligation and eagerness to preach the gospel in Rome (vv. 14–15) seems to mean more than the conversion of non-Christians to the faith.

[50] Where Paul's discussion of justification by faith is followed by the demand that those who are righteous before God pursue righteousness of life and sanctification.

182

However, his precise wording is *'to you also*[51] who are in Rome', which includes *the recipients* of the letter who have already been described as believers (cf. v. 8). In what sense, then, does he 'preach the gospel' to Christians? First, both context[52] and Pauline usage[53] require that the verb *euangelizomai* be understood here as meaning to 'preach the gospel', not to 'proclaim' or 'preach' in a general sense. Secondly, although this verb is often taken to include only initial or primary evangelism, Paul employs the *euangelion* word-group to cover the whole range of evangelistic and teaching ministry – from the initial proclamation of the gospel to the building up of believers and grounding them firmly in the faith.

On occasion, when the apostle harks back to his own preaching of the *kerygma* in the founding of churches, an evangelizing activity which aims at conversions is specially in mind (cf. 1 Cor. 4:15). But Paul did not understand his apostolic separation for the gospel (Rom. 1:1; cf. 1 Cor. 1:17) or his service in the gospel (Rom. 1:9) solely in terms of its initial proclamation. The gospel is not simply 'the initial impulse on the way to salvation' (Dunn 1988a: 34). It is the message by which men and women are finally saved. The Christian life is certainly created through the gospel (1 Cor. 4:15; Col. 1:5–6); but it is also lived in the sphere of this dynamic and authoritative message (cf. Phil. 1:27). It needs therefore to be preached to those who have already received it and become Christians. Believers do not leave the gospel behind or progress beyond it as they grow and mature in their faith. They stand fast in this *kerygma* and are being saved through it if they hold firmly

[51] Gk. *kai hymin*. It could be 'among you' if the preposition *en* is taken as original. But even this does not alleviate the problem for the expression has to do with results within the Christian community whatever else it may imply in relation to the general population in the capital.
[52] Here in v. 15, where the verb *euangelizomai* appears, it is the proclamation of the gospel that is in view, rather than some general activity of preaching. This is made clear in the immediately following words (v. 16) where Paul explains the reason for his eagerness: *'for* I am not ashamed of the gospel (*euangelion*)', NRSV (emphasis added).
[53] Paul's normal usage of the verb *euangelizomai* is against the general meaning of 'preach'. This verb, which focuses on 'the central missionary nature of [his] apostolic activity' (Schütz 1975: 39), is used by the apostle twenty-one times (Rom. 1:15; 10:15; 15:20; 1 Cor. 1:17; 9:16 [twice], 18; 15:1, 2; 2 Cor. 10:16; 11:7; Gal. 1:8 [twice], 9, 11, 16, 23; 4:13; Eph. 2:17; 3:8; 1 Thess. 3:6). Often it is employed specifically with 'gospel' as its object (1 Cor. 15:1; 2 Cor. 11:7; Gal. 1:11). But even in those contexts where the cognate noun is not present, the notion of proclaiming the gospel is in view (*cf.* Rom. 10:15 with 10:16; 2 Cor. 10:16; Gal. 4:13; 1:8; and Rom. 15:20 in the light of v. 19). Paul knows that he has been sent by Christ *to proclaim the gospel* (1 Cor. 1:17; 9:16–18). One may conclude that 'in almost every instance the verb *euangelizesthai* seems to presuppose the definition of its cognate noun' (Schütz 1975: 39). Note also his treatment of Gal. 1:9, 16, 23 and 1 Thess. 3:6.

to it (1 Cor. 15:1–2), for it is in this authoritative announcement that true hope is held out to them (Col. 1:5, 23).[54]

Paul's language, then, points to both primary evangelism and a full exposition of the gospel. The difficult expression, 'to you also', like the parallel 'among you' (v. 13), is employed rather loosely and is not limited exclusively to the readers. Accordingly, his apostolic labours will result in edification for the Roman Christians and conversions among others in the capital.

Fulfilling the gospel of Christ (Rom. 15:19)

Paul's amazing claim, 'I have fulfilled the gospel of Christ' (NRSV), is best understood along similar lines. The text cannot mean that he has preached the gospel to every single person 'from Jerusalem all the way around to Illyricum' or even to all the small towns and country districts of the lands he had evangelized. Bowers asks the question in relation to Paul's claim to have 'fulfilled the gospel': in what sort of activity would Paul 'need to engage in order to arrive at this sense of accomplishment'? His response is: 'Paul's missionary vocation finds its sense of fulfillment in the presence of firmly established churches' (Bowers 1987: 198). Proclaiming the gospel meant for Paul not simply an initial preaching or with it the reaping of converts; it included also a whole range of nurturing and strengthening activities which led to the firm establishment of congregations. So, his claim to have 'fulfilled the gospel in an arc right up to Illyricum' signified that he had established strong churches in strategic centres of this area, such as Thessalonica, Corinth and Ephesus. Further evangelistic outreach and the upbuilding of congregations lay in the hands of others. But for the apostle there was no more place for him to work in these regions, and thus he was 'free' to go up to Jerusalem and move on to Spain via Rome.

To conclude, then: the activities in which Paul engaged as he sought to fulfil his missionary commission included not only primary evangelism, through which men and women were converted, but also the founding of churches and the bringing of believers to full maturity in Christ.

---

[54] Cf. a similar usage in support of a wide-ranging series of activities being subsumed under the notion of preaching the gospel at Eph. 3:8, where God's grace given to Paul consisted in his 'bringing the Gentiles the good news (euangelisasthai) of Christ's unfathomable wealth'. Also in Col. 1:28 the public proclamation (note the parallel katangellō) of Christ as Lord is explained and developed in the subsequent words about admonition and instruction, for it is through the ongoing teaching and warning of each person that the proclamation of Christ is carried out.

Paul, the apostle to the Gentiles, and Israel in God's plan

In his key thematic statement of Romans 1 Paul declares that the gospel is the power of God for salvation *to everyone* who believes (v. 16). A note of particularism, however, is introduced immediately after this universal statement: the promises of God realized in the gospel are 'to the Jew first and then to the Greek [*i.e.* Gentile]'.[55] This priority is in line with the divine promises to Abraham and the fathers, which are foundational to God's redemptive plan (Gen. 12:1–3; cf. Is. 49:6; Rom. 9 – 11). As 'the apostle to the Gentiles' (Rom. 11:13), Paul recognized this divine priority and regularly followed the pattern of 'to the Jew first' in his missionary proclamation (Acts 18:4–6, 19; 19:8). His practice of going to the synagogue first was not driven simply by pragmatic considerations, as though he used the place where Jews regularly gathered solely as a launching pad for preaching the gospel to Gentiles.

But if the adverb 'first' draws attention to Israel's special role in salvation history, the following words, 'and also for the Greek', suggest 'the fundamental equality of Jew and Gentile in the face of the gospel' (Cranfield 1975: 91). Much of the letter to the Romans, particularly chapters 9 – 11, is given over to relating these two connected strands of universalism and particularism.

There is, however, a fundamental problem that the apostle addresses in these chapters, namely, why has Israel failed to respond to the gospel? Paul's great burden for his own people is clearly evident throughout. His 'heart's desire and prayer to God for the Israelites is that they may be saved' (10:1). Indeed, if it were possible he could wish that he himself were cursed and cut off from Christ for the sake of his brothers, those of his own race, the people of Israel (9:3). What is more, the promises of God would seem to have failed (cf. 9:6). Accordingly, God's plan for his people, Israel, and its relationship to the salvation of Gentiles, together with Paul's apostleship to the latter, are of singular importance to chapters 9 – 11.

In response to the suggestion that God's promises to his people have failed Paul shows, first of all, that 'not all who are descended from

[55] The term *Hellēn* ('Greek') here indicates broadly a non-Jew (a person who is a Gentile in view of being a Greek; *cf.* Louw and Nida §11.40). Although *Hellēn* is used in a more restricted sense in Rom. 1:14 and Col. 3:11 (which distinguishes Greeks from barbarians), here in Rom. 1:16 and the rest of Romans (2:9,10; 3:9; 10:12) the term designates non-Jews (Schreiner 1998: 62).

Israel are Israel' (9:6). Salvation was never promised in God's plan to every individual Israelite: he chose Isaac rather than Ishmael (vv. 7–9) and Jacob rather than Esau (vv. 10–13). God has complete freedom to show mercy as both Moses (9:15; Exod. 33:19) and Hosea (3:1, 5, LXX) had testified. Accordingly, he has called a new people to himself, comprising both Jews and Gentiles (Rom. 9:24), a plan that was anticipated in the Old Testament.[56]

If in Romans 9:6–29 Paul stresses the electing purpose of God, then 9:30 – 10:21 addresses the same issue from another perspective – Israel's failure to believe. Paul asks why Gentiles in such large numbers have come into a right standing with God, while Israel as a whole has not reached it (9:30 – 10:4). Gentiles have obtained righteousness by faith in response to the gospel message, but the people of Israel who have a genuine zeal for God tried to establish their own righteousness instead of submitting to the righteousness of God. They pursued the law in the wrong way, 'as from works' instead of by faith (9:31–32). Consequently, they stumbled over God's stone (Christ) and failed to believe in him. Although they heard 'the word of faith' from accredited preachers of the gospel they did not believe the message. The nation remained disobedient, despite God's patience and mercy.

In the context of a sharp contrast between the righteousness of the law and that of faith (10:5–13), Paul states that those who belong to the people of God, whether Jews or Gentiles, believe the gospel message that Jesus is Lord and confess that God has raised him from the dead (10:9–10). This message is available to all and is universally proclaimed. Ultimately, there is no distinction 'between Jew and Gentile – the same Lord is Lord of all and richly blesses all who call on him, for, "Everyone who calls on the name of the Lord will be saved"' (vv. 12–13). Through a series of rhetorical questions the apostle outlines the steps that are necessary to believe the gospel of Christ and to call on him as Lord (vv. 14–17). In the process Paul lays out fundamental principles for the work of mission (Chae 1997: 249). One cannot call on the name of the Lord without believing in him, and to do this men and women must hear of him. But they cannot hear unless someone proclaims the message to them, and for this to occur preachers need to be sent. In Romans 10:15 Paul quotes Isaiah 52:7 ('How beautiful are the feet of those who bring good news!') to show that messengers have been sent and the gospel has been proclaimed.

The great tragedy is that Israel has heard the message of the gospel –

[56] In relation to Gentiles, Hos. 2:23; 1:10 (Rom. 9:25–26) and to Jews, Is. 10:22–23; 1:9 (Rom. 9:27–29).

since it has been proclaimed to the ends of the earth (v. 18) – but has refused to believe it. Further, the nation should have known from the Old Testament that Gentiles would be included among God's people (v. 19). It was God's plan to reveal himself to those who did not seek him (v. 20) and so to provoke Israel to jealousy by including Gentiles within the sphere of his blessing.[57]

One might conclude that because Israel has been so stubborn God would finally reject his people (11:1). But Paul emphatically repudiates this suggestion: the presence of a 'remnant' chosen by grace testifies to the truth that God has not cast off his people (e.g. Deut. 31:6; Ps. 37:28, etc.). There has always been a remnant throughout history by God's electing grace, and it continues to the present. Paul's own membership of the people of God is concrete evidence of this (v. 1). The 'rest', that is the majority of Israel, however, were hardened in their sin and excluded from God's righteousness (11:7–10). The Old Testament bears witness to this hardening. Accordingly, 'Paul presently ministers in an era in which Israel is hardened and only a remnant is being saved' (Schreiner 1998: 532).

But the 'rejection' of Israel as a whole is not God's last word to his people: it is neither total (vv. 1–10) nor final (vv. 11–32). In fact, Israel's repudiation of the blessings of the gospel has led to salvation reaching the Gentiles and thus to the whole world (vv. 11–12; cf. Moo 1996: 683). This is not to suggest that God changed his salvation plan (Chae 1997: 260–261) so as to direct his saving blessings to the Gentiles. It was his plan from of old to bless 'all peoples on earth' (cf. Gen. 12:3). But if Israel's temporary hardening has led to Gentiles streaming into the people of God, and riches and reconciliation coming to the whole world, then what will Israel's fulness and acceptance be? Nothing less than 'vast riches' and 'life from the dead' (vv. 12, 15).[58]

Paul therefore glorifies his ministry as 'the apostle to the Gentiles' (11:13). He hopes that it will flourish so that his preaching of the gospel will bring more and more Gentiles to salvation, and as a result some Jews, that is, his own 'flesh and blood', will be provoked to jealousy and ultimately saved.[59] Paul's apostolic ministry is clearly

[57] 'God continues to stretch out his hands to Israel, imploring them to be saved. But Israel obstinately resists God's gracious advances' (Schreiner 1998: 532).

[58] 'Paul expects a far greater blessing upon the Gentiles when Israel experiences the fullness of the blessing of the gospel' (Chae 1997: 283).

[59] Although Cranfield, Morris and others have thought that Paul saw himself as the figure whom God would use to bring Israel to its destined 'fullness', the language 'some [Jews]' does not suggest this (cf. Moo 1996: 692).

related to Israel, but this does not mean his commission is ultimately given for the sake of Israel, as it is sometimes claimed.[60]

After warning Gentile believers not to become arrogant towards the Jews (11:17–24), the apostle turns to rehearse God's salvation-historical drama in which Israel and the Gentiles take turns on centre stage (vv. 25–32). This paragraph is the climax not only of 11:11–32, but also of Romans 9 – 11 (Moo 1996: 712), for here is a resolution of the problem raised by Israel's hardness of heart (v. 28a; 9:1–3) and God's unchangeable promises to his people (v. 28b; cf. 9:4–5; 11:1–2). The special significance of this salvation-historical restatement is underscored by its introduction as a 'mystery'. Three elements make up this mystery (vv. 25b–26a):[61] 1. 'Israel has experienced a hardening in part'; 2. 'until the full number of the Gentiles has come in'; 3. 'And so all Israel will be saved.' What particularly stands out as something new in Paul's argument (and is therefore the particular focus of the 'mystery' here), which involves a reversal in current Jewish belief, [62] is 'the sequence in which "all Israel" will be saved: Israel hardened *until* the Gentiles come in and *in this way* all Israel being saved'.[63] It is as if the order of the divine mission has effectively become 'to the Gentile first and also to the Jew'.

According to the apostle, Israel's hostility towards God and her refusal to believe the gospel (cf. 9:30 – 10:21) is itself part of the divine plan, for God has hardened them (cf. 11:7–10). This hardening, however, is both limited ('in part', v. 25b; cf. 11:3–7) and temporary ('until', v. 25b), so as to allow the Gentiles to 'come in' (v. 25b; cf. 11:11–15) and to provoke Israel to repentance (vv. 26, 27; cf. v. 11). With the arrival of 'the full number of the Gentiles' into the kingdom of God, that is, the messianic salvation, the removal of Israel's hardening is signalled. The Gentiles' 'fullness', a notion which derives from Jewish apocalyptic, involves a numerical completion. Those who become members of the people of God through faith in the Lord Jesus Christ 'are the branches who are being grafted on to the olive tree in such great numbers' (Schreiner 1998: 617).

---

[60] *Cf.* J. M. Scott (1993: 799), who thinks that the gospel Paul was commissioned to proclaim was 'the good news of Israel's restoration'. Note the criticisms of Chae 1997: 283.

[61] Paul specifies its content in three separate clauses introduced by a *hoti* clause ('that', v. 25). Many scholars have failed to see that the mystery also relates to the Gentiles, and not simply to the fact that 'all Israel will be saved'. See the discussions in Moo 1996: 712–717; Chae 1997: 272–284; and Schreiner 1998: 612–615.

[62] Stuhlmacher 1994: 171–172; Byrne 1996: 350; and Schreiner 1998: 617.

[63] Moo 1996: 716, following Wilckens and Beker.

The third element of the mystery, 'and so all Israel will be saved' (v. 26a), is the most difficult to interpret and has been a 'storm centre' in the history of the interpretation of Romans 9 – 11.[64]

1. We note that although the words 'and so' (*kai houtōs*) have been taken in a temporal sense ('and then'),[65] or as expressing consequence ('and as a result' of this process),[66] it is preferable to understand it as signifying the way or manner in which Israel would be saved ('and in this manner'),[67] that is, in accord with the process outlined in verses 11–24, and summarized in verse 25b.

2. For some, the expression 'all Israel' signifies the community of the elect, Jews and Gentiles who have believed in Jesus the Messiah.[68] But this does not fit with Paul's use of the term 'Israel' throughout the rest of chapter 11. Accordingly, most exegetes think that the expression signifies the nation of Israel as a whole, though not referring to every Jew without exception.[69] The promise, it is claimed, is that Israel will be saved as a people. It is just possible, however, that Paul is referring to 'the elect within Israel', a usage found in Romans 9:6b, 'not all who are descended from Israel [*i.e.* the nation] are Israel [the elect]'. If 'Israel' denotes the elect among Israel throughout time in 11:26, then the apostle is asserting that all elect Jews would be saved. Although this has been dismissed as a truism,[70] it does not necessarily follow if Paul has in mind the *manner* in which all Israel will be saved rather than the *fact* of its being saved.[71] The difficulty that still remains,

---

[64] Limitations of space prevent a detailed discussion of this highly disputed expression. For recent treatments of the exegetical and theological issues involved, including interactions with earlier scholarship and further bibliographical details, see Moo 1996: 719–726; Chae 1997: 272–282; Schreiner 1998: 614–623; and Wagner 1999: 341–351.

[65] In other words, Israel is hardened until the fullness of the Gentiles enters in *and then* all Israel will be saved. So Barrett and Käsemann, among others. The decisive objection against this interpretation is that a temporal meaning of *houtōs* is not found elsewhere in Greek.

[66] As a result of this process all Israel will be saved. *Cf.* Dodd, Fitzmyer and Kim, *etc.*

[67] So many commentators, including Sanday and Headlam, Cranfield, Dunn, Byrne, Moo and Wright. Note Moo's defence (1996: 719–720).

[68] This view, which harks back to Augustine, has been held by Calvin (together with many Continental Protestant theologians), J. Jeremias, R. P. Martin and N. T. Wright. Wright thinks that Gentiles 'enter' Israel, according to 11:25 (1991: 250–251).

[69] Paul writes 'all Israel', not 'every Israelite', and the difference is significant.

[70] By definition, it is argued, all the elect will be saved. Schreiner (1998: 617) dismisses this interpretation of the mystery as 'stunningly anticlimactic'. He thinks that the salvation of the remnant fits with Paul's argument in Rom. 9 and 11:1–10, but 11:11–24 suggests that 'something more than the salvation of the remnant awaits Israel'.

[71] A point Moo (1996: 722) brings out, even though he 'inclines slightly to the view that Israel in v. 26a refers to the nation generally'. Among the advocates of 'the elect

however, is the shift in the meaning of 'Israel' from the nation that is partially hardened in verse 25b to the elect in verse 26a.

3. As to the time and manner of all Israel's salvation, most claim that Paul places this event at the end when there will be a great ingathering of Jews prior to the second coming of Jesus, and after the full number of the Gentiles has entered into the people of God. This is believed to line up with the mention of Israel's 'fullness' (v. 12), 'acceptance' (v. 15) and the grafting in of the natural branches (v. 24) which contrasts with the nation's situation at the present time, and therefore must be a future event. Moreover, since Israel's current hardening will be reversed when the fullness of the Gentiles have come in, and it is unlikely that the latter's salvation would have ceased before the end, Israel's salvation must occur just before the return of the Lord Jesus. The citation of Scripture (Is. 59:20–21; 27:9) in verses 26–27 is thought to support this interpretation. Moo concludes:

> Paul's language in Rom. 11 seems deliberately calculated to restate [the] traditional hope for Israel's renewal. His point seems to be that the present situation in salvation history, in which so few Jews are being saved, cannot finally do full justice to the scriptural expectations about Israel's future. Something 'more' is to be expected; and this 'more,' Paul implies, is a large-scale conversion of Jewish people at the end of this age.[72]

However, a caveat about the timing of Israel's salvation needs to be entered. Paul's mention of the temporal sequence of the salvation of Gentiles and Israel does not necessarily mean the latter will not occur before the return of Christ in glory. Some Jews are already experiencing God's saving blessings. The 'now' of verses 30–31 indicates that (some) Jews will receive divine mercy in the present, and not simply before the parousia. Otherwise, Paul's concern to provoke Israel to jealousy and to save some through his own ministry (11:14; 1 Cor. 9:16, 19–23) would be meaningless (Chae 1997: 275–276).

What does emerge clearly, regardless of one's view of the precise timing, is that the salvation of Israel in the last days vindicates God's

---

within Israel' view are D. W. B. Robinson 1967: 94–95 and Ridderbos 1975: 358–359; and *cf.* Dumbrell 1994: 278–279.

[72] Moo 1996: 774. While acknowledging one cannot be precise about the 'exact timing of the conversion of Israel in comparison with other events of the end times', he believes that because it will take place after the salvation of the elect Gentiles 'it will be closely associated with the return of Christ in glory' (724–725).

impartiality (v. 32). At the conclusion of Romans 9 – 11 Paul again underscores the equality of Jew and Gentile in the saving plan of God. This is entirely coherent with the earlier parts of the letter where he has been at pains to show that there is a 'fundamental equality of Jew and Gentile in sinfulness (1:18 – 3:20), in justification (3:21 – 4:25), in the new status (Rom. 5 – 8)' (Chae 1997: 285). At the same time, as Robinson has claimed, the fullness of the Gentiles and the salvation of all Israel correspond 'to the two arms of the divine purpose to be achieved through the Servant of the Lord as foretold in Isaiah 49:6'.[73] The Servant's mission was not only to restore the tribes of Jacob and to raise up the preserved of Israel, but also to be a light to lighten the Gentiles and to carry God's salvation to the ends of the earth. The mystery about which Paul writes is 'that the Gentiles are both the beneficiaries of the Israelites' lapse and also the means of the salvation of those very Israelites' (D. W. B. Robinson 1967: 93).

It is no surprise, then, that Paul bursts into joy and admiration for God's merciful plan that is all of a piece with his equal dealing with Jew and Gentile for their salvation in the Lord Jesus Christ (11:33–36) (Chae 1997: 273).

The place of believers within the Pauline mission

Although the apostle makes a number of important statements in his letters about his own missionary calling and its place within God's purposes (and in this endeavour his co-workers are linked with him),[74] he does not seem, at first glance, to say a great deal about how the Christians in his congregations were to carry on his work or to be caught up with his mission and so be involved in these saving purposes of God.[75] How did Paul understand his missionary activity in relation to that of others? What are the links, if any, between his own dynamic endeavours and those of his fellow-believers? He is certainly aware and approves of the work which other Christians are doing (cf. Rom. 15:18–21). But what is his understanding of their activity in relation to his own? A related question is this: why is so little written in the Pauline letters about the need for Christians to evangelize? In an attempt to come to grips with these issues we note the following.

[73] D. W. B. Robinson 1967: 88, cited by Dumbrell 1994: 279.

[74] See especially Ollrog 1979 and E. E. Ellis 1993: 183–189.

[75] Zeller 1982: 164 claims that while Paul develops a theological understanding of his own mission, he does not expand upon that of other missionaries or other church situations.

The advance of the gospel

Paul often goes out of his way to stress the dynamic, almost personal, character of the gospel (*euangelion*; O'Brien 1974–75: 144–55). It is well-known that *gospel* within the Pauline corpus signifies not only the content of what is preached, but also the act or process of the proclamation (*euangelion* is a noun of agency). The two are closely related and in the very act of proclamation the gospel's content becomes a reality. But, in addition, Paul speaks of the gospel as a force or agency able to accomplish something, and which has a purpose towards which it moves.[76]

When the apostle refers to the fulfilment of the divine purposes, instead of focusing on what men and women are doing, he regularly highlights this *powerful advance of the gospel*. It is the divine work that the apostle frequently stresses and, although the evangelistic endeavours of Christians are mentioned from time to time, this is not where he usually puts the emphasis. So in Colossians 1 *euangelion* is a mighty, personal force working powerfully in the lives of men and women. It had come to the Colossian Christians (v. 6) and remained with them, having a firm place in their lives. Like the seed in the parable of the sower it continued to produce a vigorous fruit (Luke 8:15), not only among the Colossians themselves (Col. 1:10) but also in the rest of the world. 'Fruit-bearing' is to be understood as a crop of good deeds (cf. Phil. 1:11), while the growth of the gospel points to the increasing number of converts. The dynamic character of the gospel is accented also in 1 Thessalonians 1. Although Paul might well have written 'we came with the gospel' (cf. 2 Cor. 10:14), by stating 'our gospel came' (v. 5), he puts the emphasis on the activity of the message. The manner of its coming was truly awesome, for it was not simply in word but also 'in power and in the Holy Spirit and with full conviction'. Gospel is again regarded as a personal, living force (cf. 2:13).

An important reference in this regard is 2 Thessalonians 3:1–2, where the apostle requests his Christian friends as follows: 'brothers, pray for us'. The content of the petition is not that Paul and his colleagues may speak the word of the gospel boldly and clearly, though he might well have requested this (cf. Eph. 6:19; Col. 4:3–4); rather, it is that 'the word of the Lord may spread rapidly and be glorified everywhere, just as it is among you' (NRSV). The apostle and others will be engaged in

---

[76] In 1 Cor. 9:23 *euangelion* is employed in this dynamic sense as Paul refers to his own participation in the gospel's powerful advance (*cf.* Schütz 1975: 51–52).

preaching, but the stress is on the dynamic march of the gospel itself.[77]

Philippians 1:14–18 bears important testimony to the work of evangelism by Christian men and women in the city of Paul's imprisonment, which was probably Rome. The apostle writes confidently to his dear friends at Philippi, who had been deeply concerned about his welfare, to assure them that the things that had happened to him, namely, his imprisonment, sufferings and personal inconveniences, had surprisingly contributed to the *progress* (*prokopē*) of the gospel. That dynamic advance, which was of paramount importance to Paul, since he read his own circumstances in the light of it, is described in two ways. First, outside the Christian community his arrest and confinement were understood to be because of his union with Christ. He was not in prison as a political or civil wrong-doer; instead, his detention was a demonstration or manifestation of Christ's saving activity and thus contributed to the spread of the gospel among those who made up the praetorian guard, as well as among other Gentiles (v. 13). Secondly, others within the Christian fellowship had been given fresh stimulus for the work of evangelism (v. 14). The majority of believers in the city had already been proclaiming Christ before Paul arrived there. But now with his imprisonment their confidence in the Lord had been strengthened by his example and they had been encouraged to testify to Christ more courageously. Clearly, the preaching of the gospel is a highly significant motif in this paragraph, and Paul knows of its progress in the capital because of what he had observed.

Several important points emerge from this passage: first, the apostle's reference to Christians in Rome engaging in evangelism appears to be an incidental one, but is all the more significant for that reason. As Paul writes to his Philippian friends he expresses no surprise that these believers should engage in active outreach for the gospel. Secondly, these Christians were already evangelizing prior to his arrival in the city. Now, through Paul's witness in prison, they are galvanized into speaking the word of God with 'greater boldness and without fear'. Thirdly, the apostle obviously approved of this energetic activity. He rejoices when their resolve to evangelize is strengthened (from whatever motives: vv. 15, 17–18), and he regards their proclamation of Christ as a significant element in the advance of the gospel.

[77] In fact, the apostle has gone out of his way to make this point emphatically, for in 3:2 he swings back to the first-person-plural subject, 'and that *we* may be delivered from wicked and evil men'.

Partnership in the gospel

Several times the apostle, either by way of commendation or exhortation, refers to the Philippians' commitment to the gospel: '[I am grateful] for your active participation (*koinōnia*) in the gospel from the first day until now' (Phil. 1:5, author's translation). Although the term *koinōnia* has been taken in a passive sense, so that the whole phrase, 'your participation in the gospel', is regarded as equivalent to 'your faith' and means that they had received the *kerygma*, it is better to understand the word in an active sense, signifying 'your co-operation [in promoting] the gospel'. Paul has in mind a dynamic endeavour on the part of the Philippians. Their active partnership was with him in his ministry of the word of life to Gentiles and is to be understood in a broad sense. This co-operation is not limited to their financial help, though clearly it was in the apostle's mind, since it was referred to in verse 3 (cf. 4:15–18), and was a signal instance of their participation (*koinōnia*).

In addition to their involvement in Paul's endeavours, the Philippians were engaged in the 'same struggle' (*agōn*) for the gospel as he was (1:30), albeit *in Philippi*, and so their contending for the spread and growth of the faith signified evangelistic outreach. Likewise, their holding fast the word of life, in which Paul encourages them (2:16), included among other things their letting this explosive message have its dynamic way in and through their lives as it made its triumphal progress in Philippi. Moreover, their 'participation' also included their actual proclamation of the gospel message to outsiders (1:27, 30) and their suffering along with Paul for the gospel's sake (cf. 1:30; 4:14–15). It also included their intercessory activity on his behalf (cf. 1:19), an endeavour in which the apostle knew they were engaged at the time of his writing to them.

Paul as a model for believers

The apostle presented himself on a number of occasions in his letters as a model to be followed by his readers.[78] According to A. J. Malherbe, 'Paul's method of shaping a community was to gather converts around himself and by his own behavior to demonstrate what he taught' (Malherbe 1987: 52). In this he was following a method widely

---

[78] 1 Cor. 4:16; 10:31 – 11:1; Phil. 3:15, 17; 4:9; *cf.* 2:17; 1 Thess. 1:6; 2:14; 2 Thess. 3:7–9. For a recent examination together with bibliographical details, see Clarke 1998: 329–360.

practised by the moral philosophers, in particular. The teacher as example provided a moral paradigm.[79]

When he reminded his Christian friends of his pattern of behaviour,[80] Paul did so for practical and exhortatory purposes, since he had an ethical dimension in view. To the Philippians his example served to underscore the central exhortation of the letter ('Now, the important thing is this: live as citizens of heaven in a manner that is worthy of the gospel of Christ', Phil. 1:27; O'Brien 1992: 273–284), an injunction which is part of the leading proposition that they should stand firm in the gospel (1:27–30). However, given the close connection between the apostle's life-style and the gospel he proclaims (cf. Phil. 1:12–26; 1 Thess. 2:1–12), one may question whether there was something more to Paul's being a pattern. Did it involve a commitment to the spread of the gospel as well?

Of particular significance in this regard is 1 Corinthians 11:1, 'Follow my example, as I follow the example of Christ.' Within the context of chapters 9 – 11, and especially in the light of Paul's 'defence' in chapter 9:19–23, it is clear that the apostle's earnest desire and goal of saving men and women was an essential element in the servant pattern he adopted ('I make myself a slave to everyone, so that I might win as many as possible', 1 Cor. 9:19). Paul was committed to the good of others and he defines this in terms of saving them (10:33).

Within this stance that characterized his whole missionary career (1 Cor. 9:19–23), Paul makes the following points: first, the basis for his flexible conduct in a variety of (social) settings lay in his *freedom in Christ* and his total gospel orientation. He speaks of himself 'as being free' (v. 19), as 'not under the law' (v. 20), as 'not free from God's law but under Christ's law' (v. 21). Most interpreters agree that these four clauses are concessive ('Though I am free', *etc.*; cf. NIV, RSV, JB) with the expressions indicating Paul's freedom from the law, especially in matters of Jewish (religious) legal requirements.[81] His behaviour was

---

[79] In addition to this, according to Seneca, he offered security to those who turned to him for guidance (Seneca, *Epistle* 11.8–10). Judge (1992: 191–197) has argued, however, that 'Paul's call for imitation is unique' (191) because it arises from the context of preaching the gospel and has to do with an imitation in affliction.

[80] On the question as to whether this was consistent with Christian humility, see O'Brien 1995: 84–85.

[81] Recently, there has been considerable scholarly discussion as to whether Paul is, in this context, speaking only of his financial freedom from the Corinthians. So, for example, Fee (1987: 425–26), understands Paul to be referring to his financial independence from the Corinthians, not to an inner freedom, a freedom from sin or the law. But there are difficulties in the way of Fee's interpretation, not least of all because of the apostle's deliberate return in v. 19 to the issues of vv. 1–3, where 'freedom' is

grounded in his being a Christian, not in his apostleship as such.

Also, his overall stance of making himself a slave (9:19) was paradigmatic for the Corinthians. As one who was truly free, he was living in conformity with the example of his Lord and thus showing a truly Christian life-style. He followed the servant model of his Master (cf. Phil. 2:7); let the readers and other Christians do the same. As we have seen, the salvation of men and women was Paul's goal (1 Cor. 9:19–23). His earnest desire was to win Jews, Gentiles and weak Christians, that is, to save them completely so that they would be pure and blameless at the second coming. The Corinthians' ambitions should be the same.[82] Finally, although his overall stance of making himself a slave (v. 19) was paradigmatic for the Corinthians, the actual outworking of this for his readers might vary. Paul is not suggesting that they should engage in the same wide-ranging, apostolic ministry in which he has been involved; but each *in his or her own way and according to their personal gifts* was to have the same orientation and ambitions as Paul himself, that is, of seeking by all possible means to save some.

The Christian and spiritual warfare (Eph. 6)

Finally, as we address the question whether Paul wanted Christians in his congregations to be caught up in God's saving purposes for Gentiles or, as a related issue, whether he urged them to engage in evangelism, we turn to his statements about the spiritual warfare in Ephesians 6:10–20,[83] especially the reference to believers having their feet shod with 'the preparation of the gospel of peace' (v. 15, NRSV) and their being urged to use the sword of the Spirit, namely, the word of God, as an offensive weapon (v. 17).

These two statements (vv. 15 and 17) are part of a unique emphasis on spiritual warfare and power found in Ephesians 6:10–20 (a

---

something broader than financial independence. Harris's comment on v. 19 strikes the right balance: 'Paul was "free from all", not only in the sense that he was financially independent of his converts (vv. 12b–18), but also in the sense that he was in bondage to no human being (*cf.* 1 Cor. 7:23) and to no circumstance (*cf.* Phil. 4:11–12) and had been emancipated from sin and the law' (1999: 101–102).

[82] For detailed argument of Paul's slavery as a model for the Corinthians, see O'Brien 1995: 92–104. On the subject of slavery in general, see Harris 1999.

[83] For a recent defence of the Pauline authorship of Ephesians, see O'Brien 1999b: 4–47 (and for a detailed examination of 6:10–20, see 456–490). But if it is claimed that the letter was written by a close associate of the apostle or a member of the Pauline school, our conclusions from Eph. 6:15, 17 regarding the dynamic of the gospel and believers' involvement in it are not materially affected, since they are consistent with what we have noted elsewhere in the generally accepted Pauline letters, especially Romans and Philippians.

structurally significant paragraph in the letter)[84] where believers are
called upon to struggle against evil and personal, supernatural forces
called 'principalities and powers' (NRSV).[85] The passage brings the
theme of power to a climax by focusing on the power of God working
on behalf of believers in their struggle with the forces of evil. All
Christians are involved in a spiritual warfare (*palē*) against the powers
of darkness.[86] All are urged to put on God's own armour which he
gives to his people so that they can *stand firm* against the onslaughts of
the evil one by resistance and proclamation (vv. 10–17).[87]

In particular, they need to be outfitted with proper footwear so as to
be ready for battle (v. 15). In language obviously borrowed from Isaiah
52:7 Paul urges believers to have their feet fitted with either *a.* a
'readiness' which is bestowed by 'the gospel of peace',[88] and thereby

[84] This final section of the exhortatory material of Ephesians serves as the climax of
the letter as a whole. Here the apostle looks from a broader, cosmic perspective at the
Christian's responsibility to live in the world. Having pointed to the new and distinctive
life-style that should characterize the lives of his readers (4:1 – 6:9), not least of all
within the family (5:21 – 6:9), Paul sets forth an effective summary of his paraenesis,
reinforces his earlier exhortations in relation to the larger struggle between the forces of
good and evil, and challenges his readers to action (*cf.* O'Brien 1999b: 457–460).

[85] Note particularly the recent ground-breaking works of Arnold 1989: 103–122 and
1992: 148–160 on this issue.

[86] All the readers of this (circular?) letter are now addressed in 6:10, whereas in 5:22 –
6:9 instructions were given to the various groups in the Christian household (wives,
husbands, children, parents, *etc.*). Moreover, by speaking of the battle at v. 12 as '*our*
struggle' (which has the best manuscript support), the author identifies with his readers
(and, by implication, all Christians) in this spiritual conflict.

[87] According to Eph. 4:27, Satan seeks to gain a foothold and exert his influence over
the lives of Christians, esp. through uncontrolled anger (v. 26), but also through
falsehood (v. 25), stealing (v. 28), unwholesome talk (v. 29), indeed any conduct that is
characteristic of the 'old way of life' (v. 22). Moreover, the evil one is committed to
hindering the progress of the gospel and the fulfilment of God's plan of summing up all
things in Christ (1:10; *cf.* 3:10). He attempts by his 'insidious wiles' to turn believers
aside from pursuing the cause of Christ and achieving this goal.

[88] That is, the genitive 'of the gospel' functions as a genitive of origin. This is usually
taken to mean adopting a defensive posture, of holding fast to the position that has
already been won, of remaining steadfast against the powers of darkness and resisting
temptation. However, this still begs the question as to whether Paul's language implies
that believers are to adopt *only* a defensive stance. Certainly they are to appropriate and
preserve the gospel of peace, to withstand each and every temptation in the ethical
sphere (*cf.* Eph. 4:26–27), and to resist the diverse influences of the evil one. But
standing firm can also involve carrying the attack into enemy territory, of plundering
Satan's kingdom by announcing the promise of divine rescue to captives in the realm of
darkness. Consistent with his use of military imagery elsewhere, Paul speaks of the
weapons he uses in his warfare as being divinely powerful to demolish strongholds, to
overthrow arguments and every pretension that sets itself up against the knowledge of
God (2 Cor. 10:4). This undoubtedly involves carrying the attack into enemy territory,
which clearly means going on the offensive.

enables Christians to heed the repeated injunction to stand firm, or *b.* a 'readiness, willingness' to share the gospel[89] by those who have already appropriated it. The net difference between the two interpretations is not great, especially if the dynamic dimension to the gospel is recognized. Because all engaged in the spiritual warfare are urged to have their feet fitted with this preparation of the gospel, what is predicated of the royal messenger in Isaiah 52:7, and the Messiah himself in Ephesians 2:17, is now stated with reference to all believers. Those who have appropriated that peace for themselves have their feet fitted with this 'readiness', a preparedness to announce the gospel of peace. Paradoxically, they are prepared to announce the gospel of peace as they engage in a spiritual warfare!

The final piece of equipment in the believers' armour which Paul urges them to grasp is 'the sword of the Spirit', and this is clearly an offensive weapon (v. 17). While it obviously helped the believer's resistance, it was also a weapon of aggression. The sword of the Spirit is identified with the word of God, a term which here, as elsewhere in Paul, often signifies the gospel (cf. Rom 10:8). At verse 15 Paul spoke of the 'readiness' of the Christian warrior to make known the gospel. Now he goes a step further and mentions the power by which that gospel is successful, namely, the Spirit. 'The Word of God and the work of the Spirit are the means by which the people of God step out in defiance of Satan and rob his domain' (Arnold 1992: 157). These are the instruments by which God draws men and women into a relationship with himself, transforming their lives so as to be like his Son.

Summary

In addressing the issue of whether Paul envisaged believers in his congregations as being caught up in his mission, and therefore involved in the divine saving purposes, or whether they were telling forth the glorious news of the saving grace of God, we have observed that the

---

[89] The genitive is objective. The reasons for adopting this line are as follows: first, the noun 'signifies a state of being ready for action', and the phrase is rendered: 'in readiness (to proclaim) the good news of peace' (Louw and Nida §77.1). On this view, 'gospel' in the original is a noun of agency signifying 'to proclaim, or share the gospel [of peace]', a force which it has in more than half of its sixty other occurrences in Paul. Secondly, the context of Is. 52:7 favours this interpretation: the messenger whose beautiful feet glide over the mountain tops is ready to announce good tidings to Zion. Thirdly, the echoes of this Old Testament text earlier in Ephesians, namely at 2:17, draw attention to Christ, the herald of good tidings, who on the basis of his peace-making work on the cross, comes and announces peace to Jews and Gentiles alike. The focus is upon the proclamation of the gospel of peace to those for whom this reconciliation has been won.

apostle often highlights the powerful advance of the gospel rather than focusing on the evangelistic endeavours of Christians. At the same time, incidental references to the latter suggest that there were probably many more engaged in these activities than we might think. Certainly, the apostle does not seem to be surprised that believers in Rome were speaking the word of God courageously and fearlessly (Phil. 1:14–18), while he clearly desires that the Philippians themselves might be committed to a broad-ranging partnership in the gospel, which included a sharing the word of life with others (Phil. 1:5, 30; 2:16). He urged the Corinthians to follow his example, of making himself a slave to all (1 Cor. 9:19; 11:1), just as the Lord Jesus had done (Phil. 2:5–11). Paul was committed to the good of others, which he defines in terms of saving them (1 Cor. 10:33), and he wants his readers to follow his example. Finally, the spiritual warfare in which all Christians are engaged is to be fought with God's own armour so that we can stand firm against the onslaughts of the evil one and his principalities (Eph. 6:10–20). Among other things, believers are to have their feet fitted with 'readiness', a preparedness to announce the gospel of peace (v. 15), and to take up the sword, that is, the word of God or the gospel which the Spirit makes powerful and effective (v. 17).

Conclusions

Paul's amazing missionary career began with the most decisive event in his life – his confrontation with the risen Christ on the Damascus road when he was converted and called to be the apostle to the Gentiles. From that day on, the gospel became the determinative focus of his whole life. Paul's encounter with the risen Lord led to a paradigm shift in his thinking: he came to understand that Jesus is at the centre of God's saving purposes, and that he is Israel's Messiah, the Son of God and Lord of all. As the crucified and exalted one he bore the curse 'for us' and brought the law to an end as a way of salvation. It was God's plan that 'the blessing given to Abraham might come to the Gentiles through Christ Jesus' (Gal. 3:13–14).

The apostle understood his missionary activity to Gentiles within the context of an Old Testament expectation in which the nations would on the final day partake of God's ultimate blessings to Israel. This major point emerges in a variety of ways: Paul speaks of his apostolic self-consciousness in Old Testament prophetic-call language, aligning himself with the Isaianic Servant of the Lord and Jeremiah, two key figures in redemptive history through whom God renews his will for the salvation of Gentiles (Gal. 1). By reference to his stewardship of the mystery (Eph. 3) and the effects of his mission (when he uses cultic terms, exodus language and servant terminology and sets his ministry within an Old Testament geographic dimension: Rom. 15), Paul makes it clear that his missionary calling to preach the gospel to Gentiles is an integral part of God's redemptive plan.

Paul is totally committed to and involved in the advance of the gospel. He has been set apart for this divine *kerygma* and so he serves God wholeheartedly in this gospel of his Son. So great is Paul's passion that his readiness to proclaim it knows no limits (Rom. 1). He is convinced that it is utterly reliable, for God himself is the author of it. Moreover, the gospel is not some new-fangled message. God had promised it beforehand in the Old Testament Scriptures. They reveal his unfolding purposes in significant events of that gospel which have been announced, effected and divinely interpreted. At the centre of the apostolic gospel is the unique Son of God, the mediator of salvation between God and man, who was in his earthly life the seed of David, the Messiah. By his resurrection he has become the powerful Son of God – Jesus Christ, our Lord. The purpose of Paul's missionary endeavours, as well as that of his apostolic gospel, is 'to bring about the obedience of faith among the Gentiles for the sake of the name of Christ' (Rom. 1:5, NRSV), that is, in the fullness of time, to bring the nations into captive obedience to himself. Jesus Christ now rules over the new people of God.

The saving power of the gospel is spelled out in the light of humanity's dreadful predicament outside of Christ. The world comprising Jews and Gentiles stands under judgment. But this apparently weak and foolish message, the content of which centres on Jesus Christ, mediates the almighty power of God that leads to salvation. The saving righteousness of God has been revealed in Jesus Christ and his atoning death. Men and women are justified freely by God's grace at great cost, namely, through the redemption that is in Christ Jesus. Through Jesus' sacrificial death on the cross the divine answer to the disastrous human predicament is provided.

At significant points in his letters Paul spells out the goals of his apostleship, describing these aims in a variety of ways (1 Cor. 9:19–23; Rom. 1:5; 15:15–16). The tasks that were included within the scope of his missionary commission included primary evangelism. His ambition was to go where the gospel had not yet been preached. The apostle proclaimed the gospel and, under God, converted men and women. But he also founded churches as a necessary element in his missionary task.

Conversion to Christ meant incorporation into him, and thus membership within a Christian community. Through his practice of residential missions and his nurture of churches by teaching and admonition, it is clear that Paul sought to bring men and women to full maturity in Christ. He anticipates his converts being his joy and crown as they stand fast on the final day, so demonstrating that he had not run in vain in his ministry (2 Cor. 1:14; Gal. 2:2; Phil. 2:16; 4:1; 1 Thess. 2:19).

While Paul was called and commissioned to be the apostle to Gentiles (Rom. 11:13), he ardently prayed for the salvation of his own people. He recognized that although there has been a temporary and partial hardening of Israel which led to the blessings of salvation reaching the Gentiles and ultimately the whole world, God intends to bring his saving grace to Israel. There is a fundamental equality of Jew and Gentile in the saving plan of God. At the end of Romans 9 – 11, then, Paul bursts into joy and admiration for God's merciful plan in which Jew and Gentile alike participate in salvation in the Lord Jesus Christ (vv. 33–36).

Finally, although the apostle makes a number of important statements in his letters about his own missionary calling and its place within God's purposes, he does not appear, at first sight, to say a great deal about how the Christians in his congregations were to carry on his work or to be caught up with his mission and so be involved in these saving purposes of God. Nor does he often mention whether believers were telling forth the glorious news of the saving grace of God. Paul, however, often highlights the powerful advance of the gospel rather than focusing on the evangelistic endeavours of Christians. At the same time, there are incidental references to the latter, suggesting that more believers may have been engaged in these activities than we might think. On occasion, he presents himself as a model for his converts to follow, and while his focus is on being a slave as Christ was, it also involves being committed to the salvation of others. Further, the spiritual warfare in which all Christians are engaged means standing firm against the onslaughts of the evil one and his powers, and this leads, on the one hand, to resisting temptation and, on the other, to announcing the gospel of peace in the power of God's Spirit.

Chapter Eight

John

John's contribution to the New Testament teaching on mission is frequently overshadowed by the 'Great Commission' found at the end of Matthew's Gospel and the Pauline mission in the book of Acts. Indeed, John's concern for mission may not be as overt as that of Luke or Paul, which may explain why the Matthean-Lukan-Pauline axis has garnered the lion's share of scholarly attention.[1] Some have even argued that John has little, or even no, interest in mission.[2] Yet, as will be seen, John's interest in mission is both demonstrable and considerable.[3]

The Fourth Gospel's primary focus is the mission of Jesus: he is the one who comes into the world, accomplishes his work and returns to the Father; he is the one who descended from heaven and ascends again; he is the Sent One, who, in complete dependence and perfect obedience to his sender, fulfils the purpose for which the Father sent him.[4] He is also the shepherd-teacher who calls followers to help gather his eschatological harvest (Köstenberger 1998a: 93–140). The mission of Jesus' followers is presented within this framework. The Johannine

---

[1] Cf. e.g. Bosch 1991; and the critique by Towner (1995: 99–119), who rightly points out that Bosch's neglect of the Johannine paradigm caused his model of mission to lack the biblical element of confrontation with and rejection by the world.

[2] Cf. e.g. Kuhn 1954: 161–168; Meeks 1972: 44–72.

[3] This is already suggested by the substantial number of treatments devoted to this topic in recent decades (see the *Forschungsberichte* in Okure 1988: 7–35 and Köstenberger 1998a: 5–16). Significant discussions (in order of publication) include: Radermakers 1964: 100–121; Hahn 1965: 152–163; Bieder 1965; Kuhl 1967; McPolin 1969: 113–122; Olsson 1974: 241–248; Veloso 1975; Miranda 1976 and 1977; Bühner 1977; Prescott-Ezickson 1986; Ruiz 1986; Okure 1988; Ghiberti 1990: 185–200; Köstenberger 1998a; and Nissen 1999: 213–231.

[4] Comments such as that by McPolin (1969: 114), who maintains that 'the Father remains 'the "mission centre", the source from which all missions derive', must therefore be supplemented by the equally true assertion that Jesus is the 'mission focus' of the Fourth Gospel (not the Father). The reason for this is that Jesus, not the Father, serves as believers' model for mission as further developed below. See also the section entitled 'The Focus of Mission: Theocentric or Christocentric?' in Köstenberger 1995c: 452–453.

commissioning passage (20:21) links these missions explicitly, indicating that believers are to emulate Jesus' relationship with his sender, the Father, by carrying out their own mission in complete dependence and on obedience to Jesus, their sender (Köstenberger 1998a: 141–198).

With regard to Jesus' followers, John traces the shift of focus from the old-covenant community to the new (Pryor 1992). While he affirms the Jews' salvation-historical primacy, he chronicles their rejection of the Messiah, with the implication that this rejection would lead to the inclusion of the Gentiles in the orbit of God's salvation after Jesus' glorification. There are also clear verbal links between Jesus' mission on the one hand, and John's and Peter's missions on the other (Quast 1989). The evangelist thus maintains an overlap between Jesus' shepherding and witnessing functions and that of his chosen representatives. Moreover, the Gospel accentuates believers' need to be knit together in love, unity and mutual service, modelled closely after Jesus' relationship with the Father. It remains to develop these insights more fully below.

Jesus' mission

John portrays Jesus as utterly unique, a person possessing attributes of divinity as well as humanity and thus called to carry out a unique mission (Köstenberger 1998a: 45–52). The uniqueness of Jesus is already stressed in the Prologue, which affirms his eternal pre-existence (1:1) and unique relationship with God (*monogenēs*; 1:14, 18; cf. 3:16, 18). Jesus' pre-existence is further implied in the Gospel's many references to Jesus' 'having come',[5] to his being 'from God',[6] and in Jesus' claim to be sent (Pollard 1970: 16–17). The Gospel's primary interest lies, however, not in Jesus' ontological nature (even though Jesus' divinity is clearly assumed), but in what Jesus' unique personhood and relationship with God enabled him to do: to accomplish a mission that required a fully human and a fully divine person. This is indicated by the climax to which the Prologue builds: 'No one has ever seen God, but God the only Son, who is at the Father's side, has made him known' (1:18). Jesus' revelation of God is here rooted in his unique relationship with, and intimate knowledge of, God.[7]

---

[5] *Cf.* e.g. 5:43; 6:14; 7:28; 9:39; 10:10; 11:27; 12:46; 15:22; 18:37.

[6] *Cf.* 6:46; 7:29; 9:33; 16:27, 28; 17:8.

[7] *Cf.* Carson 1991b: 135: 'The emphasis of the Prologue, then, is on the revelation of

Jesus is characterized by John as both 'Son of Man' and 'Son of God'.[8] His is an utterly unique sonship: he alone is 'the Son of the Father' or simply 'the Son'.[9] Another hint at Jesus' deity is provided by the Johannine 'I ams', which include absolute instances of 'I am' (*egō eimi*) as well as those in the predicate nominative.[10] This designation for Jesus may allude to the divine title used for *yhwh* in Isaiah.[11] To this should be added claims by Jesus or the evangelist that Jesus is equal to God.[12] Moreover, Jesus is presented as possessing supernatural knowledge.[13] Finally, the strategic placement of references to Jesus' divinity in John's Gospel, too, underscores this claim: it is found in the introductions to both parts of the book (1:1–4; 13:1–3) and near its conclusion (20:28).[14] In sum, John presents Jesus' unique identity as the foundation for his unique mission.

Signs and works

Jesus regularly refers to his own task in terms of 'work(s)'.[15] The

---

the Word as the ultimate disclosure of God himself ... "the unique one, [himself] God" ... this unique and beloved Person has made God known ...' See also the thorough treatment in Harris 1992: 73–103. It is also worth pointing out that the term 'make known' (*exēgeisthai*) elsewhere in the New Testament means 'to narrate' (as in to give a complete account of something; *cf.* Luke 24:35; Acts 10:8; 15:12, 14; 21:19): thus 1:18 provides the framework for the entire remaining narrative. *Cf.* Louw 1968: 32–40.

[8] Son of Man: 1:51; 3:13, 14; 5:27; 6:27, 53, 62; 8:28; 9:35; 12:23; 13:31; Son of God: 1:34, 49; 3:18; 5:25; 10:36; 11:4, 27; 19:7; 20:31. The bibliography on both expressions is vast. On the Johannine 'Son of Man', see esp. Burkett 1991; Caragounis 1986; Lindars 1973: 43–60; Maddox 1974: 186–204; Moloney 1978; Smalley 1979: 278–301 (for additional bibliography, see Köstenberger 1998a: 50–51, n. 26). On Jesus as (Son of) God in the Fourth Gospel, see esp. Harris 1992: 51–129; Mastin 1975: 32–51; Matsunaga 1981: 124–145; and Howton 1963/64: 227–237.

[9] *Cf.* 3:17, 35, 36; 5:19, 20, 21, 22, 23, 25, 26; 6:40; 8:35, 36; 14:13; 17:1.

[10] Absolute uses: 6:20; 8:24, 28, 58; 13:19; 18:5; predicate nominative: 6:35, 51; 8:12 *cf.* 9:5; 10:7, 9, 11, 14; 11:25; 14:6; 15:1, 5. See esp. the monographs by Harner 1970 and Ball 1996; the article by Zimmermann 1960: 54–69, 266–276; and the treatments in Morris 1989: 107–125; R. E. Brown 1966: 533–538; and Schnackenburg 1990: 2:79–89.

[11] The Hebrew *'anî hû* is rendered by the LXX with *egō eimi* in Is. 43:10–13, 25; 45:18; 48:12; 51:12; 52:6; *cf.* Exod. 3:14.

[12] *Cf.* 5:17–18; *cf.* 1:3; 8:58; 10:30; 14:9–11, 20, 23; 17:5, 24; 20:28.

[13] *Cf.* 1:48; 2:4, 19; 3:14; 4:17–18; 6:51, 70; 8:28; 9:3; 10:15–18; 11:4, 14; 12:24, 32; 13:10–11, 38; 15:13; 20:27; 21:18–19. See Köstenberger 1999c: 69.

[14] See esp. Harris 1992: 105–129, who draws attention to the strategic placement of the references to Jesus as God in John's Gospel: 'The Prologue ends (1:18) as it begins (1:1), and the Gospel ends (20:28) as it begins (1:1), with an assertion of the deity of Jesus' (128), whereby 20:28 'forms the culmination of the entire Gospel' (129).

[15] *Ergon*: 4:34; 17:4; *erga*: 5:20, 36; 7:3, 21; 9:3, 4; 10:25, 32, 33, 37, 38; 14:10, 11, 12; 15:24. See Köstenberger 1998a: 72–73; Riedl 1973; and Ensor 1996.

evangelist, on the other hand, has selected and designated certain of Jesus' works as 'signs'.[16] The very expression 'sign' already stresses the symbolic value of a given work of Jesus with reference to his own personal characteristics. Not merely the powerful nature of an event is highlighted in John, but its significance. Particularly in the first part of the Gospel, the signs provide an important structural component together with the repeated surfacing of people's messianic expectations. From the first to the last sign, from the changing of water into wine to the raising of Lazarus, Jesus' messianic attributes are displayed. Nevertheless, 'the Jews' (that is, the Jewish nation represented by its leadership), to whom these signs were primarily directed, failed to believe (12:37–40).

The following signs can be identified (Köstenberger 1995a: 87–103):

1. the changing of water into wine (2:1–11);
2. the cleansing of the temple (2:18–21);[17]
3. the healing of the nobleman's son (4:46–54);
4. the healing of the lame man (5:1–15);
5. the feeding of the multitude (6:1–15);
6. the healing of the blind man (ch. 9); and
7. the raising of Lazarus (ch. 11).

We note that all signs are public works of Jesus, belonging to John's presentation of the earthly ministry of Jesus in chapters 1 – 12. Their primary audience is 'the Jews', and their function is temporary and salvation-historically constrained. From this it follows that Jesus' crucifixion or resurrection are not signs. These events are rather the reality to which Jesus' earlier signs point. While the working of 'signs' is limited exclusively to Jesus, 'works' terminology is shared between Jesus and the disciples (cf. esp. the 'greater works' reference in 14:12). This will be taken up further below.

The first and the last reference to *ergon* in John's Gospel are in the singular, relating to Jesus' work in its entirety (4:34; 17:4). What is this 'work' that Jesus came to do and completed? John describes Jesus' mission in terms of both revelation and redemption. Jesus came to make the Father known (1:18); at the same time, he also is 'the Lamb of God' who takes away the sin of the world (1:29, 36). Some who detect traces of gnosticism in this Gospel characterize John's portrayal

---

[16] *Sēmeion, sēmeia; cf.* esp. the purpose statement in 20:30 and the summary in 12:37. See Köstenberger 1995a: 87–103 and 1998a: 54–72 (with extensive bibliography on 55–56, n. 36); as well as Guthrie 1967: 72–83 and M. M. Thompson 1991: 89–108.

[17] On the temple cleansing as a sign of God's judgment for the Jews' lack of concern for Gentile mission, see Evans 1997: 417–442.

of Jesus primarily (or exclusively) as that of Revealer while denying the presence of the notion of atonement.[18] To be sure, the fourth evangelist largely empties Jesus' death on the cross of its shame (Osborne 1979: 80–96), casting it rather as a mere station on Jesus' return to the Father (Nicholson 1983). According to John, Jesus' death is part of his exaltation (see esp. the 'lifted-up sayings' in 3:14; 8:28; and 12:32; Thüsing 1979). However, this should not be taken to imply that the element of atonement is completely absent from John: the 'Lamb of God' will give his flesh for the world (6:51); the good shepherd gives his life for the sheep (10:11, 15, 17, 18); greater love has no-one than this, that he lay down his life for his friends (15:13; cf. 3:16).[19] Thus John, like the other evangelists, portrays Jesus' death as a death for others (*hyper*); Jesus came to 'give (eternal) life'.[20]

Glory

'Christ's mission in John's Gospel, however, fulfils a much higher purpose than simply to confer life to a sinful humanity. The ultimate objective for Jesus is to bring glory to God' (Erdmann 1998: 213–15). This underlying motivation surfaces repeatedly at the occasion of Jesus' 'signs' (9:3; 11:4, 40). Still, John makes clear that Jesus, by seeking God's approval rather than human,[21] has glory as well: glory characterized Jesus' eternal pre-existence (17:5); Isaiah saw Jesus' glory (12:41), as did the disciples (1:14; 2:11). Glory in the Fourth Gospel is therefore not exclusively or even primarily an attribute of God the Father; it is foremost of all a characteristic of the Son in whom God is glorified.[22]

John's claim is not so much that God is glorious; that was already known. It is rather that God's glory was revealed *in Jesus*, the Pre-existent One whom Isaiah had seen in his vision, and the Incarnate One whose glory the disciples saw as well. Moreover, the amazing fact was not so much Jesus' pre-existent glory but rather his *incarnate* glory. For in it God revealed his redeeming love for humanity (3:16). God's glory and his love do not stand in tension; God's love rather is part of

[18] *Cf.* Bultmann 1955: 49–69 and Forestell 1974, and the response in Turner 1990: 99–122. See also Thompson 1988 and Morris 1978: 37–53.

[19] See Carey 1981: 97–122; Matera 1988: 161–178; and the discussion in Köstenberger 1998a: 74–80.

[20] 3:16–17; 6:57–58; 10:7–10; 17:2–3. *Cf.* McPolin 1969: 118: 'the primary purpose, to which all others are subordinated, is to confer life'.

[21] *Cf.* 5:41, 44; 7:18; 8:50, 54; 12:28, 43.

[22] *Cf.* 11:4; 12:28; 13:31–32; 14:13; 17:1, 4–5. This is true esp. of Jesus' signs: see Köstenberger 1998a: 61–63.

his glory, the primary missionary motive that, in turn, brings yet further glory to God.

The disciples, in turn, are caught up in this circle of glory. Taken into the life of the triune God, its love and unity, believers are made part of God's redemptive mission in the world: endowed with the Spirit, they are to proclaim the gospel of redemption and forgiveness in Jesus' name (20:21–23). Thus Jesus will be glorified in his disciples (17:10), just as the Father was glorified in him. For by this is the Father glorified, if Jesus' followers bear fruit as proof of their discipleship (15:8). Some, like Peter, may even be called to 'glorify' God by suffering martyrdom (21:19).

It has been maintained that the focus of glory in John's Gospel is Jesus.[23] This may now be taken one step further: in the ultimate analysis, John presents Jesus' death on the cross as the climactic moment of his glorification.[24] Thus John's *theologia crucis* is a *theologia gloriae*. This perspective dramatically reverses the view that Jesus' death constituted a supreme tragedy, the death of an innocent man. Caiaphas spoke better than he knew when he said that it was better for one man to die for the people rather than for the whole nation to perish (11:50; 18:14).

Why is Jesus' death the climactic moment of Jesus' glorification for John? Because it is here that Jesus' self-humbling reaches its lowest – and thus highest – point: he who had enjoyed eternal, pre-existent glory with the Father, yielded his very self for sinners, out of pure love, extending free forgiveness to all. According to John, this downward side of his 'V-shaped' christology in fact constitutes the moment of Jesus' greatest honour, his highest exaltation; for the momentous work of salvation was entrusted to, and accomplished by, him (17:4; 19:30). Indeed, God had 'lifted up', that is, crucified as well as exalted, Jesus (3:14; 8:28; 12:32).

The sent Son

Within the framework of the Word's coming into the world, accomplishing God's purpose and returning to God (cf. Is. 55:11–12), it is the figure of the sent Son of the Father that provides the most characteristic designation of Jesus (Köstenberger 1998a: 96–121). John

---

[23] See the section entitled 'The Focus of Mission: Theocentric or Christocentric?' in Köstenberger 1995c: 452–453; and the essay related to this question by Barrett (1982: 1–18).

[24] *Cf.* 7:39; 12:16, 23; 12:28. See the bibliographic references in Köstenberger 1998a: 76, n. 100.

may have chosen this expression at least in part because of its relevance for his Jewish audience. For it was a common feature of Jewish life for a father, when seeking to safeguard the delivery of an important message, to send, not a hired servant, but a son, preferably his first-born.[25] In this cultural context, Jesus is cast as the one and only Son of his heavenly Father, who has been entrusted with the all-important mission of revealing his sender and of completing the redemptive work on behalf of humankind.

In John's sending christology, the sent one is to know the sender intimately (7:29; cf. 15:21; 17:8, 25); live in a close relationship with the sender (8:16, 18, 29; 16:32); bring glory and honour to the sender (5:23; 7:18); do the sender's will (4:34; 5:30, 38; 6:38–39) and works (5:36; 9:4); speak the sender's words (3:34; 7:16; 12:49; 14:10b, 24); follow the sender's example (13:16); be accountable to the sender (passim; cf. esp. ch. 17); bear witness to the sender (12:44–45; 13:20; 15:18–25); and exercise delegated authority (5:21–22, 27; 13:3; 17:2; 20:23).[26] John goes to great lengths to show that Jesus fulfilled all the functions of a sent one perfectly. He does so in part for the purpose of presenting Jesus as a model for his disciples to follow. When Jesus commissions his followers (20:21), he functions, for the first time in the Fourth Gospel, not as the sent one, but as one who sends others. Like Jesus, his disciples are to fulfil the manifold functions of one sent as outlined above.

The disciples' mission

It is the mission of Jesus, not that of his followers, that is central in John. Every other mission is derivative of the mission of Jesus: the mission of the Baptist, the Spirit and the disciples. The mission of the disciples, for example, is virtually never mentioned other than in the context of Jesus' mission (see esp. 17:18; 20:21). This does not mean that John considers these missions insignificant. They are important, however, only because of the larger mission of which they are a part: the mission of Jesus. Accordingly, each of them is cast in subordinate terms: the Baptist, the Spirit and the disciples are each said to be 'sent'[27] in order to 'witness' to Jesus.[28] The mission of the Baptist is

[25] *Cf.* esp. Harvey 1987: 239–250. See also Friend 1990: 18–28; Ibuki 1988: 38–81; Borgen 1983: 121–132; and Schweizer 1960: 68–76.

[26] For an interaction with the relevant literature see Köstenberger 1998a: 115–121.

[27] The Baptist: 1:6; 3:28; the Spirit: 14:26; 15:26; 16:7; the disciples: 4:38; 17:18; 20:21.

[28] The Baptist: 1:7, 8, 15, 32, 34; 3:26; the Spirit: 15:26; the disciples: 15:27.

subordinate in that it is entirely devoted to giving witness to the Pre-existent One (1:15), baptizing in water in order that Jesus may be manifested to Israel (1:31). The Spirit's mission is subordinate to that of Jesus in that the Spirit descended and remained upon Jesus at his baptism by John (1:32–33); he will remind Jesus' followers of Jesus' words (14:26), convict the world of its unbelief in Jesus (16:9), and take what belongs to Jesus and disclose it to his disciples (16:14). The disciples' mission is subordinate to the mission of Jesus, since the disciples are called (1:35–51), trained and commissioned (20:21–23) by Jesus and their task is described from beginning to end as 'following' Jesus (1:37; 21:22).

Moreover, John describes the mission of the disciples in terms of 'harvesting' (4:38), 'fruitbearing' (15:8, 16) and 'witnessing' (15:27). All of these terms place the disciples in the humble position of extending the mission of another, Jesus. The disciples are to 'harvest the crop' they did not work for (4:38). They are to 'bear fruit' they did not produce (15:8, 16). They are to do 'greater works' than Jesus in dependence on the exalted Lord who answers their prayers (14:12–13). They are to extend forgiveness or retain sins, a ministry made possible by their Lord, who presented his pierced hands and side as living proof of the completion of his own mission (20:19–23).

The disciples

John's portrayal of the new messianic community follows salvation-historical lines. This is strongly suggested by the following features (Pryor 1992):

1. The use of the term 'his own' (*hoi idioi*) in 1:11 with reference to Israel and in 13:1 with reference to Jesus' followers.
2. The insistence that Jesus' sonship is unique (*monogenēs* in 1:14, 18; 3:16, 18).
3. The claim that Jesus' glory 'dwelt among us' (that is, the new messianic community), in allusion to God's dwelling among his (old-)covenant people, Israel (1:14).
4. The implication of 1:51 that Jesus replaces Israel as the locus of the revelation of God's glory.
5. The use of 'shepherd' and 'flock' imagery for the relationship between Jesus and a community that transcends Jewish ethnic lines.
6. The Fourth Gospel's adaptation of the covenantal terminology and patterns found in the primary texts of Judaism, Exodus

and Deuteronomy.

7. The Fourth Gospel's portrayal of Jesus as the Mosaic Prophet, particularly by way of sending terminology and the patterning of chs. 13 – 17 after the book of Deuteronomy.
8. The insistence in 15:1 that Jesus is the 'true' vine embodying the true Israel.
9. Jesus' 'creation' of the new messianic community by breathing the Spirit on it (20:22).

The term *mathētēs* occurs seventy-eight times in John.[29] Most of these references are to the followers of Jesus. After their call (1:37–43), the disciples accompany Jesus (2:2, 11, 17), begin to participate in Jesus' work (4:2, 8, 27, 31, 33, 38), and gradually step into the foreground (6:3, 8, 12, 16, 22, 24, 60–71). The loyalty of Jesus' inner circle is contrasted with the unbelief of Jesus' own brothers (7:2–5). Discipleship is discussed in a number of passages (8:12, 31; 9:27–29; ch. 10). The disciples play an important role on the way to Jerusalem (9:2; 11:7–16, 54; 12:16, 21–22) and during their time of preparation and instruction in Jesus' farewell discourse (chs. 13 – 17). Judas, one of Jesus' disciples, betrays him (6:70–71; 12:4–8; 13:21–30; 17:12). Finally, the risen Jesus appears to his followers and commissions them (chs. 20 – 21; esp. 20:19–23).

It is not always clear whether the term *mathētēs* refers to the twelve or to a larger circle of Jesus' followers.[30] The term 'the twelve' is rarely used in John, and where it occurs, it does so almost incidentally (6:67–71; 20:24).[31] This seems to be one of the instances in this Gospel where John assumes his readers' knowledge of the Synoptic tradition. Nevertheless, the occurrence of the term in 6:67–71 points to 'the twelve' as those who stay with Jesus at a pivotal time in his ministry.[32] It is possible that John here draws on the symbolic correspondence between the number of Jesus' followers and the twelve tribes of Israel.

[29] The characterization of the disciples in John's Gospel coheres remarkably with the Synoptic treatment. As Schulz (1962: 137) observes, 'The use of the term *mathētēs* in the Fourth Gospel provides an impressive corroboration of this document's historical and theological accuracy.' The vast literature on disciples/discipleship in the Fourth Gospel includes Schnackenburg 1990: 203–217 and 1977: 247–256; Culpepper 1983: 99–148 (esp. 115–123, 132–144); Pryor 1988: 44–51 and 1992: 157–180; Schnelle 1991: 37–50; Schweizer 1959: 363–381; and Siker-Gieseler 1980: 199–227 (for additional bibliographic references see Köstenberger 1998a: 142–143, n. 1).

[30] *Cf.* Schulz 1962: 137–138; Schnackenburg 1990: 3:207–208; Quast 1989: 23.

[31] *Cf.* Köstenberger 1998a: 147–148; contra Bauder 1976: 489.

[32] Contra Collins (1990: 83), who claims that 'From the standpoint of the Fourth Gospel, the corporate faith of the twelve is somehow inadequate'.

Indeed, contrary to 'the twelve', who continue to follow Jesus, 'the Jews' do not. This becomes clear particularly in light of references to discipleship in the following chapters where many of 'the Jews' fail to penetrate to full faith in Jesus.[33]

In the second half of the Gospel, the emphasis is on Jesus' vision of a unified, loving, faithful, suffering and witnessing community of believers through which Jesus' mission would continue to be carried out. While only 'the twelve' were present with Jesus at the last supper (cf. Mark 14:17) and subsequently heard Jesus' farewell discourse (cf. 13:18 with 6:70), they function as representatives of later followers of Jesus so that derivatively the teachings of the discourse extend to subsequent generations of believers (cf. e.g. the 'greater works' in 14:12). Likewise, Jesus' commission in 20:21–23 is not limited to 'the twelve'. Nevertheless, they are cast in John as Jesus' first followers who were faithful to him when many fell away, the ones who were part of Jesus' inner circle and benefited from his instruction, and the ones through whose witness subsequent generations would come to believe (17:20; 20:29).

While John, like the Synoptists, uses the term 'disciples' to refer to the followers of the earthly Jesus, both in their historical particularity and in their representative function for later believers, this does not exhaust his use of the expression. As the Gospel progresses, the term is gradually widened from a physical remaining with Jesus (1:37–43) to a spiritual 'remaining' in Jesus' word (8:31) and in Jesus beyond his earthly ministry (ch. 15).[34] Already in 13:35, the designation 'disciple' is released from a following of the historical Jesus to a spiritual 'following' of him and of his example that is not constrained by boundaries of time and space. Indeed, if the circle of Jesus' disciples at times remains indefinite and ambiguous, this has a reason: the term itself is already opened up, expanded, prepared for a new point of reference. An example of this is the requirement for a disciple to remain in Jesus' word in 8:31. While the statement was originally addressed to Jews – who soon turn out to have exercised merely spurious faith in Jesus – this does not exhaust the statement's significance. Since the pronouncement is phrased in general terms, it is relevant for every potential follower of Jesus (cf. also 8:12, 51).

---

[33] *Cf.* 8:31–59; 9:1–41; 10:1–39; and 12:39–50. There is little evidence, however, that the twelve of the Fourth Gospel actually 'represent a group among Jewish Christians' in John's day, as Collins (1990: 81) contends.

[34] *Cf.* Köstenberger 1998a: 149–153; Schulz 1962: 139–142; Moreno 1971: 276–283; and Schnackenburg 1990: 3:208–209.

It may be asked whether the general Johannine practice of widening the term 'disciple' necessarily extends to post-resurrection followers of Jesus. In 15:26–27, the disciples' witnessing in conjunction with the Spirit is predicated on their having been with Jesus 'from the beginning', a possible reference to 'the twelve'. In the context of the Fourth Gospel, this points to those disciples who had been called by Jesus at the beginning of his public ministry (1:37–43) and had persevered in following him (6:60–71). But does that mean that John considers the task of witnessing to be limited to 'the twelve'? At first glance, this seems to be the case, since witnessing in this Gospel is usually related to the earthly Jesus[35] and since the term 'to witness' is in Johannine literature frequently tied to 'seeing'.[36] The significance of 'the twelve' in John's Gospel, however, is not exhausted by their historical function. As already noted, they also function as representatives of Jesus' messianic community. Thus the responsibility of witnessing, while given primarily to Jesus' first disciples, derivatively also extends to later generations of believers.[37] However, it is only on the basis of the message of the first disciples that later believers are able to bear witness themselves (cf. 17:20). Moreover, this line drawn between first and later generations of believers in John's Gospel also serves the function of authorizing the witness of the first disciples, including the witness of the writer of the Gospel himself (cf. 15:26–27).

Another important feature of John's characterization of Jesus' followers is the distinct development from the first to the second part of the Gospel. While in chapters 1 – 12 the disciples are set in relation to the earthly Jesus, chapters 13 – 21 find them as participants in the mission of the Father, the exalted Jesus and the Spirit. Their love for one another and their mission to the world are to be grounded in the Father-Son relationship Jesus maintained with his sender (cf. 13:35; 17:18; 20:21). This transformation of followers and disciples of the earthly Jesus into representatives of the exalted Jesus (cf. 13:16, 20; 15:20) is made possible by Jesus' exaltation, subsequent to his return to the Father. The second part of the Fourth Gospel also shows a change from a teacher-disciple relationship between Jesus and his followers to

[35] Cf. 1:7, 8, 15, 32, 34; 3:11, 26, 28, 32; 15:26–27; 19:35; 21:24.

[36] Cf. 3:11, 32; 19:35; 1 John 1:1–3; 4:14.

[37] Stott (1975: 48) gets the balance right when he writes, 'Our personal witness does indeed corroborate the witness of the biblical authors, especially that of the apostles. *But theirs is the primary witness*, for they were "with Jesus" and knew him, and they have borne witness to what they heard with their ears and saw with their eyes. Our witness is always secondary and subordinate to theirs.'

a more intimate relationship. This is indicated by the more endearing terms used by Jesus for his disciples: Jesus' 'own' (13:1), 'my children' (*teknia*; 13:33); 'friends' (15:13–15), 'those whom you gave me' (17:6), those who are 'mine' (17:10), 'brothers' (20:17) and 'children' (*paidia*; 21:4–5, NRSV). Even at the end of the Gospel, however, Jesus' disciples are still called to 'follow' him.

There are a number of characters in the Fourth Gospel who, besides representing historical persons, may be used by the fourth evangelist to show the issues involved in a person's becoming a disciple of Jesus or growing in such discipleship. This may even include people outside the circle of Jesus' immediate followers, such as Nicodemus, the Samaritan woman, the man born blind, or Mary and Martha. Among Jesus' disciples, reference may be made to Andrew, Nathanael, Thomas, even Judas, and above all Peter and the 'beloved disciple'. Most importantly, it is evident that John develops Peter and the 'beloved disciple' concurrently throughout his entire Gospel.[38] This may be seen as lending expression to the legitimacy of distinct personal callings: in the case of the 'beloved disciple', that of bearing witness in form of a written Gospel; in the case of Peter, in his bearing of witness by exercising pastoral oversight, culminating in a martyr's death. Both the beloved disciple and Peter also sustain a similarity with the mission of Jesus.[39]

Corporate metaphors

John uses two major metaphors for the new messianic community: that of a flock and that of branches (Köstenberger 1998a: 161–167). The metaphor of a 'flock' is commonly found in the Old Testament as a designation for God's people Israel.[40] This is the controlling image of chapter 10, where Jesus identifies himself as 'the good shepherd' and his followers as 'sheep' who hear his voice. The term 'flock' occurs in 10:16 in the context of Jesus' vision of uniting his sheep with yet 'other sheep' so that there will be 'one flock and one shepherd' (an allusion to Ezek. 34:23). The reference to the imminent 'scattering' of Jesus' disciples and the passages in chapter 17 regarding Jesus' protection of his own (e.g. 17:12) also may imply the imagery of a flock. Finally, in 21:15–17 Jesus gives Peter charge over his 'flock'.

[38] *Cf.* 1:37–42; 6:68–70; 13:6–10, 23–25, 36–38; 18:15–18, 25–27; 19:26–27, 35; 20:2–10; 21:7–24. See esp. Quast 1989; and the discussion in Köstenberger 1998a: 154–161.
[39] *Cf.* 1:18 with 13:23; 12:33 with 21:19. See Köstenberger 1998a: 159–161.
[40] *Cf.* e.g. Ps. 23; Is. 40:11; Jer. 23:1; Ezek. 34:11.

It is highly instructive to understand the relationship of John 10 to its Old Testament antecedents in Ezekiel 34:23–24 and Zechariah 13:7–9.[41] Jesus is the fulfilment of the messianic promise, the messianic shepherd in contrast to the failing leaders of the Jewish people (Schnackenburg 1990: 3:210). Remarkably, the impact of the messianic shepherd transcends the boundaries of ethnic Israel, even to the extent that ethnic Jews can be said to be not of Jesus' sheep (10:26; cf. 8:31–59). In continuity with, even escalation of, the Old Testament theme of the failure of Israel's leadership, the Jewish leaders do not believe in Jesus because they do not belong to his sheep (Schnackenburg 1990: 3:211). Those who do believe know themselves to be a new community belonging to the messianic eschatological shepherd. However, these believers, though originally almost all Jewish, no longer define themselves by their ethnic identity, but rather by their characteristic as *believers*, which opens up the possibility of membership in the messianic community to a universal and diverse group of people. Indeed, most take the 'other sheep' in 10:16 to refer to Gentiles, thus giving expression to Jesus' vision of one messianic community composed of believing Jews and Gentiles.[42]

Thus, in terms of individual discipleship as well as in terms of belonging to this messianic community, criteria for membership in this new entity have been extended beyond ethnic boundaries to assume universal dimensions. One may view the entire Gospel as an unfolding presentation of the movement from old definitions of discipleship and belonging to the people of God to a new understanding of such categories. Judaism is viewed as a system that has been transcended by the appearance of the Messiah which left Judaism an empty shell and exposed its futile adherence to customs now obsolete as well as its clinging to power that would soon be gone. Even those figures Judaism claimed as its own founding fathers, Abraham and Moses, were denied

[41] See esp. France 1970: 103–110, 148–150, 208–209, following Lamarche 1961; Bruce 1960/61: 336–353; and the discussion in Köstenberger 1998a: 134–137.

[42] *Cf.* Schnackenburg 1977: 251; Carson 1991b: 390. Martyn (1978: 115–121) hypothesizes that the 'other sheep' are Christians in other congregations who have been scattered by the persecution of the 80s. R. E. Brown (1978: 5–22) develops Martyn's thesis even further, claiming to be able to 'read off' from the text of the Fourth Gospel six different groups: the synagogue of 'the Jews'; crypto-Christians; Jewish Christians; Christians of apostolic churches; Johannine Christians; and secessionist Johannine Christians. He identifies the 'other sheep' of 10:16 with believers of apostolic churches with which the Johannine Christians hoped to be reconciled and united in the same church. While ingenious, however, these theories are too speculative and are based on too questionable a hermeneutic to merit serious consideration (see esp. Carson 1991b: 35–36, 41–45).

to it by Jesus' claim that they pointed toward himself and were preparatory for him.[43]

The second significant corporate metaphor in John is that of the 'vine' and the 'branches' (ch. 15; Corell 1958: 26–29). The barely concealed reference to Israel[44] casts Jesus as the true vine, the representative of Israel, and his disciples as the branches, participants in Jesus, the 'new' Israel (Pryor 1988: 49). Notably, it is not the messianic community that replaces Israel, but Jesus himself. The Father is the 'vinedresser' as well as the one to whose glory the disciples are to 'bear fruit'. The metaphor of the vine illustrates even more vividly than that of the shepherd and his flock the organic unity between Jesus and his disciples.[45] Significantly, the contexts in which these two metaphors occur share in common references to Jesus' death.[46] This points to the centrality of Jesus' death for the community's birth and subsequent life. More important still for the purposes of the present study, both corporate metaphors are also significant for the concept of mission. The shepherd motif of chapter 10 is applied to Peter in 21:15–17. The vine metaphor of chapter 15 is linked with references to the disciples' 'going' and bearing of fruit (cf. 15:8, 16). These two connections clearly indicate that the circle begun with Jesus' death is not closed until his redeemed community goes and accomplishes its mission.[47]

The significance of the Fourth Gospel's corporate metaphors for mission lies not so much in the imagery itself nor in the Old Testament antecedents. It rather consists of the new referents of these metaphors in contrast to their conventional references, that is, believers in Jesus the Messiah regardless of their ethnic, racial, or gender identity rather than Old Testament Israel. By establishing one sole criterion for

[43] Thus Haacker (1972) properly draws attention to the 'founder motif' in John's Gospel. It seems unwarranted, however, to characterize Jesus and Moses exclusively in these terms; the Johannine 'replacement theme' is much more multi-faceted. On Moses and exodus typology in the Fourth Gospel, see also Boismard 1993; Enz 1957: 208–215; Glasson 1963; de Jonge 1973: 160–177; Meeks 1967; Schnackenburg 1959: 622–639; and R. H. Smith 1962: 329–342.

[44] Cf. Is. 5:1–7; 27:2–6; Jer. 2:21; Ezek. 15; 19:10–14; Hos. 10:1; Ps. 80:8–16.

[45] There is a certain affinity between Johannine 'vine' imagery and the Pauline 'body of Christ' metaphor (so Schweizer 1959: 368–370; Haacker 1973: 183). However, in contrast to Paul who develops the body metaphor primarily in terms of the relationship of the various members to one another (but see Eph. 5:21–33, on which see esp. Clowney 1984: 81), John focuses on the necessary connection of each individual to Jesus.

[46] Cf. 10:11, 15, 17, 18; 15:13. See Corell 1958: 25–26.

[47] For further Johannine expressions with eschatological significance see Köstenberger 1998a: 165–166.

belonging to what is described by various corporate metaphors, that is, believing in Jesus the Messiah, and by pointing to the *world* as the destination where both Jesus and the disciples are sent (cf. 3:16; 17:18; 20:21), John reveals the universal scope of Jesus' mission and work, yet without sacrificing its historical particularity. The message for Jews and proselytes reading his Gospel would be clear: a reversal has taken place, necessitating a rethinking of categories. The issue is no longer one of others joining *Jews* in *their* special and privileged position with God, but for Jews to join the universal messianic community inaugurated by the mission of the Messiah, the Son of God, that is, *Jesus*. 'The Jews' had rejected the Messiah, but God had raised him from the dead. The effects of Jesus' death extend to the world *through the disciples* who are sent into the world to do greater works than even those Jesus did during his earthly ministry, in the power of his Spirit. The eschatological time of harvest had dawned; and the readers of the Gospel, too, should believe that the Messiah is Jesus (cf. 20:30–31; Carson 1987: 639–651).

The disciples' task

While Jesus' task is referred to in the Fourth Gospel in terms of 'works' (*erga*) and 'signs' (*sēmeia*), the range for describing his followers' task is much more limited (Köstenberger 1998a: 169–176). The disciples do not perform any 'signs' in John's Gospel.[48] There is no mention of their 'work' (in the singular). Even reference to the disciples' 'works' is limited to one, albeit very significant, instance (14:12).[49] Other passages speak of their task in terms of a harvest they are sent to reap (4:38), or an appointment to go and bear fruit (15:16). Jesus' followers are to testify to him in conjunction with the Spirit (15:26–27) and to forgive others their sins as Jesus' representatives (20:23).

One notes that the disciples' participation in Jesus' mission is discussed almost exclusively in the second part of the Gospel, except for the proleptic reference in 4:38 and the possible implications drawn from 10:16 and 12:20–32. The disciples' participation in the mission of the earthly Jesus in chapters 1 – 12 is limited to the ordinary tasks of disciples such as the buying of food (cf. 4:8) or helping Jesus to

---

[48] *Cf.* Schnackenburg 1990: 1:524: 'Thus the later heralds of the faith can only recount, attest and recall the revelation given by Jesus in "signs" (and words), which becomes thereby "present" in their own day ... But his [Jesus'] revelation, as a historical and eschatological event, is closed, and it only remains to explain it further, disclose its riches and explicate its full truth.'

[49] See Köstenberger 1998a: 171–175 and the discussion below.

distribute food and gathering leftovers (cf. 6:5–13).[50] By contrast, the disciples' participation in the exalted Jesus' mission according to chapters 13 – 21 is much more significant: the disciples will do even 'greater works' than their Master did during his own earthly mission (14:12).

The 'greater works'

In 14:12, John relates Jesus' prediction that believers will do the works he has been doing and 'even greater things than these'. What is the meaning of this startling saying? Surely Jesus is not saying that his followers will work greater miracles than the raising of Lazarus or the walking on the water? Many have taken this statement to refer to the great missionary successes of the early church narrated in the book of Acts. Is this John's point of reference? In context, one finds the explanation that these 'greater works' will be possible because Jesus is about to go 'to the Father' (14:12c). In this new era of salvation history, where Jesus becomes the object of believers' prayer and grants them their requests from his exalted heavenly position, Jesus' followers will be able to do 'greater things' even than Jesus during the time of his earthly ministry.[51]

Thus the primary point of reference appears to be an eschatological one (Nicholson 1983). The disciples will be able to do 'greater works' owing to their later placement in the history of salvation. Their work will be based on Jesus' finished work of salvation. They will be able to apply the full benefits of forgiveness and life to those who receive their message regarding the Messiah (20:23). As Barrett (1978: 460) notes, 'The death and exaltation of Jesus are the condition of the church's mission ... The work of the disciples [is] greater not because they themselves are greater but because Jesus' work is now complete.' The results of believers' mission include a broader stream of God's life-giving powers (17:2), the gathering together of the dispersed children of God (11:52), and the judgment of the unbelieving world (16:8–11).

In a sense, the reference in 14:12 elevates the future works of believers above Jesus' 'signs' of chapters 1 – 12. It also reveals Jesus' perspective of his own work in relation to that of the disciples *after* the accomplishment of his earthly mission.[52] Jesus' death and resurrection

[50] See on this aspect Köstenberger 1998c: 97–128.
[51] *Cf.* Matt. 11:11; *cf.* also 1:50; 5:20. See Bruce 1983a: 112–114, who, commenting on Matt. 11:11 (par. Luke 7:28), draws the implication that the disciples were privileged to participate in Jesus' 'new age of salvation'.
[52] Contra Dietzfelbinger (1989: 27–47) who views the 'greater works' logion merely as a later reflection on the part of the community rather than being rooted in the teaching

are thus set in the context not just of *salvation* but of *mission*. Jesus is the sower of the eschatological harvest (4:34–38) as well as the grain of wheat that falls into the ground and dies, *bearing much fruit* (12:24). Yet, in eschatological perspective, it is only the age of the Spirit that will see the disciples help gather the eschatological harvest and thus do 'greater works' even than Jesus. As one writer sums up 14:12–14, 'The disciples go forth in their mission and seek the Lord's aid therein, and in response to their prayers *he* will do through them "greater things" than in the days of his flesh, "that the Father may be glorified in the Son" – in the powerful mission that *he* continues!' (Beasley-Murray 1987: 380).

The Fourth Gospel's acknowledgment of the disciples' misunderstandings before the giving of the Spirit underscores the fact that it is the *Spirit* who accounts for the disciples' later understanding and ability. It is he who continues the revelation and work of Jesus who is now exalted. This keeps Jesus the Messiah from being merely a past chapter of history that fades from living memory for ever. Rather, the Spirit is a living Presence[53] who applies Jesus' work to the world through his representatives: by teaching and reminding them of Jesus' words (14:26; 16:13–14), by bearing witness to Jesus (15:26), and by convicting the world of its unbelief (16:8–11). Closing the gap between 30 and 90 AD, John's Gospel portrays the works of the messianic community as the continued work of the exalted Messiah, 'greater works' even than the signs performed during Jesus' earthly ministry. In a real sense, these 'greater works' are works *of the exalted Christ* through believers.

Following and being sent

A central term regarding the disciples' mission, never applied to Jesus and spanning from 1:37–43 to 21:19–21, is that of 'following'.[54] Notably, not all *keep* following Jesus (cf. e.g. 6:60–71 or 8:31–33). Before his passion, Jesus predicts that even his close disciples will be scattered and that all will leave him (16:32). Only later, by the 'reminding' ministry of the Spirit (14:26), will Jesus' disciples remember Jesus' words and understand their significance (2:22; 12:16). Thus, according to John, faithful following of Jesus is possible only

of the historical Jesus. But it is unlikely that the later community would construe such a saying that appears to elevate it above its own Lord.
[53] *Paraklētos*: 14:16, 26; 15:26; 16:7; cf. 7:37–39.
[54] See Köstenberger 1998a: 177–180; Schulz 1962: 172–175.

after the cross and Jesus' glorification.

In his use of the term 'following', John moves from literal to figurative 'following'.[55] While the opening call narrative still entails the disciples' literal following of Jesus, 8:12 asserts that those who 'follow' Jesus will not 'walk in darkness' but have 'the light of life' (that is, salvation; cf. 10:9–10). The literal and figurative meanings of 'following' are used side by side in 13:36–38. There is also a widening from the 'following' of Jesus' original disciples to that of every believer.[56] This is especially evident in chapter 10, where Jesus elaborates on the kind of trust relationship that characterizes his relationship with believers individually and corporately. John 12:26 adds to this the notion that following Jesus involves 'death' to self-interest (cf. also 21:15–23; Synoptics). In life and death, in humiliation and glory, Jesus' disciple is to be with his Master (cf. 14:3; 17;24).

The context of 12:24–26 is one of (Gentile) mission.[57] The Greeks address themselves to the disciples. Indeed, it is the disciples who will mediate access to Jesus – but not now. First comes the 'hour' of Jesus' glorification (cf. 12:23). Jesus will be 'lifted up' and draw 'all men' – that is, all *kinds* of people, Gentiles as well as Jews – to himself (12:32–33; cf. 12:24). Thus 12:32 can be taken as an indirect answer to the Greeks' question in 12:21. Paradoxically, it is through his *exaltation* that Jesus will become accessible to the Greeks. Read in connection with 14:12 and 15:16, it may be concluded that the 'following' of 12:26 includes the disciples' participation in Jesus' drawing of all people to himself after Jesus has been exalted. John 10:16, too, may imply the disciples' participation in Jesus' future mission to 'other sheep' (that is, Gentiles).

In another lesson on 'following', the fourth evangelist uses Peter to illustrate the impossibility of an adequate following of Jesus before Jesus' glorification (cf. 13:36–38). Moreover, the final pericope featuring Peter and the 'beloved disciple' indicates that there are different ways of following the crucified and risen Messiah, and that following Jesus does not *necessarily* entail *physical* death, though it entails death to self (12:26, cf. v. 24).

---

[55] *Cf.* 1:37, 40, 43, and 8:12; *cf.* also 13:13–38. See Cullmann 1948: 367; Richard 1985: 100.

[56] *Cf.* 1:37–43; 8:12; ch. 10.

[57] *Cf.* 12:20–21; *cf.* already 10:6; 11:49–52. See esp. Beutler 1990: 333–347, who notes: 'The wording of the approach of the Greeks to Jesus echoes in an astonishing way Isa 52,15 LXX': 'those to whom the news had not yet been announced about him will see, and those who have not yet heard will understand' – that is, the Gentiles (*ethnē polla*; 342); and Köstenberger (1998a: 179, n. 134) for further references.

The other significant term regarding the disciples' mission is that of being 'sent' (Köstenberger 1998a: 180–194). Unlike the term 'following', this expression overlaps with Jesus' mission (cf. esp. 17:18; 20:21). In 17:18 ('sent ... *into the world*'), the point of comparison between the missions of Jesus and his followers appears to be the way they were sent: they were set apart (cf. 10:36), equipped with the Spirit (cf. 1:34–36; 3:34) and sent out. The disciples' mission is set in relation to the world: the disciples are set apart from it (cf. 13:8–14; 15:3), equipped for service, and then sent back into it. The disciples share with Jesus an otherworldly orientation and the resulting suffering of rejection in the world (cf. esp. 15:18–27). A dark place alienated from God,[58] the world nevertheless remains an object of his love (cf. 3:16).[59] While believers need to love each other (13:34; 15:12) and to be unified (17:11, 22–23), these qualities are presented, not as ends in themselves, but as prerequisites for the believer's mission in the world.[60] Moreover, the 'destination' of the church's mission is defined not primarily in geographical but in spiritual terms.

The most important implication from the wording of 17:18 for the disciples' mission can be described thus: 'Use of the phrase *into the world* for the mission of the disciples shows that there is no *necessary* overtone of incarnation or of invasion from another world. Only the broader descriptions of the coming of the Son "into the world" betray the ontological gap that forever distances the origins of Jesus' mission from the origins of the disciples' mission' (Carson 1991b: 566). Thus seekers reading the Gospel are confronted with mutually exclusive spheres that require a choice: 'the circle of the world, in all its rebellion and lostness, and the circle of the disciples of Jesus, in all the privilege of their relationship to the living, self-disclosing, mission-ordaining, sanctifying God' (Carson 1991b: 567).

In 20:21, the point seems to be that the mission of Jesus' followers is to be guided by the same kinds of parameters that determined the sender-sent relationship between Jesus and the Father. Also, Jesus is shown to invest the disciples with authority and legitimacy.[61] The more general reference to 'sending' ties the disciples' mission to the characteristics of Jesus' relationship to his own sender, the Father. At

[58] *Cf.* 8:23–24, 34–37; 9:39–41; 15:22; 16:8–11.

[59] See the helpful survey by Woodbridge (1999: 1–31); and the interaction with Cassem (1972–73: 81–91) in Köstenberger 1998a: 187–188, n. 168.

[60] See the interaction with Popkes 1978: 63–69 in Köstenberger 1998a: 189–190.

[61] *Cf.* Schnackenburg (1990: 3:324), who maintains that while 17:18 has overtones of the disciples' being sent into a world alienated from God, 20:21 is concerned with the passing on of the *Vollmacht* (authority) and *Auftrag* (mandate) *Jesu.*

this stage, Jesus, the paradigmatic 'sent one' (9:7), turns sender. Now Jesus' followers are to embody the qualities characteristic of their Lord during his earthly mission. As Jesus did his Father's will, they have to do *Jesus'* will. As Jesus did his Father's works, they have to do *Jesus'* works. As Jesus spoke the words of his Father, they have to speak *Jesus'* words. Their relationship to their sender, Jesus, is to reflect Jesus' relationship with *his* sender.

These correspondences are explicated well by the following observations on the force of *kathōs* ('just as') in 20:21:

> The special Johannine contribution to the theology of this mission is that the Father's sending of the Son serves both as the model [the comparative aspect of *kathōs*] and the ground [the explanatory aspect of *kathōs*] for the Son's sending of the disciples. Their mission is to continue the Son's mission; and this requires that the Son must be present to them during this mission, just as the Father had to be present to the Son during his mission (R. E. Brown 1970: 1036).

This highlights the underlying continuity between Jesus and his representatives. The Son's mission does not end with his exaltation to the Father. While the form of fulfilment is to be changed, the mission will continue and be effective. The disciples are commissioned to carry on Christ's work rather than to begin a new one. Consequently, 'the disciples are not just to *represent* Jesus (thus the Jewish sending concept is transcended), they are to *re-present* him, that is, Jesus will be present in and through them in his Spirit as they fulfill their mission in the world' (Köstenberger 1998a: 191). The Spirit, too, provides a crucial element of continuity between the missions of Jesus and of the disciples: 'The risen Lord, in associating his disciples with his continuing mission in the world, bestows the Spirit, through whom his own ministry in the flesh was carried out in the power of God' (Beasley-Murray 1987: 380).[62] Finally, Jesus' commission to his followers to forgive or retain sins should probably be seen in the context of people's reception or rejection of Jesus as the Christ, that is, in the context of belief or unbelief in Jesus (Carson 1991b: 655; Bruce 1983b: 392).

---

[62] See also the contributions by Giblet (1957: 20–43), Hahn (1976: 87–106), and Stibbe (1993: 189–206).

Implications

Implications regarding the purpose of John's Gospel

Proposed solutions to the purpose of John's Gospel fall into two general categories (Köstenberger 1998a: 200–206): 1. the Fourth Gospel as *Missionsschrift*, that is, as designed to lead its recipients to faith, whatever group the author(s) may have had in mind;[63] 2. the Fourth Gospel as a *Gemeindeschrift*, as written to strengthen the already existing faith of a community of believers.[64] Among proponents of some form of the 'Johannine community hypothesis', one finds differences of opinion regarding the degree of mission-consciousness displayed in the Fourth Gospel. Some cast the 'Johannine community' in a sectarian mold,[65] others see it as quite concerned to reach out to its (Jewish and other) neighbours.[66] Finally, in recent years, the mediating view has gained popularity that John wrote his Gospel to equip believers to reach out to unbelievers.[67]

How does the present study of mission in John's Gospel inform this ongoing debate? Some selective soundings must suffice here.[68] First, the mission of Jesus, not the mission of Jesus' followers, is the focal point of John's mission presentation. This, together with the considerable amount of material on mission found in this Gospel, renders radical sectarian views of the Fourth Gospel rather implausible. At the same time, John did not merely set forth a self-contained christological portrait. He rather relates the missions of Jesus and of his disciples to

---

[63] So Bornhäuser 1928; Oehler 1936, 1941 and 1957; Oepke 1941: 4–26; van Unnik 1959: 382–411; J. A. T. Robinson 1959–60: 117–131; and more recently Carson 1991b.

[64] See e.g. Schnackenburg 1963: 240–264; Conzelmann 1967: 362; and many others.

[65] See esp. the very influential contribution by Meeks (1972: 44–72); but note the strong refutation by Schnackenburg (1984: 58–72) and the comments in Carson (1991b: 88); and Kuhn (1954: 167–168).

[66] Onuki (1984) conjectures that the Fourth Gospel represents the 'Johannine community's' reflection on its current situation with the purpose of its reintegration into the community. Rensberger (1988), taking his cue from Onuki, argues that the Gospel had a *kathartic* function in the life of the 'Johannine community' leading to a renewed focus on the community's mission: 'The function of the Fourth Gospel, then, is to enable the community to step back from its situation of rejection, reflect upon it in the light of the fate of Jesus, and to be *sent out again with its faith renewed*' (144). Okure (1988: 232) believes that the Fourth Gospel was written by a group within the 'Johannine community' that sought to stir up fellow group members to greater faith and missionary zeal. For a more detailed treatment see Köstenberger 1998a: 205–206.

[67] So e.g. Witherington 1995: 29–32 and Bauckham 1997.

[68] For a more detailed discussion and bibliographic references, see Köstenberger 1995c: 445–464 and 1998a: 199–220.

each other, characterizing Jesus' mission in a way that is relevant for the mission of his followers.

Second, John's distinction between the community of believers and 'the Jews' (chs. 1 – 12) on the one hand and 'the world' (chs. 13 – 21) on the other should be understood not primarily along sociological but salvation-historical lines.[69] This is suggested, for example, by the evangelist's insistence at the end of the first part of his Gospel that the Jewish rejection of the signs-working Messiah fulfilled Isaianic prophecy. Likewise, John's corporate metaphors are built upon Old Testament metaphors for God's people Israel, thus pointing to a salvation-historical linkage between the old and the new messianic community (Pryor 1992). This shifts the focus significantly away from inner-community matters to larger salvation-historical dimensions.

Third, John's perspective, besides being configured along salvation-historical lines, embraces at the same time a realistic attitude towards 'the Jews' during the earthly Jesus' mission and 'the world' at the time of the mission of the later community, and an interest in a mission to the world. Thus the author's horizon appears to have encompassed the world, not merely his own community.

Fourth, when some strong separating lines are drawn, this may reflect a concern to delineate as clearly as possible who is, and is not, part of the new messianic community. This, in turn, would not merely be meaningful in the aftermath of a struggle between the 'Johannine community' and an alleged Jewish parent synagogue; it would also be an important prerequisite for missionizing diaspora Jews and proselytes, since only a clear demonstration of the differences between Judaism and the new messianic community would necessitate the choice of the latter over the former. A missionary purpose of John's Gospel, whether direct or indirect, remains therefore a good possibility. Certainly this seems to be the more natural reading of the Gospel's purpose statement in 20:30–31: 'but these are written that you may believe that *Jesus* is the Christ, the Son of God, and that by believing you may have life in his name'.[70]

Implications for the mission of the contemporary church

The overarching implication for the mission of the contemporary church from the present study is its *need to see itself more consciously in relation to the mission of Jesus*. The fourth evangelist conceived of the mission of the Christian community as ultimately the mission of *the*

[69] Contra Meeks, Onuki, Rensberger, *et al.*
[70] See Carson 1987: 639–651 (critiqued by Fee 1992: 2193–2205).

exalted Jesus carried out through his followers. As is apparent also in Paul's teaching on the headship of Christ over his church, Jesus has not relinquished the ultimate control and direction of the mission of the church (cf. also Matt. 28:18–20). Rather than operating on the basis of marketing surveys or mere human strategizing, the contemporary church therefore needs to subordinate itself consciously to the salvation-historical purposes Jesus seeks to pursue in our day.

The fourth evangelist's teaching on mission *calls the church to greater humility* in the conception of its task. The church is not to function alongside Jesus, or even as a replacement of him. It rather remains a church under orders. Its main role is the extension of forgiveness in Jesus' name to repentant sinners (cf. 20:23) and the proclamation of the gospel message (cf. 17:20). This proclamation should be given credibility by the relationship of the church's members. A humble servant spirit (cf. 13:1–5) and mutual love (cf. 13:35; 15:13) and unity (cf. 17:21, 23, 25) need to be pursued, should the church's mission be successful.

Another implication for the church's mission from John's Gospel is the *need to acknowledge anew the sovereignty of God in its mission.* The fourth evangelist's affirmation that the rejection of Jesus by his own people, including his crucifixion, occurred according to God's predestinatory counsel, should give the church new strength especially in parts of the world where it is currently suffering. The assurance permeating the Fourth Gospel that God draws people to himself and that he 'gives' people to Jesus, too, should encourage the church in its resolve to proclaim the gospel. Moreover, as the church carries out its mission, it can be assured that all of the resources needed for its outreach will be provided (cf. 14:13; 15:7, 16b).

The mission of God in this world *cannot be thwarted.* Even sinful human resistance to God's salvific plans is incorporated into God's inscrutable predestinatory counsel. Thus the world's rejection of the church and its mission should not cause the church to reject the world. On the contrary, Jesus' followers must bear witness to Jesus (cf. 15:18–27). Like Jesus, they are sent into the world (cf. 17:18). The church's mission, however, is to be based on a spiritually separated life, one that is based on God's word (17:17). John's Gospel provides a timely reminder that the church must preach Jesus as the *only* way to the Father (cf. 14:6) regardless of the popularity of this message in its modern context. While dialogue and contextualization are important, inappropriate accommodation or compromise must be avoided.

One final lesson that emerges from a study of the Fourth Gospel's mission theology is that *the church's mission is not to be carried out as an individualistic enterprise.* The mission should rather be undergirded by the corporate life of the community, as believers reflect God's love and unity.[71] Where direct proclamation of the word may initially fail to persuade, the more indirect approach of providing an example of loving, unified relationships may provide the needed corroboration for mission to succeed. Moreover, the Christian community is to follow its calling to represent Christ actively in the world. A merely passive reflection of Christ in the community's life falls short of the church's mandate.[72]

Conclusion

The above study of John's presentation of Jesus' mission showed that the fourth evangelist conceived of Jesus as unique. Jesus, a unique person combining within himself attributes of divinity as well as humanity, was called to carry out a unique mission, culminating in his 'exaltation' and 'glorification' and his founding of the new messianic community. The implications for an age where pluralism makes rapid gains are profound (Carson 1996). It seems difficult to see how anyone who takes his or her cue from the biblical material can dispute that the New Testament writers viewed Jesus as unique in his personhood and redemptive work.[73]

For the fourth evangelist, God's work for humanity is centred in Christ's cross-work[74] and in his revelation of God in word and work (cf. 1:14, 18; the 'signs'). The paradigm for the church's mission is to be the sender–sent relationship sustained between God the Father and Jesus the Son during the latter's earthly ministry (cf. 20:21). The church's obedient response needs to mirror Jesus' in his total dependence upon God. At the same time, John conceives of the church's mission in more humble terms than in analogy with Christ's incarnation, affirming the uniqueness of the Word's becoming flesh and of Christ's salvific work.[75]

---

[71] *Cf.* 13:34–35; 15:12; 17:11, 20–26.

[72] *Cf.* 15:16; 17:18; 20:21.

[73] *Cf.* e.g. 1:14, 18; 3:16; 14:6.

[74] *Cf.* 3:13–17; 4:34; 6:51–58; 8:28; 10:11, 15, 17–18; 12:32; 17:4; 19:30.

[75] *Cf.* 1:14, 18; 3:16, 18. *Cf.* Köstenberger 1995c: 453–455, esp. 454: 'John seems far too concerned to preserve Jesus' ontological uniqueness to make his incarnation the model for the church's mission.' Contra, most recently, Nissen 1999: 229–230.

Chapter Nine

The General Epistles and Revelation[1]

Treatments of mission in the biblical writings tend to set aside the General Epistles and Revelation, because they do not seem to be directly concerned with mission if such is defined too narrowly.[2] Apart from a few exceptional passages, these writings do not feature sending terminology, a 'Great Commission', or overt exhortations to evangelistic outreach. Their primary concerns are rather bound up with defending the Christian gospel against heresy and equipping believers to respond appropriately to suffering and persecution. In one very important sense, these activities are not mission. For without the interpretive word (that is, the gospel of forgiveness and salvation in Christ), Christian behaviour by itself remains insufficient to lead people to a saving knowledge of the Lord Jesus Christ.

Nevertheless, it seems appropriate to discuss the contribution made by the General Epistles and Revelation to the Bible's teaching on mission. For in order for the gospel to be proclaimed persuasively and with God's saving power, it must be preserved pure. And if Christians fail to adorn their verbal message with the witness of a godly life and proper relationships, this is bound to have a negative effect on their active outreach to unbelievers. How else, for instance, are we to understand Peter's exhortation to the wives of unbelieving husbands to be submissive to them so that they may be won over 'without words by

---

[1] This chapter represents a revision of Köstenberger 1995b and 1998b.

[2] Senior and Stuhlmueller (1983: 297–305) focus on 1 Peter and Revelation while giving little attention to Hebrews (see briefly 309–310); Hahn's treatment (1965: 137–143) is confined to a few cursory references to 1 Peter. See also Bosch (1991: 55), who focuses on the contributions by Matthew, Luke and Paul, arguing that these three New Testament authors are 'representative of first-century missionary thinking and practice'. The Scripture index to Bosch's work includes references to three passages in 1 Peter and to one passage in Revelation, while there is not a single reference to the book of Hebrews in Bosch's work, which extends to over five hundred pages. This exclusive focus on the Matthean-Lukan-Pauline axis of mission in the New Testament results in a marginalization of the contributions of books such as 1 Peter. Bosch's otherwise fine recent article (1993: 175–192) likewise does not contain a single reference to the General Epistles or Revelation.

the behaviour of their wives'? In what follows, we will first deal with writings that are primarily devoted to the defence of the gospel (2 Peter, Jude and 1 – 3 John). After this, we will discuss the contribution made to a biblical theology of mission by the epistle to the Hebrews, 1 Peter and the book of Revelation.

The preservation of orthodoxy in 2 Peter, Jude and 1 – 3 John

2 Peter and Jude

Both Jude and Peter deal with false teachers who practise unrighteous, licentious living while claiming to possess superior spirituality (Jude 4; 2 Pet. 2:13–14, 18–22). Jude denounces 'godless men who change the grace of our God into a licence for immorality and deny Jesus Christ our only Sovereign and Lord', while Peter apparently deals with a more specific and quite unique doctrinal aberration: teachers who deny the reality of divine intervention in history, be it in the past through a flood or in the future through Christ's second coming and a judgment by fire (2 Pet. 3:3–7).

This is not the place to engage in a more detailed exposition of the message of these books. Suffice it to say that, in their desire to preserve orthodoxy in the churches entrusted to them, both Jude and Peter clear the ground, as it were, for the church's outreach. For while they do not engage in mission directly, they help ensure the continued purity of the gospel message. This, in turn, is an important prerequisite for an effective missionary enterprise.[3]

1 John

To understand the first epistle of John adequately one must look at it against the backdrop of a proto-gnostic heresy which had entered the church through some who had since left it (2:19). The letter was apparently written in an effort to undo the harm done by those false teachers and to reassure the bewildered and confused members of the congregation who were left behind. Thus the epistle represents, not an exhortation to mission, but an effort to provide pastoral counsel after a dangerous Christian heresy had shaken the church. John's message revolves primarily around the issues of proper doctrine and the identity of believers.

In terms of doctrine, John is supremely concerned to uphold apostolic

---

[3] See further the implications drawn at the end of this section.

christological teaching against gnostic distortions. This entails defence of the incarnation (1:7; 4:2; 2 John 7) as well as of Christ's universal atonement for sins (2:2; cf. 4:10). Underlying both emphases is a firm conviction regarding the reality of sin and Christ's willingness and ability to extend forgiveness upon confession of sin (1:9; 2:1; cf. John 20:23). Thoroughly biblical christological and soteriological teaching remains crucial and indispensable in dealing with other religions that may be open to *aspects* of Christian teaching (such as in the ethical realm) or may be willing to acknowledge that Jesus was a prophet from God while refusing to embrace the Bible's message on Christ and salvation in its entirety.

Regarding the identity of believers, John focuses primarily on ontological realities that apply to all true believers, such as their regeneration (3:1-2, 9-10; 4:4, 6; 5:18-19; cf. John 3:3, 5), possession of the Holy Spirit (2:20, 27) and of eternal life (5:11-12) and the availability of forgiveness of sin (1:9; 2:1). In dealing with adherents of other religions, therefore, Christians need not be in the least intimidated by other forms of spirituality that claim intimate knowledge and communion with God. Christianity is a religion for everyone, not merely for a spiritual elite initiated into certain religious rites or blessed with esoteric knowledge of divine secrets, as was the case in the mystery religions that flourished in that day.

2 – 3 John

Like 1 John, John's second and third epistles are concerned with believers 'walking in truth' (2 John 4; 3 John 3–4) and 'loving one another' (2 John 5). But they add one new element: that of extending or rejecting hospitality to false teachers (2 John 9–11; 3 John 5–11). In his second epistle, John is emphatic that no 'official welcome' must be given to those 'official teachers' who are 'dedicated missionaries of error' (Stott 1988: 215). In light of the devastating eternal consequences of false doctrine (in the present case, a denial of the incarnation) on people's lives, it is imperative not to provide any encouragement to those who perpetrate it. Moreover, hospitality in this regard means more than inviting such a teacher over for a meal; it amounts to furnishing him with a base for his work, including financial assistance and support, and thus making common cause in the gospel (Thompson 1992: 160).

The situation addressed in John's third epistle is different again. Locked in a struggle for authority, John ('the elder') confronts a local church official named Diotrephes who not only refused to extend hospitality to any travelling missionaries associated with John but even forbade other church members to do so. If anyone ignored his directives, he put them out of the church (3 John 9–11). The purpose of the letter is to encourage Gaius, who has shown such proper hospitality, to continue to do so and to strengthen his hand in light of Diotrephes' efforts to intimidate him. This curious incident shows that the criterion used in the matter of extending hospitality to travelling teachers must not be motivated by sheer power hunger or arbitrary enforcement of doctrinal conformity to certain church leaders' views. Rather, the underlying purpose of John's instructions is to ensure that the church supports only the propagation of those views that are in keeping with the apostolic gospel.

Implications

Several insights relevant for the mission of the contemporary church emerge from the materials considered above. At least three such lessons can be gleaned from the epistles of Jude and 2 Peter.

2 Peter and Jude

First, the church must *renew its zeal in contending for the faith* 'once for all entrusted to the saints' (Jude 3). In an age when doctrinal distinctives are frequently surrendered for the sake of so-called 'evangelical unity', it must be kept in mind that Christianity is a historic faith that must be preserved rather than changed according to modern-day sensibilities. Those who rise up to defend orthodox biblical Christianity need not be divisive, as is increasingly alleged, but may rather be faithful, responsible, courageous servants of Christ who take seriously his call to preserve not just the church's unity, but also its doctrinal distinctives.

Second, believers should *consider the results of rebellion against God*. As Jude points out, the history of God's people shows that false teachers were severely judged by God; it will be no different for those who teach unorthodox doctrine in our day. As a result, believers should face up to their responsibility to discern false teaching and distance themselves from those who perpetrate it.

Third, Jude and Peter provide helpful instruction on *dealing with infiltrators of Christian congregations* who seek to sway believers away from the faith.[4] If the spiritual well-being of a congregation is in

---

[4] It may be inferred from Jude 12 ('These men are blemishes at your love feasts') that these false teachers were actually present among the congregation during times of

jeopardy, the concern of the church leadership for its members may necessitate the removal of false teachers from the community once the heterodox nature of their teaching has been established.

Jude and 2 Peter thus constitute reminders of an essential *prerequisite* for mission: that of zeal for historic biblical Christianity. It is imperative to define carefully the parameters of orthodoxy and to defend the particular distinctives of the Christian faith in order for mission to be meaningful. Without a well-defined, clearly delineated gospel, mission will become increasingly ineffective, if not entirely meaningless. Jude and 2 Peter thus highlight the crucial connection between a concern for doctrinal orthodoxy and mission, between theological fidelity and gospel proclamation.

We turn briefly to a discussion of the contemporary relevance of John's epistles for the church's mission.

1 John

When John does not call his audience to direct verbal engagement with the world, this may at least in part be due to his conviction that the world is caught up in its sinful blindness and hardened in its opposition to Christ, believers and the gospel (cf. 2:15–17). John's message to his readers is not an exhortation to enhanced apologetic efforts, but a call to perseverance, holiness, full assurance and brotherly love. Prophetically, John insists that a person's true beliefs will be apparent in that person's actions, whether good or evil. Truthful lives thus make a telling statement to the surrounding world, while people living a lie betray their message by their deeds. This underscores the need for the credibility of the church's witness.

In an age of pragmatism and pluralism, John calls the church to a return to the simplicity and clarity of biblical teaching on the Christian faith. Effective gospel proclamation must be undergirded by constant vigilance in preserving the purity of the Christian message. Our praxis (mission) must be rooted in ontological realities: a vibrant biblical christology and soteriology, and a proper understanding of the identity of believers in Christ and in this world. John is not hostile towards the world, but he reminds us that the world is ultimately hostile to *us* as Christians. This should warn us against both a complacent accommodation to the world and undue optimism as we seek to engage it in terms of the gospel.

---

worship, that they were not just members but teachers (*cf.* 11–13), and that they sought to impart their prophecies and teachings during these meetings.

2 – 3 John

While the issue addressed in John's second and third epistles (that of extending or rejecting hospitality to false teachers) is less pressing in an age of ample hotel accommodation – but note the continued dependence of missionaries on local private hospitality in many parts of the world – we must continue to heed the principle invoked by John: 'Anyone who welcomes him [that is, fails to exercise proper discernment regarding the unorthodox character of someone's teaching] shares in his wicked works' (2 John 11). Believers must discern the content of people's teaching and refuse to have any part in the propagation of unorthodox doctrine. This is an element sadly lacking in vast segments of the contemporary church (Marshall 1978b: 74).

Adorning the gospel in the midst of adversity: Hebrews, 1 Peter and Revelation

We turn now to the writings that deal with mission more directly: Hebrews, 1 Peter and Revelation. Before considering each book separately, it may be helpful to note a few commonalities. To begin with, all three of these books deal with the issue of how the church and individual believers should respond to suffering and persecution during the second half of the first century AD, be it in the empire's capital or in the provinces of Asia Minor.[5] According to the respective authors, believers work out their Christian faith in adverse circumstances through submission to authority, non-retaliation, love of enemies, harmonious, loving and unified relationships within the church, recognition of the heavenly calling of believers, and perseverance. In light of the challenges at hand, one finds little *direct* exhortation to the verbal proclamation of the gospel.[6] These writings do, however, reflect a concern for believers' witness by way of a godly life in the midst of a largely hostile environment, in the hope that thus some may be won to the faith. Like Old Testament Israel, the New Testament church is to fulfil a mediatorial function between God and larger humanity.[7]

All three books also accentuate the temporary nature of believers'

---

[5] *Cf.* Heb. 10:23, 32–39; 12:1–13; 13:12–13; 1 Pet. 1:6–7; 2:13–17; 3:13–18; 4:12–19; 5:1, 7–10; Rev., passim.

[6] Yet these writings everywhere assume 'the great doctrines of the faith' (Wells 2000: 211).

[7] *Cf.* 1 Pet. 2:5, 9; Rev. 1:6; 5:10; 20:6; *cf.* Exod. 19:6. See the discussion of Israel and the exodus in ch. 2 of the present book.

earthly existence and their essential foreignness in this world.[8] The followers of Christ are sojourners, aliens and pilgrims, pursuing the path toward their permanent home, heaven (Heb. 11:9, 13; 1 Pet. 1:1, 17; 2:11). Christian living in general, and the suffering of persecution for one's faith in particular, are thus set into a pointedly eschatological perspective. In light of Christ's imminent return, the transitory nature of believers' afflictions is brought into sharper focus. This perspective renders hardships more bearable, focusing attention on the rewards of eternal fellowship with Christ promised to those who persevere. Those who suffer shame will be divinely honoured.[9] Moreover, all three writings feature an increased emphasis on God's final judgment.[10] This eschatological perspective determines the framework for the church's ordering of its external relationships. In the midst of their suffering, believers are reminded of their enduring heavenly inheritance, which puts their ordeal in proper perspective: it is merely temporary, and it should be seen as an opportunity for witness. This encompasses a variety of earthly relationships: as slaves of unbelieving masters, as wives of unbelieving husbands, as citizens of an anti-Christian state, believers are to 'submit' while testifying courageously to their Lord.

Finally, all three authors accentuate the supremacy and uniqueness of Christ. According to the writer of Hebrews, Jesus is the captain of our salvation, the once-for-all sacrifice, the great high priest. For Peter, Jesus is the suffering servant of Isaiah who, in fulfilment of Old Testament typology, 'bore our sins in his body on the cross'. For the author of Revelation, Jesus is the faithful witness, the Lamb who alone is worthy to open the scroll that contains the prophecies of the entire book, and the one who is entrusted with God's judgment.

Hebrews

The book of Hebrews may appear to be an unlikely candidate to be consulted regarding its teaching on mission. Most think of this epistle as solely concerned, not with the church's relationship to the world, but with internal matters. However, it was precisely because of external pressures and persecution for Christ's sake that some were apparently

---

[8] For the emphasis on the identity of believers (that is, their elect status) in 1 Peter, see Wells 2000: 211–213, 215–216.

[9] On shame and honour in Hebrews, see deSilva 1995; on shame and honour in 1 Peter, see Elliott 1995: 166–178.

[10] The Gk. terms for 'judge' (verb: *krinō*; noun: *kritēs*) or 'judgment' (*krisis*) are found in Heb. 9:27; 10:27, 30; 12:23; 13:4; 1 Pet. 1:17; 2:23; 4:5, 6; Rev. 6:10; 11:18; 14:7; 16:5, 7; 18:8, 10, 20; 19:2 (bis), 11; 20:12, 13. To this should be added references to the '[last] day' (Heb. 10:25; 1 Pet. 2:12; Rev. 16:14). *Cf.* Hahn 1965: 142.

tempted to revert to Judaism in order to escape such affliction. The epistle appears to be directed towards a congregation in danger of drifting from its Christian faith back to Judaism. Probably written in Rome (13:14; Bruce 1990c: 13–14; W. L. Lane 1991a: lviii–lx), the epistle was composed by an unknown second-generation believer (2:3; W. L. Lane 1991a: lxii), perhaps shortly before the destruction of the Jerusalem temple in AD 70 (Bruce 1990c: 20–22). In the face of temptation to apostatize from the faith, probably due to the threat of imminent suffering, the author sets out to convince his readers of the superiority of Jesus and of the priesthood he instituted. The letter thus serves to confirm the commitments of a community that had already suffered a certain degree of religious and social ostracism, while insisting that those values require engagement in, not separation from, an antagonistic society (Attridge 1990: 211–226).

The supremacy of Jesus

The author of Hebrews demonstrates Jesus' unique role in God's plan of salvation in no uncertain terms. The book opens with a number of startling claims regarding the supremacy of the revelation brought by Jesus, and regarding the superior work and nature of Jesus. God's revelation in Jesus is superior, since God in ancient days spoke through prophets, while, in the last days, he spoke to us in revelation involving 'a son' (1:1–2).[11] Jesus' work is superior, since, through him, God made the ages (1:2). Jesus also made purification from sin and sat down at the right hand of the Majesty on high (1:2–3). Jesus' nature, too, is superior, since he is the radiant splendour of God's glory and the exact representation of his nature (1:3). Finally, he is superior to other spirit beings (angels, including Satan; see 2:14), in nature, calling and authority (1:4 – 2:18).[12]

Jesus is presented as the great high priest (5:1 – 10:39; cf. 2:17), who was given an eternal priesthood according to the order of Melchizedek (5:1 – 7:28) and who instituted a new, superior covenant (8:1 – 10:39). The writer of Hebrews draws the implication that when Jesus 'sat down' (1:3; 8:1; 10:12; 12:2), this indicated that there remained no further need for sacrifice. Complete atonement had been rendered (9:23–28). The question of how to deal effectively with sin is crucial, and Hebrews provides a powerful answer: Jesus has dealt with sin decisively once and for all. He has overcome the power of Satan. Regarding Israel, the extensive quotes of Jeremiah 31:31–34 and 31:33

[11] On God as 'the one who speaks', see Köstenberger 1998b.
[12] Quoting esp. 2 Sam. 7:14; Pss. 2:7; 8:4–6; 110:1.

with reference to Jesus (cf. 8:8–12; 10:16–17) imply that, now that a 'new' covenant has been made, the 'old' covenant is obsolete and no longer effective, so that Jews should find the fulfilment of God's promise of an eschatological covenant in Jesus.[13]

Witness terminology and the metaphor of a race

Usually, one thinks of the term 'witness' in the New Testament as something the church is enjoined to do with regard to Jesus Christ. In Hebrews, however, 'witness' terminology is never applied to believers in the active sense of the term, that is, as a call for them to bear witness. Rather, it is God who bears witness to the faith of previous believers (11:2, 4, 5, 39; 12:1). In the 'faith chapter' of Hebrews (ch. 11), Abraham, Moses and many other Old Testament examples are cited in order to make clear that believers in God must be willing to renounce all earthly ties in favour of following the God who called them.[14] The many verbal and allusive parallels to the intertestamental book of 2 Maccabees in 12:1–3 indicate, together with the exhortation of 12:4, that the author conceives of the Christian 'witness' as one who is prepared to 'resist to the point of shedding blood'. This certainly was true for many of the believers mentioned in 11:32–38 as well as for the martyrs of the Maccabean period. When facing the prospect of persecution, the Hebrew believers should therefore be inspired by the 'great cloud of witnesses' who had gone – and suffered – before them (12:1), with Jesus, 'the author and perfecter of our faith, who ... endured such opposition from sinful men', as the supreme forerunner (12:1–3; cf. 2:10; 6:20). Followers of Christ are to 'hold firmly to the faith we profess' (4:14; 10:23) according to the example of 'the Apostle and High Priest' of their faith (3:1).

By using the metaphor of a 'race', even that of a marathon, the author urges his audience to view suffering as a form of divine discipline designed to perfect them as sons (12:5–11), just as Jesus himself learned obedience through suffering (cf. 2:10, 17–18; 5:7–9). This mindset would help believers persevere in their struggle as they 'ran the race' by fixing their eyes on Jesus, just as he had fixed his eyes on God. Christians' primary focus should therefore not be on the world, but on Jesus, on God. The community's and the individual Christian's faithful practice of obedience is thus an essential prerequisite for mission.

---

[13] See already the discussion of 'The restoration of Israel and the new covenant' in ch. 2 above.

[14] See the discussion of the call of Abram in ch. 2 of this book.

Christians as 'pilgrims' who despise shame for the sake of a higher honour

What is the identity of believers in this world? How might one describe their relationship to the world in which they live? According to the author of Hebrews, Christians are pilgrims, exiles in search of a homeland, a better country, of 'a city prepared by God' (11:13–16; cf. 12:22; Johnsson 1978). The pilgrimage to an earthly sanctuary is replaced by people's pilgrimage to a lasting heavenly sanctuary (6:19–20). Israel's unbelief during the exodus is to serve as a warning against the Hebrews' disbelief during their new exodus (3:7 – 4:11; cf. 1 Cor. 10:6, 11). Abraham, on the other hand, is presented as a model pilgrim: he set out not knowing where he was going, acting upon nothing but God's word of promise, living in tents like a foreigner, looking ahead to a permanent home, not in Palestine, but in heaven (11:8–10).[15] Moses, likewise, scorned the fleeting pleasures of this world (11:24–29). According to the pattern set by Abraham and Moses, the readers of Hebrews were sojourners embarking on a new exodus, with their way led, not by Joshua (4:8; Gk. *Iēsous*), but by Jesus (cf. 2:10; 12:2; Gk. *Iēsous*). As the author of Hebrews argues, the Old Testament already contains the acknowledgment that, even after Israel had entered the Promised Land, there continued to remain a future rest for God's people (3:7 – 4:11; cf. Ps. 95:7–11).

As pilgrims in this world, believers are to despise shame in order to gain higher, heavenly honour (deSilva 1995). The climactic exhortation of the entire book, transcending even 12:1–3, is found in 13:13. After affirming that Jesus suffered outside the gate, the author exhorts his audience, 'Let us then, go to him outside the camp, bearing the disgrace he bore' (13:13; cf. 10:25–26).[16] Remarkably, conceptualities involving the 'temple' have been eclipsed in Hebrews by 'tent' and 'camp' terminologies. Christians are to count it a privilege to follow the one 'who for the joy set before him endured the cross, despising the shame' (12:2). Their mission is to have its root in this radical discipleship which reveals itself in their close association with Christ, not just in his glory, but also in his sufferings (cf. 1 Pet. 1:11–12; 5:1).

---

[15] *Cf.* Schick 1989: 375. Schick's article is highly suggestive at many points, but in one point he surely overstates his case when he claims that Hebrews presents believers as *priestly* pilgrims. Pilgrims they may be, but, according to Hebrews, only Jesus is a priest.

[16] See the extensive discussion in W. L. Lane 1991b: 542–546.

Implications

The book of Hebrews has no direct equivalent to Matthew's 'Great Commission'. But this does not mean that the epistle's author did not believe in the necessity of Christian outreach. Rather, it is assumed that believers' identity as followers, even disciples, of Christ will entail suffering which, in turn, will require the bearing of witness. While there are no clear lines of demarcation between verbal gospel proclamation and the witness of a godly life (whether in the form of godliness in persecution or some other form of 'bearing the disgrace he bore'), the two sustain an intricate relationship with each other. For it is assumed that believers in Christ have confessed their faith to the outside world and that they are identified with their Christian profession whether their witness in a given instance entails specific verbal testimony or various forms of the witness of a godly life. Similar to Peter in his first epistle, the author of Hebrews upholds Christ as believers' ultimate example in suffering. If Christ was willing to endure the cross for the joy set before him, so should his followers be. In all things, Christ has shown the way.

Significantly, the writer's exhortation for believers to go to Jesus 'outside the camp' and to bear suffering with him accentuates Christians' call to be 'outsiders', choosing, not the easy road of material prosperity, but the path of the cross, of self-denying, death-defying discipleship and, if called for, even social ostracism. This letter's message is especially meaningful for a church called to suffer for Christ's sake or tempted to religious compromise in order to escape persecution.

1 Peter

Believers' status as 'resident aliens'

Like the letter to the Hebrews, Peter's first epistle portrays believers as pilgrims in this world. Christians are sojourners, 'resident aliens'.[17] The letter was probably written to believers 'dispersed'[18] in Asia Minor at the onset of a major persecution in the early 60s AD. In all likelihood,

---

[17] *Cf.* 1:1: *parepidēmois*; 1:17: *paroikias*; 2:11: *paroikous kai parepidēmous*; *cf.* Heb. 11:13: *xenoi kai parepidēmoi*; 11:9: *parōikēsen*; and Phil. 3:20: *politeuma en ouranois*. The overall approach taken by Elliott (1966 and 1982), while providing many suggestive insights, is invalidated by the author's practice of imposing sociological categories onto the text. *Cf.* Chin 1991: 96–112 and Feldmeier 1992.

[18] Chevallier (1974: 387–400) argues that, for Peter, living in the diaspora is not accidental and deplorable but symbolizes the state of Christians in the world. They are not cut off from non-Christian society but remain engaged in the very name of their faith, seeking to draw in non-believers by virtue of their good conduct (2:12).

Peter wrote from Rome (5:13) – where such persecution may already
have begun – in order to prepare his readers for imminent suffering
(4:12). Christians are viewed as 'disgraced yet graced' (Elliott 1995:
166–178) and reminded of the dignity and honour they already enjoy as
members of God's household. They are also enjoined to solidarity with
their shamed but divinely honoured Lord Jesus Christ.[19]

By referring to the location where he lives at the time of writing as
'Babylon' (5:13), Peter symbolically refers to Rome as the antitype to
the nation that was responsible for Israel's exile, a metaphor already
found in Jewish intertestamental literature (cf. e.g. *Sibylline Oracles*
5.143, 159; *4 Ezra* and *2 Baruch*, passim), developed even more fully
in Revelation.[20] Peter, who identifies himself as a 'witness of Christ's
sufferings' (5:1), would soon be martyred himself, thus providing, like
Jesus, an example of suffering that others could follow (cf. John 21:15–
23).

An eschatological framework

A strong eschatological component flavours the entire epistle,
especially in light of the church's suffering and persecution.[21] This
pervasive eschatological thrust, in turn, is tied to the notion of mission
(O'Connor 1991: 23). Peter reminds Christians in the diaspora of their
imperishable inheritance kept in heaven (1:4), assuring them that they
are, by the power of God, guarded through faith for a salvation to be
revealed on the last day (1:5). Thus believers are to rejoice in their
hope, even though they may have to endure various trials in this world,
'for a little while' (1:6). Christians are, however, not alone in their
sufferings; there is a solidarity among believers in all the world (5:9; cf.
5:1; 2:21–25).

Peter's message to his readers is that their 'home', that is, their
identity, is found in the 'family of God' (4:17), which is the fellowship
of God's people, a 'spiritual house' (2:5). Paradoxically, these 'resident
aliens' are also God's 'chosen people' (2:9; cf. 1:1–2). Peter's

[19] On the cultural implications of 1 Peter, see esp. Volf (1994: 15–30), who, in
interaction with E. Troeltsch and H. R. Niebuhr, claims that 1 Peter speaks more
pointedly and comprehensively to the problem of 'Christ and culture' than any other
New Testament text.
[20] *Cf.* Rev. 14:8; 16:19; 17:5; 18:2, 10, 21. *Cf.* Michaels 1988: 311; O'Connor 1991:
17–26. *Cf.* the code name of 'Kittim' for the Romans in the Qumran scrolls (e.g.
1QpHab. 1:14–16; 1QM, passim). It should be acknowledged that some dispute the
identification of 'Babylon' with Rome in 1 Pet. 5:13.
[21] *Cf.* Selwyn (1956: 394): 'there is no book in the New Testament where the
eschatology is more closely integrated with the teaching of the document as a whole'.

characterization of his recipients' identity in those terms represents an effort to equip the church for the fulfilment of its mission. Rather than being discouraged by their powerlessness, uprootedness and abuse from the world, Christians receive hope and strength in their faith and vision (O'Connor 1991: 20). Thus empowered, believers are made ready to minister to an often abusive world rather than adopting a defensive 'siege mentality' (Senior and Stuhlmueller 1983: 299).

Transference of old-covenant categories

What is the relationship between the roles assigned to Israel and the church with regard to mission? Does Peter conceive of these primarily in terms of continuity or of discontinuity? God's promises to his Old Testament covenant people of a physical land, inheritance and descendants are transformed in Peter's first epistle into expectations of eternal realities, so that believers' present experience is placed into an eschatological perspective. Categories reserved in the Old Testament for Israel are now freely transferred to God's 'new people' (2:9–10; Steuernagel 1986: 8–18). Peter's vision of the church's mission likewise appears to take its cue from the Old Testament concept of Israel as a mediatorial body and a light to the nations.[22]

Peter perceives the believing community's presence in the world from the vantage point of mission, stressing its identity as a witnessing body analogous to Israel's intended function (P. J. Robinson 1989: 176–187). The transference of covenant categories from God's old-covenant community to his new in 2:9–10 climaxes in the purpose statement of 2:9: 'that you may declare the praises of him who called you out of darkness into his wonderful light', a quotation from the eschatological passage of Isaiah 43:21.[23] Moreover, believers are to keep their

---

[22] Cf. Exod. 19:6 and Is. 43:20, quoted in 1 Pet. 2:9; cf. Is. 49:6. This does not imply that God intended Israel to be 'a nation of evangelists and foreign missionaries', engaging in 'cross-cultural' or foreign mission as we understand it today (here we agree with Goldsworthy 1996: 7). See the discussion under 'The question of Israel's "mission" to the nations' in ch. 2 above.

[23] According to Wells (2000: 227–228), the phrase 'proclaim the excellencies' refers to declaring God's glory and praise as well as his great deeds: the exodus echoed in the liberation from Babylonian captivity, and the eschatological 'exodus', that is, Jesus' death and resurrection. Thus 'proclaiming God's excellencies' means nothing other than preaching the gospel (see the references provided by Wells on p. 229). However, Wells erects a false dichotomy when she maintains, 'The aim of the church is not to make converts. Rather, it is to glorify God' (229). Is it not possible to glorify God *by making converts*? Michaels (1988: 110–111) holds that the present passage refers to 'worship, not missionary activity'; believers are recounting the wonderful (saving) acts of God. However, the line between worship and missions should not be drawn too sharply. Moreover, even Michaels acknowledges that the phrase 'of him who called you out of

behaviour excellent among the nations, so that 'though they accuse you of doing wrong, they may see your good deeds and glorify God on the day he visits us' (2:12). The proclamation of God's excellencies must be undergirded by 'excellent behaviour', not now by Old Testament Israel among the Gentiles, but by the new-covenant community in the unbelieving world surrounding it.[24]

Holiness and submission

The transference of Old Testament categories to God's new-covenant people also involves the need for New Testament believers to be holy as God is holy. The entire section of 1:13 – 2:10 is devoted to Peter's exhortation to his readers to live a holy, spiritually set-apart life.[25] Indeed, 'No part of the New Testament speaks out more eloquently ... on [the] theme of holiness of life as a way of Christian witness [as does 1 Peter]' (O'Connor 1991: 17). Significantly, this exhortation to holiness, rather than being focused on believers' relationship with God or with one another, is directed towards their responsibility to reflect God's character in the midst of an unbelieving world.

The injunction is grounded in God's command to the people he called out from slavery in Egypt to be holy and set apart for him.[26] While the external expressions of such distinctness (*i.e.* dietary, ritual and ceremonial laws) have been largely rendered obsolete, the need for God's people to live a distinct Christian life-style and to abstain from both physical and spiritual adultery remains.[27] By living holy lives, Christians reveal to the surrounding world God's very own nature, just as Israel was called to do. A failure to do so, today as then, amounts to a failure to commend the gospel of Christ by our lives. Notably, the power for living a holy life is not drawn from one's own moral capacity, but derives from Christ's redemption (1:18–23).

Not only this; even believers' *submission to earthly authorities*, whether civil, economic, familial or ecclesial authorities (2:13, 18; 3:1; 5:1, 5), is *necessary ultimately for mission*, a frequently overlooked

---

darkness into his wonderful light' refers to conversion, which thus constitutes the backdrop for the present statement.

[24] Wells 2000: 229: 'exemplary conduct ... is clearly public and missionary in intent ... The Christian mission is the outworking of Christians living out their difference [from the world]'.

[25] See here esp. Wells (2000: 216–231), who discusses 1 Peter in the context of Israel's call to holiness, including missionary implications.

[26] *Cf.* 1:15–16, quoting Lev. 11:44, 45; 19:2; and 20:7.

[27] *Cf.* 1:14, 18; 2:1, 11–12; 4:3–4, 15; *cf.* Matt. 5 – 7.

fact.[28] Mission provides a powerful rationale not only for believers to submit to governing authorities (2:13) or economic superiors (2:18), but also for wives to submit to husbands (3:1) and for younger men in the church to submit to elders (5:5). In each case, the same word, *hypotassō* ('submit'), is used.[29] Christian wives may hope to win over any unbelieving husbands by their submissive behaviour 'without a word' (3:1). In a society where women were usually expected to adopt their husband's religion, Christian wives in mixed marriages were in a very vulnerable position indeed. Husbands, in turn, are to treat their wives with understanding, as fellow-heirs of grace (3:7), while the entire congregation is to humble itself under God (5:6).

Following in the footsteps of Christ, their example in suffering, believers are to entrust themselves to God. He will restore and strengthen those in minority positions, whether Christian citizens in an ungodly society, Christian slaves suffering from the abuse of people in authority over them, or Christian wives who have to live with their unbelieving husbands (5:10). Apart from the glory of God, a primary motive for proper submission to authorities is the Christian community's witness in the surrounding unbelieving world.[30]

Believers' suffering and the example of Jesus

The terms 'suffering' or 'suffer' are found in every chapter of Peter's first epistle.[31] This corresponds to the frequency of words for 'hope'.[32] The theme of 'hope in suffering' is therefore central to the epistle.

[28] The effort by Senior and Stuhlmueller (1983: 310, n. 5) to interpret 'submit' in 2:13 exclusively in terms of 'participation' and 'involvement' in the world in contrast to 'non-involvement' is reductionistic and misses the denotation of the term for a possible connotation (cf. 300–301 and 311, n. 8). This is evident by the use of the same term used for 'submit' in the context of slave–master (2:13) and wife–husband relationships (3:1–6). Clearly, for example, wives are not merely encouraged to 'participate' in their marriages, but to reflect, by their proper submission to authority, their Christian faith even under the improper use of authority, setting their Christian witness above their desire for immediate vindication and liberation.

[29] It will not do to set aside the implications from this passage for husband–wife relationships by reducing the thrust to a 'pattern of courageous witness and redemptive suffering', as Senior and Stuhlmueller do (1983: 301), nor is there any basis to argue for a shift in meaning from 'subjection to authority' in 2:13 to 'considerate submission to others' in 3:1 (Richardson 1987: 70–80). While the larger context is frequently not given adequate attention in the passage's interpretation, 'context' should not be permitted to overwhelm the explicit teaching of the passage or empty it of its clear implication, that is, that wives are to adopt a submissive stance toward their husbands, even unbelieving ones.

[30] Cf. 2:13, 18; 3:1, 8 leading up to 3:15–18.

[31] *Pathēma, paschō*: 1:11; 2:19, 20, 21, 23; 3:14, 17, 18; 4:1, 13, 15, 19; 5:1, 9, 10.

[32] Cf. 1:3, 13, 21; 3:5, 15.

Interestingly, the author uses a general term for persecution, *peirasmos*.[33] In 1:6, Peter vaguely speaks of 'various trials', while 4:12 refers to an imminent 'fiery ordeal'.[34]

Against this backdrop of persecution, Peter reminds his readers that they have been set apart by God's Spirit (1:2) and redeemed with the precious blood of Christ (1:18–19), in order that they might 'declare the praises of him who called you out of darkness into his wonderful light' (2:9). Believers are persecuted because they are different from the rest of the society in which they live (4:4). They are God's people and therefore ought not to be surprised when they are subjected to suffering. What is more, they are actually 'called' to suffer (2:21), and they are to rejoice in the fact that their suffering occurs for the cause of Christ (1:6–7; 4:13–14). And by all means, let their suffering come as a result of doing good, not evil (2:20; 3:13–17; 4:15–16).

In this context, Peter presents Jesus not merely as Lord and Saviour, but also, like the author of Hebrews, as believers' supreme example in suffering.[35] Indeed, patient suffering on the part of Christians may even lead some to God. This is the implication of Peter's linking of the exhortation to suffer for doing what is right (3:17) with the explanatory statement, 'For Christ died for sins once for all, the righteous for the unrighteous, to bring you to God' (3:18). While Peter's focus is on Christians' appropriate attitude towards suffering, their response to it, he does not therefore neglect to point to their need to be prepared to give an answer to those who ask them (3:15).

Implications

Peter's teaching about mission, besides being influenced by the context of suffering, presents Christianity as a 'working man's religion'. Lofty Christian concepts and virtues are brought down to earth and are applied to everyday relationships, be it at work or at home. No sphere of life is to be exempt from obedience to Christ. This vision was revived during the Protestant Reformation, when great emphasis was once again placed on living out one's Christian faith in everyday life. However, even in this arena of mission, there are risks, especially that of conforming to the world in which one lives (cf. Rom. 12:2; 13:13–14). If there is no difference between Christians and non-Christians in

---

[33] *Cf.* 1:6; 4:12; *cf.* Jas. 1:2; 2 Pet. 2:9; Rev. 3:10.

[34] *Pyrōsis*; *cf. dia pyros* in 1:7; elsewhere in the New Testament only of the eschatological destruction of evil 'Babylon' by fire in Rev. 18:9, 18; *cf.* Josephus, *Ant.* 1.203 with reference to the destruction of Sodom. For a detailed discussion of *pyrōsis* in 1 Pet. 4:12, see esp. Michaels 1988: 260–262.

[35] *Cf.* 2:21–25 echoing Is. 53; *cf.* Heb. 12:1–3.

the way they live (as is all too often the case in contemporary society), their witness will remain ineffectual.[36] There will be no reason for questions concerning the hope of Christians (3:15). Peter believes that the Christian lifestyle, if it is a consistently holy lifestyle, has certain unique qualities which will render gospel proclamation attractive.

Revelation

The book of Revelation, best classified as a prophetic-apocalyptic epistle (Ladd 1957: 192–200), presents the reader with a powerful vision of the results of the Christian mission at the end of time. Representatives from all the nations will be gathered around God's throne, worshipping him. At the end of time, the die will have been cast. Those who have believed in Christ and who have persevered until the end will be saved, and the wicked will be judged. Thus mission, as the church's crucial task in the interim between Christ's first and second comings (cf. Mark 13:10; Matt. 24:14), will have come to an end. This points to the limited time-frame for mission, stressing its urgency as well as its ultimate purpose, that is, the gathering of a diverse representation of redeemed humanity for the worship and praise of God.[37] The righteous will be vindicated, the wicked will be judged, and Christ will reign as the eternal king. This eschatological, apocalyptic vision given to John[38] is to sustain the suffering church in

[36] *Cf.* Volf 1994: 15–30, who speaks of the missionary distance reflected in 1 Peter in terms of a 'soft difference', taking on the form of witness and invitation of the surrounding culture to consider and accept the Christian gospel message.

[37] *Cf.* 1:7; 4:10–11; 5:9; 7:4–17; 14:1–5.

[38] Contemporary scholarship largely rejects the notion that John's Gospel and Revelation were written by the same author. Schüssler-Fiorenza (1985: 107) speaks for many when she maintains that these writings 'represent opposite eschatological options'. Still, most proponents of the 'Johannine community hypothesis' believe both documents were produced by this group. But if the types of eschatology found in the Fourth Gospel and Revelation are indeed as irreconcilable as is frequently alleged, how could they have come from within the same circle? And if they could have come from the same circle, why not from the same author, even John? There are in fact significant theological affinities between both writings, including the christological designations 'Lamb' (*amnos*: John 1:29, 36; *arnion*: Rev. 5:6, 8, 12, 13; *etc.*) and 'Word' (John 1:1, 14; Rev. 19:13), the eschatological metaphors of shepherding and living water (John 4:14; 6:35; 7:37–38; Rev. 7:17; 21:6; 22:1, 17), the motif of God's dwelling with men (*skenō*: John 1:14; Rev. 7:15; 12:12; 13:6; 21:3), references to the absence of the temple (John 2:19, 21; 4:20–26; Rev. 21:22), 'witness' (*martyreō, martyria*) and 'glory' (*doxa, doxazō*) terminologies, a concern for believers' perseverance (John: *menō*; Rev.: *nikaō, hypomonē*), the significance of the number seven (John: signs, 'I am' sayings; Rev.: seals, trumpets, bowls), and the citation of Zech. 12:10 in both John 19:37 and Rev. 1:7. While the case cannot be argued for here, there seems no good reason to reject the joint authorship of the Fourth Gospel and Revelation from the outset esp. when considering

Asia Minor in its struggle at the end of the first century.[39]

Probably written during the reign of the Roman emperor Domitian AD 81–96,[40] the book may best be described as a call for 'patient endurance on the part of the saints' (14:12). Notably, it is Jesus, the crucified, risen and exalted Lord, who reveals the prophecies of this book to the suffering church. The Jesus who overcame suffering, even death, the Lamb who was also the Lion, is now encouraging his suffering saints from heaven to persevere until the end and to preserve purity and faithfulness in an unclean society characterized by compromise. He presents visions of a world with no more suffering, pain and death (21:4), telling believers to fix their hope on the eternal world awaiting them. Indeed, there is another world, even more real and permanent than the realities in this present life, which are merely temporary and transitional. This kind of vision is never more meaningful than for a church that is suffering.

Witness terminology and the conversion of the nations

The book is replete with allusions to the Old Testament, indicating that the new-covenant community inherits the eschatological vision of the future initially given to God's old covenant people Israel. Interestingly, Zechariah 12:10, an apocalyptic passage applied by John to Christ's first coming (cf. John 19:37), is here reapplied to his second coming (cf. 1:7). John's mission concept is expressed primarily through the

---

the different genres and occasions for writing. See further Guthrie 1990: 937–948; Carson, Moo and Morris 1992: 472–473.

[39] In recent years, scholarship on the book of Revelation has increasingly emphasized apocalypticism as a socio-political function. While this has led to considerable advances in reconstructing the putative life-setting of the document, it has issued in a neglect of the theological and eschatological dimensions of the work, including its rich christology and the numerous allusions to the Old Testament which establish firm covenantal links along salvation-historical lines. The book also claims to be prophecy (1:3; 22:18–19), and thus has both a forthtelling and a foretelling component, neither of which should be downplayed. Unfortunately, the treatment by Senior and Stuhlmueller (1983: 302–305), by following recent trends rather uncritically, shares some of the weaknesses just mentioned.

[40] The earliest attestation comes from Irenaeus, *Adv. Haer.* 5.30.3, who comments that Revelation was written 'almost in our own generation, at the end of the reign of Domitian' (quoted in Guthrie 1990: 956). Domitian expected his subjects to address him as *dominus et deus* ('lord and god'; *cf.* Suetonius, *Dom.* 13; Martial, *Epig.* 9.56.3), which stood in direct contradiction with the Christian confession of Jesus (*cf.* John 20:29). See esp. the discussion in Hemer 1986: 9–11; 213–214, n. 1; and 216, n. 22. See also Guthrie 1990: 956–962; Carson, Moo and Morris 1992: 473–476; Mounce 1998: 15–21; and the conclusion by Beale 1999: 27.

'witness' motif, a term that undergoes a permutation from 'testimony' to a person's dying for the faith as a 'martyr'.[41]

Bauckham has recently argued persuasively that the question of the conversion of the nations is at the centre of the prophetic message of Revelation (Bauckham 1993: 238–337).[42] He draws attention particularly to the following passages:

1. Revelation 14:6–7, where the usual terminology, 'the inhabitants of the earth', is changed to 'those who live on the earth', which indicates that the latter group, unlike the former, is still a potential prospect for conversion; the passage also contains an allusion to Psalm 96:2b, with Psalm 96 being the first of a string of psalms celebrating Yahweh's universal lordship.

2. Revelation 11:1–4, the account of the two witnesses (cf. esp. 11:5–6), where Moses and Elijah, both of whom confronted pagan rulers and religions, serve as the Old Testament models, but where the two witnesses transcend both, since they die a martyr's death, something neither Moses nor Elijah did, with Elijah (and Moses, according to tradition) not having died at all.

3. Revelation 14:14-16, the vision of the grain harvest: an image, not of judgment, but of the gathering of the converted from the nations into the kingdom of God.

4. Revelation 15:2–4, the Song of Moses, a piece of careful exegesis of Exodus 15:1–18 with reference to Psalms 86:8–10; 98:1–2; 105:1; Jeremiah 10:6–7; and Isaiah 12:1–6. As Bauckham contends, in this final period, God does not deliver his faithful people *by the slaughter of their enemies*, as he did in the days of Moses, Elijah and Esther, but instead will allow them *to be slain by their enemies* in order to bring the nations to repentance and faith. In this way, those ransomed by the sacrifice of the Lamb are now called themselves to sacrifice in order to participate also in his victory, giving it universal effect.[43]

Thus believers' witness is the quintessential prerequisite for the conversion of the nations. At this 'climax of prophecy', suffering and

[41] See already Heb. 12:1, 4. *Cf.* Vassiliadis 1985: 129–134; and Trites 1973: 72–80.

[42] But see now the perceptive critique and refinement by Schnabel (1999) including his discussion of Rev. 11:3–13; 14:14–16; 15:2–4; 21:1–8; 22:2. As Schnabel rightly points out, the book of Revelation 'does not predict the conversion of all humanity – whether this be a conversion of all individual human beings or a conversion of nations ... [but rather] the decisive victory which Jesus will finally win over the hostile powers and over the people who follow them when he returns (19:11–21)'.

[43] Pilgrim (1989: 242) contends that the book of Revelation does not shut 'the door completely to anyone, even the rebellious kings and their deceived followers', but this flies in the face of passages such as Rev. 21:8.

martyrdom are placed in an eternal perspective. Jesus is the prime witness, the proto-martyr (1:5; 3:14; cf. 11:3; 14:6; 17:6; 19:11; 22:16, 20); he is also the firstborn from the dead, the Lamb of God, and co-equal with the Father.[44] Reference is also made to Antipas, 'the faithful witness' (2:13), and to the 'two witnesses' who testify before the inhabitants of the earth for 1,260 days and then are killed on account of their testimony (11:3, 7).[45] John the seer, too, is said to testify (1:2; 20:18).

Like Peter, John introduces himself as a 'fellow-sharer in the tribulation and kingdom and endurance in Jesus' (1:9; cf. 1 Pet. 5:1–2). 'The testimony of Jesus' (1:2, 9; 12:17; 19:10 [bis]; 20:4), that is, believers' testimony *to* Jesus, with a possible martyrological nuance, 'unto death' (Vassiliadis 1985: 129–134), is presented as a prophetic act that discloses God's truth in a world adamant in its opposition to God. In the final days, it is not mission, but 'holding to the testimony of Jesus' that is needed, for 'the one who overcomes' and 'endures' is the one who will be rewarded eternally.[46]

Nevertheless, 'witness' terminology clearly involves not mere indifference to the world's fate, but the proclamation of a divine message (cf. 14:6 where an angel proclaims an eternal gospel to all nations). Also, exhortations to five of the seven churches, or individuals in them, to repent, clearly indicate that the seer still allows

[44] *Cf.* the recent contribution by Hengel (1996: 159–175), who argues that in Revelation there is not only an exaltation christology but also a pre-existence christology, similar to John's Gospel. Revelation presupposes a concept of incarnation and attributes divine dignity to the Son as the sacrificial Lamb in communion with the Father.

[45] *Cf.* Poucouta 1988: 38–57, who argues that the lampstand in the inaugural vision, the letters of Rev. 1 – 3, and in 11:1–13, expresses the church's mission as prophetic witness; and Giblin 1984: 433–459. Miller (1998: 235) claims that the image of the 144,000 in 7:4–8 represents a 'band of missionaries' set apart for a 'final world-wide thrust'. He contends that the 144,000 are distinct from the innumerable company which follows (7:9–17) and that 'the sealing and sending of the 144,000 (7:2–8)' fulfil God's global plan of salvation, eliciting 'another overwhelming scene of worship and praise in heaven (7:9–14)'. But there is no 'sending' or commissioning of the 144,000 in 7:2–8, as Miller claims, nor is there any evidence at all that the 144,000 were in fact 'missionaries'. As Ladd (1972: 111–12) makes clear, the purpose of the sealing of the 144,000, reminiscent of events during the plagues in Egypt and Israel's exodus, is the church's deliverance from God's wrath about to fall on 'those people who did not have the seal of God on their foreheads' (9:4; *cf.* 16:2). Contrary to Miller, the 144,000 of 7:2–8 are therefore not a 'band of missionaries' set apart for a 'final world-wide thrust'. The scene rather represents a symbolic depiction of the church's protection from God's wrath.

[46] 'Overcomes': *nikaō*; 2:7, 11, 17, 26; 3:5, 12, 21 [bis]; 21:7; 'endures': *hypomenō/hypomonē;* 1:9; 2:2, 3, 19; 3:10; 13:10; 14:12; *cf.* Heb. 10:32, 36; 12:1, 2, 3, 7; 1 Pet. 2:20 [bis].

room for conversion (2:5, 16, 21–22; 3:3, 19). The unrepentant attitude of those confronted with the gospel in Revelation also functions as the foil for John's 'justification of God', theodicy (Osborne 1993: 63–77). Finally, the church is, as in 1 Peter, presented as a priestly kingdom,[47] indicating its mediatorial function for the world.

John's vision presents the Messianic community as a woman who, after having given birth to a son (Christ), flees into the wilderness to escape persecution, but there is nurtured by God (12:1–17). Satan is cast as a dragon (cf. Satan as a roaring lion in 1 Pet. 5:8). 'Babylon', that is, Rome, is powerfully portrayed as 'the great prostitute' with whom the kings of the earth committed acts of immorality, 'the woman dressed in purple and scarlet ... drunk with the blood of the saints, the blood of those who bore testimony to Jesus' (17:1–6). Witness in such a context must not lead to defilement (cf. 14:4). While Peter's first epistle still emphasizes discriminate participation in society, the seer here focuses on non-participation in activities associated with the pervasive emperor cult (Senior and Stuhlmueller 1983: 305; deSilva 1991: 185–208). Revelation may thus be likened to a subversive underground tract, seeking to strengthen believers against the controlling power by holding before them a vision of the end, where, in a complete reversal of contemporary circumstances, Rome will get her due while Christians will be completely vindicated. Only faith could sustain a vision so entirely contrary to people's current experience. As in Hebrews and 1 Peter, only infinitely more gloriously, Jesus is presented as believers' supreme example in suffering.

Other mission emphases in the four visions given to John[48]

Apart from 'witness' terminology, the book of Revelation employs several other motifs to express concern for the church's mission. Part of John's first vision (1:9 – 3:22) are the letters to the seven churches (2:1 – 3:22). The general emphasis of these messages is on the imminence of Christ's return (e.g. 1:3; 3:11), and hence on the importance of believers' uncompromising perseverance in holding fast to the testimony of Jesus. In the case of the church in John's day, the Roman empire with its decadent emperor-worship was in view, but the exhortations expressed in the seven letters also have powerful

[47] Cf. 1:6; 5:10; 20:6; cf. Exod. 19:6; Is. 61:6; cf. 1 Pet. 2:5, 9.
[48] On the typical apocalyptic structural convention 'in the Spirit' (cf. Rev. 1:10–11; 4:1–2; 17:1–3; and 21:9–10) in relation to the book's overall structure, see C. R. Smith (1994: 373–393), who points out that John receives his visions 'in the Spirit' on Patmos, in heaven, in the wilderness and on a mountaintop respectively.

implications for the church's witness in a pluralistic world of any age. For John, ungodly politico-economic systems are ultimately manifestations of the spirit of the Antichrist. The seer's emphasis on Christians' need to persevere faithfully until the end is paralleled by the stress of the writer of Hebrews on the necessity of believers' holding fast to their confession[49] and of their endurance in the face of suffering.

Among the adversaries of the churches in Asia Minor referred to in the seven letters are 'the Jews' – called a 'synagogue of Satan' in 2:9 and 3:9 – though the book as a whole suggests that major opposition is arising from the Roman empire. Satan is clearly presented in the entire book as the ultimate enemy of Christ (cf. 2:9, 10, 13, 24; 3:9; passim). Reference is also made to the 'Nicolaitans' (2:6, 15) and to 'the woman Jezebel', who taught idolatry and sexual immorality in Thyatira (2:20; cf. 2:14; Hemer 1986).[50] Churches are exhorted to rekindle their 'first love' (2:4), not to fear suffering (2:10), to be faithful unto death (2:10), to be mindful of their citizenship in the new Jerusalem (3:12; cf. Heb. 12:22: 'heavenly Jerusalem'), and to face up to their spiritual morbidity (3:1) and poverty (3:17). In an allusion to Proverbs 3:12 (cf. similarly Heb. 12:6), in 3:19 Christ exhorts the Laodicean believers to repent. He is presented as shut out, standing at the door knocking, longing for fellowship, a clear indictment of the church's eschatological state of apostasy (3:20).

In John's second vision, the so-called 'throne-room vision' (4:1 – 16:21), God's judgment upon the wicked and his vindication of the martyrs and saints are presented against the backdrop of the heavenly worship of God and the Lamb. This judgment is first revealed (the seven 'seals'; 6:1 – 8:5), then announced (the seven 'trumpets'; 8:6 – 11:19), and finally executed (the seven 'bowls'; 16:1–21). John's third vision has as its content the fall of Babylon, the marriage supper of the Lamb, Jesus' execution of judgment and his thousand-year reign, as well as the defeat of Satan, the great, white throne of judgment and the new heaven and the new earth (17:1 – 21:8). The fourth vision displays the new Jerusalem (21:9 – 22:5) and the coming of Christ (22:6–21).[51] In these visions, God's eschatological judgment is the dark backdrop against which the vindication of his saints takes place. God's judgment,

---

[49] *Cf.* e.g. Heb. 3:1; 4:14; 12:1–4; see also the frequent warnings against apostasy.

[50] On the Nicolaitans, *cf.* esp. Fox 1994: 485–496. See also Klauck (1992: 153–182), who argues that the relation (proximity or distance) between the Christian communities and pagan urban society was the book's major concern (*cf.* 18:4: 'Come out of her, my people').

[51] See already the discussion of 'new heaven and new earth' language in Is. 66:18–24 in the concluding section of ch. 2 above.

too, however, is presented ultimately in a positive light, as a display of the impeccable righteousness and justice of God which cannot be thwarted by anyone, be it Satan and his demons, or persistent unbelief and refusal to repent.[52]

Implications

The book of Revelation invokes a multitude of powerful images. It is full of apocalyptic symbolisms depicting God's vindication of his saints and his execution of judgment on the wicked. John clearly portrays the central role of the crucified and risen Christ in judgment and rule; the participation of the church in Christ's rule; the universality of believers and their worship; the glory awaiting those who faithfully endure suffering; the condemnation of sexual and spiritual immorality, of compromise, cowardice, complacency, lies, materialism, homosexuality and other sins.

This is the vision by which the contemporary church needs to be transformed. Its primary accountability is to its God, not to the surrounding world. The identification figure for the church's witness, even unto death, is Jesus Christ himself.[53] It is worthy of note that the three writings under consideration share a common apocalyptic element.[54] What Revelation adds is the notion that there would be a time with no more mission (contra J. C. Smith 1984: 70). As indicated by the prophetic perfect, the choices will have been made. All that remains to be done is for history to be concluded. This, too, is part of God's plan.

Conclusion

The writings surveyed here teach, each in its own way, that the Christian mission is firmly based upon the conviction that Jesus Christ is the unique Saviour of all those who receive the gospel. The nature of believers' witness may differ, ranging from life witness (including martyrdom) to verbal proclamation, but the belief undergirding such witness is that, unless people hear the gospel and believe in Christ, they will spend eternity separated from God and Christ. To persevere until the end really matters, and to resist spiritual compromise is vital

---

[52] Contrary to Miller (1998), 22:17 does *not* refer to 'the present witness of the church'. The scene rather depicts the eternal state.

[53] Other witnesses include Antipas, the two witnesses and those already in heaven; *cf.* Heb. 12:1.

[54] *Cf.* Heb. 12:18–29; 1 Pet. 1:7, 13; 2:12; 4:13; Rev., passim.

indeed, since there will be eternal ramifications regarding a person's faithfulness or failure to represent the truth.

We conclude with the following observations:

1. Mission will be affected by a church's historical, cultural and social circumstances. Depending on its particular situation, the church's verbal proclamation may go forth unhindered or be rendered more difficult through persecution. Even in the latter instance, however, verbal gospel proclamation remains imperative, though a godly response to suffering may take on increased significance as well (Heb. 12:14; 1 Pet. 2:12; 3:15).

2. Believers' response to suffering and persecution at the hands of individual unbelievers or by political authorities is a significant statement to the world of believers' identity in Christ, and those who suffer shame in this world will be divinely honoured.[55]

3. Mission must be understood from an eschatological perspective. Believers are pilgrims and resident aliens walking the fine line between submission to authorities and courageous witness to their Lord (esp. 1 Pet.).

4. The defence of the historic, orthodox, apostolic, biblical Christian faith is an important *prerequisite* for mission (2 Pet.; Jude; 1 – 3 John). If the gospel proclaimed in the church's preaching is not the gospel of Scripture, mission will remain largely ineffectual.

The bedrock convictions of the writings considered in this chapter expose the shallowness of recent contemporary attempts to refashion the Christian message in the image of secular societal developments. The writers of 2 Peter, Jude and 1 – 3 John display great zeal and passion for the preservation of the orthodox faith. The authors of Hebrews, 1 Peter and Revelation assign supreme significance to believers' perseverance in their faith, even if that determination severely limits their opportunity for 'religious dialogue'. Ultimately, it is not missionary appeal but the vindication of God's sovereign righteousness that is of supreme importance, both in Christ's first coming at the cross and at his second coming. Not human obduracy and sin but divine righteousness will have the last word.

---

[55] *Cf.* Heb. 10:23, 32–39; 12:1–13; 13:12–13; 1 Pet. 1:6–7; 2:13–17; 3:13–18; 4:12–19; 5:1, 7–10.

Chapter Ten

Concluding synthesis

It is now time to draw together the various strands of mission teaching in Scripture and to conclude the present investigation with some final observations.

Summary of findings

The following biblical-theological sketch on mission shows the multi-faceted yet unified nature of the scriptural teaching on this vital motif. There is an inherent dynamic and progression in the unfolding of the divine mission to save humanity from a profound spiritual predicament. At the same time, all aspects of this mission in its various dimensions can be traced back to the heart of a loving God and his redemptive initiative in his Son, the Lord Jesus Christ.

The Old Testament

There was no 'mission' in the Garden of Eden and there will be no 'mission' in the new heavens and the new earth (though the results of 'mission' will be evident). From the first glimmer of the gospel in Genesis 3:15 to the end of this age, however, mission is necessitated by humanity's fall into sin and need for a Saviour, and is made possible only by the saving initiative of God in Christ.

Genesis

Once fallen, humanity lies under the wrath of God. Adam's relationship with God, his mate and others is severely affected, while the exercise of dominion over creation through work and procreation is characterized by frustration and pain. The increasing spread of sin is depicted in the narratives following the fall. Yet God remains faithful to his creation, entering into covenants with Noah (9:9–13) and Abraham (12:1–3; cf. 15:1–8; ch. 17). The latter is summoned to leave his native country on the basis of God's promise of a land, seed and blessing. Ultimately, this blessing extends not merely to Abraham's physical descendants but to

251

all who are 'children of Abraham' through faith (Gal. 3:6–9, 26–29; Rom. 4:16–17). The Abrahamic covenant provides the framework for God's dealings with humanity for the rest of biblical history, which culminates in the new covenant instituted by Abraham's 'seed', Jesus Christ (Gal. 3:16).

The exodus and Israel's role among the nations

Once the Israelites have been delivered from bondage in Egypt, they are to be God's treasured possession out of all nations, 'a kingdom of priests and a holy nation' (Exod. 19:5–6). Israel is called because the whole earth belongs to Yahweh. His people, who are set apart to serve him as a holy God, are to mediate his presence and blessings to the surrounding nations. This does not mean that Israel is enjoined to engage in intentional cross-cultural mission. Rather, as the recipient of the divine blessings, the nation is to exalt God in its life and worship, attracting individuals from among the nations *historically* by incorporation and *eschatologically* by ingathering. Thus Rahab and her family and Ruth the Moabitess become part of Israel. Also, the Mosaic legislation makes special provision for the *gēr*, the alien residing in Israel (cf. Exod. 12:48; 22:21). But intermarriage with foreigners is frequently limited, particularly in the post-exilic period (Neh. 13:23–27; Ezra 9 – 10). Overall, incorporation in Old Testament times related to a small number of individuals, while a large-scale ingathering of Gentiles was not expected until the end times (cf. esp. Is. 56:8).

The Davidic kingship and the eschatological pilgrimage of the nations

In 2 Samuel 7:13, David is assured by God that his kingdom will be established for ever. The establishment of the Davidic kingship is crucial for an understanding of Yahweh's rule over the nations and the fulfilment of his covenant promises to Abraham. During the reign of David's son, Solomon, various promises to Abraham and David are fulfilled: the Promised Land is fully conquered, Israel becomes a great nation, and the Jerusalem temple is built (cf. Deut. 12:5–11). Jerusalem becomes a world centre, epitomized by the Queen of Sheba's visit to the city. This visit serves as a paradigm for the eschatological pilgrimage of the nations to Zion in later prophecy (Is. 2:2–4; 60 – 62; cf. Mic. 4:1–5; Pss. 36:8–9; 50:2). Zion, in turn, is depicted in some Old Testament apocalyptic passages as the centre of the new creation (Is. 35:1–10; 65:17–18).

In the last days, the nations will flock to Jerusalem to learn about

Yahweh and his ways (Is. 2:2–3; cf. Zech. 8:20–23; Mic. 4:1–2). As they come, they bring the scattered children of Israel with them (Is. 60:2–9). In an amazing reversal, the nations submit to Israel (v. 14), bring their wealth into the city (vv. 11–22) and join in the worship of Yahweh, whose people they have now become. Thus the prophet's admonition, 'Turn to me and be saved, all you ends of the earth' (Is. 45:22), is fulfilled. Significantly, this ingathering of Gentiles is depicted as an eschatological event, effected by God, not Israel. Moreover, the mode of this ingathering is attraction (the nations come to Israel), not active outreach (Israel going to the nations). In addition to the anticipation of the universal scope of eschatological salvation, several prophetic books envision the restoration of a remnant of Israel, including the inauguration of a new covenant (cf. esp. Jer. 31:31–34).

The Isaianic Servant of the Lord

The Servant of Yahweh, who features in the four 'Servant songs' of Isaiah (42:1–4; 49:1–6; 50:4–9; 52:13 – 53:12; cf. 61:1–3), is one of the most important Old Testament figures whose ministry pertains to both Israel and the nations. While the Servant's work is in the first instance related to the redemption of Jerusalem and Israel's return to the holy city, his work will affect the entire world. The sequence of the Servant's ministry, directed initially to Israel but resulting in blessing for the nations, follows a pattern similar to the Abrahamic promises and constitutes a partial fulfilment of these. The Servant's death, which is clearly set forth in Isaiah 52:13 – 53:12, will not be the end of his career. God adds his 'Amen' to his work by raising and exalting him (53:10–12). The Servant will be satisfied with the results of his sacrifice and bring many into a right relationship with God (v. 11). His ministry was for pagans (52:13–15) and Israelites (53:1–6), witnesses and hearers, insiders and outsiders. Ultimately, however, it is for one group: 'transgressors' – many of them. The Servant is the instrument of God's grace to sinners and the key to the extension of the divine salvation to the ends of the earth.

The paradox concerning the identity of the Servant will not be resolved fully until the coming of Jesus of Nazareth, who is both the expected Messiah and the one who fulfils Israel's destiny. In the Gospels, Israel's role of world mission, which was forfeited through disobedience, is transferred to Jesus.

The nations in the Psalms

The nations represent the great mass of humanity in rebellion against

God and subject to divine judgment (Ps. 10:16). Yet they are still within the Creator's plan of grace, since he intends to bring blessing to the nations of the world. Fundamental to this inclusion of the nations is Israel's role as the people of God in whose privileges the nations will be invited to join. In the enthronement psalms (Pss. 47; 93; 96–97; 99), Zion is the permanent centre of the worship of Yahweh in Israel. Like the tabernacle and Mt Sinai before it, Zion is holy because of Yahweh's presence, and if his people are 'holy' because of Yahweh's presence in Zion, then Israel is separated from the nations (cf. Ps. 78). Salvation for them must therefore involve their coming out of the world to Zion in order to worship the Lord in the end times (Pss. 72:8–11; 102:12–22).

The second-temple period

Traditionally, the view largely prevailed that second-temple Judaism engaged in mission. If that were the case, the early church's mission would have operated within the parameters already established by Judaism. However, if mission is defined as a conscious, deliberate, organized and extensive effort to convert others to one's religion by way of evangelization or proselytization, it is doubtful whether this kind of activity was characteristic of second-temple Judaism. For while the Jewish religion was doubtless successful in attracting converts or proselytes, the initiative in such instances usually lay with Gentiles who desired to join Judaism; conversions were not usually the result of intentional Jewish missionary efforts. This is not contradicted by Matthew 23:15, where Jesus censures the Pharisees for their misguided zeal in proselytization.

Second-temple Judaism, therefore, should therefore not be regarded as a missionary religion. The operative paradigm was one of attraction rather than intentional outreach. While Jews did allow sympathizers and proselytes to participate in their religious practices to a certain extent, they were primarily preoccupied with national or sectarian concerns. The inclusion of Gentiles in the orbit of God's salvation was not expected until the end times as a special work of God, a view that prevented intertestamental Jews from actively reaching out to Gentiles. The missions of Jesus and the early church thus did not merely build upon Jewish precedent but replaced the old paradigm of mission with a new mode of outreach.

The New Testament

If Mark was the first to write a Gospel, mission gradually moves to the forefront of the Gospel tradition. Nevertheless, the Gospels are transitional in that they portray Jesus as still focused on his mission to Israel. It is the death and resurrection of Jesus together with Pentecost and the subsequent events recorded in the book of Acts that open the floodgates and render the Christian mission a truly universal phenomenon. Here Paul's teaching and practice take centre stage.

Mark

Mark focuses his message on the mission of Jesus, the Son of God (Mark 1:1). While Jesus' ministry is directed primarily to the Jews (cf. esp. 7:27a), he does have occasional contact with Gentiles, albeit always at their initiative (5:1–20; 7:24–30). Towards the end of the book, reference is made to the future proclamation of the gospel to the Gentiles (13:10; 14:9) and the fulfilment of Isaiah's vision of the temple as a house of prayer *for all nations* (11:17, quoting Is. 56:7). The Gospel's climactic christological confession is uttered, not by a Jew, but by a Roman Gentile (Mark 15:39).

Despite portraying Jesus as open to minister to individual Gentiles who approach him and as envisioning a future mission to the Gentiles, however, Mark does not show Jesus as embarking on a 'Gentile mission'. Rather, he presents him as following the pattern of Old Testament (and intertestamental) Israel, whose presence was to attract the surrounding nations to her God without going out of her way to reach them. While Jesus is shown to send out the twelve as part of their preparation for ministry (6:7–13), there is little sustained emphasis on their mission. Rather, they are portrayed as grappling, often unsuccessfully, with understanding who Jesus is (e.g. 6:49–52).

Matthew

Matthew's Gospel, while generally cohering with Mark's portrayal, transcends the latter by ending his Gospel with the Great Commission, the risen Christ's command to his followers to disciple the nations. Also, he grounds the missions of Jesus and of his disciples more explicitly in the Old Testament antecedents. According to Matthew, Jesus the Messiah fulfilled Israel's destiny as the representative, paradigmatic Son of God, with the result that God's blessings to the nations, promised to Abraham, are to come to fruition through Jesus in the mission of his followers.

Like the other evangelists, Matthew portrays Jesus' mission as proceeding along salvation-historical lines: first to the Jews, then to the Gentiles. While Jesus' disciples prior to the resurrection are instructed to limit their mission to Israel (10:5–6; 15:24), the Great Commission extends their summons to all the nations. Occasionally in Matthew Jesus ministers to Gentiles, but never at his own initiative (cf. e.g. 8:5–13; 15:24–27). Towards the end of his Gospel, Matthew refers to the preaching of the 'gospel of the kingdom' as a witness to all the nations (24:14; cf. also 26:13; Mark 13:10).

Like Mark's Gospel, Matthew's account focuses on Jesus' mission, which includes the preparation of his followers for ministry. But unlike Mark, Matthew does not end on a note of doubt and fear; rather, he shows Jesus on a Galilean mountain, surveying the territory like a conquering general, assuring his followers of his unlimited authority in heaven as well as on earth, and commanding them to spread the victorious, glorious news of the gospel to all the nations. Matthew thus ends on a note of triumph and joyous expectation: the community of Jesus, with its conquering general at its side, is sent on a worldwide mission.

Luke-Acts

Luke's Gospel tells the story of Jesus and his salvation; the book of Acts traces the movement of that salvation to the Gentiles. The first volume begins with a summary of God's promises to Israel about to be fulfilled in Jesus. This sets the stage for the second volume which presents the regathering of 'Israel' and her mission as a light to the nations. The infancy narratives of Luke 1 – 2 indicate that Israel's hopes for a Saviour of David's line are about to be realized (1:30–35; cf. 2 Sam. 7:12–13). Through the birth of Jesus, God will restore Israel and fulfil his purposes for Abraham and his descendants. The Abrahamic promises, however, are brought to fulfilment in those who fear God (1:50–55), not in national Israel. Further, according to the third evangelist, the Lord's Messiah accomplishes the role of Yahweh's Servant (2:32; 4:18–19; cf. Is. 42:6; 49:6–9; 61:1–2).

Luke's genealogy reaches beyond Abraham to Adam (Luke 3:23–28; contrast Matt. 1:1–17), pointing to Jesus' identification with all people, not just Israel. Jesus' healing of the centurion's servant, his first encounter with a Gentile in Luke's Gospel, foreshadows the expansion of his ministry to the Gentiles (7:1–10). He chooses and commissions first the twelve, then the seventy(-two) to be involved in his mission to Israel, and this embraces a ministry of preaching and healing (6:12–15; 9:1–2; 10:1–24). Two Lukan parables, told during the extended 'travel narrative' (9:51 – 19:28), envisage Gentile participation in the messianic banquet (13:28–30; 14:23–24). After Jerusalem's rejection of her Messiah, the risen Christ commissions his disciples to proclaim the forgiveness of sins in his name to all nations (24:44–49).

In comparison with Mark and Matthew, Luke portrays Jesus' mission in more overtly universal terms, that is, as ultimately directed also towards the Gentiles. But like his Synoptic counterparts, Luke maintains the historical fact that Jesus did not actively reach out to Gentiles during his earthly ministry. Unlike the other Synoptists, however, Luke composes a second volume, and there makes clear that the boundaries still in place prior to Jesus' crucifixion and resurrection are removed subsequent to the outpouring of the Spirit at Pentecost.

Luke's second volume presents what 'Jesus continued to do and teach' (cf. 1:1) by his Spirit through the early church led by the apostles. This establishes the subtle but vital point that Jesus, even after his ascension, has not disappeared from the scene; rather, from his exalted position at the Father's right hand, he continues to direct and oversee the divine mission. Luke's account traces the progress of gospel proclamation from Jerusalem – the centre from which the word of the Lord goes forth – to Judea and Samaria, and even 'to the ends of the earth' (1:8). In a major paradigm shift from a centripetal movement (men and women coming to Israel) to a centrifugal one (God's people going out to others), the twelve are to function as 'witnesses' to Israel and subsequently Paul as a 'witness' to the Gentiles.

Events with major significance for the mission recorded in the book of Acts include Pentecost and the gift of the Spirit (Acts 2), Stephen's martyrdom (ch. 7), the spread of the gospel to Judea and Samaria (8:4–40), Paul's conversion and commission (9:1–31), Cornelius and the Gentiles (10:1 – 11:18), Paul's first missionary journey (13:1 – 14:28) and the Council of Jerusalem (15:1–35). The last has been depicted as 'the most crucial chapter in the whole book' since it describes the turning point in Luke's story. The threat to the expansion of the gospel to the Gentiles is turned around so that the Christian mission now extends to Western Asia and Europe.

Nothing can hinder the irresistible progress of the gospel, and God's people, through his Spirit, overcome all obstacles. Paul and Barnabas continue the ministry of the Servant, for they are now the 'light for the Gentiles' (13:47, quoting Is. 49:6, a passage applied to Jesus in Luke 2:32), and while proclamation still begins with the Jews (3:26; 13:46; 18:5; 28:25–28), no distinction is now made between them and Gentiles concerning salvation and reception into God's people: faith in Jesus as Lord is all that is required (e.g. 16:31). The conclusion of Luke's second volume describes an open-ended mission to Jews and Gentiles (28:17–31). This reminds readers of an unfinished task and the urgency of being identified with the ongoing advance of the gospel of salvation.

Paul

From the time of his conversion and calling on the road to Damascus, the gospel, that is, the authoritative and gracious message of salvation in the Lord Jesus Christ, became the determinative focus of Paul's whole life (Acts 9). His encounter with the risen Christ led to a 'paradigm shift' in his thinking: he came to understand that Jesus is at the centre of God's saving purposes, and that he is Israel's Messiah, the Son of God and Lord of all. As the crucified and exalted one, he bore the curse 'for us' and brought the law to an end as a way of salvation. It was God's plan that 'the blessing given to Abraham might come to the Gentiles through Jesus Christ' (Gal. 3:13–14).

The apostle understood his missionary activity to Gentiles within the context of an Old Testament expectation in which the nations would on the final day partake of God's ultimate blessings to Israel. Paul knew that he was entrusted with God's 'mystery', the eschatological revelation that now Jews and Gentiles alike were gathered together into one body, the church (Rom. 16:25–26; Eph. 2:1 – 3:13; Col. 1:25–27).

Paul was totally committed to and involved in the advance of the gospel. He had been set apart for this divine *kērygma* and so he served God wholeheartedly in this gospel of his Son. So great was Paul's passion that his readiness to proclaim it knows no limits (Rom. 1). He is convinced that it is utterly reliable, for God himself is the author of it. At the centre of the apostolic gospel is the unique Son of God, the mediator of salvation between God and man, who was in his earthly life the seed of David, the Messiah. By his resurrection he has become the powerful Son of God – Jesus Christ, our Lord (vv. 3–4). The saving power of the gospel is spelled out in the light of humanity's dreadful predicament outside of Christ. The world comprising Jews and Gentiles stands under judgment (1:18 – 3:20), but this apparently weak and foolish message, the content of which centres on Jesus Christ, mediates the almighty power of God that leads to salvation (1:16–17).

The purpose of Paul's missionary endeavours, as well as that of his apostolic gospel, is 'for his [Jesus'] name's sake ... to call people from among the Gentiles to the obedience that comes from faith' (Rom. 1:5), that is, in the fullness of time, to bring the nations into captive obedience to himself. Jesus Christ now rules over the new people of God. The first task included within the scope of his missionary commission was primary evangelism. Paul's ambition was to go where the gospel had not yet been preached (Rom. 15:20–21). His strategy focused on preaching and evangelizing Jews as well as Gentile proselytes and God-fearers in local synagogues. The apostle proclaimed the gospel and, under God, converted men and women.

But he also founded churches as a necessary element in his missionary task. Paul's aim was to establish Christian congregations in strategic (mostly urban) centres from where the gospel could spread further to the surrounding regions. Conversion to Christ meant incorporation into him, and thus membership within a Christian community. Furthermore, through his practice of residential missions and his nurture of churches by teaching and admonition, it is clear that Paul sought to bring men and women to full maturity in Christ. He anticipates that his converts will be his joy and crown as they stand fast on the final day, so demonstrating that he had not run in vain in his ministry (2 Cor. 1:14; Gal. 2:2; Phil. 2:16; 4:1; 1 Thess. 2:19). In the Pastoral Epistles, Paul emphasizes that God is the Saviour of all (1 Tim. 2:3–4; 4:10; Titus 2:10–11; 3:4) and provides the post-apostolic church with a pattern of organization and qualifications for its leadership.

While Paul was called and commissioned to be the apostle to Gentiles (Rom. 11:13), he ardently prayed for the salvation of his own people. He recognized that although there has been a temporary and partial hardening of Israel which led to the extension of the blessings of salvation to the Gentiles and ultimately the whole world, God intends to bring his saving grace to Israel. There is a fundamental equality of Jew and Gentile in the saving plan of God. At the end of Romans 9 – 11, then, the apostle bursts into joy and admiration for God's merciful plan in which Jew and Gentile alike participate in salvation in the Lord Jesus Christ (11:33–36).

The apostle's writings stand in close relationship with those of Luke, his associate in travels and ministry (see the 'we' passages in Acts). Both are united in their focus on reaching Gentiles. Both also share a strategic mindset that seeks to promote Christianity in ever-widening concentric circles, in Paul's case all the way to Spain (Rom. 15:24). Paul's writings wrestle in particular with Jewish unbelief; the relationship between Jews and Gentiles in the church; the nature of the gospel in relation to law; and the implications of Christ's death and resurrection for the life of the believer.

With regard to mission, it is evident that this motif is not equally predominant in all of Paul's letters. It seems that in certain instances Paul had to focus primarily on internal struggles or believers' lack of maturity so that he could not develop the theme of mission more fully (e.g. Gal. or 1 – 2 Cor.). In other instances, however, Paul involves his recipients more directly in mission work, such as in the case of the

259

Philippians, whom he calls 'partners' in ministry (Phil. 1:5, 27; 2:16; 4:10–19), presenting himself as a model for his converts to follow (1 Cor. 9:19 – 11:1). In relation to the spiritual warfare in which all Christians are engaged, he urges his readers to stand firm against the onslaughts of the evil one and his powers, and this involves resisting temptation (see Eph. 4:27) and announcing the gospel of peace in the power of God's Spirit (Eph. 6:10–20, esp. 15, 17). Overall, the Pauline mission takes centre stage in Paul's epistles, with the Pauline churches being expected to do their part to spread the gospel within their sphere of influence.[1]

John

John shares with Luke the conviction that the mission of the earthly Jesus is continued in the mission of the exalted Jesus through his followers. However, while Luke writes two programmatic volumes, John accomplishes the same purpose in one. His teaching on mission focuses on Jesus who, as the sent Son, fulfils his redemptive mission in complete dependence on and obedience to the Father 'who sent' him (e.g. 4:34). While the first part of John's Gospel shows Jesus' rejection by his own people Israel (1:11), the second part focuses on his preparation of his new-covenant community to continue his mission following his crucifixion and resurrection (chs. 13 – 17).

Anticipating his exaltation to the Father, Jesus promises to send 'another helper' (14:16) and to answer prayer in his name (14:13–14). He calls on his followers to glorify him by 'going' and bearing fruit (15:16) as they bear witness together with the Spirit (15:26–27). Love and unity are to be characteristic of these believers (13:34–35; 15:12, 17; 17:20–26). In the Johannine commissioning narrative, the crucified and risen Lord, the Sent One, now turned sender, breathes his Spirit on the disciples and charges them to proclaim forgiveness of sins in his name (20:21–23). The wording of Jesus' commission, 'As the Father has sent me, I am sending you' (20:21), makes his own relationship with the Father the basic paradigm for the disciples' relationship with Jesus in the pursuit of their mission. Finally, the Gospel's declared purpose is that many might believe (that is, come to first-time faith) in Jesus (20:30–31).

---

[1] In the Pastoral Epistles Paul combats false teaching by encouraging behaviour that is consistent with the standards of the gospel (1 Tim. 1:11). A godly life-style is pleasing to 'God our Saviour, who wants all to be saved and to come to a knowledge of the truth' (2:3–4). Such behaviour provides an example for mission-minded Christians in all generations who, in a desire to win many, seek to make the doctrine of God more attractive (Titus 2:10).

Of all the Gospels, John attempts the most conscious theological reflection regarding the relationship between the mission of Jesus and that of his disciples. However, John does not teach an 'incarnational model'. To the contrary, he portrays the Word-become-flesh as unique in every respect (1:14, 18; 3:16, 18). While Jesus' mission was tied up with the final, decisive revelation and redemption, the disciples are to serve as his representatives, proclaiming him as the Way, the Truth and the Life, and as the one through whom forgiveness of sins and eternal life are now available. John also offers a profound reflection on the way in which Jesus' followers remain connected with their Lord after his exaltation. They are linked with him in a living relationship which enables them to bear fruit (ch. 15), and they are joint witnesses with the Spirit who mediates Jesus' presence to them (15:26–27).

The General Epistles

In their struggle with heretical teaching, Jude, 2 Peter and 1 – 3 John display an essential prerequisite for mission: zeal for the 'faith that was once for all entrusted to the saints' (Jude 3). John's second and third epistles deal with the issue of extending or refusing hospitality to false teachers. But it is Hebrews and 1 Peter that contribute most to a biblical theology of mission. Addressing a congregation in danger of reverting to Judaism, the author of Hebrews contends that God's final revelation occurred in his Son, Jesus (1:1–3), and that his readers neglect 'such a great salvation' at grave peril (2:3; the 'warning passages'). Christians are portrayed as running a race following their forerunner, Jesus, into heaven (6:20; 12:1–3, 12–13). They are cast as pilgrims and exiles in search of a homeland, a better country and a 'city prepared by God' (11:13–16; cf. 12:22). As followers of the one who endured great hostility from sinners (12:3), believers are not to be afraid to suffer and to identify openly with their crucified Lord (13:13; cf. 10:25–26).

Like the author of Hebrews, Peter describes believers as sojourners and 'resident aliens' in this world (1 Pet. 1:1, 17; 2:11; cf. Heb. 11:9, 13). He exhorts his readers to view their suffering from an eschatological perspective: they are to be mindful that an imperishable inheritance awaits them in heaven and that they are shielded by faith through God's power until their salvation will be revealed on the last day (1 Pet. 1:4–5). The believing community is shown to fulfil the calling of Old Testament Israel which was to 'declare the praises' of God as a mediatorial body (2:5–9; cf. Is. 43:21). Believers' mission is to take on the form of verbal witness (1 Pet. 2:9; 3:15), undergirded by a holy, spiritually separated life (1:13 – 2:10), a God-glorifying response to suffering (esp. 2:13–25; 3:8–18b) and proper submission to earthly authorities (2:13, 18; 3:1; 5:1, 5).

Revelation

The book of Revelation depicts the result of mission: people from every tribe and nation gathered in heaven to worship God and the Lamb (1:7; 4:10–11; 5:9; 7:4–17; 14:1–5). This marks the fulfilment of God's covenants with Abraham (all nations are blessed in his seed, Christ) and David (the exalted Lord is the eternal ruler of his people). The entire book, including the seven letters in chapters 2 and 3, challenges believers to renewed spiritual zeal and commitment and exhorts them to persevere in their suffering (cf. 14:12). The seer's apocalyptic visions depict an eternal state free from pain, suffering and death (21:4). This indicates that creation has come full circle, with the Edenic state not merely restored but superseded. God's vindication of the righteous (martyrs) and his judgment of the wicked are shown to serve the purpose of theodicy. John's visions are cast in terms of the pervasive evil influence of the Roman Empire ('the whore Babylon', chs. 17 – 18), a precursor of the Antichrist. The concluding chapters depicting the 'new Jerusalem' and the new heavens and the new earth portray the restoration of God's created order and the fulfilment of the divine purposes for his chosen people.

To sum up, Revelation is not primarily concerned with exhorting believers to engage in mission. Its purpose is rather to put believers' present suffering in eternal perspective. The eternal state will witness a radical reversal of power and worship: while currently the perverse and corrupt Beast wields control and exercises its seductive influence, Christ at his coming will judge the evil world-system and lead his saints to triumph. Even unbelief and stubborn rebellion are shown ultimately to serve the purpose of bringing glory to God. For in light of the world's committed refusal to accept God's salvation, God is shown to be justified in pronouncing its final condemnation. All mission has come to an end, and it becomes clear that mission is in fact a means to an end, the end being a total focus on the worship and the glory of God in our Lord Jesus Christ.

Some concluding observations and implications

God's saving plan is the overarching message of the Bible

Our study of the biblical revelation has demonstrated clearly that the divine plan of extending salvation to the ends of the earth is the major thrust of the Scriptures from beginning to end. If the first indications of God's purposes for the world appear in the creation account of Genesis 1, and subsequently in the call of Abram (Gen. 12) which is profoundly related to God's dealings with the nations, then the Bible ends with a vision of 'a great multitude that no-one could count, from every nation, tribe, people and language, standing before the throne and in front of the Lamb' praising in a loud voice and saying, 'Salvation belongs to our God, who sits on the throne, and to the Lamb' (Rev. 7:9–10; cf. 14:6). God's saving plan for the whole world forms a grand frame around the entire story of Scripture. His mission is bound up with his salvation which moves from creation to new creation. Its focus is on God's gracious movement to save a desperately needy world that is in rebellion against him and which stands under his righteous judgment. The Lord of the Scriptures is a missionary God who reaches out to the lost, and sends his servants, and particularly his beloved Son, to achieve his gracious purposes of salvation. In the final paragraph of Isaiah 66, which describes an eschatological vision of staggering proportions, the Lord himself is the missionary who gathers and rescues people from all nations in order that they may see his glory (vv. 18–24).

The appropriate response of those who have come to understand and experience the saving grace of God in his Son should be one of wonder, awe and gratitude to him, our mighty God. And since the ultimate goal of the divine mission is the glory of God – that he might be known and honoured for who he really is – then what better way to express this than in Paul's doxology of Romans 11:33–36?

> Oh, the depth of the riches of the wisdom and knowledge of God!
>> How unsearchable his judgments,
>> and his paths beyond tracing out!
> 'Who has known the mind of the Lord?
>> Or who has been his counsellor?'
> 'Who has ever given to God,
>> that God should repay him?'
> For from him and through him and to him are all things.
>> To him be the glory for ever!
>>> Amen.

The mission of Jesus in God's plan

At the centre of God's saving purposes is Jesus the Messiah, in whom the Old Testament Scriptures have been fulfilled. In his Son Jesus, whom he has sent to this world, God has confirmed his earlier promises to Israel and brought the nation's history to a climax. The salvation which the Lord Jesus Christ brings is in fulfilment of the divine promises made to Abraham and the fathers, to Israel and to the house of his servant David. Through the Saviour's birth, the divine word by which Israel would be a blessing to the world is brought to fruition (Luke 1 – 2). As God's Son, Jesus is Israel's Messiah who replays the story of the nation's experience in the wilderness, in what amounts to a new exodus (Luke 4:1–13). At the same time his relationship to all humanity is as their representative, since he is the 'Son of Adam, the Son of God' (Luke 3:38).

So within the divine saving plan the basic and foundational *mission* is that of Jesus who has been sent by God to Israel (Luke 4:16–30), and subsequently, through his witnesses, to the Gentiles (Luke 24:45–49). Anointed by the Holy Spirit (Luke 4:18–19), Jesus is conscious that he has been sent from heaven for his mission to 'preach the good news' of God's rule, and to proclaim 'release' to the captives, a release which is first and foremost 'the forgiveness of sins'. In other words, it is a picture of total forgiveness and salvation just as the expression had become in Isaiah 61.

According to John's Gospel, Jesus is a unique person who is both fully divine (John 1:14, 18) and fully human, and therefore perfectly qualified to carry out his unique mission. This culminates in his 'exaltation' and 'glorification'. For the fourth evangelist God's action on behalf of humanity is centred in Christ's work on the cross (John 3:13–17; 4:34; 6:51–58; 10:11, 15, 17–18), and in his revelation of God himself in word and deed (cf. 1:14, 18). In accordance with the divine purpose, Jesus' mission leads to suffering and death. What is written in Scripture about him finds fulfilment (cf. Is. 53): he is numbered with the transgressors, and dies in Jerusalem, rejected as Messiah and Son of Man on earth, but vindicated in heaven. His death, resurrection and ascension are the climactic events of history.

Contemporary Christians need to recognize that Jesus' mission is the fundamental mission in the Scriptures. He is the Messiah and Lord who has fulfilled the purposes of God through his coming, and especially in his death and resurrection. Our own great indebtedness to him is obvious. He is the one who has announced to us the good news of God's rule, and on the basis of his death he has brought forgiveness of sins and salvation to needy men and women.

The mission of others: Jesus sends his witnesses to continue his mission

Although the foundational mission during his earthly ministry was Jesus, being sent by God to Israel (Luke 4:16–30; cf. 20:13), the twelve disciples and the seventy-two are intimately involved with Jesus in his mission to Israel and play a key role within it (Luke 9:1–6; 10:1–24). They are sent by the one who is himself sent from God. Jesus did not embark on a universal mission during the course of his earthly ministry, but there are hints and anticipations throughout that his saving work will have worldwide repercussions (Matt. 8:5–13; 15:24–27; Mark 5:1–20; 7:24–30; Luke 4:24–27; 13:28–30; 14:23–24).

Likewise, after his death and resurrection, with the way now open for repentance and the forgiveness of sins to be proclaimed in his name to all the nations (Luke 24:47), the sending of Jesus by the Father is still the *essential mission.* There is now, however, a major development within the story as to how God's saving purposes for Israel and the nations are to be realized. Jesus' universal mission, which is grounded in his death and resurrection (v. 46), is to be effected by his disciples as *witnesses* to the gospel after he returns to the Father (v. 49; cf. Acts 1:8, 22; 2:32; etc.). They have been chosen by him, and are to be equipped by the Holy Spirit for this task (Luke 24:49; cf. Acts 1:4–5, 8). The twelve are to be his witnesses 'in Jerusalem, and in all Judea and Samaria, and to the ends of the earth' (Acts 1:8, 22). They will bear testimony to Israel (2:22; 13:31; cf. 10:36–39), while later, Paul, who is included among the number of witnesses, takes the testimony to the ends of the earth, that is, to the Gentiles (9:15; 22:14–15; 26:16).

God sent the risen Jesus, his servant (Acts 3:13, 26; cf. Is. 53:12), to bring blessing to 'all peoples on earth', in the first instance to Israel (the 'heirs of the prophets and of the covenant', v. 25), then to the Gentiles (v. 26). It is through the witness of the apostles that God sends his Son (note Peter's own testimony in Acts 3). By listening to this witness, the hearers can now respond to Jesus, the prophet like Moses (v. 22). The mission of Jesus, in which he is sent first to Israel and then to the Gentiles, takes place in and through the testimony of the twelve and later Paul's witness, with the result that Jesus is received by those who hear and believe.

The same fundamental points, in different terms, are made in Matthew 28:18–20, where the disciples are commissioned by Jesus to make disciples of *all the nations,* and in the Gospel of John, where the mission of the disciples derives from the mission of Jesus. They are called (John 1:35–51), trained and commissioned (20:21–23) by Jesus, and their task is described from beginning to end as 'following Jesus' (1:37; 21:22).

Several implications flow from the fact of Jesus' foundational mission leading to others being sent by him to engage in his mission. First, contemporary Christians need to recognize that the mission which really matters in God's sight is not ours but that of Jesus. Matthew, Luke and John conceive of the mission of God's people as ultimately the mission of the exalted Jesus carried out by his followers in and through the power of the Holy Spirit. The Son who has been sent has not relinquished the ultimate control and direction of this mission (cf. Matt. 28:18–20). Accordingly, at the turn of the millennium we need consciously to identify ourselves, both individually and corporately, with Jesus' mission and gracious saving purposes for men and women in our day.

Secondly, recognizing the foundational nature of his mission should lead to a greater humility on our part as God's people in the tasks we undertake in his name. The church does not operate alongside, or even as a replacement for, Jesus. We are God's people under orders. Our proclamation of the forgiveness of sins in Jesus' name should be accompanied by a humble spirit (cf. John 13:1–5), mutual love (cf. 13:35; 15:13) and unity (17:21, 23, 25).

The sovereignty of God in mission

Given that the divine plan of salvation reaching the ends of the earth is the major thrust of the Scriptures, moving from creation to new creation, it is not surprising that the same Scriptures assert from beginning to end God's lordship in mission and salvation. This dimension clearly has been evident throughout each of the preceding chapters, from God's creation of the world through to the climactic events surrounding the breaking in of his kingdom in the ministry of Jesus and his apostles. God has mightily and powerfully sent his Son to seek and to save the lost (Luke 19:10; cf. 4:18–10), and intimately involved in this mission of salvation were Jesus' apostolic witnesses.

Several related aspects of God's sovereignty in mission have important implications for our ongoing and contemporary mission, particularly in a context where pluralism has made rapid gains.

First, God's sovereignty in mission is especially evident in the progress of the word of the gospel. In the book of Acts, this theme, which has already been anticipated within the broad scope of Jesus' ministry in Luke's Gospel and set up in Acts 1:1–11, is a major motif

266

and 'provides the main story-line of Acts'.[2] It is confirmed throughout Luke's second volume at critical points in the narrative by summaries which stress how impressive and far-reaching this advance of the gospel is. Yet this is no triumphalistic advance, for the word of God and its messengers encounter hostility and persecution that are pervasive and constant. In spite of the opposition, however, nothing can ultimately hinder the irresistible progress of the gospel, for God is the one who is sovereignly at work. He has ordained, planned, guided and supported this dynamic advance. Throughout Acts the 'word of God', the content of which is the 'kingdom of God' and the 'salvation of God', depends for its progress on the purpose, will and plan of God.[3] And this word does not return empty. Like God's word in Isaiah 55, it will accomplish what he desires, and achieve the purpose for which he sends it (v. 11). Similar points, as we have already seen, are made about God's sovereignty in mission by the apostle Paul in relation to the saving power of the gospel (Rom. 1:16–17; 3:21–26) and its dynamic advance (Phil. 1:14–18; Col. 1:6, 10; 1 Thess. 1:5; 2:13; 2 Thess. 3:1–2).

Secondly, and related to the first implication, the mission of God in this world cannot be thwarted. The rejection of Jesus by his own people, a rejection that culminates in the cross, occurred within the predeterminate counsel of God. Sinful human resistance to the divine plan of salvation is overruled and used by the sovereign Lord of history to achieve his own purposes. The world's rejection of God's people and their mission in Christ's name is not the final word. Believers should not respond in like manner and reject the world. Instead, we are to be firm in our resolve to proclaim the gospel as we bear testimony to Jesus (cf. John 15:18–27), knowing that the sovereign Lord draws people to himself. As believers carry out this mission, we are assured that all the resources needed for this outreach will be provided, and God's purposes finally will triumph.

The advance of the gospel leads to the founding of settled Christian communities

The New Testament makes it plain that the mission of Jesus, in which the apostles and others were engaged, was not concluded when men and women, Jews and Gentiles, were converted or brought into an initial saving relationship with God. We have already seen, particularly in Acts and the letters of Paul, that the advance of the gospel or the

[2] Rosner 1998: 215–233, esp. 215.
[3] Rosner 1998: 224.

progress of the word of God leads to the founding of settled Christian communities. The apostolic documents of the New Testament bear witness to a wide-ranging series of activities that result in believers' being built up in Christ, and formed into vibrant Christian congregations. This is particularly evident in the case of Paul. He was engaged in primary evangelism and proclaimed the message of the grace of God so that men and women were converted, but he also founded churches and sought to bring believers to full maturity in Christ as a necessary element in his missionary task. Conversion to Christ meant incorporation into a Christian community. Paul anticipates his converts being his joy and crown, as they stand fast on the final day, thereby showing that he had not run in vain in his ministry.

Similarly, the theological instructions and warnings of the General Epistles, particularly 1 Peter and Hebrews, which urge Christians to view their sufferings from an eschatological perspective and so glorify God in their response, are intended to strengthen them in leading holy, separated lives as they bear witness and declare the praises of him who called them out of darkness into his wonderful light (1 Pet. 2:9). Peter and the author of Hebrews were committed in their teaching and admonition to bringing believers to full maturity in Christ.

If the apostolic model is to be followed by missionaries in the contemporary scene, then the initial proclamation of the gospel and the winning of converts does not conclude the missionary task. Forming believers into mature Christian congregations, providing theological and pastoral counsel against dangers arising from inside and outside churches, strengthening believers both individually and corporately as they face suffering and persecution, so that they will stand fast in the Lord, all fall within the scope of what is involved in continuing the mission of the exalted Lord Jesus Christ.

Mission and the final goal

We have understood the notion of 'mission' (which, strictly speaking, is not a biblical term) as intimately bound up with God's saving plan that moves from creation to new creation, and as framing the entire story of Scripture. It has to do with God's salvation reaching the ends of the earth: that is, his gracious movement in his Son, the Lord Jesus Christ, to rescue a desperately needy world that is in rebellion against him and stands under his righteous judgment. Clearly the *notion* of 'sending' is central to any treatment of mission, but by this we do not simply mean the *instances* of the *sending terminology* in both Old and

New Testaments. Rather, our focus has been on the *concept* of sending, within the above-mentioned biblical-theological framework, and this has necessitated our looking at related issues, such as: who sends? For what purposes? What activities fall within the sphere of the sending? And what are the long-range goals of mission?

The Lord of the Scriptures is a missionary God who not only reaches out and gathers the lost but also sends his servants, and particularly his beloved Son, to achieve his gracious saving purposes. As many have rightly observed, the most important mission in the Scriptures is the *missio Dei*. Jesus Christ is the 'missionary' *par excellence*: the basic and foundational mission is his. He has been sent by the Father to effect forgiveness and salvation, especially through his death and resurrection (cf. Luke 4:18–19; 24:46–47), and then to announce it to Jews and Gentiles alike. In fulfilment of the Servant's role his task is to bring (or, perhaps, *be*) God's salvation to the ends of the earth.

The mission of the exalted Jesus is accomplished through the witness of the apostles in the power of the Holy Spirit. The one who is himself sent by God sends his representatives to bear testimony to his salvation, to announce the forgiveness of sins and to make disciples of all nations. In other words, his witnesses continue the mission of Jesus by declaring to men and women everywhere the glorious gospel of the grace of God. As the Father has sent him, so Jesus sends them. Moreover, this testimony to Jesus and his saving work involves a wide-ranging series of activities that result in believers being built up in Christ and formed into Christian congregations. It is not limited simply to primary evangelism and its immediate results. Conversion to Christ necessarily involved incorporation into a Christian community.

Contemporary disciples who follow in the footsteps of the apostles and first witnesses are caught up in God's majestic saving plan, and because of their identity with Jesus they continue his mission. Its focus is the apostolic gospel which is proclaimed under the sovereignty of God, in full acknowledgment of the supremacy of the Lord Jesus and through the power of the Holy Spirit. This mission of God's people within the world is to be understood within an eschatological perspective, that is, it is grounded in the saving events of the gospel and keeps an eye on the final goal – the gathering of men and women from every nation, tribe, people and language before the throne of God and the Lamb.

In this era between the 'already' and the 'not yet' God's people are a body of pilgrims and resident aliens. They suffer and are persecuted for the sake of Christ's name, but in the midst of this they are to follow his example, demonstrating patience and a gentle spirit and showing that ultimately they do not belong to the world. Moreover, the gospel must be preserved pure if it is to be proclaimed persuasively and with God's saving power. And Christians should adorn that gospel with their godly lifestyle and proper relationships, if their spoken words are not to have negative effects on unbelievers.

Finally, continuing the mission of Jesus in the contemporary context will involve the nurture and pastoral care of men and women by feeding them with the word of God so that those who have come into a relationship with Christ will be brought to maturity in him and will stand fast before their Lord on the final day.

Appendix
Paul's use of *euangelion*[1]

Introduction

The *euangel-* word group turns up in the Pauline corpus on some eighty-four occasions: the noun *euangelion* ('gospel') is used some sixty times, the verb *euangelizomai* ('preach the gospel') twenty-one times, with the noun *euangelistēs* ('evangelist') occurring twice (Eph. 4:11; 2 Tim. 4:5) and the related verb *proeuangelizomai* ('preach the gospel beforehand') once (at Gal. 3:8). Surprisingly, these terms appear less frequently in the rest of the New Testament. For example, *euangelion* turns up on only sixteen other occasions, half of which are in Mark, while the verb *euangelizomai* (apart from the ten instances in Luke's Gospel and the fifteen in Acts) occurs only eight additional times.

In general, *euangelion* served as a label to express in summary fashion the message that Paul announced to the world of his day (Rom. 1:1).[2] Although the term and its cognates occupied a significant place in Pauline teaching, he was not the first to employ this language. Prior to his ministry *euangelion* was already a technical term in early Christian vocabulary to denote the authoritative news of Jesus Christ.

The Graeco-Roman world

Euangelion originally signified 'the reward' given to a messenger for his tidings, especially his good news which brought relief to his recipients. The term then came to be used of the message itself. While

---

[1] Note esp. Stuhlmacher 1968, 1991a: 1–25, 1991b: 149–172; and Dunn 1998: 163–169.

[2] 'Gospel' became 'a central concept of Paul's theology; it was for the apostle the principal, theologically-charged motif in his mission preaching' (Wilckens 1978: 74).

271

SALVATION TO THE ENDS OF THE EARTH

occasionally signifying political and private messages, it had importance as a message of victory and this was often understood as a gift of the gods. On such occasions sacrifices were offered to the gods out of gratitude and in order to secure the benefits proclaimed by the 'good news'.

Of special importance are those instances of the plural *euangelia* in the language of the imperial cult to describe the emperor's birth, coming of age or enthronement as well as his speeches, decrees and acts that were regarded as the 'glad tidings' which brought the long-hoped-for fulfilment of the yearnings of the world for happiness and peace. The oft-quoted Calendar Inscription from Priene (in Asia Minor) says 'the birthday of the god [= Augustus] was for the world the beginning of *good tidings* owing to him'. The proclamation of these tidings does not simply herald the new era; it actually brings it about. While earlier scholarship was inclined to interpret the early Christians' use of the singular *euangelion* against this background of the imperial cult, this assessment is currently regarded as unlikely: in the latter context only the plural (*euangelia*) appears, not a technical singular, while the New Testament itself gives no evidence of a political or polemical orientation.

The Old Testament background

Of greater significance than the imperial cult for an understanding of the background to Paul's thought is the cognate verb *euangelizomai* (particularly in Is. 40 – 66) which comes to stand for the Hebrew *biśśēr*, 'to announce, tell, deliver a (good or bad) message' (e.g. 1 Kgs. 1:42; Jer. 20:15). This verb is used in the Psalms (40:9[10]; 68:11[12]; 96:2ff.) and Isaiah (41:27; 52:7) to herald Yahweh's victory over the world and his kingly rule. With his enthronement (cf. esp. Ps. 96) and his return to Zion (Is. 40 – 55) a new era begins. The messenger of good tidings, the *meḇaśśēr* (rendered by *ho euangelizomenos* in the LXX), announces this new era of God's rule and inaugurates it by his word. The Lord has become king (Is. 52:7; cf. 40:9; 41:27) and his reign extends over the whole earth (Ps. 96:2ff.). Peace and salvation have now come. In the mouth of his messengers God himself speaks and through this divine proclamation the new age begins.

Jesus and his disciples

Jesus understood his own sending in the light of Isaiah 61:1–2, for according to Matthew 11:2–6 he regarded his healing miracles and his preaching as a fulfilment of this Old Testament text (cf. Is. 35).[3] He saw himself as the messianic evangelist of the poor (Matt. 11:5), fulfilling the role of the *mᵉbaśśēr* ('messenger of good tidings') of whom Isaiah 61:1 speaks. His preaching of God's kingly rule (Mark 1:15) is the *bᵉśôrâ* ('message of peace') of Isaiah 52:7 ('How beautiful on the mountains are the feet of those who bring good news, who proclaim peace, who bring good tidings, who proclaim salvation, who say to Zion, "Your God reigns!"'). His gospel announcement is the *šᵉmû'a* ('report') of Isaiah 53:1, that is, the saving message of God's coming. The term *euangelion* is attributed to Jesus by the evangelists on a number of occasions (Mark 1:15; 8:35; 10:29; 13:10; 14:9; Matt. 4:23; 9:35; 24:14; 26:13). Further, Jesus appears not only as the messenger and the author of the message; he is at the same time the subject, the one of whom the message speaks. It is therefore not surprising that the New Testament writers apply the term *euangelion* to describe the message of salvation that is connected with the coming of Jesus. He is the messenger who announces the arrival of peace and salvation with the coming of God himself.

Jesus' disciples shared in his proclamation and saw their task as a continuation of that of the *mᵉbaśśēr* ('messenger') of Isaiah 61:1–3 and 52:7 (cf. Matt. 10:1–16; Luke 9:6).

Early Christian preaching

Both the singular noun 'gospel' and the cognate verb were employed to describe the early Christian preaching of the coming of God's rule as evidenced in the coming of Jesus, his death and resurrection (cf. Acts 5:32), a gospel that was for both Jew and Gentile alike. The mission preaching of Peter is referred to by means of *euangelion* (Acts 15:7; cf. that of Paul: Acts 20:24), while in Acts 10:36–43, where the account of Peter's preaching the gospel to Cornelius is reported, the verb 'preach the gospel' is used in a significant way. Echoes of Isaiah 52:7 (cf. Nah. 1:15) can be heard, while God himself is named as the messenger (*euangelizomenos*) of peace through Jesus Christ (Acts 10:36).

Summary conclusion

Prior to Paul's ministry, *euangelion* was already a technical term in

---

[3] See the careful treatment of this by Stuhlmacher 1991a: 20–21.

early Christian vocabulary to denote the authoritative news of Jesus Christ. The apostle's frequent use of the noun 'gospel' without any qualifiers indicates that he was taking over phraseology already familiar to his readers. They knew what the content of the gospel was (cf. 1 Cor. 15:1–11). The noun could describe the activity of preaching the gospel as well as the content of the message.

The Christian use of the word derives from Jesus' own ministry in which the verb form was established in dependence on Isaiah 61:1–2 (cf. 40:9; 52:7). Jesus understood his own ministry as a fulfilment of the role of the *m^ebaśśēr* of Isaiah. He is the messenger who announces the arrival of peace and salvation with the coming of God himself. Further, Jesus' disciples shared in his proclamation and saw their task as a continuation of that of the *m^ebaśśēr* of Isaiah 61:1–3 and 52:7.

Bibliography

Alexander, T. D. (1994), 'Abraham Re-assessed Theologically: The Abraham Narrative and the New Testament Understanding of Justification by Faith', in R. S. Hess, G. J. Wenham and P. E. Satterthwaite (eds.), *He Swore an Oath: Biblical Themes from Genesis 12 – 50*, Carlisle/Grand Rapids: Paternoster/Baker, 7–28.

—— (1997), 'Further Observations on the Term "Seed" in Genesis', *TynB* 48, 363–367.

—— (1998), 'Royal Expectations in Genesis to Kings: Their Importance for Biblical Theology', *TynB* 49, 191–212.

Allen, L. C. (1976), *The Books of Joel, Obadiah, Jonah and Micah*, London: Hodder and Stoughton.

Allison, D. C., Jr (1989), 'Who will Come from East and West? Observations on Matt. 8.11–12 – Luke 13.28–29', *IBS* 11, 158–170.

—— (1993), *The New Moses: A Matthean Typology*, Minneapolis: Fortress.

Alt, A. (1951), 'Die Stätten des Wirkens Jesu in Galiläa', *Zeitschrift des deutschen Palästina-Vereins* 68, 51–72.

Arias, M. (1991), 'Church in the World: Rethinking the Great Commission', *TToday* 47, 410–418.

Arnold, C. E. (1989), *Ephesians: Power and Magic: The Concept of Power in Ephesians in Light of its Historical Setting*, SNTSMS 63, Cambridge: Cambridge University Press.

—— (1992), *Powers of Darkness*, Leicester: IVP.

Attridge, H. W. (1990), 'Paraenesis in a Homily (*logos parakl$se2s*): The Possible Location of, and Socialization in, the "Epistle to the Hebrews"', *Semeia* 50, 211–226.

Aus, R. D. (1979), 'Paul's Travel Plans to Spain and the "Full Number of the Gentiles" of Rom. xi 25', *NovT* 21, 232–262.

Axenfeld, K. (1904), 'Die jüdische Propaganda als Vorläuferin und Wegbereiterin der urchristlichen Mission', in *Missionswissenschaftliche Studien: Festschrift zum 70. Geburtstag des Herrn Prof. D. Dr. Gustav Warneck*, Berlin: Martin Warneck, 1–80.

Bailey, D. P. (1999), 'Jesus as the Mercy Seat', unpublished PhD thesis, Cambridge.

Balch, D. L. (1998), 'Attitudes toward Foreigners in 2 Maccabees, Eupolemus, Esther, Aristeas, and Luke-Acts', in A. J. Malherbe, F. W. Norris and J. W. Thompson (eds.), *The Early Church in Its Context: Essays in Honor of Everett Ferguson*, NovTSup 90, Leiden: Brill, 22–47.

Ball, D. M. (1996), *'I Am' in John's Gospel: Literary Function, Background and Theological Implications*, JSNTSS 124, Sheffield: Sheffield Academic Press.

Barclay, J. (1996), *Jews in the Mediterranean Diaspora from Alexander to Trajan (323 BCE – 117 CE)*, Edinburgh: T. and T. Clark.

Barrett, C. K. (1978), *The Gospel According to St. John*, 2nd ed., Philadelphia: Westminster.

—— (1982), 'Christocentric or Theocentric? Observations on the Theological Method of the Fourth Gospel', in *Essays on John*, Philadelphia: Westminster, 1–18.

—— (1988), 'The Gentile Mission as an Eschatological Phenomenon', in W. H. Gloer (ed.), *Eschatology and the New Testament: Essays in Honor of George Raymond Beasley-Murray*, Peabody, MA: Hendrickson, 65–75.

—— (1994, 1998), *The Acts of the Apostles*, ICC, 2 vols., Edinburgh: T. and T. Clark.

Barth, K. (1961), 'An Exegetical Study of Matthew 28:16–20', in G. H. Anderson (ed.), *The Theology of the Christian Mission*, Nashville/New York: Abingdon, 55–71.

Bauckham, R. (1993), *The Climax of Prophecy*, Edinburgh: T. and T. Clark.

—— (1995), 'James and the Jerusalem Church', in R. Bauckham (ed.), *The Book of Acts in Its First Century Setting* 4: *The Book of Acts in Its Palestinian Setting*, Grand Rapids/Carlisle: Eerdmans/Paternoster, 415–480.

——(1996), 'James and the Gentiles (Acts 15.13–21)', in B. Witherington (ed.), *History, Literature and Society in the Book of Acts*, Cambridge: Cambridge University Press, 154–184.

—— (1997), *The Gospels for All Christians: Rethinking the Gospel Audiences*, Grand Rapids: Eerdmans.

Bauder, W. (1976), 'Disciple', in C. Brown (ed.), *The New International Dictionary of New Testament Theology* 1, Grand Rapids: Zondervan, 480–494.

Bauer, D. R. (1988), *The Structure of Matthew's Gospel: A Study in Literary Design*, JSNTSS 31, Sheffield: Almond.

Bavinck, J. H. (1960), *An Introduction to the Science of Missions*,

Philadelphia: Presbyterian and Reformed.

Bayer, H. F. (1998), 'The Preaching of Peter in Acts', in I. H. Marshall and D. Peterson (eds.), *Witness to the Gospel: The Theology of Acts*, Grand Rapids/Cambridge: Eerdmans, 257–274.

Beale, G. K. (1997), 'The Eschatological Conception of New Testament Theology', in K. E. Brower and M. W. Elliott (eds.), *'The Reader Must Understand': Eschatology in Bible and Theology*, Leicester: IVP, 11–52.

—— (1999), *The Book of Revelation*, NIGTC, Grand Rapids: Eerdmans.

Beare, F. W. (1981), *The Gospel According to Matthew*, San Francisco: Harper and Row.

Beasley-Murray, G. R. (1987), *John*, WBC 36, Waco, TX: Word.

Bedell, C. H. (1998), 'Mission in Intertestamental Judaism', in W. J. Larkin and J. F. Williams (eds.), *Mission in the New Testament: An Evangelical Approach*, Maryknoll, NY: Orbis.

Best, E. (1984), 'The Revelation to Evangelize the Gentiles', *JTS* 35, 1–30.

Betz, H. D. (1994), 'Jesus and the Cynics: Survey and Analysis of a Hypothesis', *JR* 74, 453–475.

Beutler, J. (1990), 'Greeks Come to See Jesus (John 12, 20f)', *Bib* 71, 333–347.

Bieder, W. (1965), *Gottes Sendung und der missionarische Auftrag nach Matthäus, Lukas, Paulus, und Johannes*, ThStud 82, Zürich: EVZ.

Blauw, J. (1962), *The Missionary Nature of the Church: A Survey of the Biblical Theology of Mission*, London: Lutterworth.

Blomberg, C. L. (1992), *Matthew*, NAC 22, Nashville: Broadman.

Blue, B. (1998), 'The Influence of Jewish Worship on Luke's Presentation of the Early Church', in I. H. Marshall and D. Peterson (eds.), *Witness to the Gospel: The Theology of Acts*, Grand Rapids/Cambridge: Eerdmans, 473–497.

Bock, D. L. (1994, 1996), *Luke*, 2 vols., BECNT, Grand Rapids: Baker.

Bockmuehl, M. N. A. (1990), *Revelation and Mystery in Ancient Judaism and Pauline Christianity*, WUNT 36, Tübingen: Mohr-Siebeck.

Boismard, M.-E. (1993), *Moses or Jesus: An Essay in Johannine Christology*, trans. B. T. Viviano, Minneapolis: Fortress.

Bolt, P. G. (1998), 'Mission and Witness', in I. H. Marshall and D. Peterson (eds.), *Witness to the Gospel: The Theology of Acts*, Grand

Rapids/Cambridge: Eerdmans, 191–214.

—— (forthcoming), 'Following Jesus and Fishing for People: Evangelistic Mission in the Third Millennium', *Explorations* 12, 1–37.

Boobyer, G. H. (1952–53), 'Galilee and Galileans in St Mark's Gospel', *BJRL* 25, 334–348.

—— (1953), 'The Miracles of the Loaves and the Gentiles in St Mark's Gospel', *SJT* 6, 77–87.

Boomershine, T. E. (1981), 'Mark 16:8 and the Apostolic Commission', *JBL* 100, 225–239.

Borgen, P. (1983), 'God's Agent in the Fourth Gospel', in *Logos Was the True Light and Other Essays on the Gospel of John*, Trondheim: Tapir, 121–132.

—— (1996), *Early Christianity and Hellenistic Judaism*, Edinburgh: T. and T. Clark.

Bornhäuser, K. (1928), *Das Johannesevangelium: Eine Missionsschrift für Israel*, BFCT 2/15, Gütersloh: Bertelsmann.

Bornkamm, G. (1970), 'Der Auferstandene und der Irdische', in G. Bornkamm, G. Barth and H. J. Held, *Überlieferung und Auslegung im Matthäusevangelium*, WMANT 1, 6th ed., Neukirchen: Kreis Moers, x–xx.

—— (1971), 'The Risen Lord and the Earthly Jesus: Matthew 28.16–20', in James M. Robinson (ed.), *The Future of Our Religious Past: Essays in Honour of Rudolf Bultmann*, London: SCM, 203–229.

Bornkamm, G., G. Barth and H. J. Held (1963), *Tradition and Interpretation in Matthew*, London: SCM.

Bosch, D. J. (1983), 'The Structure of Mission: An Exposition of Matthew 28:16–20', in W. R. Shenk (ed.), *Exploring Church Growth*, Grand Rapids: Eerdmans, 218–248.

—— (1991), *Transforming Mission: Paradigm Shifts in Theology of Mission*, American Society of Missiology Series 16, Maryknoll, NY: Orbis.

—— (1993), 'Reflections on Biblical Models of Mission', in J. M. Phillips and R. T. Coote (eds.), *Toward the 21st Century in Christian Mission*, Grand Rapids: Eerdmans, 175–192.

Botha, J. (1988), 'Christian and Society in 1 Peter: Critical Solidarity', *Scriptura* 24, 27–37.

Bowers, W. P. (1976), 'Studies in Paul's Understanding of his Mission', unpublished PhD thesis, Cambridge.

—— (1980), 'Paul and Religious Propaganda in the First Century', *NovT* 22, 317–323.

—— (1987), 'Fulfilling the Gospel: The Scope of the Pauline Mission', *JETS* 30, 185–198.

—— (1993), 'Mission', in G. F. Hawthorne and R. P. Martin (eds.), *Dictionary of Paul and His Letters*, Downers Grove/Leicester: IVP, 608–619.

Braun, W. (1995), *Feasting and Social Rhetoric in Luke 14*, SNTSMS 85, Cambridge: Cambridge University Press.

Brawley, R. L. (1990), *Centering on God: Method and Message in Luke-Acts*, Louisville: Westminster/John Knox.

—— (1994), 'The Blessing of all the Families of the Earth: Jesus and Covenant Traditions in Luke-Acts', in E. H. Lovering (ed.), *Society of Biblical Literature 1994 Seminary Papers*, Atlanta: Scholars, 252–268.

Bright, J. (1955), *The Kingdom of God in Bible and Church*, London: Lutterworth.

Brooks, O. S. (1981), 'Matthew xxviii 16–20 and the Design of the First Gospel', *JSNT* 10, 2–18.

Brosend, W. F. (1996), 'The means of absent ends', in B. Witherington (ed.), *History, Literature and Society in the Book of Acts*, Cambridge: Cambridge University Press, 348–362.

Brown, R. E. (1966, 1970), *The Gospel according to John*, 2 vols., New York: Doubleday.

—— (1968), *The Semitic Background of the Term 'Mystery' in the New Testament*, Philadelphia: Fortress.

—— (1977), *The Birth of the Messiah*, Garden City, NY: Doubleday.

—— (1978), '"Other Sheep Not of This Fold': The Johannine Perspective on Christian Diversity in the Late First Century', *JBL* 97, 5–22.

Brown, S. (1977), 'The Two-fold Representation of the Mission in Matthew's Gospel', *ST* 31, 21–32.

—— (1980), 'The Matthean Community and the Gentile Mission', *NovT* 22, 193–221.

Bruce, F. F. (1960–61), 'The Book of Zechariah and the Passion Narrative', *BJRL* 43, 336–353.

—— (1961), *The Epistle to the Ephesians*, London: Pickering and Inglis.

—— (1983a), *The Hard Sayings of Jesus*, Downers Grove: IVP.

—— (1983b), *The Gospel of John*, Grand Rapids: Eerdmans.

—— (1988), *The Book of Acts*, rev. ed., NICNT, Grand Rapids: Eerdmans.

—— (1990a), 'Luke's Presentation of the Spirit in Acts', *CTR* 54, 15–29.

—— (1990b), *The Acts of the Apostles*, 3rd ed., Grand Rapids: Eerdmans.

—— (1990c), *The Epistle to the Hebrews*, rev. ed., NICNT, Grand Rapids: Eerdmans.

Bühner, J. A. (1977), *Der Gesandte und sein Weg im 4. Evangelium: Die kultur- und religionsgeschichtliche Entwicklung*, WUNT 2/2, Tübingen: Mohr-Siebeck.

Bultmann, R. (1951, 1955), *Theology of the New Testament*, 2 vols., New York: Charles Scribner's Sons, 1955.

Burkett, D. (1991), *The Son of Man in the Gospel of John*, JSNTSS 56, Sheffield: JSOT.

Byrne, B. (1996), *Romans*, Sacra Pagina 6, Collegeville, MN: Glazier, Liturgical.

Caragounis, C. C. (1986), *The Son of Man*, WUNT 38, Tübingen: Mohr-Siebeck.

Carey, G. L. (1981), 'The Lamb of God and Atonement Theories', *TynB* 32, 97–122.

Cargal, T. B. (1991), ' "His blood be upon us and upon our children": A Matthean *double entendre*?' *NTS* 37, 101–112.

Carroll, J. T. (1988), *Response to the End of History: Eschatology and Situation in Luke-Acts*, SBLDS 92, Atlanta: Scholars.

Carson, D. A. (1984), 'Matthew', *The Expositor's Bible Commentary* 8, Grand Rapids: Zondervan, 1–599.

—— (1987), 'The Purpose of the Fourth Gospel: Jn 20:31 Reconsidered', *JBL* 106, 639–651.

—— (1991a), 'The Role of Exegesis in Systematic Theology', in J. D. Woodbridge and T. E. McComiskey (eds.), *Doing Theology in Today's World: Essays in Honor of Kenneth S. Kantzer*, Grand Rapids: Zondervan, 39–76.

—— (1991b), *The Gospel According to John*, Grand Rapids: Eerdmans.

—— (1995), 'Current Issues in Biblical Theology: A New Testament Perspective', *BBR* 5, 17–41.

—— (1996), *The Gagging of God: Christianity Confronts Pluralism*, Grand Rapids: Zondervan.

Carson, D. A., D. J. Moo and L. Morris (1992), *An Introduction to the New Testament*, Grand Rapids: Zondervan.

Cassem, N. H. (1972–73), 'A Grammatical and Contextual Inventory of the Use of *kosmos* in the Johannine Cosmic Theology', *NTS* 19, 81–91.

Chae, D. J.-S. (1997), *Paul as Apostle to the Gentiles: His Apostolic Self-Awareness and its Influence on the Soteriological Argument of*

Romans, Carlisle: Paternoster.

Chevallier, M.-A. (1974), 'Condition et vocation des chrétiens en diaspora: remarques exégétiques sur la 1re *Épître de Pierre*', *RevScRel* 48, 387–400.

Chin, M. (1991), 'A Heavenly Home for the Homeless: Aliens and Strangers in 1 Peter', *TynB* 42, 96–112.

Clark, A. C. (1998), 'The Role of the Apostles', in I. H. Marshall and D. Peterson (eds.), *Witness to the Gospel: The Theology of Acts*, Grand Rapids/Cambridge: Eerdmans, 169–190.

Clarke, A. D. (1998), ' "Be Imitators of Me": Paul's Model of Leadership', *TynB* 49, 329–360.

Clowney, E. P. (1984), 'Interpreting the Biblical Models of the Church: A Hermeneutical Deepening of Ecclesiology', in D. A. Carson (ed.), *Biblical Interpretation and the Church*, Exeter: Paternoster, 64–109.

Cohen, S. J. D. (1992), 'Was Judaism in Antiquity a Missionary Religion?', in M. Mor (ed.), *Jewish Assimilation, Acculturation and Accommodation: Past Traditions, Current Issues, and Future Prospects*, Lanham, MD: University Press of America, 14–23.

Collins J. (1997), 'A Syntactical Note (Genesis 3:15): Is the Woman's Seed Singular or Plural?', *TynB* 48:139–148.

Collins, R. F. (1990), *These Things Have Been Written – Studies on the Fourth Gospel*, Louvain/Grand Rapids: Peeters/Eerdmans.

Conzelmann, H. (1967), *Grundriß des Theologie des Neuen Testaments*, München: Chr. Kaiser.

—— (1992), *Gentiles – Jews – Christians: Polemics and Apologetics in the Greco-Roman Era*, Minneapolis: Fortress.

Corell, A. (1958), *Consummatum Est: Eschatology and Church in the Gospel of St John*, London: SPCK.

Corley, B. (1997), 'Interpreting Paul's Conversion – Then and Now', in R. N. Longenecker (ed.), *The Road from Damascus: The Impact of Paul's Conversion on His Life, Thought, and Ministry*, Grand Rapids/Cambridge: Eerdmans, 1–17.

Cranfield, C. E. B. (1959), *The Gospel According to Saint Mark*, Cambridge: Cambridge University Press.

—— (1975, 1979), *The Epistle to the Romans*, 2 vols., Edinburgh: T. and T. Clark.

Cullmann, O. (1948), 'Der johanneische Gebrauch doppeldeutiger Ausdrücke als Schlüssel zum Verständnis des 4. Evangeliums', *TZ* 4, 360–372.

Culpepper, R. A. (1983), *The Anatomy of the Fourth Gospel: A Study in Literary Design*, Philadelphia: Fortress.

Culver, R. D. (1968), 'What is the Church's Commission? Some Exegetical Issues in Matthew 28:16-20', *BibSac* 125: 239–253.

Dalbert, P. (1954), *Die Theologie der hellenistisch-jüdischen Missionsliteratur unter Ausschluß von Philo und Josephus*, Hamburg: Reich.

Darr, J. A. (1992), *On Character Building: The Reader and the Rhetoric of Characterization in Luke-Acts*, Louisville: Westminster/John Knox.

Davies, G. I. (1989), 'The Destiny of the Nations in the Book of Isaiah', in J. Vermeylen (ed.), *The Book of Isaiah*, Leuven: Leuven University Press, 93–120.

Davies, W. D., and D. C. Allison (1988, 1991, 1997), *The Gospel According to St. Matthew*, ICC, 3 vols., Edinburgh: T. and T. Clark.

De Ridder, R. R. (1975), *Discipling the Nations*, Grand Rapids: Baker.

deSilva, D. A. (1991), 'The "Image of the Beast" and the Christians in Asia Minor: Escalation of Sectarian Tension in Revelation 13', *TrinJ* 12 NS, 185–208.

—— (1995), *Despising Shame: Honor Discourse and Community Maintenance in the Epistle to the Hebrews*, SBLDS 152, Atlanta, GA: Scholars.

Dietzfelbinger, C. (1989), 'Die größeren Werke (Joh. 14.12f)', *NTS* 35, 27–47.

Dobbie, R. (1962), 'The Biblical Foundation of the Mission of the Church: Old Testament', *IRM* 51, 196–205.

Dodd, C. H. (1952), *According to the Scriptures: The Substructure of New Testament Theology*, Digswell Place: J. Nisbet.

Dollar, H. E. (1993), *A Biblical-Missiological Exploration of the Cross-Cultural Dimensions in Luke-Acts*, San Francisco: Edwin Mellen.

Donahue, J. R. (1973), *Are You the Christ?*, SBLDS 10, Missoula, MT: SBL.

—— (1983), *The Theology and Setting of Discipleship in the Gospel of Mark*, Milwaukee, WI: Marquette University Press.

Donaldson, T. L. (1985), *Jesus on the Mountain: A Study in Matthean Typology*, JSNTSS 8, Sheffield: JSOT.

—— (1997a), 'Israelite, Convert, Apostle to the Gentiles: The Origin of Paul's Gentile Mission', in R. N. Longenecker (ed.), *The Road from Damascus: The Impact of Paul's Conversion on His Life, Thought, and Ministry*, Grand Rapids/Cambridge: Eerdmans, 62–84.

—— (1997b), *Paul and the Gentiles: Remapping the Apostle's Convictional World*, Minneapolis: Fortress.

Dumbrell, W. J. (1984), *Covenant and Creation: An Old Testament Covenantal Theology*, Exeter: Paternoster.

—— (1994), *The Search for Order: Biblical Eschatology in Focus*, Grand Rapids: Baker.

Dunn, J. D. G. (1987), ' "A Light to the Gentiles": The Significance of the Damascus Road Christophany for Paul', in L. D. Hurst and N. T. Wright (eds.), *The Glory of Christ in the New Testament*, Oxford: Clarendon, 251–266.

—— (1988a, 1988b), *Romans 1 – 8*, *Romans 9 – 16*, Dallas: Word.

—— (1990), *Unity and Diversity in the New Testament: An Enquiry into the Character of Earliest Christianity*, 2nd ed., London/Philadelphia: SCM/Trinity International.

—— (1998), *The Theology of Paul the Apostle*, Grand Rapids/Cambridge: Eerdmans.

Eddy, P. R. (1996), 'Jesus as Diogenes? Reflections on the Cynic Jesus Thesis', *JBL* 115, 449–469.

Egelkraut, H. L. (1976), *Jesus' Mission to Jerusalem: A Redaction-Critical Study of the Travel Narrative in the Gospel of Luke, Lk. 9.51 – 19.48*, Frankfurt: Peter Lang.

Elliott, J. H. (1966), *The Elect and the Holy*, NovTSup 12, Leiden: Brill.

—— (1982), *A Home for the Homeless: A Sociological Exegesis of 1 Peter, Its Situation and Strategy*, London: SCM.

—— (1995), 'Disgraced Yet Graced. The Gospel according to 1 Peter in the Key of Honor and Shame', *BTB* 25, 166–178.

Ellis, E. E. (1993), 'Paul and his Coworkers', in G. F. Hawthorne and R. P. Martin (eds.), *Dictionary of Paul and His Letters*, Downers Grove/Leicester: IVP, 183–189.

Ellis, I. P. (1967–68), 'But Some Doubted', *NTS* 14, 574–580.

Ensor, P. W. (1996), *Jesus and His 'Works'*, WUNT 85, Tübingen: Mohr-Siebeck.

Enz, J. J. (1957), 'The Book of Exodus as a Literary Type for the Gospel of John', *JBL* 76, 208–215.

Erdmann, M. (1998), 'Mission in John's Gospel and Letters', in W. J. Larkin and J. F. Williams (eds.), *Mission in the New Testament: An Evangelical Approach*, Maryknoll, NY: Orbis, 207–226.

Evans, C. A. (1997), 'From "House of Prayer" to "Cave of Robbers": Jesus' Prophetic Criticism of the Temple Establishment', in C. A. Evans and S. Talmon (eds.), *The Quest for Context and Meaning*, Leiden: Brill, 417–442.

Evans, C. A. and J. A. Sanders (1993), *Luke and Scripture: The*

Function of Sacred Tradition in Luke-Acts, Minneapolis: Fortress.

Farrer, A. (1951), *A Study in St Mark*, Westminster: Dacre.

Farris, S. (1985), *The Hymns of Luke's Infancy Narrative: Their Origin, Meaning and Significance*, JSNTSS 9, Sheffield: JSOT.

Fee, G. D. (1987), *The First Epistle to the Corinthians*, NICNT, Grand Rapids: Eerdmans.

—— (1992), 'On the Text and Meaning of John 20.30–31', in F. van Segbroeck, C. M. Tuckett, G. van Belle, and J. Verheyden (eds.), *The Four Gospels 1992; Festschrift Frans Neirynck*, BETL C, vol. 3, Leuven: Leuven University Press, 2193–2205.

Feldman, L. H. (1950), 'Jewish "Sympathisers" in Classical Literature and Inscriptions', *TAPA* 81, 200–208.

—— (1993), *Jew and Gentile in the Ancient World: Attitudes and Interactions from Alexander to Justinian*, Princeton, NJ: Princeton University Press.

Feldmeier, R. (1992), *Die Christen als Fremde: Die Metapher der Fremde in der antiken Welt, im Urchristentum und im 1 Petrusbrief*, WUNT 64, Tübingen: Mohr-Siebeck.

Fernando, A. (1998), *Ephesians: NIV Application Commentary*, Grand Rapids: Zondervan.

Finn, T. M. (1985), 'The God-fearers Reconsidered', *CBQ* 47, 75–84.

Fitzmyer, J. A. (1965), 'Anti-Semitism and the Cry of "All the People"', *TS* 26, 667–671.

—— (1981), *The Gospel according to Luke (I–IX)*, AB, New York: Doubleday.

—— (1998), *The Acts of the Apostles*, AB, New York: Doubleday.

Flusser, D. (1987), 'Paganism in Palestine', in *The Jewish People in the First Century: Historical Geography, Political History, Social, Cultural and Religious Life and Institutions*, CRINT 1/2, Philadelphia: Fortress, 1065–1100.

—— (1992), 'Jesus and Judaism: Jewish Perspectives', in H. W. Attridge and G. Hata (eds.), *Eusebius, Christianity, and Judaism*, Leiden: Brill, 80–109.

Ford, J. M. (1990), 'Persecution and Martyrdom in the Book of Revelation', *BibToday* 28, 141–146.

Forestell, J. T. (1974), *The Word of the Cross: Salvation as Revelation in the Fourth Gospel*, AnBib 57, Rome: Biblical Institute Press.

Fox, K. A. (1994), 'The Nicolaitans, Nicolaus and the early Church', *SR* 23, 485–496.

France, R. T. (1970), *Jesus and the Old Testament: His Application of Old Testament Passages to Himself and His Mission*, London:

Tyndale.

—— (1985), *Matthew*, TNTC, Leicester/Grand Rapids: IVP/Eerdmans.

—— (1989), *Matthew: Evangelist and Teacher*, Grand Rapids: Zondervan.

Frankemölle, H. (1982), 'Zur Theologie der Mission im Matthäusevangelium', in Karl Kertelge (ed.), *Mission im Neuen Testament*, QD 93, Herder: Freiburg/Basel/Vienna, 93–129.

Franklin, E. (1975), *Christ the Lord: A Study in the Purpose and Theology of Luke-Acts*, London: SPCK.

Freed, E. D. (1987), 'The Women in Matthew's Genealogy', *JSNT* 29, 3–19.

Friedländer, M. (1903), *Geschichte der jüdischen Apologetik als Vorgeschichte des Christentums*, Zürich: C. Schmidt.

Friend, H. S. (1990), 'Like Father, Like Son: A Discussion of the Concept of Agency in Halakah and John', *Ashland Theological Journal* 21, 18–28.

Friesen, A. (1998), *Erasmus, the Anabaptists, and the Great Commission*, Grand Rapids/Cambridge: Eerdmans.

Fung, R. Y. K. (1988), *The Epistle to the Galatians*, NICNT, Grand Rapids: Eerdmans.

Garland, D. E. (1979), *The Intention of Matthew 23*, NovTSup 52, Leiden: Brill.

Garlington, D. B. (1990), 'The Obedience of Faith in the Letter to the Romans. Part I: The Meaning of *hypakoē pisteōs* (Rom 1:5; 16:26)', *WTJ* 52, 201–224.

—— (1991), *'The Obedience of Faith': A Pauline Phrase in Historical Context*, WUNT 38, Tübingen: Mohr-Siebeck.

Gaventa, B. R. (1982), ' "You Will be My Witnesses": Aspects of Mission in Acts of the Apostles', *Missiology* 10, 413–425.

—— (1986), *From Darkness to Light: Aspects of Conversion in the New Testament*, Philadelphia: Fortress.

Georgi, D. (1986), *The Opponents of Paul in Second Corinthians*, Edinburgh: T. and T. Clark.

Ghiberti, G. (1990), 'Missione di Gesù e di discepoli nel quarto Vangelo', *Ricerche Storico Bibliche* 2, 185–200.

Gibbs, J. M. (1963–64), 'Purpose and Pattern in Matthew's Use of the Title "Son of David" ', *NTS* 10, 446–464.

Giblet, J. (1957), 'Les promesses de l'Esprit et la mission des apôtres dans les Évangiles', *Irénikon* 30, 5–43.

Giblin, C. H. (1984), 'Revelation 11:1–13: Its Form, Function, and Contextual Integration', *NTS* 30, 433–459.

Gibson, R. J. (ed.) (1998), *Interpreting God's Plan: Biblical Theology and the Pastor*, Explorations 11, Carlisle/Adelaide: Paternoster/Openbook.

Gill, A. (1991), 'Beyond the Boundaries: Marcan Mission Perspectives for Today's Church', in Paul Beasley-Murray (ed.), *Mission to the World*, Didcot, Oxford: Baptist Historical Society, 35–41.

Glasson, F. (1963), *Moses in the Fourth Gospel*, SBT 40, London: SCM.

Goldsworthy, G. (1996), 'The Great Indicative: An Aspect of a Biblical Theology of Mission', *RTR* 55, 2–13.

Goodman, M. (1989), 'Proselytising in Rabbinic Judaism', *JJS* 40, 175–185.

―― (1994), *Mission and Conversion: Proselytizing in the Religious History of the Roman Empire*, Oxford: Clarendon.

Green, J. B. (1992), 'Proclaiming Repentance and Forgiveness of Sins to all Nations: A Biblical Perspective on the Church's Mission', in A. G. Padgett (ed.), *The Mission of the Church in Methodist Perspective: The World is My Parish*, Studies in the History of Missions 10, Lewiston/Queenston/Lampeter: Edwin Mellen, 13–43.

――(1994), 'Good News to Whom? Jesus and the Poor in the Gospel of Luke', in J. B. Green and M. Turner (eds.), *Jesus of Nazareth: Lord and Christ: Essays on the Historical Jesus and New Testament Christology*, Grand Rapids: Eerdmans, 59–74.

―― (1997a), *The Gospel of Luke*, NICNT, Grand Rapids: Eerdmans.

―― (1997b), 'Cornelius', in R. P. Martin and P. H. Davids (eds.), *Dictionary of the Later New Testament and Its Developments*, Downers Grove/Leicester: IVP, 243–245.

―― (1998), ' "Salvation to the End of the Earth" (Acts 13:47): God as Saviour in the Acts of the Apostles', in I. H. Marshall and D. Peterson (eds.), *Witness to the Gospel: The Theology of Acts*, Grand Rapids/Cambridge: Eerdmans, 83–106.

Gressmann, H. (1924), 'Heidnische Mission in der Werdezeit des Christentums', *Zeitschrift für Missionskunde und Missionswissenschaft* 39, 10–24.

Guelich, R. A. (1989), *Mark 1 – 8:26*, WBC 34A, Dallas, TX: Word.

―― (1992), 'Mark, Gospel of', in J. B. Green, S. McKnight, I. H. Marshall (eds.), *Dictionary of Jesus and the Gospels*, Downers Grove/Leicester: IVP, 512–525.

Gundry, R. H. (1993), *Mark: A Commentary on His Apology for the Cross*, Grand Rapids: Eerdmans.

―― (1994), *Matthew: A Commentary on His Handbook for a Mixed*

Church under Persecution, 2nd ed., Grand Rapids: Eerdmans.

Guthrie, D. (1967), 'The Importance of Signs in the Fourth Gospel', *Vox Evangelica* V, 72–83.

—— (1990), *Introduction to the New Testament*, 4th ed., Leicester/Downers Grove: IVP.

Haacker, K. (1972), *Die Stiftung des Heils: Untersuchungen zur Struktur der johanneischen Theologie*, Arbeiten zur Theologie 1/47, Stuttgart: Calwer.

—— (1973), 'Jesus und die Kirche nach Johannes', *TZ* 29, 179–201.

Haenchen, E. (1971), *The Acts of the Apostles*, Oxford: Blackwell.

Hafemann, S. J. (1995), *Paul, Moses and the History of Israel: The Letter/Spirit Contrast and the Argument from Scripture in 2 Corinthians 3*, WUNT 81, Tübingen: Mohr-Siebeck.

Hagner, D. A. (1993), *Matthew 1 – 13*, WBC 33A, Dallas, TX: Word.

—— (1995), *Matthew 14 – 28*, WBC 33B, Dallas, TX: Word.

Hahn, F. (1965), *Mission in the New Testament*, SBT 47, London: SCM.

—— (1976), 'Sendung des Geistes – Sendung der Jünger: Die pneumatologische Dimension des Missionsauftrages nach dem Zeugnis des Neuen Testamentes', in P.-G. Müller and W. Stenger (eds.), *Universales Christentum angesichts einer pluralen Welt*, Beiträge zur Religionstheologie 1, Freiburg im Breisgau: Herder, 430–438.

—— (1980), 'Der Sendungsauftrag des Auferstandenen: Matthäus 28, 16–20', in T. Sundermeier (ed.), *Fides pro mundi vita: Missionstheologie heute: Hans-Werner Gensichen zum 65. Geburtstag*, Gütersloh: Mohn, 28–43.

Hansen, G. W. (1998), 'The Preaching and Defence of Paul', in I. H. Marshall and D. Peterson (eds.), *Witness to the Gospel: The Theology of Acts*, Grand Rapids/Cambridge: Eerdmans, 295–324.

Hare, D. R. A. and D. J. Harrington (1975), 'Make Disciples of All the Gentiles (Matt. 28:19)', *CBQ* 37, 359–369.

Harnack, A. (1924), *Mission und Ausbreitung des Christentums in den ersten drei Jahrhunderten*, 4th ed., Leipzig: Hinrichsche Buchhandlung.

—— (1972), *The Mission and Expansion of Christianity in the First Three Centuries*, Gloucester, MA: Peter Smith.

Harner, P. B. (1970), *The 'I Am' of the Fourth Gospel*, Philadelphia: Fortress.

Harris, M. J. (1992), *Jesus as God: The New Testament Use of Theos in Reference to Jesus*, Grand Rapids: Baker.

—— (1999), *Slave of Christ: A New Testament Metaphor for Total Devotion to Christ*, NSBT, Leicester: Apollos.

Harvey, A. E. (1987), 'Christ as Agent', in L. D. Hurst and N. T. Wright (eds.), *The Glory of Christ in the New Testament*, Oxford: Clarendon, 239–250.

Hays, R. B. (1989), *Echoes of Scripture in the Letters of Paul*, New Haven: Yale University Press.

Hedlund, R. E. (1991), *The Mission of the Church in the World: A Biblical Theology*, Grand Rapids: Baker.

Hedrick, C. W. (1981), 'Paul's Conversion/Call: A Comparative Analysis of the Three Reports in Acts', *JBL* 100, 415–432.

Hemer, C. J. (1986), *The Letters to the Seven Churches of Asia in their Local Setting*, JSNTSS 11, Sheffield: JSOT.

Hengel, M. (1974), *Judaism and Hellenism: Studies in their Encounter in Palestine during the Early Hellenistic Period*, Philadelphia: Fortress.

—— (1983), 'The Origins of the Christian Mission', in *Between Jesus and Paul*, London: SCM, 48–64.

—— (1986), *Acts and the History of Earliest Christianity*, London: SCM.

—— (1991), 'Literary, Theological, and Historical Problems in the Gospel of Mark', in Peter Stuhlmacher (ed.), *The Gospel and the Gospels*, Grand Rapids: Eerdmans, 209–251.

—— (1995), 'The Geography of Palestine in Acts', in R. Bauckham (ed.), *The Book of Acts in Its First Century Setting* 4: *The Book of Acts in Its Palestinian Setting*, Grand Rapids/Carlisle: Eerdmans/Paternoster, 27–78.

—— (1996), 'Die Throngemeinschaft des Lammes mit Gott in der Johannesapokalypse', *TBei* 27, 159–175.

Howell, D. N. (1998), 'Mission in Paul's Epistles: Genesis, Pattern, and Dynamics', in W. J. Larkin and J. F. Williams (eds.), *Mission in the New Testament: An Evangelical Approach*, Maryknoll, NY: Orbis, 63–91.

Howton, D. J. (1963–64), ' "Son of God" in the Fourth Gospel', *NTS* 10, 227–237.

Hugenberger, G. P. (1995), 'The Servant of the Lord in the Servant Songs of Isaiah', in P. E. Satterthwaite, R. S. Hess and G. J. Wenham (eds.), *The Lord's Anointed: Interpretation of Old Testament Messianic Texts*, Carlisle: Paternoster/Grand Rapids: Baker, 105–140.

Hultgren, A. J. (1985), *Paul's Gospel and Mission: The Outlook from his Letter to the Romans*, Philadelphia: Fortress.

Hurtado, L. W. (1988), *One God, One Lord: Early Christian Devotion and Ancient Jewish Monotheism*, Philadelphia: Fortress.

Ibuki, Y. (1988), 'Die Doxa des Gesandten – Studie zur johanneischen Christologie', in M. Sekine and A. Satake (eds.), *Annual of the Japanese Biblical Institute* 14, Tokyo: Yamamoto Shoten, 38–81.

Jeremias, J. (1958), *Jesus' Promise to the Nations*, SBT 24, London: SCM.

—— (1971), *New Testament Theology: The Proclamation of Jesus*, trans. J. Bowden, New York: Macmillan.

Jervell, J. (1972), *Luke and the People of God: A New Look on Luke-Acts*, Minneapolis: Augsburg.

—— (1984), *The Unknown Paul: Essays on Luke-Acts and the Early Christian History*, Minneapolis: Augsburg.

—— (1998), *Die Apostelgeschichte*, KEK, Göttingen: Vandenhoeck und Ruprecht.

Johnson, D. E. (1990), 'Jesus against the Idols: The Use of Isaianic Servant Songs in the Missiology of Acts, *WTJ* 52, 343–353.

Johnson, L. T. (1977), *The Literary Function of Possessions in Luke-Acts*, SBLDS 39, Missoula, MT: Scholars.

Johnsson, W. G. (1978), 'The Pilgrimage Motif in the Book of Hebrews', *JBL* 97, 239–251.

Jonge, M. de (1972–73), 'Jewish Expectations about the "Messiah" According to the Fourth Gospel', *NTS* 19, 246–270.

—— (1973), 'Jesus as Prophet and King in the Fourth Gospel', *ETL* 49, 160–177.

—— (1977), *Jesus: Stranger from Heaven and Son of God*, Missoula, MT: Scholars.

Judge, E. A. (1992), 'The Teacher as Moral Exemplar in Paul and in the Inscriptions of Ephesus', in D. Peterson and J. Pryor (eds.), *In the Fullness of Time: Biblical Studies in Honour of Archbishop Donald Robinson*, Homebush West, NSW: Lancer, 185–201.

Juel, D. (1977), *Messiah and Temple*, SBLDS 31, Missoula, MT: SBL.

—— (1986), 'Making Disciples: The Mission of the Church in the Gospel According to Matthew', in W. Stumme (ed.), *Bible and Mission*, Minneapolis: Augsburg, 75–86.

Kaiser, W. C., Jr (1981), 'Israel's Missionary Call', in R. D. Winter and S. C. Hawthorne (eds.), *Perspectives on the World Christian Movement: A Reader*, Pasadena, CA: William Carey Library, 25–34.

—— (2000), *Mission in the Old Testament: Israel as a Light to the Nations*, Grand Rapids: Baker.

Kanagaranj, J. J. (1997), 'The Poor in the Gospels and the Good News Proclaimed to Them', *Themelios* 23, 40–58.

Käsemann, E. (1980), *Commentary on Romans*, Grand Rapids: Eerdmans.

Kasting, H. (1969), *Die Anfänge der urchristlichen Mission*, München: Chr. Kaiser.

Kato, Z. (1986), *Die Völkermission im Markusevangelium*, EHS XXIII/252, Bern/Frankfurt am Maine/New York: Peter Lang.

Keathley, K. D. (1997), 'The Two Phases of Mission in Matthew', Wake Forest, NC: unpublished seminar paper.

Keener, C. S. (1999), *A Commentary on the Gospel of Matthew*, Grand Rapids/Cambridge: Eerdmans.

Kelber, W. (1974), *The Kingdom in Mark*, Philadelphia: Fortress.

Kiddle, M. (1934), 'The Death of Jesus and the Admission of the Gentiles in St Mark', *JTS* 35, 45–50.

Kilpatrick, G. D. (1946), *The Origins of the Gospel According to St Matthew*, Oxford: Clarendon.

—— (1955), 'The Gentile Mission in Mark and Mark 13:9–11', in D. E. Nineham (ed.), *Studies in the Gospels: Essays in Memory of R. H. Lightfoot*, Oxford: Blackwell, 145–158.

Kim, S. (1982), *The Origin of Paul's Gospel*, Grand Rapids: Eerdmans.

—— (1997), 'God Reconciled His Enemy to Himself: The Origin of Paul's Concept of Reconciliation', in R. N. Longenecker (ed.), *The Road from Damascus: The Impact of Paul's Conversion on His Life, Thought, and Ministry*, Grand Rapids/Cambridge: Eerdmans.

Kingsbury, J. D. (1973), *Matthew*, 2nd ed., Philadelphia: Fortress.

—— (1974), 'The Composition and Christology of Matt 28:16–20', *JBL* 93, 573–584.

Klauck, H.-J. (1992), 'Das Sendschreiben nach Pargamon und der Kaiserkult in der Johannesoffenbarung', *Bib* 73, 153–182.

Knox, J. (1964), 'Romans 15:14–33 and Paul's Conception of his Apostolic Mission', *JBL* 83, 1–11.

Köstenberger, A. J. (1995a), 'The Seventh Johannine Sign: A Study in John's Christology', *BBR* 5, 87–103.

—— (1995b), 'The Contribution of the General Epistles and Revelation to a Biblical Theology of Religions', in Edward Rommen and Harold A. Netland (eds.), *Christianity and the Religions: An Evangelical Theology of Religions*, EMS Missiological Monographs 2, Pasadena, CA: William Carey, 113–140.

—— (1995c), 'The Challenge of a Systematized Biblical Theology:

Missiological Insights from the Gospel of John', *Missiology* 23, 445–464.

—— (1998a), *The Missions of Jesus and the Disciples According to the Fourth Gospel: With Implications for the Fourth Gospel's Purpose and the Mission of the Contemporary Church*, Grand Rapids: Eerdmans.

—— (1998b), 'Mission in the General Epistles', in W. J. Larkin Jr and J. F. Williams (eds.), *Mission in the New Testament: An Evangelical Approach*, Maryknoll, NY: Orbis, 189–206.

—— (1998c), 'Jesus as Rabbi in the Fourth Gospel', *BBR* 8, 97–128.

—— (1999a), 'The Place of Mission in New Testament Theology: An Attempt to Determine the Significance of Mission Within the Scope of the New Testament's Message as a Whole', *Missiology* 27, 347–362.

—— (1999b), 'The Two Johannine Verbs for Sending: A Study of John's Use of Words with Reference to General Linguistic Theory', in S. E. Porter and D. A. Carson (eds.), *Linguistics and the New Testament: Critical Junctures*, JSNTSS 168, Sheffield: Sheffield Academic Press.

—— (1999c), *Encountering John: The Gospel in Historical, Literary, and Theological Perspective*, EBS, Grand Rapids: Baker.

—— (2000a), 'Mission', in D. Alexander and B. Rosner (eds.), *New Dictionary of Biblical Theology*, Leicester: IVP.

—— (2000b), 'Vielfalt und Einheit des Neuen Testaments', in H.-W. Neudorfer and E. J. Schnabel (eds.), *Das Studium des Neuen Testaments 2: Spezialprobleme*, Wuppertal/Giessen: R. Brockhaus/Brunnen.

Kraabel, A. T. (1981), 'The Disappearance of the "God-fearers"', *Numen* 28, 113–126.

—— (1992), 'The Roman Diaspora: Six Questionable Assumptions', in J. A. Overman and R. S. MacLennan (eds.), *Diaspora Jews and Judaism: Essays in Honor of, and in Dialogue with, A. Thomas Kraabel*, South Florida Studies in the History of Judaism 41, Atlanta, GA: Scholars, 9–14.

—— (1994), 'Immigrants, Exiles, Expatriates, and Missionaries', in L. Bormann, K. del Tredici and A. Standhartinger (eds.), *Religious Propaganda and Missionary Competition in the New Testament World: Essays Honoring Dieter Georgi*, Leiden: Brill, 71–88.

Kuhl, J. (1967), *Die Sendung Jesu und der Kirche nach dem Johannes-Evangelium*, Studia Instituti Missiologica Societatis Verbi Domini 11, St Augustin: Steyler.

Kuhn, K. G. (1954), 'Das Problem der Mission in der Urchristenheit',

EMZ 11, 161–168.

Kupp, D. D. (1996), *Matthew's Emmanuel: Divine Presence and God's People in the First Gospel*, SNTSMS 90, Cambridge: Cambridge University Press.

Kvalbein, H. (1988), '"Go therefore and make disciples": The Concept of Discipleship in the New Testament', *Themelios* 13, 48–53.

Ladd, G. E. (1957), 'Why Not Prophetic-Apocalyptic?' *JBL* 76, 192–200.

—— (1972), *A Commentary on the Revelation of John*, Grand Rapids: Eerdmans.

—— (1993), *A Theology of the New Testament*, rev. ed., Grand Rapids: Eerdmans.

LaGrand, J. (1999), *The Earliest Christian Mission to 'All Nations' in the Light of Matthew's Gospel*, Grand Rapids/Cambridge: Eerdmans.

Lake, K. (1933), 'Proselytes and God-fearers', in F. J. Foakes-Jackson and K. Lake (eds.), *The Beginnings of Christianity* I: *The Acts of the Apostles*, London: Macmillan, 5:85–88.

Lamarche, P. (1961), *Zacharie IX – XIV: Structure Litteraire et Messianisme*, Paris: J. Gabalda.

Lane, T. J. (1996), *Luke and the Gentile Mission: Gospel Anticipates Acts*, New York/Bern/Frankfurt: Peter Lang.

Lane, W. L. (1974), *The Gospel According to Mark*, NICNT, Grand Rapids: Eerdmans.

—— (1991a), *Hebrews 1 – 8*, WBC 47A, Dallas, TX: Word.

—— (1991b), *Hebrews 9 – 13*, WBC 47B, Dallas, TX: Word.

Lange, J. (1973), *Das Erscheinen des Auferstandenen im Evangelium nach Matthäus*, FB 11, Würzburg: Echter.

Larkin, W. J., Jr (1998), 'Mission in Luke', in *Mission in the New Testament: An Evangelical Approach*, Maryknoll, NY: Orbis, 152–169.

Larkin, W. J., Jr, and J. F. Williams (eds.) (1998), *Mission in the New Testament: An Evangelical Approach*, Maryknoll, NY: Orbis.

Legrand, L. (1964), 'Was Jesus Mission-Minded?' *Indian Ecclesiastical Studies* 3, 87–104, 190–207.

—— (1990), *Unity and Plurality: Mission in the Bible*, Maryknoll, NY: Orbis.

Levinskaya, I. (1996), *The Book of Acts in Its First Century Setting* 5: *The Book of Acts in Its Diaspora Setting*, Grand Rapids/Carlisle: Eerdmans/Paternoster.

Lewis, A. H. (1972), 'Jehovah's International Love', *JETS* 15, 87–92.

Liefeld, W. L. (1967), 'The Wandering Preacher as a Social Figure in the Roman Empire', PhD thesis, Columbia University.

Lincoln, A. T. (1989), 'The Promise and the Failure: Mark 16:7, 8', *JBL* 108, 283–300.

Lindars, B. (1973), 'The Son of Man in the Johannine Christology', in B. Lindars and S. S. Smalley (eds.), *Christ and Spirit: In Honour of C. F. D. Moule*, London: SCM, 43–60.

Loader, W. (1996), 'Challenged at the Boundaries: A Conservative Jesus in Mark's Tradition', *JSNT* 63, 45–61.

Longenecker, R. N. (1981), 'The Acts of the Apostles', *The Expositor's Bible Commentary* 9, Grand Rapids: Zondervan, 207–573.

—— (ed.) (1997a), *The Road from Damascus: The Impact of Paul's Conversion on His Life, Thought, and Ministry*, Grand Rapids/ Cambridge: Eerdmans.

—— (1997b), 'A Realized Hope, a New Commitment, and a Developed Proclamation: Paul and Jesus', in R. N. Longenecker (ed.), *The Road from Damascus: The Impact of Paul's Conversion on His Life, Thought, and Ministry*, Grand Rapids/Cambridge: Eerdmans, 18–42.

Louw, J. P. (1968), 'Narrator of the Father – *exēgeisthai* and related terms in Johannine Christology', *Neot* 2, 32–40.

Louw, J. P., and E. A. Nida (1988, 1989), *Greek–English Lexicon of the New Testament Based on Semantic Domains*, 2 vols., New York: United Bible Societies.

Luz, U. (1989), *Matthew 1 – 7*, trans. W. C. Linss, Minneapolis: Fortress.

McConville, G. (1992), 'Jerusalem in the Old Testament', in P. W. L. Walker (ed.), *Jerusalem Past and Present in the Purposes of God*, Cambridge: Tyndale House, 21–51.

McKnight, S. (1986), 'New Shepherds for Israel: An Historical and Critical Study of Matthew 9:35 – 11:1', unpublished PhD thesis, Nottingham.

—— (1991), *A Light Among the Gentiles: Jewish Missionary Activity in the Second Temple Period*, Minneapolis: Fortress.

—— (1993), 'A Loyal Critic: Matthew's Polemic with Judaism in Theological Perspective', in C. A. Evans and D. A. Hagner (eds.), *Anti-Semitism and Early Christianity: Issues of Polemic and Faith*, Minneapolis: Fortress, 55–79.

—— (forthcoming), 'Jewish Missionary Activity: The Evidence of Demographics and Synagogues', in A.-J. Levine and R. Pervo (eds.), *Jewish Proselytism*, Perspectives in Ancient Judaism, Lanham, MD:

University Press of America.

McNicol, A. (1989), 'Discipleship as Mission: A Missing Dimension in Contemporary Discussion on Matthew 28:18–20', *Christian Studies* 10, 27–47.

McPolin, J. (1969), 'Mission in the Fourth Gospel', *ITQ* 36, 113–122.

Maddox, R. L. (1974), 'The Function of the Son of Man in the Gospel of John', in R. J. Banks (ed.), *Reconciliation and Hope: New Testament Essays on Atonement and Eschatology Presented to L. L. Morris on his 60th Birthday*, Exeter/Grand Rapids: Paternoster/Eerdmans, 186–204.

Maier, G. (1994), *Biblical Hermeneutics*, trans. R. W. Yarbrough, Wheaton, IL: Crossway.

Malbon, E. S. (1983), 'Fallible Followers: Women and Men in the Gospel of Mark', *Semeia* 28, 29–48.

Malherbe, A. J. (1987), *Paul and the Thessalonians*, Philadelphia: Fortress.

Manson, W. (1953), 'The Biblical Doctrine of Mission', *IRM* 42, 257–265.

Marguerat, D. (1993), 'The End of Acts (28.16–31) and the Rhetoric of Silence', in S. E. Porter and T. H. Olbricht (eds.), *Rhetoric and the New Testament: Essays from the 1992 Heidelberg Conference*, JSNTSS 90, Sheffield: Sheffield Academic Press, 74–89.

Marshall, I. H. (1978a), *The Gospel of Luke*, NIGTC, Grand Rapids: Eerdmans.

—— (1978b), *The Epistles of John*, NICNT, Grand Rapids: Eerdmans.

—— (1980), *The Acts of the Apostles: An Introduction and Commentary*, TNTC, Leicester/Grand Rapids: IVP/Eerdmans.

—— (1993), 'Acts and the "Former Treatise"', in B. W. Winter and A. D. Clarke (eds.), *The Book of Acts in Its First Century Setting*.1: *The Book of Acts in Its Ancient Literary Setting*, Grand Rapids/Carlisle: Eerdmans/Paternoster, 163–182.

—— (1997), 'A New Understanding of the Present and the Future: Paul and Eschatology', in R. N. Longenecker (ed.), *The Road from Damascus: The Impact of Paul's Conversion on His Life, Thought, and Ministry*, Grand Rapids/Cambridge: Eerdmans, 43–61.

Martens, E. A. (1994), *God's Design: A Focus on Old Testament Theology*, Grand Rapids/Leicester: Baker/IVP.

Martin, R. (1993), *Mark: Evangelist and Theologian*, Grand Rapids: Zondervan.

Martin-Achard, R. (1962), *A Light to the Nations*, Edinburgh: Oliver and Boyd.

Martyn, J. L. (1978), *The Gospel of John in Christian History: Essays for Interpreters*, New York: Paulist.

Marxsen, W. (1969), *Mark the Evangelist: Studies on the Redaction History of the Gospel*, Nashville: Abingdon.

Mastin, B. (1975), 'A Neglected Feature of the Christology of the Fourth Gospel', *NTS* 22, 32–51.

Matera, F. J. (1988), ' "On Behalf of Others", "Cleansing", "Return": Johannine Images for Jesus' Death', *Louvain Studies* 13, 161–178.

Matson, D. L. (1996), *Household Narratives in Acts: Pattern and Interpretation*, JSNTSS 123, Sheffield: Sheffield Academic Press.

Matsunaga, K. (1981), 'The "Theos" Christology as the Ultimate Confession of the Fourth Gospel', in M. Sekine and A. Satake (eds.), *Annual of the Japanese Biblical Institute* 7, Tokyo: Yamamoto Shoten, 124–145.

Meeks, W. A. (1967), *The Prophet-King: Moses Traditions and the Johannine Christology*, NovTSup 14, Leiden: Brill.

—— (1972), 'The Man from Heaven in Johannine Sectarianism', *JBL* 91, 44–72.

Meier, J. P. (1976), *Law and History in Matthew's Gospel: A Redactional Study of Mt. 5:17–48*, AnBib 71, Rome: Biblical Institute Press.

—— (1977a), 'Two Disputed Questions in Matt 28:16–20', *JBL* 96, 407–424.

—— (1977b), 'Nations of Gentiles in Matthew 28:19?' *CBQ* 39, 94–102.

Menzies, R. P. (1994), *Empowered for Witness: The Spirit in Luke-Acts*, JPTSS 6, Sheffield: Sheffield Academic Press.

Metzger, B. M. (1994), *A Textual Commentary on the Greek New Testament*, Stuttgart: Deutsche Bibelgesellschaft.

Meye, R. (1969), 'Mark 16:8 – The Ending of Mark's Gospel', *BibRes* 14, 33–43.

Michaels, J. R. (1988), *1 Peter*, WBC 49, Waco, TX: Word.

Michel, O. (1983), 'The Conclusion of Matthew's Gospel: A Contribution to the History of the Easter Message', in G. Stanton (ed.), *The Interpretation of Matthew*, IRT 3, Philadelphia: Fortress, 30–41.

Miller, J. V. (1998), 'Mission in Revelation', in W. J. Larkin and J. F. Williams (eds.), *Mission in the New Testament: An Evangelical Approach*, Maryknoll, NY: Orbis, 227–238.

Milton, H. (1962), 'The Structure of the Prologue to St Matthew's Gospel', *JBL* 81, 175–181.

Minear, P. (1971), 'Gratitude and Mission in the Epistle to the Romans', in *The Obedience of Faith*, SBT 2/19, London: SCM, 102–110.

Miranda, P. (1976), *Der Vater der mich gesandt hat. Religionsgeschichtliche Untersuchungen zu den johanneischen Sendungsformeln: Zugleich ein Beitrag zur johanneischen Christologie und Ekklesiologie*, EHS 23/7, 2nd ed., Frankfurt am Main: Peter Lang.

—— (1977), *Die Sendung Jesu im vierten Evangelium: Religions- und theologiegeschichtliche Untersuchungen zu den Sendungsformeln*, SBS 87, Stuttgart: Katholisches Bibelwerk.

Moberly, R. W. L. (1983), *At the Mountain of God: Story and Theology in Exodus 32 – 34*, Sheffield: JSOT.

Molland, E. (1934), *Das paulinische Euangelion: Das Wort und die Sache*, Oslo: Dybwad.

Moloney, F. J. (1978), *The Johannine Son of Man*, 2nd ed., Rome: Libreria Ateneo Salesiano.

Moo, D. J. (1996), *The Epistle to the Romans*, NICNT, Grand Rapids/Cambridge: Eerdmans.

Moore, G. F. (1927), *Judaism in the First Centuries of the Christian Era: The Age of the Tannaim*, Cambridge, MA: Harvard University Press.

Moore, T. S. (1997a), 'The Lucan Great Commission and the Isaianic Servant', *BibSac* 154, 47–60.

—— (1997b), '"To the End of the Earth": The Geographical and Ethnic Universalism of Acts 1:8 in Light of Isaianic Influence on Luke', *JETS* 40, 389–399.

Moreno, R. (1971), 'El discípulo de Jerucristo, según el evangelio de S. Juan', *Estudios bíblicos* 30, 269–311.

Morris, L. L. (1978), 'The Jesus of Saint John', in R. A. Guelich (ed.), *Unity and Diversity in New Testament Theology: Essays in Honor of George E. Ladd*, Grand Rapids: Eerdmans, 37–53.

—— (1988), *The Epistle to the Romans*, Grand Rapids/Leicester: Eerdmans/IVP.

—— (1989), *Jesus Is the Christ: Studies in the Theology of John*, Grand Rapids: Eerdmans.

Motyer, J. A. (1993), *The Prophecy of Isaiah*, Leicester: IVP.

Mounce, R. H. (1985), *Matthew*, GNC, San Francisco: Harper and Row.

—— (1998), *The Book of Revelation*, rev. ed., NICNT, Grand Rapids: Eerdmans.

Muilenburg, J. (1965), 'Abraham and the Nations: Blessing and World

History', *Int* 19, 387–398.

Munck, J. (1959), *Paul and the Salvation of Mankind*, London: SCM.

Munro, G. (1996), 'The Place of the Nations in God's Plan According to the Book of Psalms', unpublished seminar paper, Moore College.

Neudorfer, H.-W. (1998), 'The Speech of Stephen', in I. H. Marshall and D. Peterson (eds.), *Witness to the Gospel: The Theology of Acts*, Grand Rapids/Cambridge: Eerdmans, 275–294.

Neusner, J., W. S. Green and E. Frerichs (1987), *Judaisms and their Messiahs at the Turn of the Christian Era*, Cambridge: Cambridge University Press.

Nicholson, G. C. (1983), *Death as Departure: The Johannine Descent–Ascent Schema*, SBLDS 63, Chico, CA: Scholars.

Nissen, J. (1999), 'Mission in the Fourth Gospel: Historical and Hermeneutical Perspectives', in J. Nissen and S. Pedersen (eds.), *New Readings in John. Literary and Theological Perspectives*, JSNTSS 182, Sheffield: Academic Press, 213–231.

Nock, A. D. (1972), *Essays on Religion and the Ancient World*, Cambridge, MA: Harvard University Press.

Nolland, J. (1989, 1993a, 1993b), *Luke 1 – 9:20, Luke 9:21 – 18:34, Luke 18:35 – 24:53*, WBC 35A, 35B, 35C, 3 vols, Dallas: Word.

O'Brien, P. T. (1974–75), 'Thanksgiving and the Gospel in Paul', *NTS* 21, 144–155.

—— (1976), 'The Great Commission of Matthew 28:18–20: A Missionary Mandate or Not?' *RTR* 35, 66–71.

—— (1992), 'The Gospel and Godly Models in Philippians', in M. J. Wilkins and T. Paige (eds.), *Worship, Theology and Ministry in the Early Church: Essays in Honor of Professor Ralph P. Martin*, JSNTSS 87, Sheffield: Sheffield Academic Press, 273–284.

—— (1995), *Gospel and Mission in the Writings of Paul: An Exegetical and Theological Analysis*, Grand Rapids/Carlisle: Eerdmans/Paternoster.

—— (1999a), 'Mission, Witness and the Coming of the Spirit', *BBR* 9, 203–214.

—— (1999b), *The Letter to the Ephesians*, PNTC, Grand Rapids/Leicester: Eerdmans/IVP.

O'Connor, D. (1991), 'Holiness of Life as a Way of Christian Witness', *IRM* 80, 17–26.

O'Toole, R. F. (1978), *Acts 26: The Christological Climax of Paul's Defense (Acts 22:1 – 26:32)*, AnBib 78, Rome: Pontifical Biblical Institute.

Oehler, W. (1936), *Das Johannesevangelium, eine Missionsschrift für die Welt, der Gemeinde ausgelegt*, Gütersloh: Bertelsmann.

—— (1941), *Zum Missionscharakter des Johannesevangeliums*, Gütersloh: Bertelsmann.

—— (1957), *Das Johannesevangelium, eine Missionsschrift für die Welt*, 3 vols., Württemberg: Buchhandlung der Evangelischen Missionsschule Unterweissach.

Oepke, A. (1941), 'Das missionarische Christuszeugnis des Johannesevangeliums', *EMZ* 2, 4–26.

Okure, T. (1988), *The Johannine Approach to Mission: A Contextual Study of John 4:1–42*, WUNT 31, Tübingen: Mohr-Siebeck.

Ollenberger, B. C. (1987), *Zion, The City of the Great King: A Theological Symbol of the Jerusalem Cult*, Sheffield: JSOT.

Ollrog, W. H. (1979), *Paulus und seine Mitarbeiter: Untersuchungen zur Theorie und Praxis der paulinischen Mission*, WMANT 50, Neukirchen-Vluyn: Neukirchener.

Olsson, B. (1974), 'Excursus III: Mission in Jn', in *Structure and Meaning in the Fourth Gospel: A Text-Linguistic Analysis of John 2:1–11 and 4:1–42*, ConBNT 6, Lund: Gleerup, 241–248.

Onuki, T. (1984), *Gemeinde und Welt im Johannesevangelium: Ein Beitrag zur Frage nach der theologischen und pragmatischen Funktion des johanneischen 'Dualismus'*, WMANT 56, Neukirchen-Vluyn: Neukirchener.

Osborne, G. R. (1976), 'Redaction Criticism and the Great Commission: A Case Study Toward a Biblical Understanding of Inerrancy', *JETS* 19, 73–85.

—— (1978), 'The Evangelical and *Traditionsgeschichte*', *JETS* 21, 117–130.

—— (1979), 'Redactional Trajectories in the Crucifixion Narrative', *EQ* 51, 80–96.

—— (1984), *The Resurrection Narratives: A Redactional Study*, Grand Rapids: Baker.

—— (1993), 'Theodicy in the Apocalypse', *TrinJ* 14 NS, 63–77.

Oswalt, J. N. (1991), 'The Mission of Israel to the Nations', in W. V. Crockett and J. G. Sigountos (eds.), *Through No Fault of Their Own? The Fate of Those Who Have Never Heard*, Grand Rapids: Baker, 85–95.

Overman, J. A. (1990), *Matthew's Gospel and Formative Judaism: The Social World of the Matthean Community*, Minneapolis: Fortress.

—— (1996), *Church and Community in Crisis: The Gospel According to Matthew*, Valley Forge, PA: Trinity Press International.

Paget, J. C. (1996), 'Jewish Proselytism at the Time of Christian Origins: Chimera or Reality?' *JSNT* 62, 65–103.

Palmer, D. W. (1993), 'Mission to Jews and Gentiles in the Last Episode of Acts', *RTR* 52, 62–73.

Pao, D. W. C. (1998), 'Acts and the Isaianic New Exodus', unpublished PhD thesis, Harvard.

Park, E. C. (1995), *The Mission Discourse in Matthew's Interpretation*, WUNT 2/81, Tübingen: Mohr-Siebeck.

Parsons, M. C. (1987), *The Departure of Jesus in Luke-Acts: The Ascension Narratives in Context*, JSNTSS 21, Sheffield: JSOT.

Payne, D. F. (1995), 'The Meaning of Mission in Isaiah 40–55', in A. Billington, T. Lane and M. Turner (eds.), *Mission and Meaning: Essays Presented to Peter Cotterell*, Carlisle: Paternoster, 3–11.

Pedersen, S. (1985), 'Theologische Überlegungen zur Isagogik des Römerbriefes', *ZNW* 76, 47–67.

Penney, J. M. (1997), *The Missionary Emphasis of Lukan Pneumatology*, JPTSS 12, Sheffield: Sheffield Academic Press.

Persson, L. (1980), 'The Gentile Mission in the Markan Interpolation (Mark 7:1 – 8:26)', *Bangalore Theological Forum* 12, 44–49.

Pesch, R. (1980), *Das Markusevangelium*, HTKNT, Freiburg: Herder.

Petersen, N. (1980), 'When Is the End Not the End?' *Int* 34, 151–166.

Peterson, D. G. (1992), *Engaging with God: A Biblical Theology of Worship*, Leicester: Apollos.

—— (1993), 'The Motif of Fulfilment and the Purpose of Luke-Acts', in B. W. Winter and A. D. Clarke (eds.), *The Book of Acts in Its First Century Setting* 1: *The Book of Acts in Its Ancient Literary Setting*, Grand Rapids: Eerdmans, 83–104.

Phillips, J. M. (1990), 'Three Models for Christian Mission', *IBMR* 14, 18–24.

Pilgrim, W. E. (1989), 'Universalism in the Apocalypse', *WW* 9, 235–243.

Piper, J. (1993), *Let the Nations be Glad!*, Grand Rapids: Baker.

Polhill, J. B. (1992), *Acts*, NAC, Nashville: Broadman.

Pollard, T. E. (1970), *Johannine Christology and the Early Church*, SNTSMS 13, Cambridge: Cambridge University Press.

Popkes, W. (1978), 'Zum Verständnis der Mission bei Johannes', *Zeitschrift für Mission* 4, 63–69.

Poucouta, P. (1988), 'La mission prophétique de l'Église dans l'Apocalypse johannique', *NRT* 110, 38–57.

Powell, M. A. (1994), 'The Mission of Jesus and the Mission of the Church in the Gospel of Matthew', *Trinity Seminary Review* 16, 77–89.

Prescott-Ezickson, R. (1986), 'The Sending Motif in the Gospel of John: Implications for the Theology of Mission', PhD thesis, Louisville, KY: Southern Baptist Theological Seminary.

Pryor, J. W. (1988), 'Covenant and Community in John's Gospel', *RTR* 47, 44–51.

—— (1992), *John: Evangelist of the Covenant People*, Downers Grove: IVP.

Quast, K. (1989), *Peter and the Beloved Disciple: Figures for a Community in Crisis*, JSNTSS 32, Sheffield: JSOT.

Radermakers, J. (1964), 'Mission et Apostolat dans l'Évangile Johannique', in F. L. Cross (ed.), *SE II*/1, TU 87, Berlin: Akademie, 100–121.

Radl, W. (1986), 'Alle Mühe umsonst? Paulus und der Gottesknecht', in A. Vanhoye (ed.), *L'Apôtre Paul*, Leuven: University Press, 144–149.

Rapinchuk, M. (1994), 'Is Matthew 23:15 Proof of Jewish Missionary Activity? A Preliminary Response and Suggested Reading', unpublished seminar paper, Deerfield, IL: Trinity Evangelical Divinity School.

—— (1996), 'The End of the Exile: A Neglected Aspect of Matthean Christological Typology', PhD thesis, Deerfield, IL: Trinity Evangelical Divinity School.

Rapske, B. (1998), 'Opposition to the Plan of God and Persecution', in I. H. Marshall and D. Peterson (eds.), *Witness to the Gospel: The Theology of Acts*, Grand Rapids/Cambridge: Eerdmans, 235–256.

Rensberger, D. (1988), *Overcoming the World: Politics and Community in the Gospel of John*, London: SPCK.

Rhoads, D. (1995), 'Mission in the Gospel of Mark', *CurTM* 22: 340–355.

Richard, E. (1985), 'Expressions of Double Meaning and Their Function in the Gospel of John', *NTS* 31, 96–112.

Richardson, R. L., Jr (1987), 'From "Subjection to Authority" to "Mutual Submission": The Ethic of Subordination in 1 Peter', *Faith and Mission* 4, 70–80.

Ridderbos, H. (1975), *Paul: An Outline of his Theology*, Grand Rapids: Eerdmans.

Riedd, J. (1973), *Das Heilswerk Jesu nach Johannes*, Freiburger Theologische Studien 93, Freiburg im Breisgau: Herder.

Riesner, R. (1991), 'Jesus as Preacher and Teacher', in H. Wansborough (ed.), *Jesus and the Oral Gospel Traditions*, Sheffield: JSOT, 185–210.

—— (1998), *Paul's Early Period: Chronology, Mission Strategy, Theology*, Grand Rapids/Cambridge: Eerdmans.

Riggenbach, E. (1903), *Der trinitarische Taufbefehl Matth. 28,19 nach seiner ursprünglichen Textgestalt und seiner Authentie untersucht*, BFCT, Gütersloh: C. Bertelsmann.

Robinson, D. W. B. (1967), 'The Salvation of Israel in Romans 9 – 11', *RTR* 26, 81–96.

—— (1974), 'The Priesthood of Paul in the Gospel of Hope', in R. J. Banks (ed.), *Reconciliation and Hope: New Testament Essays on Atonement and Eschatology presented to L. L. Morris on his 60th Birthday*, Exeter: Paternoster, 231–245.

Robinson, J. A. T. (1959–60), 'The Destination and Purpose of St John's Gospel', *NTS* 6, 117–131.

Robinson, P. J. (1989), 'Some Missiological Perspectives from 1 Peter 2:4–10', *Missionalia* 17, 176–187.

Rogers, C. (1973), 'The Great Commission', *BibSac* 130, 258–267.

Rosen, F. and G. Bertram (1929), *Die Juden und Phönizier: Das antike Judentum als Missionsreligion und die Entstehung der jüdischen Diaspora*, Tübingen: Mohr.

Rosner, B. (1998), 'The Progress of the Word', in I. H. Marshall and D. Peterson (eds.), *Witness to the Gospel: The Theology of Acts*, Grand Rapids/Cambridge: Eerdmans, 215–233.

Rowley, H. H. (1945), *The Missionary Message of the Old Testament*, London: Carey.

Ruíz, M. R. (1986), *Der Missionsgedanke des Johannesevangeliums: Ein Beitrag zur johanneischen Soteriologie und Ekklesiologie*, FB 55, Würzburg: Echter.

Sailhamer, J. H. (1992), *The Pentateuch as Narrative*, Grand Rapids: Zondervan.

Saldarini, A. J. (1994), *Matthew's Christian-Jewish Community*, Chicago: Chicago University Press.

Sanders, J. T. (1987), *The Jews in Luke-Acts*, London/Philadelphia: SCM/Fortress.

Sandmel, S. (1969), *The First Christian Century*, New York: Oxford University Press.

Sandnes, K. O. (1991), *Paul – One of the Prophets? A Contribution to the Apostle's Self-Understanding*, WUNT 43, Tübingen: Mohr-Siebeck.

Satterthwaite, P. E. (1993), 'Acts against the Background of Classical Rhetoric', in B. W. Winter and A. D. Clarke (eds.), *The Book of Acts in Its First Century Setting* 1: *The Book of Acts in Its Ancient Literary*

Setting, Grand Rapids: Eerdmans, 337–379.

—— (1995), 'David in the Books of Samuel: A Messianic Hope?' in P. E. Satterthwaite, R. S. Hess and G. J. Wenham (eds.), *The Lord's Anointed. Interpretation of Old Testament Messianic Texts*, Carlisle /Grand Rapids: Paternoster/Baker, 41–65.

Scaer, D. P. (1991), 'The Relation of Matthew 28:16–20 to the Rest of the Gospel', *Concordia Theological Quarterly* 55, 245–266.

Schick, E. A. (1989), 'Priestly Pilgrims: Mission Outside the Camp in Hebrews', *CurTM* 16, 372–376.

Schiffman, L. H. (1997), 'Non-Jews in the Dead Sea Scrolls', in C. A. Evans and S. Talmon (eds.), *The Quest for Context and Meaning*, Leiden: Brill, 153–171.

Schlatter, A. (1906), *Die Geschichte Israels von Alexander dem Großen bis Hadrian*, 2nd ed., Calwer/Stuttgart: Verlag der Vereinsbuchhandlung.

—— (1948), *Der Evangelist Matthäus*, Stuttgart: Calwer.

—— (1997), *The History of the Christ: The Foundation for New Testament Theology*, trans. A. J. Köstenberger, Grand Rapids: Baker.

—— (1999 [1922]), *The Theology of the Apostles: The Development of New Testament Theology*, trans. A. J. Köstenberger, Grand Rapids: Baker.

Schnabel, E. J. (1994), 'Jesus and the Beginnings of the Mission to the Gentiles', in J. B. Green and M. Turner (eds.), *Jesus of Nazareth: Lord and Christ*, Grand Rapids: Eerdmans, 37–58.

—— (1997), 'Mission, Early Non-Pauline', in R. P. Martin and P. H. Davids (eds.), *Dictionary of the Later New Testament and Its Developments*, Downers Grove/Leicester: IVP, 752–775.

—— (1999), 'John and the Future of the Nations', paper presented at the annual meeting of the Evangelical Theological Society, Danvers, MA, 1–23.

Schnackenburg, R. (1959), 'Die Erwartung des "Propheten" nach dem Neuen Testament und den Qumran-Texten', in F. L. Cross (ed.), *SE I*, TU 73, Berlin: Akademie, 622–639.

—— (1963), 'Die Messiasfrage im Johannesevangelium', in J. Blinzler, O. Kuss and F. Mußner (eds.), *Neutestamentliche Aufsätze: Festschrift für Josef Schmid*, Regensburg: F. Pustet, 240–264.

—— (1977), 'Is There a Johannine Ecclesiology?', in M. J. Taylor (ed.), *A Companion to John: Readings in Johannine Theology*, New York: Alba, 247–256.

—— (1984), 'Der Missionsgedanke des Johannesevangeliums im heutigen Horizont', in *Das Johannesevangelium 4: Ergänzende*

Auslegungen und Exkurse, HTKNT, Freiburg im Breisgau: Herder, 58–72.

—— (1990), *The Gospel According to St John*, 3 vols., New York: Crossroad.

Schnelle, U. (1991), 'Johanneische Ekklesiologie', *NTS* 37, 37–50.

Schreiner, T. R. (1998), *Romans*, BECNT, Grand Rapids: Baker.

Schulz, A. (1962), *Nachfolgen und Nachahmen: Studien über das Verhältnis der neutestamentlichen Jüngerschaft zur urchristlichen Vorbildethik*, SANT VI, München: Kösel.

Schürer, E. (1973, 1979, 1986, 1987), *The History of the Jewish People in the Age of Jesus Christ (175 BC – AD 135)*, 4 vols, rev. ed., Edinburgh: T. and T. Clark.

Schüssler Fiorenza, E. (1972), *Priester für Gott: Studien zum Herrschafts- und Priestermotiv in der Apokalypse*, NTAbh 7, Münster: Aschendorff.

—— (1976), 'Miracles, Mission, and Apologetics: An Introduction', in E. Schüssler Fiorenza (ed.), *Aspects of Religious Propaganda in Judaism and Early Christianity*, Notre Dame: University of Notre Dame Press, 1–25.

—— (1985), *The Book of Revelation: Justice and Judgment*, Philadelphia: Fortress.

Schütz, J. H. (1975), *Paul and the Anatomy of Apostolic Authority*, SNTSMS 26, Cambridge: Cambridge University Press.

Schweizer, E. (1959), 'Der Kirchenbegriff im Evangelium und den Briefen des Johannes', in K. Aland et al. (eds.), *SE*, TU 73, Berlin: Akademie, 363–381.

—— (1960), 'Jesus as the One Obedient in Suffering and Therefore Exalted to the Father', in *Lordship and Discipleship*, SBT 28, Naperville, IL, 68–76.

Scobie, C. H. H. (1984), 'Jesus or Paul? The Origin of the Universal Mission of the Christian Church', in P. Richardson and J. C. Hurd (eds.), *From Jesus to Paul: Studies in Honour of F. W. Beare*, Waterloo, ON: Wilfred Laurier University Press, 47–60.

—— (1992), 'Israel and the Nations: An Essay in Biblical Theology', *TynB* 43, 283–305.

Scott, J. J., Jr (1990), 'Gentiles and the Ministry of Jesus', *JETS* 33, 161–169.

—— (1995), *Customs and Controversies: Intertestamental Jewish Backgrounds of the New Testament*, Grand Rapids: Baker.

Scott, J. M. (1993), 'Restoration of Israel', in G. F. Hawthorne and R. P. Martin (eds.), *Dictionary of Paul and His Letters*, Downers

Grove/Leicester: IVP, 796–805.

—— (1994), 'Luke's Geographical Horizon', in D. W. J. Gill and C. Gempf (eds.), *The Book of Acts in Its First Century Setting 2: The Book of Acts in Its Graeco-Roman Setting*, Grand Rapids/Carlisle: Eerdmans/Paternoster, 483–544.

—— (1995), *Paul and the Nations: The Old Testament and Jewish Background of Paul's Mission to the Nations with Special Reference to the Destination of Galatians*, WUNT 84, Tübingen: Mohr-Siebeck.

Seccombe, D. P. (1982), *Possessions and the Poor in Luke-Acts*, SNTU 6, Linz: A. Fuchs.

Seifrid, M. A. (1992), *Justification by Faith: The Origin and Development of a Central Pauline Theme*, NovTSup 68, Leiden: Brill.

—— (2000), *Christ, our Righteousness: Paul's Theology of Justification*, NSBT, Leicester/Downers Grove: Apollos/IVP.

Selwyn, E. G. (1956), 'Eschatology in 1 Peter', in W. D. Davies and D. Daube (eds.), *The Background of the New Testament and its Eschatology*, Cambridge: Cambridge University Press, 394–401.

Senior, D. (1984), 'The Struggle to be Universal: Mission as Vantage Point for New Testament Investigation', *CBQ* 46, 63–81.

Senior, D. and C. Stuhlmueller (1983), *The Biblical Foundations for Mission*, Maryknoll, NY: Orbis.

Shepherd, W. H. (1994), *The Narrative Function of the Holy Spirit as Character in Luke-Acts*, SBLDS 147, Atlanta: Scholars.

Siker-Gieseler, J. S. (1980), 'Disciples and Discipleship in the Fourth Gospel: A Canonical Approach', *SBT* 10, 199–227.

Sim, D. C. (1995), 'The Gospel of Matthew and the Gentiles', *JSNT* 57, 19–48.

Smalley, S. S. (1979), 'The Johannine Son of Man Sayings', *NTS* 15, 278–301.

Smith, C. R. (1994), 'The Structure of the Book of Revelation in Light of Apocalyptic Literary Conventions', *NovT* 36, 373–393.

Smith, J. C. (1984), 'Missions in Revelation: Research in Progress', in D. Priest Jr (ed.), *Unto the Uttermost: Missions in the Christian Churches – Churches of Christ*, Pasadena, CA: William Carey.

Smith, R. H. (1962), 'Exodus Typology in the Fourth Gospel', *JBL* 81, 329–342.

—— (1995), 'Why John Wrote the Apocalypse (Rev 1:9)', *CurTM* 22, 356–361.

Soards, M. (1994), *The Speeches in Acts: Their Content, Context, and*

Concerns, Louisville: Westminster/John Knox.

Spencer, F. S. (1992), *The Portrait of Philip in Acts: A Study of Roles and Relations*, JSNTSS 67, Sheffield: Sheffield Academic Press.

Squires, J. T. (1993), *The Plan of God in Luke-Acts*, SNTSMS 76, Cambridge: Cambridge University Press.

—— (1998a), 'The Plan of God in the Acts of the Apostles', in I. H. Marshall and D. Peterson (eds.), *Witness to the Gospel: The Theology of Acts*, Grand Rapids/Cambridge: Eerdmans, 19–39.

—— (1998b), 'The Function of Acts 8.4 – 12.25', *NTS* 44, 608–617.

Stanton, G. (1985), 'The Origin and Purpose of Matthew's Gospel: Matthean Scholarship from 1945 to 1980', in W. Haase (ed.), *Aufstieg und Niedergang der römischen Welt. Principat* II.25.3, Berlin/New York: de Gruyter, 1889–1951.

Stein, R. H. (1973–74), 'A Short Note on Mark xiv.28 and xvi.7', *NTS* 20, 445–452.

—— (1992), *Luke*, NAC 24, Nashville: Broadman.

Stendahl, K. (1976), *Paul among Jews and Gentiles and Other Essays*, Philadelphia: Fortress.

Stenschke, C. (1998), 'The Need for Salvation', in I. H. Marshall and D. Peterson (eds.), *Witness to the Gospel: The Theology of Acts*, Grand Rapids/Cambridge: Eerdmans, 125–144.

Steuernagel, V. R. (1986), 'An Exiled Community as a Missionary Community. A Study based on 1 Peter 2:9,10', *Evangelical Review of Theology* 10, 8–18.

Stibbe, M. (1993), '"Return to Sender": A Structuralist Approach to John's Gospel', *Biblical Interpretation* 1, 189–206.

Stock, K. (1978), 'Das Bekenntnis des Centurion. Mk 15,39 im Rahmen des Markusevangeliums', *ZTK* 100, 289–301.

—— (1982), 'Theologie der Mission bei Markus', in K. Kertelge (ed.), *Mission im Neuen Testament*, QD 93, Herder: Freiburg/Basel/Vienna, 130–144.

Stolz, F. (1972), 'Zeichen und Wunder. Die prophetische Legitimation und ihre Geschichte', *ZTK* 69, 125–144.

Stott, J. R. W. (1975), *Christian Mission in the Modern World*, London: Church Pastoral Aid Society.

—— (1979), *The Message of Ephesians: God's New Society*, Leicester: IVP.

—— (1988), *The Letters of John*, rev. ed., TNTC, Leicester/Grand Rapids: IVP/Eerdmans.

—— (1990), *The Message of Acts: To the Ends of the Earth*, Leicester/Downers Grove: IVP.

—— (1991), 'An Open Letter to David Hesselgrave', *Trinity World Forum* 16/3, 1–2.

Strauss, M. L. (1995), *The Davidic Messiah in Luke-Acts: The Promise and its Fulfillment in Lukan Christology*, JSNTSS 110, Sheffield: Sheffield Academic Press.

Stronstad, R. (1984), *The Charismatic Theology of Saint Luke*, Peabody, MA: Hendrickson.

Stuart, D. (1987), *Hosea-Jonah*, Waco, TX: Word.

Stuhlmacher, P. (1968), *Das paulinische Evangelium I: Vorgeschichte*, FRLANT 95, Göttingen: Vandenhoeck und Ruprecht.

—— (1991a), 'The Theme: The Gospel and the Gospels', in P. Stuhlmacher (ed.), *The Gospel and the Gospels*, Grand Rapids: Eerdmans, 1–25.

—— (1991b), 'The Pauline Gospel', in P. Stuhlmacher (ed.), *The Gospel and the Gospels*, Grand Rapids: Eerdmans, 149–172.

—— (1994), *Paul's Letter to the Romans: A Commentary*, Louisville, KY: Westminster/John Knox.

Sundkler, B. (1937), 'Jésus et les païens', in B. Sundkler and A. Fridrichsen (eds.), *Contributions à l'étude de la pensée missionnaire dans le Nouveau Testament*, Arbeiten und Mitteilungen aus dem neutestamentlichen Seminar zu Uppsala VI, Uppsala: Das neutestamentliche Seminar zu Uppsala, 1–38.

Swartley, W. M. (1997), 'The Role of Women in Mark's Gospel: A Narrative Analysis', *BTB* 27, 16–22.

Talbert, C. H. (1974), *Literary Patterns, Theological Themes, and the Genre of Luke-Acts*, SBLMS 20, Missoula, MT: Scholars.

Tan, K. H. (1997), *The Zion Traditions and the Aims of Jesus*, SNTSMS 91, Cambridge: Cambridge University Press.

Tannehill, R. C. (1986, 1990), *The Narrative Unity of Luke-Acts: A Literary Interpretation*, 2 vols., Philadelphia: Fortress.

Tcherikover, V. (1956), 'Jewish Apologetic Literature Reconsidered', *Eos* 48, 169–193.

Telford, W. (1985), 'Introduction: The Gospel of Mark', in W. Telford (ed.), *The Interpretation of Mark*, IRT 7, Philadelphia: Fortress, 1–41.

Thompson, J. W. (1971), 'The Gentile Mission as an Eschatological Necessity', *ResQ* 14, 18–27.

Thompson, M. M. (1988), *The Humanity of Jesus in the Fourth Gospel*, Philadelphia: Fortress.

—— (1991), 'Signs and Faith in the Fourth Gospel', *BBR* 1, 89–108.

—— (1992), *1 – 3 John*, IVPNTC, Downers Grove/Leicester: IVP.

Thüsing, W. (1979), *Die Erhöhung und Verherrlichung Jesu im Johannesevangelium*, NTAbh 21, 1/2, Münster: Aschendorff.

Tiede, D. L. (1986), 'The Exaltation of Jesus and the Restoration of Israel in Acts 1', *HTR* 79, 278–286.

Towner, P. H. (1995), 'Paradigms Lost: Mission to the *Kosmos* in John and in David Bosch's Biblical Models of Mission', *EQ* 67, 99–119.

—— (1998), 'Mission Practice and Theology under Construction', in I. H. Marshall and D. Peterson (eds.), *Witness to the Gospel: The Theology of Acts*, Grand Rapids/Cambridge: Eerdmans, 417–436.

—— (1999), 'Romans 13:1–7 and Paul's Missiological Perspective: A Call to Rhetorical Quietism or Transformation?', in B. S. Soderlund and N. T. Wright (eds.), *Romans and the People of God: Essays in Honor of Gordon D. Fee on the Occasion of his 65th Birthday*, Grand Rapids/Cambridge: Eerdmans, 149–169.

Trites, A. A. (1973), '*Martys* and Martyrdom in the Apocalypse: A Semantic Study', *NovT* 15, 72–80.

—— (1977), *The New Testament Concept of Witness*, SNTSMS 31, Cambridge: Cambridge University Press.

Turner, M. (1990), 'Atonement and the Death of Jesus in John: Some Questions to Bultmann and Forestell', *EQ* 62, 99–122.

—— (1996a), *Power from on High: The Spirit in Israel's Restoration and Witness in Luke-Acts*, JPTSS 9, Sheffield: Sheffield Academic Press.

—— (1996b), *The Holy Spirit and Spiritual Gifts: Then and Now*, Carlisle: Paternoster.

Tyson, J. B. (1992), *Images of Judaism in Luke-Acts*, Columbia: University of South Carolina.

Unnik, W. C. van (1959), 'The Purpose of St. John's Gospel', in K. Aland *et al.* (eds.), *SE I*, TU 73, Berlin: Akademie, 382–411.

Van Canghe, J. (1972), 'La Galilée dans l'évangile de Marc: un lieu théologique?' *RB* 79, 59–72.

Vassiliadis, P. (1985), 'The Translation of *Martyria I$sou* in Revelation', *BT* 36, 129–134.

Veloso, M. (1975), *El Compromiso Cristiano: Un Estudio Sobre la Actualidad Misionera en el Evangelio de San Juan*, Buenos Aires: Zunino Ediciones.

Verkuyl, J. (1978), *Contemporary Missiology: An Introduction*, Grand Rapids: Eerdmans.

Verseput, D. J. (1994), 'Jesus' Pilgrimage to Jerusalem and Encounter in the Temple: A Geographical Motif in Matthew's Gospel', *NovT* 36, 105–121.

Volf, M. (1994), 'Soft Difference: Theological Reflections on the Relation Between Church and Culture in 1 Peter', *Ex Auditu* 10, 15–30.

Wagner, J. R. (1997), 'The Role of Isaianic Traditions in Paul's Missionary Theology: Romans', *SBL Abstracts*, Atlanta: Scholars, 71–72.

—— (1998), 'The Heralds of Isaiah and the Mission of Paul: An Investigation of Paul's Use of Isaiah 51 – 55 in Romans', in W. H. Bellinger and W. R. Farmer (eds.), *Jesus and the Suffering Servant: Isaiah 53 and Christian Origins*, Harrisburg, PA: Trinity Press International, 193–222.

—— (1999), ' "Who Has Believed Our Message?": Paul and Isaiah "In Concert" in the Letter to the Romans', unpublished PhD thesis, Duke University.

Walker, P. W. L. (1996), *Jesus and the Holy City: New Testament Perspectives on Jerusalem*, Grand Rapids: Eerdmans.

Walker, R. (1967), *Die Heilsgeschichte im ersten Evangelium*, FRLANT 91, Göttingen: Vandenhoeck und Ruprecht.

Watts, R. E. (1990), 'Consolation or Confrontation? Isaiah 40 – 55 and the Delay of the New Exodus', *TynB* 41, 31–59.

—— (1995), *Isaiah's New Exodus and Mark*, WUNT 88, Tübingen: Mohr-Siebeck.

Webb, B. (1996), *The Message of Isaiah: On Eagles' Wings*, Leicester/Downers Grove: IVP.

Wefald, E. K. (1995), 'The Separate Gentile Mission in Mark: A Narrative Explanation of Markan Geography, the Two Feeding Accounts and Exorcisms', *JSNT* 60, 3–26.

Wells, J. B. (2000), *God's Holy People: A Theme in Biblical Theology*, JSOTSS 305, Sheffield: Sheffield Academic Press.

Wenham, D. (1993), 'Unity and Diversity in the New Testament', in G. E. Ladd (ed.), *A Theology of the New Testament*, rev. ed., Grand Rapids: Eerdmans, 684–719.

Wenham, G. J. (1987), *Genesis 1 – 15*, WBC 1, Waco, TX: Word.

—— (1994), 'The Face at the Bottom of the Well: Hidden Agendas of the Pentateuchal Commentator', in R. S. Hess, G. J. Wenham and P. E. Satterthwaite (eds.), *He Swore an Oath: Biblical Themes from Genesis 12 – 50*, Carlisle: Paternoster/Grand Rapids: Baker, 185–209.

Westerholm, S. (1997), 'Sinai as Viewed from Damascus: Paul's Reevaluation of the Mosaic Law', in R. N. Longenecker (ed.), *The Road from Damascus: The Impact of Paul's Conversion on His Life,*

Thought, and Ministry, Grand Rapids/Cambridge: Eerdmans, 147–165.

Westermann, C. (1969), *Isaiah 40 – 66*, London: SCM.

—— (1984), *Genesis 1 – 11*, London: SPCK.

Widbin, H. W. (1991), 'Salvation for People Outside Israel's Covenant?' in W. V. Crockett and J. G. Sigountos (eds.), *Through No Fault of Their Own? The Fate of Those Who Have Never Heard*, Grand Rapids: Baker, 73–83.

Wilckens, U. (1978), *Der Brief an die Römer. Röm 1 – 5*, Zürich/Einsiedeln/Köln: Benziger.

—— (1982), *Der Brief an die Römer. Röm 12 – 16*, EKK 6, Zürich/Einsiedeln/Köln: Benziger.

Wilcox, M. (1981), 'The God-fearers in Acts: A Reconsideration', *JSNT* 13, 102–122.

Williams, J. F. (1998), 'Mission in Mark', in W. J. Larkin Jr and J. F. Williams (eds.), *Mission in the New Testament: An Evangelical Approach*, Maryknoll, NY: Orbis, 137–151.

Williams, S. K. (1980), 'The "Righteousness of God" in Romans', *JBL* 99, 241–290.

Wilson, A. (1986), *The Nations in Deutero-Isaiah: A Study on Composition and Structure*, Lewiston, NY: Edwin Mellen.

Wilson, S. G. (1973), *The Gentiles and the Gentile Mission in Luke-Acts*, SNTSMS 23, Cambridge: Cambridge University Press, 1–28.

—— (1983), *Luke and the Law*, SNTSMS 50, Cambridge: Cambridge University Press.

Witherington, B. (1995), *John's Wisdom*, Louisville, KY: Westminster/John Knox.

—— (1998), *The Acts of the Apostles: A Socio-Rhetorical Commentary*, Grand Rapids/Carlisle: Eerdmans/Paternoster.

Witherup, R. D. (1993), 'Cornelius Over and Over and Over Again: Functional Redundancy in the Acts of the Apostles', *JSNT* 49, 45–66.

Wolff, H. W. (1966), 'The Kerygma of the Yahwist', *Int* 20, 131–158.

Woodbridge, P. (1999), ' "The World" in the Fourth Gospel', in D. Peterson (ed.), *Witness to the World*, Carlisle: Paternoster, 1–31.

Woodhouse, J. W. (1987), 'Signs and Wonders in the Bible', in R. Doyle (ed.), *Signs and Wonders and Evangelicals*, Homebush West, NSW: Lancer, 17–35.

Wright, G. E. (1961), 'The Old Testament Basis for the Christian Mission', in G. H. Anderson (ed.), *The Theology of the Christian Mission*, London: SCM, 17–30.

Wright, N. T. (1991), *The Climax of the Covenant: Christ and the Law in Pauline Theology*, Edinburgh: T. and T. Clark.

—— (1996), *Jesus and the Victory of God*, Minneapolis: Fortress.

Zehnle, R. L. (1971), *Peter's Pentecostal Discourse: Tradition and Lukan Reinterpretation in Peter's Speeches of Acts 2 and 3*, SBLMS 15, Nashville: Abingdon.

Zeller, D. (1976), *Juden und Heiden in der Mission des Paulus*, Stuttgart: Katholisches Bibelwerk.

—— (1982), 'Theologie der Mission bei Paulus', in K. Kertelge (ed.), *Mission im Neuen Testament*, Freiburg/Basel/Wien: Herder, 164–189.

Zimmermann, H. (1960), 'Das absolute *egō eimi* als neutestamentliche Offenbarungsformel', *BZ* 4, 54–69, 266–276.

Index of authors

Index of Scripture and other ancient references

Old Testament

328

337

341

Index of subjects

INDEX OF SUBJECTS

witness terminology and the
conversion of the nations,
244–247

salvation history, *see* approach
'salvation to the ends of the
earth', *see* approach, title
second-temple Judaism
a missionary religion?, 56–
70, 254
implications for mission in the
NT, 68–70
nature of, 60–61
overall assessment, 64–68
Servant of the Lord, the
in the Gospels and Acts,
82, 95, 113–114, 125–126,
130, 137–138, 142, 144,
148, 153, 257
in Paul, 165–166, 170, 200
introduction of, 46–47
ministry of, 45–50
Servant songs, 45–50, 253
suffering of, 48–50, 95
task of, 47–48
šālîaḥ (messenger), 93
Sinai, see Mt Sinai
Solomon, 38, 40, 252
song of Moses, 32, 245
song of Simeon, 113
sovereignty of God in mission,
225, 250, 266–267
Spirit, the, 43–44, 116, 128, 130–
135, 139–140, 143, 150,

157, 158, 209–211, 213,
219, 222
spiritual warfare, 196–198
suffering Servant, *see* Servant of
the Lord

temple, the
building of, 40
destruction of, 52, 84
God's glory in, 51
heavenly temple, 137
house of prayer for all the
nations, 78–79, 99–100
vision of, 43–44
Ten Commandments, 36
tenants of the vineyard parable,
79, 98–99

universal mission, 44, 47, 114,
124, 157–158, 185, 215

vicegerent, 26, 40

witness terminology:
in Hebrews, 235
in John, 213
in Luke-Acts, 124, 126,
128–130, 133, 135, 137,
139, 141–142, 147–148,
151, 156, 158
in the NT, 265–266
in Revelation, 244–247
regarding Israel, 34, 49–50

Zion, see Mt Zion

351